BRITISH SHAREHOLDER MEETINGS IN THE LONG NINETEENTH CENTURY

BRITISH SHAREHOLDER MEETINGS IN THE LONG NINETEENTH CENTURY

Edited by
Timothy Alborn

Routledge
Taylor & Francis Group
LONDON AND NEW YORK

First published 2024
by Routledge
4 Park Square, Milton Park, Abingdon, Oxon OX14 4RN

and by Routledge
605 Third Avenue, New York, NY 10158

Routledge is an imprint of the Taylor & Francis Group, an informa business

British Library Cataloguing-in-Publication Data
A catalogue record for this book is available from the British Library

ISBN: 978-1-032-01211-7 (hbk)
ISBN: 978-1-003-17771-5 (ebk)

DOI: 10.4324/9781003177715

Typeset in Times New Roman
by Apex CoVantage, LLC

CONTENTS

ACKNOWLEDGMENTS

In September 2020, Rachel Douglas at Routledge contacted me to ask if I would be interested in compiling a "historical resources" volume on "companies and business in nineteenth-century Britain." Since writing about British companies more than two decades earlier, I had periodically thought about putting together a collection of shareholder meeting reports, a type of source that I had frequently used in that book. Rachel's invitation inspired me to carry out that plan – and her patience permitted me to put it off for two more years while I finished writing another book for Routledge. Robin Pearson, whose work (and that of his colleagues) appears throughout my endnotes in this volume, provided encouragement and information at the outset, and later, gave me valuable feedback on the book's introduction. I also gained from conversations with Jeff Gramm and Peter Buck. Simon Alexander, finally, who took over from Rachel as my editor in autumn of 2022, has done an amazing job keeping me on track and answering my random questions.

The Graduate Center at the City University of New York provided me with funds to hire a research assistant for this project. My thanks go out to Rashmi, who helped track down information for the dozens of annotations that needed to be attached to each meeting report. And last but not least, my wife Alix Cooper and our two cats, Victoria and Albert, have been a constant source of warm companionship as I scoured the internet for details on obscure shareholders and the arcana of corporate governance.

INTRODUCTION

The participation of shareholders in corporate governance, in the past and present and across several national contexts, has long been a focus of attention for historians, economists, and scholars of business organization. In the British context, Mark Freeman, Robin Pearson, and James Taylor, both in collaboration and in single-authored works, have written extensively on "shareholder democracies," exploring companies' legal structure, constituents, and cultural context.[1] Many historians have explored similar themes in other regions or in comparison with the British case.[2] Most of this work has relied on archival material that provides a quantitative record of shareholders, legal documents that reveal corporate constitutions, contemporary commentary on governance, or printed material produced by companies.[3] Although some work has also analyzed the annual or half-yearly general shareholder meeting as a key moment of exchange among managers, directors, and investors, this source has mostly continued to be underutilized by historians of corporate governance. This has been the case, despite the fact that coverage of such meetings in print media was uniquely detailed during the nineteenth century, compared either to earlier times or the present day.

One reason why few scholars have factored this type of source into their work is methodological: corporate governance has mainly been studied either from an economic, managerial, or legal perspective, which tends to downplay the performative aspect of companies in modern life.[4] Another is the tendency of historians (and literary critics) to use Google Books and subscription databases to extend their research into this sort of corner – and that strategy is less likely to succeed in the case of shareholder meetings, since most of these were reported in trade journals that have often not yet been fully digitized.[5] One goal of this collection is to make such sources more accessible and to place them in their political and economic contexts. Besides filling a gap, this collection raises new questions about how private corporations developed into being such dominant forces in the world today. Although shareholder meetings comprised only one of many facets of companies' intersections with their publics during the nineteenth century, they regularly provided an often highly anticipated form of theater, marked by a set of standard features that paralleled the political news that readers encountered in adjacent newspaper and magazine columns as well as government documents, with comparable, if less obvious, impact on their lives.

Accounts of shareholder meetings, which often stretched for many pages in the back of trade journals, sometimes included the company's annual report, written by several board members and "authored" by the board as a whole; this often took the balance sheet as its proof text, with celebratory or exculpatory annotations.[6] Even if the report itself was omitted, its contents could usually be inferred from the chair's introductory gloss. Although most such reports provided little more than a cursory financial statement and additional procedural arrangements, many commented more widely on political or social issues. This was especially the case with avowedly political firms such as the East India Company, but railways, utilities, and manufacturing companies also often sprinkled social commentary into their annual reports.[7] Finally, readers could learn at least some information about what a company's investors thought about its performance as well as its leadership's response to such opinions. They could learn much more on the occasions when shareholders convened investigative committees, which drew attention to management shortcomings and offered parallels to Parliamentary select committees, both in the hearings themselves and the resulting reports.[8]

The number of published accounts of British shareholder meetings increased steadily over the course of the nineteenth century. Partly, this was related to changes in reporting practices and media (which are discussed later), and partly, to an overall increase in the number of joint-stock companies. Before 1825, the so-called Bubble Act limited new companies to those that formed with a royal charter or Act of Parliament or by means of an unwieldy deed of settlement.[9] The repeal of that law, together with new laws enabling joint-stock banks in England and Ireland, ushered in periodic waves of new company formation, starting with the 125 firms (out of 620 that were projected) that survived the "mania" of 1825.[10] By 1844, more than a thousand British companies existed, a number that doubled over the next ten years and tripled again by 1865. This explosive growth followed new laws in the 1850s that liberalized reporting requirements and enabled firms to limit the liability of their investors. Although many of these were "private companies" (converted partnerships with few shareholders), many sectors – including mining and commercial real estate – attracted millions in share capital during this period.[11] A final wave of company formation, centered on such industries as brewing, rubber, and cotton manufacturing, took place in the 1880s and 1890s.[12]

Each new wave of companies accompanied a diffusion of share ownership, most notably during the "railway mania" of the mid-1840s and following the rise of provincial stock exchanges, syndicates, and company promoters later in the century.[13] At mid-century share ownership was already very diffuse, though investors had relatively few options regarding sectors: 80% of all share capital was held in railways, banks, and insurance companies. As companies formed in more sectors after 1850, share ownership dispersed across larger constituencies – though much of this was due to a shift away from land and public securities among "the affluent elite" rather than true "democratization."[14] One recent survey of companies that formed after 1862 found that directors and owners with at least a 10% stake in companies held only 18.5% of shares on average (translating into just 16.1% of votes), and many of these firms' largest shareholders stayed out of governance. Dispersion of shares meant dispersion of liability, and it was no coincidence that it was greatest in the finance and insurance sectors – which needed to assure customers that they could meet calls on their capital. Many of the industrial companies that formed after 1880, in contrast, which were often converted family firms, retained ownership in relatively fewer hands.[15]

For the most part, British companies after 1825 operated with relatively few regulatory constraints. Most company law between 1825 and 1862 loosened restraints on corporate accountability, although the Joint Stock Companies Act of 1844 did come with minimal publicity requirements. Mandatory publication of accounts only survived until 1856, to be replaced by model articles of association that recommended but did not require annual audits. It was not until 1900 that a new law compelled companies to submit their accounts to an annual shareholder-appointed audit.[16] Most other regulations, which appeared sporadically over the course of the century, were sector-specific. Frustration with railways led customers and labor unions to lobby for a series of piecemeal laws between 1868 and 1906. Similar developments played out in companies that provided water and gas lighting to cities and towns, culminating in a municipalization movement after 1880. Instability in the insurance sector, which had been a prime motivator of the 1844 law, prompted unprecedented publicity requirements in the Life Assurance Companies Act of 1870, which also introduced novel methods for winding up insolvent firms.[17]

THE SHAREHOLDER MEETING

In most cases, nineteenth-century companies held "ordinary general meetings" (or OGMs) for shareholders once or twice a year, which they announced in circulars or adverts in local newspapers and trade magazines. Directors or shareholders could also call a "special general meeting" (SGM) to debate a specific point of policy. Quorums for these meetings varied widely, but by mid-century, on average, a minimum of 10% of the shareholders needed to attend SGMs and half of that for OGMs; the latter figure had declined from closer to 20% in the eighteenth century. Although actual attendance sometimes exceeded these quorums, this typically only occurred in a company's early years or in times of crisis. This was the case even in such a consequential body as the East India Company's Court of Proprietors, which, as one shareholder scolded in 1853, "ought to be able to get more than twenty persons out of 1,700 to attend."[18] The meeting's official governance function was to approve the directors' report, which typically occurred with little debate. For the most part – and in contrast to "proxy wars" waged by shareholder activists in the twentieth century – management could blunt any dissent that did emerge by collecting proxy votes from less engaged constituents.[19]

The first speaker at nearly every shareholder meeting was the chairman of the board, who often spoke at length before giving way to fellow directors, only then opening the floor to other shareholders. In some cases, the firm's salaried general manager would also speak, especially in railways and banks.[20] The average company board before 1850 sported twelve directors, a number that fell below eight by 1883. As was the case in Parliament, nearly all companies imposed a property qualification to serve on their boards, which increased from an average of £482 worth of shares in the eighteenth century to more than £1000 after 1820.[21] Although companies earlier in the nineteenth century tried to limit directors from serving on multiple boards, this was largely a lost cause by 1881, when 30% of directors sat on more than one board and nearly 300 sat on more than four.[22] By the turn of the century, the "professional director" had emerged, typically a retired businessman with enough time on his hands to serve on several boards and who, in the words of one trade journal, "had probably only a small interest in the company, but who clearly knew his work."[23]

Speaking before a gathered assembly came easily to many directors, who often gave similar speeches as political candidates or in Parliament. In 1881, more than 30% of House of Commons members sat on the board of at least one company (including 93 on railways and 77 on insurance companies), as well as another hundred members of the House of Lords.[24] Such "ruling-class directors" comprised nearly 10% of boards, on average, with higher proportions in the financial and transport sectors. Reasons for appointing MPs and aristocrats as directors varied. For railways, political connections were vital at the outset in securing property rights, then later, were valued for lobbying against customer and labor activism. For companies that settled or governed British colonies, director-MPs were essential to align the company's interests with those of cabinet officials.[25] There is also evidence that politicians' or aristocrats' social connections could be useful when a provincial firm tried to raise capital in London – although evidence for this is mixed, and from early on, such appointments notoriously came with the risky opportunity cost of poor oversight.[26]

Although only a tiny percentage of shareholders ever spoke at any given meeting, there was a wide variety among those who did. What they said was usually pro forma, rarely elevating the temperature in the room; but occasionally, serious contention erupted, accompanying inflection points in a company's history. As the *Bankers' Magazine* noted in 1853, even prosperous firms included investors who "were always bold enough to give free vent to their opinions, and to arraign, in a friendly manner . . . the chairmen of the day."[27] Such men (and they were almost always men) might include wealthy merchants or landowners who had a direct financial stake in the company's success – or self-appointed representatives of a company's customer base who attended to air complaints about prices, policies, or service. One type of speaker who exercised this role in an official capacity was the auditor, who was typically elected by shareholders, either from within their body or (especially later in the century) selected from an independent accounting firm. Although auditors were intended to improve transparency by forcing firms to submit their accounts to expert scrutiny, in practice, they often conspired with directors to conceal inconvenient information.[28]

Among the more entertaining, if usually less consequential, speakers at many shareholder meetings were the gadflies, who serially regaled companies with pet peeves.[29] Several examples are included in this volume, including William Clark in the Welsh Iron and Coal Company, Malcolm Lewin and W. S. Jones in the East India Company, Charles Beavis in the Great Western Railway, and an array of abolitionists in the Imperial Brazilian Mining Company. Occasionally, when their complaints converged with more general investor dissatisfaction, gadflies could exert a major impact on governance. Much more often, other shareholders merely tolerated them. What directors could not do was prevent them from speaking, since most companies permitted that privilege to anyone who purchased a set number of shares; and, as one of the abolitionists told the IBMC shareholder who asked why he had not sold his shares in a slave-owning company: "I will keep them, to endeavour to use any power or influence which I have to set at liberty the slaves."[30] Newspaper reporters (and historians), for their part, could count on gadflies to provide colorful commentary – as when the retired navy captain George Watts, who spoke at the London and North Western Railway meeting in this volume, once called a different railway "an abortion, with a crooked back and a crooked snout, conceived in cupidity and begotten in fraud."[31]

For two centuries before British women won the vote in political elections, they routinely cast votes for company directors – and indeed, women were typically not excluded by companies' constitutions to serve as directors themselves, although no evidence of this happening before 1900 has surfaced. The early eighteenth century was something of a golden age for women investors, who comprised close to 20% of companies' investors and more than that in some firms. This proportion declined to just 7% between 1780 and 1825 but bounced back to 20% by 1850, and women comprised 30% of the investors in a sample of British companies that formed between 1900 and 1910, holding 20% of the firms' stock.[32] Partly owing to their lower overall numbers but mainly owing to social conventions, it is next-to-impossible to find examples of women speaking at British shareholder meetings for much of the nineteenth century. After 1900, this was starting to change, though only gradually. In 1903, the *Railway News* reported meetings by three different railways and one insurance company, at which five "lady shareholders" spoke, as well as several others in which the chairman welcomed the "ladies and gentlemen" who were present. Notably, none of these mentioned the woman's name, whereas male speakers were almost always referred to by name.[33]

Early in the nineteenth century, when most companies were based in London, they almost always selected meeting sites from an array of city taverns that rented rooms for political, commercial, and social gatherings. Among the meetings reprinted in this volume, seven of eight prior to 1845 met in one of these taverns, including the City of London, Crown and Anchor, George and Vulture, and London Tavern; the exception was the Bank of England, which came equipped with its own majestic meeting quarters. The London Tavern, which had the same architect as the Bank and the East India Company, was the most popular of these. Opening in 1767, it featured several large dining rooms and had space for up to 900 people in its ballroom; it was lauded as the "City temple of gastronomy" early in the century but was demolished and replaced by a bank in 1876.[34] The Crown and Anchor, which hosted the meeting of the Drury Lane Theatre recounted in this volume, combined radical politics with "fashionable sociability" in an elegant structure off the Strand. The George and Vulture, which stood near the Royal Exchange, had long been a well-frequented coffee house; when it converted to a pub after 1750, it hosted Hell-fire Club meetings along with an assortment of guilds and companies.[35]

A sample of 173 railway company meetings from the summer of 1846, when the "railway mania" was at its height, provides a snapshot of the variety of sites available for shareholders to assemble and discuss the fate of their capital at mid-century. In London, where nearly half of these firms met, the London Tavern remained a favorite location: 40 different railways met there, ranging from established lines such as the Eastern Counties (which also met there in 1849, in the meeting reported in this volume) to smaller firms such as the Bandon and Bantry. In the provinces, a more random assortment of inns and hotels availed railways of their services, including Gibbs's Royal Hotel in Edinburgh, the White Lion Hotel in Bristol, and the Palatine Hotel in Leeds. Many other companies, anticipating smaller gatherings, made do with their head offices, while some (especially in the provinces) met in public spaces such as court houses, guildhalls, and "the large room of the Town Hall" in Oldham. Finally, a few took advantage of recently constructed railway stations or accompanying hotels, as when the South Eastern met in "the Large Room over the Booking Offices at the London-Bridge Station," or when the London and Northwestern met at the world's first-ever railway hotel, which it had built next to Euston Station.[36]

The same pattern remained in place at the end of the century, with the exception that two new buildings had replaced the London Tavern as venues of choice for shareholder meetings in the City of London. The Cannon Street Hotel, originally known as the City Terminus, had been erected by the South Eastern Railway in 1867 next to its station, a location that made it easier for out-of-town shareholders to attend meetings. Six of the nine London shareholder meetings featured in this volume that met after 1880 took place there, and in a sample of 1067 such meetings from *The Statist* in the first half of 1896, more than half either took place there (23%) or at Winchester House (34%) – a five-story City office building that had been erected in 1886. Railways held more of their meetings at their own stations after 1870, including (in this volume) the Great Western's meeting at Paddington in 1891.[37] Banks, which erected increasingly palatial buildings as they grew wealthier, met in purpose-built meeting spaces more often than had been the case earlier in the century; among meetings included in this volume, that was the case for the Liverpool Union in 1891 and the London and Westminster in 1909. Finally, municipal spaces continued to be used, especially in the provinces and where events required it, as when 300 City of Glasgow Bank shareholders met at the Glasgow City Hall after that bank failed in 1878.

Reports of shareholder meetings appeared in numerous British periodicals. Starting in the late eighteenth century, companies would run adverts recording matters of policy that had been determined at their meetings; newspapers only sent reporters to uniquely consequential company meetings, such as those held by the Bank of England. By the 1820s, newspapers – and by the 1830s, trade journals such as the *Railway Magazine*, the *Mining Journal*, and the *Bankers' Magazine* – sent reporters to take notes on company proceedings, which translated into more detailed coverage over the course of the century. Since these typically did not provide full transcripts of the company's annual report, firms started to print the report in paid advertisements by the end of the century. Around the same time, it became more common, especially in trade journals, to publish the full text of company chairmen's speeches, as opposed to brief summaries.[38] These developments roughly paralleled the reporting of Parliamentary debates during the nineteenth century, both in terms of the gradual appearance of day-after press coverage and details concerning official committee reports.[39]

Although most of these reports did not stand in the way of company directors' efforts to celebrate progress and minimize shortcomings, journalists did often cover meetings in ways that depicted companies more critically. Already in 1826, when a wave of scandals accompanied a stock market crash, many firms tried to ban reporters from attending, lest their stories would add fuel to the fire. Once such witnesses did achieve the right to attend meetings regularly, their independent reporting had the capacity to "regulate markets" by amplifying shareholder dissent and tarnishing the reputation of badly behaving company executives.[40] Examples of that style of reporting in this volume include accounts of meetings held by the United Chilian Mining Company and the Welsh Iron and Coal Company in 1826, the Eastern Counties Railway in 1849, and the City of Glasgow Bank in 1878. Reporters at these meetings noted that the United Chilean shareholders "expected not to be any longer humbugged" and that the Eastern Counties directors "were received with mingled groans, hisses, and cheers" upon entering the thronged London Tavern ballroom.[41]

OUTLINE OF THE BOOK

This book is divided into four parts. "Doing Business" includes reports for ten different companies that met between 1811 and 1906. "Political Companies" includes reports of seven different meetings held by the Bank of England during the tumultuous years of 1797 and 1798 as well as meetings held by the Imperial Brazilian Mining Company in 1841, the New Zealand Company in 1846, the East India Company in 1857, and the British South Africa Company in 1898. "Mergers and Acquisitions" includes reports on four newly combined companies between 1846 and 1909. Finally, "Bubbles and Failures" includes reports on five different companies as they faced insolvency between 1826 and 1882. Each report (or set of reports) appears chronologically within each section and is prefaced by a short introduction providing specific details about the company in question as well as more general economic and political context. The reports themselves are annotated with notes providing details on as many meeting participants on whom information could be found and on events or locales mentioned in the discussions. (Available biographical information varies depending on the stature of the shareholders, and not all meeting reports identify all the participants by name.)[42]

The first and largest section, "Doing Business," provides illustrative examples of companies at different stages of their careers – including newly formed firms, long-standing private firms shortly after they went public, and companies in times of crisis. It also provides a cross-section of British companies in various sectors. By far the three largest of these were insurance, banking, and railways – the first two from the eighteenth century and the third from the 1830s and all spawning new companies into the twentieth century. Different aspects of these are on display below in shareholder meetings by the Norwich Union Fire Insurance Company (1818) and Casualty Insurance Company (1908); the National Provincial Bank (1834) and Liverpool Union Bank (1891); and the Eastern Counties Railway (1849) and Great Western Railway (1891). Three other sectors stand out for experiencing short spurts of intensive company formation at different points in time: mining in the 1820s, brewing in the 1880s, and rubber (along with bicycles) in the 1890s. Exemplary shareholder meetings in this section were held by Welsh Iron and Coal (1826), Guinness (1887), and Dunlop (1896).[43]

The insurance meetings discussed in this section feature one mutual firm (the Norwich Union) and one "proprietary" firm, in which share capital guaranteed benefit payments; in the first case, the customers played the governance role typically reserved for shareholders. The case of Casualty Insurance reveals a different trend in insurance that gained momentum after 1900 – the rise of the "composite" company that combined multiple branches of insurance under one roof; Casualty fell prey to this trend a few years after its inaugural meeting.[44] The bank meetings featured in this section took place at two key moments in British banking history: this first in 1834, when joint-stock banks were first allowed to form in London, and the second in 1891, when banking companies flexed their financial muscles by supporting a bailout of the private investment bank Barings. The two railway meetings likewise illustrate two signal moments in Victorian railway history. The Eastern Counties meeting, where an absent George Hudson avoided the wrath of his shareholders, took place two years after a flurry of new investment came crashing to the ground, leaving in its wake masses of angry investors. The Great Western meeting occurred at a time when railways dominated the British landscape but also faced increasing agitation from customers and employees.

The Welsh Iron and Coal Company's meeting in 1826 illustrates one of the "boardroom scandals" that James Taylor recently surveyed in his book of the same name. Truculent exchanges between directors, shareholders, and an investor-appointed auditor testify to the volatile climate that surrounded Britain's first major boom in company formation as well as some of the ins and outs of mining-related land purchase in Britain. The Guinness meeting showcases one of Britain's most successful businesses shortly after it had made the transition from a family firm to a publicly traded company in 1887; a similar meeting unfolded a decade later when Dunlop, a leader in the newly prosperous rubber tire industry, added to its share capital through the machinations of the controversial promoter Ernest Hooley. A final example in this section concerns the Drury Lane Theatre, which held a meeting in 1811 to discuss rebuilding in the wake of a fire and was an outlier in many regards. A throwback to the seventeenth century, its closely held shares attracted funds from some of London's leading Regency-era playwrights, poets, and radical politicians.

Part 2, "Political Companies," includes meetings held by companies that either possessed a renewable government charter, found themselves intersecting with hotly disputed political issues, or both. At a structural level, relating to elections, fiduciary responsibilities, and constituencies, all companies are political in important senses of the word.[45] Some, however, especially during the centuries between 1600 and 1900, were far more political than others, since they added to the task of internal corporate governance that of governing whole territories or centrally assisting the state's capacity to do so. These "company-states," in the words of a recent survey, "made the modern world" by combining "quintessential sovereign prerogatives with the classic features of the modern corporation."[46] Although such firms were a Europe-wide phenomenon – France and the Netherlands also pursued territorial expansion by utilizing the corporate form – Britain was uniquely persistent, and also uniquely successful, in this endeavor, starting with the English East India Company in 1601 and lasting until the eve of decolonization in the 1960s.

The Bank of England meetings in this volume reveal the ongoing debates over Parliament's decision in 1797 to suspend the company's obligation to redeem its paper money with gold – while also occasioning early demands by shareholders for more transparency in how the Bank reported its accounts. The meeting of the Imperial Brazilian Mining Company was an example of a "special general meeting," called, in this case, by a vocal minority of shareholders who opposed the company's reliance on slave labor to excavate and process gold in Brazil. The New Zealand Company meeting displays the firm on the verge of dissolution, as its actions in settling the new colony conflicted with the government's policies for keeping peace with its Māori population. Similarly, the East India Company meeting included in this section occurred shortly after the Sepoi Rebellion in 1857 and shortly before it ceased to govern the subcontinent. Finally, the 1898 meeting of the British South Africa Company was a political event: Cecil Rhodes's speech attracted more than 30,000 shareholders (only a tiny fraction of whom could fit inside the Cannon Street Hotel) and offered a detailed glimpse into British colonial policy, shortly before the outbreak of the Second Anglo-Boer War.

Part 3, "Mergers and Acquisitions," explores what happened when two companies merged – or when one acquired another – and shareholders from both firms met to approve the transaction. Although this usually went smoothly enough, mergers were seldom free of dissent and often sparked vocal opposition from shareholders in one or both companies. Some of these mergers foreshadowed consolidation, which transpired in British railways after 1845 and banks during the 1890s, in both cases presaging long-term stability. Others reflected instability in the sector in question: an example was the rapid-fire merger movement among life insurance companies in the 1860s, which led to a sector-wide meltdown. A final set of acquisitions marked the inevitable outcome of company failures, as surviving firms sought to scoop up a bankrupt competitor's business at the cheapest rate. At meetings following a merger, the company's new leadership – typically drawing from two or more previously constituted boards – introduced shareholders to their new bedfellows and tried to calm frayed nerves.

Examples of the first type of merger in this volume include the London and North Western Railway, which converted three already-powerful lines into one of Britain's largest and most influential companies and set industry standards while controlling rail traffic between London and Manchester. Another, the Alliance and Dublin Consumers' Gas, combined Dublin's three gas suppliers into a single monopoly and delivered on promised profits while holding enough local political sway to fend off criticisms about inefficiencies, inequities, and corruption. Finally, when the London and County Bank merged with the London and Westminster in 1909, the resulting behemoth joined a small club of "Big Five" joint stock banks that dominated British retail finance for the next century. An example of the second two types of merger concerned the Medical Invalid and General Life Assurance Company, which was still reeling from Indian losses in the wake of the Sepoi Rebellion when the Albert stepped in with a generous purchase offer. And that, in hindsight, proved to be a poisoned chalice for the first company's shareholders, who paid the price when the Albert failed a decade later.

The final section, "Bubbles and Failures," presents examples of shareholder meetings (and in one case, policyholder meetings) when business was in a shambles. Companies in their death throes inevitably experienced rancorous meetings, as investors pointed fingers, contemplated escalating calls on their capital, and wrangled with each other over who should bear the brunt of the burden. Such meetings tended to yield more heat than light – the real story behind the failure often emerged, if at all, only after lengthy legal battles and patient forensic accounting. But they contributed to public skepticism about the efficiency and morality of companies, provided fodder to novelists and muckraking journalists, and entertained readers who wandered into their newspaper's business pages.[47] Public interest in such meetings was heightened when celebrity directors were involved, as was the case with the railway contractor Sir Morton Peto at the London, Chatham and Dover Railway (LCDR) meeting in 1866; or when the failed company had achieved local prominence, as was the case in 1878 with the once-proud City of Glasgow Bank.

When British companies failed during the nineteenth century, it was either the result of radically imperfect information, bad timing, or both. As investment opportunities steadily expanded over the course of the century, shareholders' ability to distinguish between hits and misses steadily diminished – especially in the growing array of companies with foreign or colonial interests. And a regular cycle of financial crises ensured that even relatively safe bets were seldom immune from the collateral damage inflicted by a market-wide meltdown. The first such crash occurred in 1825, when money flowed from British public credit into foreign loans and company shares. Two such "bubbles" from this era, the United Chilean Mining Company and the Chilean Mining Company, open this section, followed by the LCDR (which actually survived its flirtation with insolvency) and the City of Glasgow Bank. A fourth example is a pair of meetings held by policyholders of the Great Britain Mutual Life Assurance Society in 1881, which tested the limits of the Life Assurance Companies Act that had passed a decade earlier.

Notes

1 Mark Freeman, Robin Pearson and James Taylor, *Shareholder Democracies?: Corporate Governance in Britain and Ireland before 1850* (Chicago: University of Chicago Press, 2012); Robin Pearson, "Shareholder Democracies? English Stock Companies and the Politics of Corporate Governance during the Industrial Revolution," *English Historical Review* 117 (2002): 840–866; James Taylor, *Creating Capitalism: Joint-Stock Enterprise in British Politics and Culture, 1800–1870* (Woodbridge: Boydell, 2006); James Taylor, *Boardroom Scandal: The Criminalization of Company Fraud in Nineteenth-Century Britain* (Oxford: Oxford University Press, 2013); see also Ron Harris, *Industrializing English Law: Entrepreneurship and Business Organization, 1720–1844* (Cambridge: Cambridge University Press, 2000); Timothy L. Alborn, *Conceiving Companies: Joint-Stock Politics in Victorian England* (London: Routledge, 1998); and Paul Johnson, *Making the Market: Victorian Origins of Corporate Capitalism* (Cambridge: Cambridge University Press, 2010).

2 Colleen Dunlavy, "Corporate Governance in Late 19th-Century Europe and the US: The Case of Shareholder Voting Rights," in *Comparative Corporate Governance: The State of the Art and Emerging Research*, ed. K.J. Hopt et al. (Oxford: Clarendon Press, 1998), 5–39; Alex Preda, "The Rise of the Popular Investor: Financial Knowledge and Investing in England and France, 1840–1880," *Sociological Quarterly* 42 (2001): 205–232; Janette Rutterford, "The Shareholder Voice: British and American Accents, 1890–1965," *Enterprise and Society* 13 (2012): 120–153; Susan Watson, *The Making of the Modern Company* (Oxford: Hart Publishing, 2022).

3 On prospectuses, see Janette Rutterford, "'Propositions Put Forward by Quite Honest Men': Company Prospectuses and their Contents, 1856 to 1940," *Business History* 53 (2011): 866–899.

4 See Alborn, *Conceiving* Companies, 258 and *passim* for this diagnosis (although this tendency has been less prevalent lately than it was in the 1990s).

5 Although Google Books has filled much of this gap over the years, its search algorithms can still make it difficult to find relevant sources in such periodicals and there remain important missing links.

6 Timothy L. Alborn, "Persuading by the Numbers: The Balance Sheet in Late-Victorian Financial Journalism," in *New Economics and its Writing*, ed. John Davis (Durham: Duke University Press, 1998), 212–230.

7 In this volume, see all the meetings in the "Political Companies" section and also the Great Western Railway. For other examples, see Josephine Maltby, "Hadfields Ltd: Its Annual General Meetings 1903–1939 and their Relevance for Contemporary Corporate Social Reporting," *British Accounting Review* 36 (2004): 415–439.

8 Janette Rutterford and Leslie Hannah, "The Unsung Activists: UK Shareholder Investigation Committees, 1888–1940," *Business History Review* 96 (2022): 741–775.

9 On this era of company formation, see especially Harris, *Industrializing English Law* and Andreas Televantos, *Capitalism Before Corporations: The Morality of Business Associations and the Roots of Commercial Equity and Law* (Oxford: Oxford University Press, 2020).

10 Lucy Newton, "The Birth of Joint-Stock Banking: England and New England Compared," *Business History* Review 84 (2010): 27–52; Henry English, *A Complete View of the Joint Stock Companies, formed during the Years 1824 and 1825* (London: Boosey and Sons, 1827).

11 H. A. Shannon, "The First Five Thousand Limited Companies and Their Duration," *Economic History* 2 (1932), 420–423; Ron Harris, "The Private Origins of the Private Company: Britain 1862–1907," *Oxford Journal of Legal Studies* 33 (2013): 339–378. The laws in question were the Limited Liability Act of 1856 (19 and 20 Vict., c. 47), a second act that permitted banks to form with limited liability in 1858 (21 and 22 Vict., c. 91) and the consolidating Companies Act of 1862 (25 and 26 Vict., c. 89).

12 P.L. Payne, "The Emergence of the Large-Scale Company in Great Britain, 1870–1914," *Economic History Review* 20 (1967): 519–542.

13 Gareth Campbell and John D. Turner, "Dispelling the Myth of the Naïve Investor during the Railway Mania, 1845–1846," *Business History Review* 86 (2012): 3–41; W. A. Thomas, *The Provincial Stock Exchanges* (London: Frank Cass, 1973); R. C. Michie, "Options, Concessions, Syndicates, and the Provision of Venture Capital, 1880–1913," *Business History* 23 (1981): 147–164; John Armstrong, "The Rise and Fall of the Company Promoter and the Financing of British Industry," in *Capitalism in a Mature Economy Financial Institutions, Capital Exports and British Industry, 1870–1939*, ed. J. J. Van Helten and Y. Cassis (Aldershot: Edward Elgar, 1990), 115–138.

14 Josephine Maltby et al., "The Evidence for 'Democratization' of Share Ownership in Great Britain in the Early Twentieth Century," in *Men, Women, and Money: Perspectives on Gender, Wealth and Investment, 1850–1930*, ed. David R. Green et al. (Oxford: Oxford University Press, 2011), 185–206.

15 Graeme G. Acheson et. al., "Corporate Ownership and Control in Victorian Britain," *Economic History Review* 68 (2015): 911–936; Graeme G. Acheson, Gareth Campbell, and John D. Turner, "Active Controllers or Wealthy Rentiers? Large Shareholders in Victorian Public Companies," *Business History Review* 89 (2015): 661–691. See also Donna Loftus, "Capital and Community: Limited Liability and Attempts to Democratize the Market in Mid-Nineteenth Century England," *Victorian Studies* 45 (2002): 93–120.

16 Taylor, *Creating Capitalism*, 135–175; John Richard Edwards, *A History of Corporate Financial Reporting in Britain* (London: Routledge, 2019), 126–133; Rob McQueen, *A Social History of Company Law: Great Britain and the Australian Colonies 1854–1920* (Farnham: Ashgate, 2009), 17–176.

17 Alborn, *Conceiving Companies*, 225–256; James Foreman-Peck and Robert Millward, *Public and Private Ownership of British Industry, 1820–1990* (Oxford: Clarendon Press, 1994), 81–91, 162–191; Timothy Alborn, *Regulated Lives: Life Insurance and British Society, 1800–1914* (Toronto: University of Toronto Press, 2009), 54–75.

18 Freeman, Pearson, and Taylor, *Shareholder Democracies?*, 165–170; E. K. Newman, "The Origin and Development of Company Meeting Reports," *Journal of Advertising History* 6 (1983): 6; *Debates at the East India House* (London: privately printed, 1858), 202 (Malcolm Lewin). Most, but not all, of the reports in this volume are of OGMs as opposed to SGMs.

19 Freeman, Pearson, and Taylor, *Shareholder Democracies?*, 154–165, 241–247. On "proxy wars" in the US context, see Jeff Gramm, *Dear Chairman: Boardroom Battles and the Rise of Shareholder Activism* (New York: Harper Business, 2016).
20 On railway managers, see Terence R. Gourvish, "A British Business Elite: The Chief Executive Managers of the Railway Industry, 1850–1922," *Business History Review* 47 (1973): 289–316; on bank managers see Timothy L. Alborn, "The Moral of the Failed Bank: Professional Plots in the Victorian Money Market," *Victorian Studies* 38 (1995): 199–225.
21 Freeman, Pearson, and Taylor, *Shareholder Democracies?*, 77–83, 93–102; Gareth Campbell and John D. Turner, "Substitutes for Legal Protection: Corporate Governance and Dividends in Victorian Britain," *Economic History Review* 64 (2011), 581–583.
22 *The Directory of Directors, 1881* (London: Thomas Skinner, 1881). 2098 directors out of 7083 served on more than one board, including 288 who held at least five directorships.
23 "The Professional Director," *Financial Review* 8 (1904), 783.
24 *Directory of Directors, 1881*: in this sample, 201 Members of the House of Commons (out of 652) held 444 directorships and 107 members of the House of Lords held 196 directorships. Ten meeting chairs in this volume served in either the House of Commons or Lords.
25 Campbell and Turner, "Substitutes for Legal Protection," 587–588; David Judge, *Representation: Theory and Practice in Britain* (London: Routledge, 1999), 102–103; Fabio Braggion and Lyndon Moore, "The Economic Benefits of Political Connections in Late Victorian Britain," *Journal of Economic History* 73 (2013): 142–176; Alborn, *Conceiving Companies*, 173–256. Judge reports that there were 145 "railway MPs" in 1841, 179 in 1867, and 90 in 1886.
26 Shima Amini and Steven Toms, "Accessing Capital Markets: Aristocrats and New Share Issues in the British Bicycle Boom of the 1890s," *Business History* 60 (2018): 231–256; Richard S. Grossman and Masami Imai, "Taking the Lord's Name in Vain: The Impact of Connected Directors on 19th Century British Banks," *Explorations in Economic History* 59 (2016): 75–93.
27 "The Meeting of Joint-Stock Banks," *Bankers' Magazine* 13 (1853), 178.
28 Freeman, Pearson, and Taylor, *Shareholder Democracies?*, 227–239; Derek Matthews, Malcolm Anderson, and John Richard Edwards, *The Priesthood of Industry: The Rise of the Professional Accountant in British Management* (Oxford: Oxford University Press, 1998), 89–141.
29 A few historians have discussed corporate gadflies in passing, though seldom in a sustained fashion. See James Taylor, *Boardroom Scandal*, 24–34; Rutterford, "The Shareholder Voice," 138–147; Tim Bowley, *Activist Shareholders in Corporate Governance: The Australian Experience and its Comparative Implications* (Oxford: Hart, 2023), 47–56.
30 "Imperial Brazilian Mining Company," *Anti-Slavery Reporter*, 2 June 1841 (Richard Fry).
31 David Ross, *George and Robert Stephenson: A Passion for Success* (Stroud: The History Press, 2010), 168.
32 Freeman, Pearson, and Taylor, *Shareholder Democracies?*, 94, 125–126; Graeme G. Acheson, Gareth Campbell, and John D. Turner, "Who Financed the Expansion of the Equity Market? Shareholder Clienteles in Victorian Britain," *Business History* 59 (2017): 607–637. See also Anne Laurence, Josephine Maltby, and Janette Rutterford, eds., *Women and their Money, 1700–1950: Essays on Women and Finance* (London: Routledge, 2009); Nancy Henry, *Women, Literature and Finance in Victorian Britain: Cultures of Investment* (Cham: Palgrave Macmillan, 2018). On British women investors up to 1750, see Amy Froide, *Silent Partners: Women as Public Investors during Britain's Financial Revolution, 1690–1750* (Oxford: Oxford University Press, 2017).

33 *Railway News* 79 (1903), 290, 293–294, 328, 414, reports of meetings held by the Great Western, Great Northern, and London and North-Western Railways and the Railway Passengers' Assurance Company. Freeman, Pearson and Taylor report that women "participated in GMs infrequently and in small numbers" before 1850: *Shareholder Democracies?*, 127.

34 Rachel Cowgill, "'Wise Men from the East': Mozart's Operas and their Advocates in Early Nineteenth-Century London," in *Music and British Culture 1785–1914*, ed. Christina Bashford and Leanne Langley (Oxford: Oxford University Press, 2000), 59–60; Edward Callow, *Old London Taverns: Historical, Descriptive and Reminiscent* (New York: Brentano's, 1901), 77–81; *Hand-book to London As It Is* (London: John Murray, 1876), 297.

35 Ian Newman, *The Romantic Tavern: Literature and Conviviality in the Age of Revolution* (Cambridge: Cambridge University Press, 2019), 68–107; Ralph Nevill, *London Clubs: Their History and Treasures* (London: Lancour Press, 2008), 18–20.

36 *Herapath's Railway Magazine* 8 (1846), 833–1248 *passim* and notices in 15 August and 19 September. On the Euston Hotel, which the London and Birmingham Railway had opened in 1838 next to its terminus, see Taylor, *Creating Capitalism*, 36.

37 John Christopher, *London's Historic Railway Stations Through Time* (Stroud: Amberley Publishing, 2015), 123; "Winchester House in Old Broad Street," londonpicturearchive.org.uk; *Statist* 37 (1896), *passim*. In the *Statist* sample, 25 railway companies held meetings at their London terminus.

38 Newman, "The Origin and Development of Company Meeting Reports," 6–14. For a survey of the railway press, which includes a discussion of shareholder meetings, see John E. C. Palmer and Harold W. Paar, "Transport," in *Victorian Periodicals and Victorian Society*, ed. J. Don Vahn and Rosemary T. VanArsdel (Toronto: University of Toronto Press, 1994), 179–198.

39 On Parliamentary debates, see Dror Wahrman, "Virtual Representation: Parliamentary Reporting and Languages of Class in the 1790s," *Past and Present* 136 (1992): 83–113. On Parliamentary reports (i.e., Blue Books), see Oz Frankel, *States of Inquiry: Social Investigations and Print Culture in Nineteenth-Century Britain and the United States* (Baltimore: Johns Hopkins University Press, 2006).

40 James Taylor, "Privacy, Publicity, and Reputation: How the Press Regulated the Market in Nineteenth Century England," *Business History Review* 87 (2013): 679–701.

41 "United Chilean Mining Company," *Times* 18 April 1826; "Eastern Counties Railway," *London Standard* 1 March 1849.

42 Notes are not included for people and events who are sufficiently discussed in the document's introduction.

43 Another important sector was public utilities, including gas and water starting in the 1820s and, after 1880, electricity and tramways; in this volume, see the meeting of the Alliance and Dublin Gas Company discussed below.

44 Alborn, *Regulated Lives*, 46–51.

45 Freeman, Pearson, and Taylor, *Shareholder Democracies?*; Alborn, *Conceiving Companies*.

46 Andrew Phillips and J.C. Sharman, *Outsourcing Empire: How Company-States Made the Modern World* (Princeton: Princeton University Press, 2020), 2. See also Philip Stern, *Empire, Incorporated: The Corporations That Built British Colonialism* (Cambridge, MA: Harvard University Press, 2023).

47 See especially Taylor, *Boardroom Scandal*; also, Alborn, "The Moral of the Failed Bank."

Part 1

DOING BUSINESS

Editorial Headnote

Drury Lane Theatre (1811)

A theatre has stood between Catherine Street (formerly Bridges Street) and Drury Lane in London's West End since 1663. That year, Thomas Killigrew, a favorite of Charles II, converted a riding school into Restoration England's first Theatre Royal. After a fire destroyed this theatre in 1674, Christopher Wren designed a new one on the same spot, with seating capacity for around 1000 patrons.[1] Following David Garrick's illustrious tenure as the Drury Lane's manager between 1747 and 1775, Richard Brinsley Sheridan debt-financed a "radical reconstruction" in 1794 at a cost of £200,000. The Radical MP and celebrated playwright, who had made his name at the rival Covent Garden Theatre in the 1780s, turned the theatre into a reliably profitable, if not terribly adventurous, production company.[2] Through 1809, shares in the firm were closely held in a few hands. Although Charles II had intended Killigrew's patent to be handed down through his heirs, a "stock and derivatives market" soon developed, with transferable "building shares" that earned rental income and "profit shares" that divided earnings among the manager and actors.[3]

Sheridan's new Drury Lane Theatre had barely reached adolescence when it burned down on 24 February 1809. No lives were lost, and the fire did not spread beyond the theatre's confines. The building had been insured for only £41,500 by five insurance companies (the Imperial, British, Globe, Hope, and Eagle), and in a single day, observed the *Morning Chronicle*, "several hundred persons [were] thrown out of bread."[4] With the fire, the ownership of the theatre passed from Sheridan, who was already on the verge of insolvency, to a group put together by Samuel Whitbread. Whitbread, who had inherited Britain's largest brewery in 1796, had established himself as a leading Radical MP by the early 1800s. He secured passage of a private Act of Parliament in 1810 enabling the establishment of a new joint-stock company for the purpose of rebuilding the theatre. By October 1811, he managed to raise £300,000 in £100 shares spread among 134 investors, including £112,000 to cover construction, £40,000 to buy out Sheridan's patent, and the rest to repay the debenture-holders who had lent Sheridan money for rebuilding the theatre in 1794. Less than a year later, thanks in large part to the expert management of the builder, Henry Rowles, Whitfield opened the new theatre with a performance of *Hamlet*.[5]

This final act of Whitbread's life was brief and ended tragically, when he fatally slit his throat in 1815. Controversy swirled around every aspect of the new Drury Lane, including thc choice of its architect (the inexperienced Benjamin Wyatt), an effort in Parliament to build a third patent theatre to rival Drury Lane and Covent Garden, and clamor from Sheridan's friends, who thought he had been ill-treated by Whitbread's circle. Whitbread's closest associates, though fiercely loyal, were also headstrong and strikingly young, even for the theatre business: the rakish poet Lord Byron and his friend Douglas Kinneard were just out of college, while the novelist Matthew Lewis was still in his 30s. Wyatt's design for the new theatre, which still stands today, put pressure on Whitbread to stage spectacular (and expensive) shows that could fill its expanded seating. Two months before he ended his life, Whitbread resigned as chairman, complaining of the "jarring concerns" the theatre regularly caused him.[6]

Notes

1 Simon Trussler, *The Cambridge Illustrated History of British Theatre* (Cambridge: Cambridge University Press, 1994), 119–121.

2 Leslie Ritchie, *David Garrick and the Mediation of Celebrity* (Cambridge: Cambridge University Press, 2019); Katherine Worth, *Sheridan and Goldsmith* (London: Macmillan, 1992), 33.

3 Mattie Burkert, *Speculative Enterprise: Public Theaters and Financial Markets in London, 1688–1763* (Charlottesville: University of Virginia Press, 2021), 11–12.

4 *Morning Chronicle* 25 Feb 1809; *Lancashire Gazette* 4 May 1809.

5 Rand Carter, "The Drury Lane Theatres of Henry Holland and Benjamin Dean Wyatt," *Journal of the Society of Architectural Historians* 26 (1967), 207; Dean Rapp, *Samuel Whitbread (1764–1815): A Social and Political Study* (New York: Garland, 1987), 463–467; Roger Fulford, *Samuel Whitbread 1764–1815: A Study in Opposition* (London: Macmillan, 1967), 281–284.

6 Iain Mackintosh, "The Rise and Fall of the Georgian Playhouse 1714–1830 – A Cautionary Tale," *AA Files* 4 (1983), 26; Carter, "The Drury Lane Theatres," 207–216; Rapp, *Samuel Whitbread*, 470–471; Fulford, *Samuel Whitbread*, 279–283, 288–307.

1

DRURY LANE THEATRE

Source: Drury Lane Theatre (1811), *Morning Post*, 31 October 1811

DRURY-LANE THEATRE

A General Meeting of the Subscribers to the New Theatre yesterday took place at the Crown and Anchor Tavern.

Mr. WHITBREAD[1] took the Chair at about half-past one, and immediately opened the business. He felt it necessary to repeat some of the statements made on the former day, as it was enjoined by the Act of Parliament. On this day it was proper to state, that the Subscribers were expected to withdraw, or to confirm their subscriptions. It was necessary to come to a conclusion; and those who ratified the proceedings of the first meeting, now were bound henceforth to continue their subscriptions. The Act of Parliament did not require that at the first meeting the subject should be gone into at such length as it had been gone into; but the Committee were of opinion, that they would but ill have done their duty, had they called a meeting on the subject of rebuilding Drury-lane Theatre merely as a matter of form. He begged to be allowed again to state so much of the former report as related to the claims on the Theatre, though he thought it not necessary to state them as fully as on the former occasion. The Hon. Gentleman then proceeded to recapitulate the substance of the report of the Committee, as also the Resolutions of the last meeting, which we have already laid before the public. He then proceeded to read the new report of the Committee, which set forth, that in pursuance of the Resolutions passed at the last general meeting, they had proceeded to pursue the adjustment of the remaining claims of the New Renters. Of these, since their last meeting, to 191 were added 5, making, in the whole, 196, who had acceded to the terms proposed, out of 234 persons concerned. Of these, one was an Officer of high rank in the West Indies; another, a Gentleman of great weight in the City. The 3000*l.* Shareholders were next spoken of; of these, one, and one only, still refused to come into the proposed arrangement. One person, who on a former occasion, had given up a claim of 150*l.* had misunderstood the business, and in consequence retracted what he had then advanced. They were, however, in treaty with the party alluded to, and the Committee were in hopes it would be satisfactorily settled. The Committee were happy to say, that among the numerous body with whom they were concerned,

DOI: 10.4324/9781003177715-2

widely dispersed as they were, this was almost the only instance of misconception that had occurred. The next point related to the trust of Mr. Adams, which remained in the same state as on the former meeting. Another private box had been claimed since their last. In justice to the claimant it was proper to state, that the claim had been preferred in the most amicable manner. This claim, however, they were of opinion, could not be maintained. A new claim had been preferred on the preceding day, which they had not yet been able to take into consideration. The adjustment with the Proprietors remained as before entered into an agreement to convey the whole of the property to the new Subscribers. They were content to have no concern whatever in the new property, in consideration of their receiving the sums named for their compensation by the Committee, or such portion of them as, after all the affairs of the concern had been settled, should appear to be due to them. They would be happy to remove every obstacle that it might be in their power to do away; and they desired that no difficulty might be made about paying them the sums adjudged to them as compensation, according to the terms of the statute, as, rather than any inconvenience should be thus occasioned to the new Company, they would cheerfully wait till the new theatre was completed. The Hon. Gentleman then proceeded to state that the model submitted to the Committee by Mr. B. Wyatt,[2] had been preferred, and repeated their expression of regret at finding themselves obliged to reject performances so truly meritorious as were those produced by the other architects, who had favoured them with designs. The Committee had thought it proper to do nothing till the expence of the whole was ascertained. An agreement had been entered into by Mr. Rowles[3] to build the theatre. He had entered into securities, himself in the penalty of 20,000*l.* and two others in 5000*l.* each, to have the new theatre ready to open on or before Oct. 1, 1812. The whole of the expence, including the furnishing of the boxes, &c. was estimated at less than 125,000*l.* Of this the sum of 112,000*l.* was to be paid to Mr. Rowles for building the Theatre, and 12,500*l.* were allowed for the expences of surveyors, decorations, &c. making in the whole the sum above stated, 125,000*l.* The act provided, that it should be begun by Michaelmas, 1811, and completed by October, 1812. In consequence of this, the ground had been taken possession of, and the necessary work commenced. For this purpose, they had drawn part of the sums due to the concern from the Fire Offices, which, it was hoped, would suffice till a new application could be made to Parliament to ratify the present arrangements. Till that could be done, the subscription fund was to remain untouched; increasing by the accumulation of interest instead of being diminished. Notwithstanding all that had been done by the Committee had been approved of by the first meeting, they had taken no new step of importance, as they had thought it right not to incur the most trifling expence till the resolutions of that day were notified by the decision of the present meeting. The subscription had been considerably increased since the last meeting, and now might be said to amount to 120,000*l.* It might now, notwithstanding all the disadvantages under which it had commenced, be expected to soon still farther be augmented, as many persons who had not yet contributed to it, had pledged themselves to subscribe. The model which they had chosen was open for inspection; and any criticism with which they might be favoured, and by which it might be improved, would be thankfully received.

Mr. LEWIS[4] then submitted two Resolutions to the Meeting confirming the arrangements made, and expressing confidence in the Committee, [for which see advertisement.] These were unanimously carried.

On the motion of Mr. LEWIS, a few copies of the Reports of the Committee were ordered to be printed.

Mr. LEWIS now moved the Thanks of the Meeting to the SHERIDANS,[5] for their handsome conduct.

On the question being put from the Chair,

The Hon. Mr. D. KINNAIRD[6] gave it as his opinion that it was incumbent on them to come to the proposed Vote of Thanks, as those who were the objects of it had been much abused out of doors. Their enemies had represented the whole of the proceedings on the subject as being intended ultimately for the benefit of the SHERIDANS. The best refutation of this would be a short statement of the nature of the concern. The whole of the property of a confirmed monopoly was conveyed to the new Company, with a lease of 99 years, for about 8000*l.* per annum. The value of it might be properly appreciated, when he stated that some years ago a theatrical speculator had offered to Mr. SHERIDAN an annuity of 19,000*l.* a year for the use of the property, at the same time engaging to pay all debts. He thought it as good a speculation as ever was entered into, and if his opinion were asked of it by a customer, as a banker he would say so. This sentiment he strongly repeated, and declared he was ready to prove by his actions, that what he had stated, he believed to be true.

Mr. P. MOORE[7] spoke at some length in praise of the disinterested conduct of Mr. SHERIDAN and his Son, corroborated the statement of the last speaker, and had no doubt of the success of the undertaking.

The thanks of the Meeting were then given to Mr. WHITBREAD.

Mr. WHITBREAD felt extremely gratified at the notice which had been taken of him by the Meeting. He had been assiduous in his labours, but the only object of his exertions was to gain their approbation, and obtaining that, he gained that which was the stimulus to his exertions, the sum of his hopes, and the bounds of his ambition. That alone was the interest which he had in this concern; gaining that, he was rich in his Drury Law property; disappointed, he was a loser by his speculation. – The attacks which had been made on him for the part which he had taken in this business, were singularly impotent and ridiculously feeble. He had been represented to be a person who had a great deal at stake and who was in no common degree personally interested in the success of the undertaking. These calumnies were lost in their own extravagance, as the only object of his ambition, and the only prospect of reward by which he could possibly have been dazzled, was the hope of proving himself worthy of their confidence, and of the confidence of the public.

The meeting then broke up, with an understanding that an intimation would be given by the Committee when next they had any thing of importance to communicate to the Subscribers.

Notes

1 Samuel Whitbread (1764–1815), whose father Samuel was Britain's leading brewer and a wealthy landowner, won his father's safe Bedford seat in Parliament in 1790, which he held for the rest of his life as an influential member of the Whig (and later Radical) opposition. Among other causes, he advocated parliamentary reform, abolition of the slave trade, and religious toleration. He inherited his father's brewery in 1796, but within four years, farmed the management of it out to partners; between the brewery and the land, he earned more than £20,000 a year.

2 Benjamin Wyatt (1775–1855), son of the architect James Wyatt (1746–1813), lived in India between 1797–1803 and was private secretary to the future Duke of Wellington from 1807 to 1809. He had just started his career as an architect, working for his father, when he won the Drury Lane competition. The Prince Regent praised the new theatre, which would prove to be his only major architectural achievement. Though he continued to win commissions through the 1830s, including many from Wellington, he spent the last two decades of his life in poverty.

3 Henry Rowles (1777–1840), builder, trained with the architect Henry Holland and formed a partnership with his uncle Alexander Copland in 1807. His contracts through 1821, when he retired and sat on several company boards, included the East India Docks (1806), East India College (1807), Drury Lane Theatre (1811), and Royal Mint (1818).

4 Matthew Gregory Lewis (1775–1818) was a writer and Radical politician. His gothic novel *The Monk* (1795) earned him both infamy and celebrity, which brought access to London's literati and high society. He wrote several plays between 1797 and 1811, the first of which, *Castle Spectre* (1797), was a hit at Drury Lane and secured a close attachment to that theatre. In 1812, he inherited his father's Jamaican plantations and spent the rest of his short life lobbying for the improved treatment of Jamaican slaves.

5 Richard Brinsley Sheridan (1751–1816), after being disinherited for marrying the singer Eliza Linley in 1773, supported his family by writing and, between 1774 and 1778, borrowing money to buy a majority share in the Drury Lane Theatre. His prolific career as an actor, writer and theatre manager remained intertwined with radical politics and romantic intrigue for the rest of his life. The Drury Lane fire coincided with a £1500 lawsuit against his son Tom (1775–1817) stemming from Tom's affair with a married woman. Saddled by additional debts, he agreed to sell his and Tom's share of the theatre to Whitbread – but this did not prevent him spending the rest of his life in and out of debtor's prison, due partly to Whitbread's refusal to part with all the funds he owed Sheridan. Tom Sheridan, meanwhile, also in debt and poor health, took a post in South Africa in 1813, where he died of consumption.

6 Douglas Kinnaird (1788–1830) attended Eton and Göttingen before earning his MA at Trinity College, Cambridge, in 1811. He later briefly served in Parliament as a Radical and was a friend and patron of Lord Byron.

7 Peter Moore (1753–1828) worked as a clerk in India from 1769 to 1785; back in England, he hosted Whig political gatherings at his Middlesex manor house, befriending Sheridan and Edmund Burke, and entered Parliament as a radical Whig in 1803. Through Sheridan, he became actively involved in the Drury Lane Theatre. He sat on

its management committee and its board of trustees; raised funds to rebuild it in 1810; opposed a charter for a rival theatre in Parliament in 1811; and sat on its board of directors in 1815. After losing his seat in Parliament in 1826, the resulting exposure to creditors forced him to live his final two years in France.

Editorial Headnote

Norwich Union Fire and Annuity Office (1818)

Although not a shareholder meeting, the gathering of Norwich Union Fire (NUF) policyholders and other "concerned . . . private gentlemen" at London's George and Vulture Tavern bore many characteristics of such meetings, reflecting the blurry boundary between shareholders and policyholders in nineteenth-century British insurance. This was especially the case where (as with the NUF) the company was established on a mutual basis, whereby policyholders elected directors and voted on corporate governance issues. At the time of the meeting, the NUF had just completed its second decade as one of Britain's first provincial mutual fire insurance offices. Mutualism was common enough in life insurance, where most risks took decades to fall due, but it was more hazardous in the fire sector, which was dominated by London firms – including the century-old Sun, London Assurance, and Royal Exchange companies, with several more joining these after 1790. The NUF meeting in 1818 indicated the challenges facing a mutual fire insurer when it ventured into this London market, which the NUF did when it opened a branch there in 1815.[1]

These challenges multiplied when the company's irascible founder and secretary, Thomas Bignold, joined the mix. Bignold had been selling fire insurance out of Norwich since 1785: the NUF was his third office, and he added a sister life insurance company in 1808. After a falling out with his directors in 1815, they replaced him with his son Samuel and exiled him to London to build the firm's business there, but he soon gained a reputation (abetted by his London rivals) of denying claims on flimsy grounds. This was the context for a stormy series of meetings in 1818, which resulted in Thomas Bignold's ouster and the NUF temporarily withdrawing from the London market.[2] Three years after the meeting in 1818, the NUF converted to a "proprietary" office, in which share capital guaranteed payment of policies and shareholders replaced policyholders in governance, and resumed its London branch in 1823.[3] The NUF continued to be a presence in London for the rest of the century, though of a middling sort – ranking 20th out of 64 companies in London premium income in 1874. A thriving American business, however, kept it among the top ten British fire insurers through 1900.[4] The life office remained in Norwich and developed into one of Britain's leading provincial insurers: after a series of late-twentieth-century acquisitions, it changed its name to Aviva and, today, stands as Britain's second-largest insurer, with over £650 million in assets, and 12th-wealthiest insurer in the world.[5]

Notes

1 R. J. Ryan, "A History of the Norwich Union Fire and Life Insurance Societies from 1797 to 1914" (Ph.D. Dissertation, University of East Anglia, 1983), 154–159, 205.

2 Robert Bignold, *Five Generations of the Bignold Family* (London: B.T. Batsford, 1948).5–30; Robert Blake, *Esto Perpetua: The Norwich Union Life Assurance Society* (Norwich: privately published, 1958), 15–26.

3 Ryan, "A History of the Norwich Union Fire and Life," 225–229; Blake, *Esto Perpetua*, 28.

4 Cornelius Walford, *Insurance Cyclopaedia* (London: Layton, 1871–1880), 4: 156; Ryan, "A History of the Norwich Union Fire and Life Insurance Societies" 823–824.

5 Blake, *Esto Perpetua*, 35–36; "Best's Rankings: World's Largest Insurers – 2022 Edition," *Best's Review* (online).

2

NORWICH UNION FIRE AND ANNUITY OFFICE

Sources: Norwich Union Fire and Annuity Office (1818), *London Times*, 24 July 1818; *Morning* Post, 29 July 1818

NORWICH UNION FIRE AND ANNUITY OFFICE

A meeting took place yesterday morning, at the George and Vulture tavern, of private gentlemen, manufacturers, and others, holding policies, or otherwise concerned in the above establishment, to take into consideration the spirit and manner of some of its late proceedings in regard to those persons who had claims upon it. About fifty gentlemen were present. Mr. Alderman Thorp[1] was in the chair. Some curious facts were adduced on this occasion, which, if their correctness may be depended on, will direct a considerable degree of public odium towards the conductors of the Norwich Union. Several persons present stated the treatment to which they had been exposed, and the difficulties they had encountered before they were able to obtain satisfaction of their demands. It was said to have been the practice, at least in London, to oppose every obstacle to claimants, to offer sums far short of what was really due, and on a day being fixed for final payment, still to evade by every possible means the final settlement. Individuals of great respectability have frequently had their veracity impeached by them without cause, have undergone cross-examinations, and even been subjected to the imputation of fraud and dishonesty without the smallest ground whatever. The London agent is said to have told one of the gentlemen present, that the company have a fund of 30,000*l.* for defraying the expense of litigations. Few of the noblemen and gentlemen whose names appeared in their policies and circular letters, had any concern in the company, and in some instances the sanction of their names had been obtained in a surreptitious manner. As a proof of the importance and necessity of inquiry into the concerns of this company, it was stated that they are liable, on policies of insurance against fire, to the amount of 40,000,000*l.*; and were responsible upon life annuities to the extent of 25,125,000*l.* yearly. A series of resolutions, expressing the sense entertained by the meeting of the conduct of the Norwich Union, and its determination to proceed, for the public benefit, to a strict investigation of all the circumstances connected with it, were read and passed unanimously. A committee was appointed, with power to add to its number, to conduct the business. A gentleman named Lovell,[2] the agent to the Norwich Union for the town of Birmingham, was present in the room during the whole of

DOI: 10.4324/9781003177715-3

the proceedings, at the desire, as we understood, of the Directors of the Norwich Union. Mr. Lovell expressed his conviction of their general wish to render justice to the public, but did not offer any contradiction of the facts related to the meeting.

The cases adduced to show the manner in which the business of this insurance-company had been conducted were numerous; we give, as a specimen, that of Stubbs, a linen-draper, in Fleet-market, related by Mr. Rothwell, one of the creditors.

Stubbs was insured with the Norwich Union for 3,000*l.* and suffered a total loss by fire. On application for the payment of the sum insured, on which his solvency depended, he experienced much difficulty in establishing his claims and in coming to a proper understanding with the office. The affair was taken up by his creditors, who made enquiry at other insurance-offices, when they learned that the obstacles and delays of the Union-office were considered unusual, and very different from the liberal spirit generally acted upon; they had an interview on the subject with the London agent, who treated them very cavalierly.

After some time an offer was made to Stubbs of 1,700*l.*, little more than half his claim. This was of course rejected. After a further delay the offer was increased to 2,200*l.*, but this was also refused. An arbitration was then agreed on, and after infinite trouble, caused chiefly by the London agent, who demanded in the first instance, that the arbitrator should not be a lawyer, and afterwards insisted on the contrary, Stubbs obtained an award for something more than 2,900*l.* A day was then fixed on for the payment, but on application the London agent was not to be found, having, as it appeared, set out for Norwich. Stubbs was advised to follow him, and did so, arriving at Norwich soon after the London agent, whom he traced to the Mail, in which he had taken a place to return to London, and they both came back by the same vehicle, Stubbs being an outside and the agent an inside passenger. Stubbs, it appears, had a very intelligent legal friend, who advised all his actions; and the arrest of the agent was recommended, which was effected with some difficulty, and then, and not till then, the money was paid. Stubbs was literally saved from bankruptcy by the vigilance of his friends. Mr. Rothwell, in concluding his account, observed that the principles on which the Norwich Union conducted its business appeared to him highly reprehensible, and a proper subject for public notice.

Morning Post 29 July 1818

NORWICH UNION FIRE AND LIFE INSURANCE

On Monday last, a meeting took place at the York Hotel, Bridge-street, Blackfriars, for the purpose of taking into consideration the charges lately preferred against the Norwich Union Office. The meeting consisted of Gentlemen highly respectable, and Insurers in the Office to the amount of more than half a million of property.

THOMAS BENSLEY,[3] Esq. was called to the Chair.

Mr. SAMUEL BIGNOLD,[4] Secretary for the Country Department, informed the meeting, that as soon as the resolutions which had been passed at the George and

Vulture Tavern, appeared in the Newspapers, he felt it his duty to communicate them to the Board of Directors at Norwich; the Board had met in consequence, and came to certain resolutions, a copy of which he then read. – They stated in substance, that the Board did not consider the Society fairly treated by the meeting at the George and Vulture. – That it was their principle to pay due and ready attention to all claims made upon them, and that they would continue so to do – that the justice and impartiality of their decisions were acknowledged by Committees, formed of the most respectable individuals throughout all parts of the Country. The resolutions concluded by recommending the appointment of a more numerous London Committee, to inquire into, and adjust any claims that might exist in that Department.

Mr. S. BIGNOLD proceeded to state, that there was on the part of the Board no desire to conceal any thing. It was its wish that both the principles and conduct of the Institution might receive as much publicity as possible. The Directors desired that this Institution should be, as it were, a house of glass, through which every person might see: they were not fearful of scrutiny. Every source of intelligence connected with the Office, its books, and the state of its funds, would be open to inspection. Close investigation had already been made at Norwich, by deputations commissioned for that purpose, from Birmingham, Dublin, Bristol, and other places; and it was the wish of the Board that the same system of inquiry should be pursued by the Committee they had proposed to have established in London.

GEORGE BEDFORD, Esq. of Bedford-row, then proposed several resolutions.

JOHN HANSON, Esq. of Kensington, said, he attended there as well for himself as for his father, they being both considerable Insurers, and that he expected to hear some answer to the charges which had been lately circulated. The *ipse dixit* of the Board, however respectable, was not enough to satisfy him. The calumnies spread abroad (for such he believed them to be), should be removed in a more effectual manner. The concern would then go on better, and the public be more confident, and of course more contented.

FRANCIS KEMBLE, Esq.[5] of Philpot-lane, said, that however he might approve of the Resolutions so far as they went, he was not of opinion that they went far enough. He attended there as an independent Insurer, unconnected with the Norwich Office in point of interest, but still desirous that a fair investigation should take place. The Meeting at which its concerns had been lately made the subject of discussion, was not one from which much impartiality could be expected; he would confess there was a time when the prejudices existing against the Norwich Union Office had their full weight upon his mind, but further inquiry and better information had enabled him to shake them off. He was now an Insurer to a considerable amount, and should probably, as opportunity offered, increase his stake in the concern. Inquiry could not be prejudicial. Whatever might be his feelings as an individual, it was unquestionably due to the Members and to those Gentlemen who had lent their names to this Institution, that full, free, and impartial investigation should take place; that the slightest taint of unfairness or impropriety of conduct that might adhere to it should be removed. It was an Institution so beneficial in its tendency, if duly administered, that it was entitled to the most serious regard. He had always, in common with every person connected with inland trade, felt inclined cordially to encourage Insurance Establishments, and so far was he from objecting to the large profits made by some Offices, that he should cheerfully contribute to them if the advantages of Insurance were not to be obtained on terms much more favourable. Though the Norwich Institution was not established for purposes of profit as other Offices were, he had not the least doubt of its stability, because its large returns were only in proportion to the profits shared by other Offices, yet to the generality of Insurers the price of security was a minor consideration; but a prompt settlement of claims, was of the utmost importance. If the great object of security could not be in the slightest degree questioned whether the probable return of premium was 5*l*. or 95*l*. per cent. the Insurer would not be satisfied. The conduct of the Norwich Office in all parts of the country was most liberal and satisfactory. He believed that exclusive of the metropolis, its insurances amounted to between 35 and 40 millions, and that there was not in this extensive range a single outstanding claim. The Insurances in the London department amounted to only four millions, yet on that, several claims were yet unadjusted. It was due to the parties themselves, who managed the affairs in that district, to give them the opportunity of explaining from whence this circumstance arose. It was but justice to say that he imputed no improper motive to the management of the London department. It was impossible, indeed, that any unworthy motive could have influenced their conduct, inasmuch as they had no private interest; but it could not be denied that there were apparent errors of judgment, which must be explained. From some cause or other it appeared that the streams of liberality which issued from the fountain-head at Norwich to nourish and fructify the country departments, were dammed up, and intercepted from the London insurers. It was impossible that he should have any prejudices against the London Companies – the son of an original and most active Director of the Phœnix – the nephew of one of the founders and most zealous Directors of the Imperial – the nephew of one Director of the Albion – the partner of another – and the friend of very many Directors of that and other Offices, he must nevertheless confess that it appeared to him, that the head and front of the offending of the Norwich Office, was, that it gave for nothing to the public, that security, by the sale of which the other Offices derived a large profit. It would be nothing to prove, even though it might easily be done, that the motives from which the proceedings at the George and Vulture originated, were very different from those which had been avowed. With regard to the errors imputed to the Managers of the London department their motive he did not mean to question, but he believed the feeling to be universal, that inquiry was necessary. In one instance a verdict had been obtained against the Office, but the amount was not immediately paid. Some time was certainly allowed by law, but it was not liberal, nor did it evince that spirit which would alone justify an appeal to a Jury, to avail themselves after its decision of the law's delay. He was not a London Insurer, but although it was owing to private friendship towards a Manager of a Country department that he had not effected his Policy in town, he found that Insurances to a large amount were effected on London property, by persons approving the principle of the Norwich Union, in the same circuitous mode; and although he endeavoured amongst London friends, to promote the interest of the Norwich Union Office, he had not succeeded, in consequence of the system of management prevailing there. The Board were bound to disavow or to explain the proceedings of their Agents. Some claims were refused that appeared to him from the statements of them which had gone forth, to be perfectly equitable in themselves, and if such errors were continued, the concern could not go on prosperously. In what he had stated, he had no doubt that he expressed the sentiments of the London Insurers, with many of whom he had accidentally communicated.

Mr. BIGNOLD, sen.[6] regretted that charges preferred against his management should be listened to by any considerable insurer; and added, that being himself the person with whom the idea of promoting the prompt adjustment of claims by means of Committees had originated, he might reasonably contend that this did not look like a wish to create delay, or to withhold payments. There being at first but few insurers in London, it was not judged necessary to form a Committee there; but he had himself suggested and been desirous of it, long previous to the reports which had lately appeared in the Newspapers. It should not be forgotten that all these reports *were ex parte*. When the documents connected with the subject were produced, he had no doubt but they would clear him of all imputation.

FREDERICK SAVORY, Esq.[7] of the House of Savory, Towgood, and Co. Bankers, Bristol, said, he was the acting Member of the Society for the Bristol District, and he had great pleasure in stating to so respectable a Meeting, that the instructions he had received from the Board, were to act towards claimants upon the most liberal principles. He could further assure them, that no unsettled claim upon the Office existed in Bristol, or any of the Counties under his superintendence; nor as he verily believed, were there any to be found unadjusted out of London. Being himself a large insurer, and his father being Chairman of the Bristol Committee, he of course, felt a deep interest in the reports lately circulated. He came up to London on purpose to ascertain whether the charges made referred to the general practice of the Office, or were confined to London. He had been some time before to Norwich; had conversed about the Office with the most respectable men there; had informed himself of the state of the funds, and of the system of conduct pursued by the Board, and he felt no doubt that the prejudices existing against the Society were without foundation. From this conviction he had recommended the Institution to his friends; and having lately been through twenty-seven different counties in the kingdom, he had every where found the Society rising in estimation, and the conduct of its Managers spoken of in the highest terms. The increase of business was, in his judgment, a sufficient proof of the just and liberal principles upon which it was conducted. In the County of Norfolk the amount insured had risen from one to four millions, and in Bristol, during the last two years, it increased not less than one million and a half.

Mr. LOVELL, the Acting Member for the Birmingham district, spoke in similar terms of the general estimation and growing importance of the Society, in the Midland Counties, and that no outstanding claims existed there within his knowledge.

SAMUEL BROOKE, Esq., of Lamb's Conduit-street, said, that very satisfactory testimony had certainly been borne to the liberality and general good management which prevailed in the Country Departments of the Institution; but he spoke as a Londoner, and must contend that this was no answer to the complaints which had been made, and the dissatisfaction which had arisen in the Metropolis. For his part, he could wish that a Committee should be appointed, for the express purpose of examining into the grounds of this dissatisfaction, and that no Resolution should be passed by the present Meeting, but what was confined to that object.

JOHN MIDDLETON, Esq.,[8] of Skinner-street, said, that neither the general conduct nor the stability of the Institution had been at all questioned, and he agreed entirely with the last Speaker, that the attention of the Meeting should be confined to the subject of the late alledged grievances in London. He then moved a Resolution, for the appointment of a Committee for that particular object, which, after some further discussion, was finally put and carried.

Notes

1 John Thomas Thorp (died 1835) was a London draper. He served as a London common councilman from 1812 to 1817, alderman from 1817 to 1835, and Lord Mayor in 1820–21.

2 Edward B. Lovell was a partner in the bank Lovell, Goode, and Stubbs, and, with the brass-founder Charles Juxon, was the NUF district agent in Birmingham.

3 Thomas Bensley (1759–1835) was a London printer who apprenticed with his father and took over the shop on his father's death in 1789. He printed numerous bibles and scientific treatises and pioneered a new lithographic printing technique in 1807. His shop suffered two devastating fires, one in 1807 and the other in 1819.

4 Samuel Bignold (1791–1875) was the third son of Thomas Bignold and took over as secretary of the NUF in 1814 and Norwich Union Life in 1818, both of which positions he held until his death. He briefly represented Norwich in Parliament in the 1850s.

5 Francis Kemble was a wholesale grocer and tea dealer and governor of two asylums. His father, also Francis Kemble, a wealthy director, trustee, and customer of Phoenix Fire, died in 1800.

6 Thomas Bignold (1761–1835) settled in Norwich in 1783 and was a wine and spirit merchant before founding the Norwich Union General Insurance Company in 1792; he left that to found the NUF five years later. After his dismissal from NUF in 1818, he founded the short-lived National Union Mutual Association in London, then retired to Norwich.

7 Frederick Savery was a partner with William Towgood (died 1835) in Savery, Towgood and Co., Bristol bankers.

8 John Middleton was a London stationer, also governor of the Asylum for the Support and Education of the Deaf and Dumb Children of the Poor and for the Society of Friends of Foreigners in Distress.

Editorial Headnote

Welsh Iron and Coal Company (1826)

Although historians of the British speculative mania of 1825 typically focus on Latin America, the vast majority of new companies that formed at that time attracted money for prosaically British projects such as town improvement, shipbuilding, and flour mills. Even mining, which raised so many exotic Latin American hopes, generated a larger number of company flotations (though far less capital) in Britain than abroad.[1] One such venture was the Welsh Iron and Coal Mining Company (WICMC), concocted by John Wilks, Jr., who promoted equally disastrous mining ventures in Ireland, Devon, and Cornwall. As a scathing auditor's report revealed, Wilks and his associates had skimmed thousands of pounds from paid-up capital that had been intended to purchase and mine an absentee landlord's estate in North Wales. Leading the charge against Wilks was William Clark, a clerk-turned-stockbroker who added the WICMC to a long list of companies he called to task for bilking him and his clients. Although his actions as a corporate gadfly did succeed in riling up other shareholders, they mainly just entertained the public and annoyed judges. At a different mining company meeting, Wilks discredited Clark by exposing his recent commitment to a lunatic asylum, while judges typically blamed Clark and his fellow travelers for being sore losers, claiming that they had appealed to the law only after their speculations had turned sour.[2]

In a different sense, Clark and other disgruntled investors did succeed in shaping the public's perception of company promoters as dishonest scoundrels. As Clark bragged at a different company meeting in 1827, he had "succeeded in covering these directors with shame, and driving them out of society." The fact that reporters gained access to the WICMC meeting in August 1826 was itself a tribute to the shareholders' tenacity in foiling the directors' continued efforts to hush up their questionable activities. Besides being outvoted on the matter of reporters' access, the chair, Peter Moore, also failed to prevent the auditor, William Venning, from reading his report. Such stormy confrontations were typical of shareholder meetings across England during 1826 and 1827. Although some of Wilks's closest colleagues – most notably, Lord Palmerston – survived the crash with their reputations unscathed, others were not so lucky. When Wilks's other speculative schemes also failed, he entered Parliament in 1826 to avoid debtor's prison but was forced to move to Paris in 1828 after continued charges of forgery and theft. He persisted in such activities there and again upon returning to London in 1840. Moore, his partner in scandal, fared even worse: his unsuccessful bid to retain his seat in Parliament in 1826 resulted in bankruptcy and exile in France, where he died two years later.[3]

Notes

1 Henry English, *A Complete View of the Joint Stock Companies, formed during the Years 1824 and 1825* (London: Boosey and Sons, 1827).

2 James Taylor, *Boardroom Scandal: The Criminalization of Company Fraud in Nineteenth-Century Britain* (Oxford: Oxford University Press, 2013), 24–34. For a breezy account of the WICMC's misfortunes, from the perspective of the architect who designed its company town near Wrexham, see Charles Dickens, ed., *The Life of Charles James Mathews: Chiefly Autobiographical* (London: Macmillan and Co., 1879), 1: 170–176.

3 Taylor, *Boardroom Scandal*, 30, 39–40; James Taylor, "Privacy, Publicity, and Reputation: How the Press Regulated the Market in Nineteenth-Century England," *Business History Review* 87 (2013), 687.

3

WELSH IRON AND COAL COMPANY

Source: Welsh Iron and Coal Company (1826), *London Times*, 28 August 1826

WELSH IRON COMPANY

On Saturday a meeting of this company took place at the London Tavern, for the purpose, as the advertisement expressed it, of examining the accounts and investigating the concern. Mr. John Wilks, jun.'s,[1] connexion with this company, rendered the meeting one of no common interest, particularly as Mr. William Clark[2] has been elected an auditor; and it was reported that some extraordinary expenditure had taken place, which it would be matter of difficulty to account for.

Our reporter was refused admission upon presenting himself at the door, upon which a sharp discussion took place within, upon the proposition for allowing the members of the press to attend. Mr. Clark proposed that the reporters be forthwith admitted. Mr. Peter Moore[3] and Mr. Langslow[4] opposed the motion, which was carried by a majority of 29 to 3.

Mr. PETER MOORE was in the chair.

The CHAIRMAN, seeing a vast pile of books and documents upon the table, represented the inconvenience which must attend the public examination of such a variety of information, and at such a place.

Mr. LANGSLOW submitted the impracticability of the thing. He suggested the propriety of appointing a committee of proprietors, who held no office, to investigate the accounts at the office, and he proposed a resolution to that effect.

Mr. SELBY agreed that it would be advisable to appoint such a committee. He rejoiced that the newspapers would have accounts of what took place, as he understood the abuses were most enormous; and he trusted that an endeavour would be made to get a restitution of the money, which, in his opinion, had been so dishonourably obtained from the proprietors.

Mr. W. CLARK said, that the auditors had made some progress, and were ready with a report for the proprietors.

Mr. LANGSLOW rose to oppose the reading of any thing that had not an immediate reference to the expressed object of the meeting.

The CHAIRMAN rose to put the first resolution, which, after a great deal of exceedingly unnecessary discussion, was agreed to. Mr. Langslow was at different times accused of raising frivolous objections, for the purpose of occasioning

DOI: 10.4324/9781003177715-4

delay. Mr. Clark was anxious to read the report of the auditors, and the proprietors were still more anxious to hear it read; but Mr. Langslow persevered in opposition, and was joined by Mr. Peter Moore, who frequently smote the table, and threatened to leave the room if the meeting did not act legally and constitutionally.

The balance-sheet was then read, from which it appeared that the sum of 102,170*l.* 10*s.* 11*d.* had been received and expended since the formation of the company, one item of which expenditure (Mr. Wilks's bill) amounted to as much as 3,514*l.*

Mr. HARRIS then moved that the report of the auditors be read.

Mr. LANGSLOW and Mr. PETER MOORE resolutely opposed the motion, and called aloud to the shareholders to abide by the deed of settlement, and not act in violation of the law. (Laughter.)

Several Shareholders. – We are satisfied of the legality of entertaining the proposition just made.

Mr. LANGSLOW said, the deed stated that the auditors should make a report to the Directors, not to the proprietors. Now, a report of the former kind had not been made, and any other would be in contravention of the deed.

Mr. CLARK said, that if the Directors were ashamed of nothing, their anxiety was the most unaccountable thing in the world. All he could state was, that if the proprietors were not put in possession of the contents of the report, they must remain in ignorance of facts which it was highly essential they should know. (Cries of "Go on Mr. Clark; read it as part of your speech, if the Chairman is so squeamish.")

Mr. PETER MOORE here struck the table a violent blow, and again called to the proprietors to look to the deed of settlement.

A Shareholder. – I ask you, Mr. Moore, whether the deed has not been violated by the Directors taking enormous sums of money?

Mr. J. CAMPBELL. – I believe that not one guinea has been taken by the Directors that was not according to the deed.

Mr. P. MOORE. – I'll have the deed read: (A laugh; "for the deed is enormously long.)

Shareholders. – It is only for the purpose of delay that these objections are made – let it be put to the vote.

Mr. PETER MOORE (hitting the table hard.) – I'll go according to law.

Mr. VENNING,[5] finding that the opposition to reading the report of the auditors was likely to continue, read it as a part of his speech. The leading features of it are as follow: –

The titles to the company's estates in Wales were, the auditors believed, secured to the company, although the conveyances were not completed from causes which appeared to them unsatisfactory, and for an explanation thereon, they begged to refer to the solicitor of the company. It behoved them to state, that great irregularities had taken place in the various purchase monies, by which the company's property had been exposed to much risk, especially as a payment of 12,500*l.* for the Coad Talon estate[6] to Mr. Jones, had been made to, and withheld by, Mr.

John Wilks, junior, who had appropriated it to his own private purposes, and by a contrivance, some months afterwards, obtained from Mr. Jones his receipt to the company, for the money, giving his own acceptances at distant dates to Mr. Jones, which acceptances had never been paid. On the subject of shares, it appeared that 7,983 had been issued to the proprietors, and that 3,000 were originally reserved and appropriated to the Directors and other officers of the company; about 2,000 of which the deposits had never been paid upon, notwithstanding that three of the directors – namely, Lord Teynham,[7] Mr. Peter Moore, and Mr. William Kershaw[8] – had each received from Mr. Wilks the sum of 500*l.* for their respective interests in the same. This could only be attributed to the fact of the shares afterwards going to a discount. In the balance sheet laid before the former meeting on the 31st of January last, two sums, making together 1,114*l.* 7*s.* 6*d.*, were charged to the debit of the company for premiums and brokerage upon letters and scrip receipts for shares purchased through Messrs. Edmonds, and Woolf, and Marjoribanks, and Co.,[9] in the months of February and March, 1825; and in the month of March, 1825, 630 shares were sold in the name and for the benefit of the company through Mr. Charles Danvers (whose partner, Mr. Kent,[10] was at the time a Director of the company) at premiums from 2¼ to 4 per share, producing a net profit of 1,713*l.* 15*s.*, which sum is not carried to the credit of the company; and there is reason to believe that other shares were sold at considerable profit about the same time, which they (the auditors) were unable to give a distinct account of, from the unaccountable absence of the company's share committee minute book, which had been withheld from them. Extracts had, however, been fortunately preserved by the former auditors, by which it appeared that six of the Directors, who formed the committee of accounts, met only 21 times in the eleven months ending the 31st of December, 1825, for the purpose of their duty as a committee of accounts, but they attended no less than 181 times as a committee of shares. There was also a deficiency of 290*l.* upon the account of instalments on shares, of which the company had been deprived from causes which, after much investigation, they were wholly unable to trace to its proper source. The auditors then directed particular attention to the expenses attending the establishing and management of the company, which expenses appeared to them most unnecessary and prodigal: and the same observation would apply to a part of the establishment in Wales. The report concludes with earnestly recommending a system of retrenchment and future economy that should comprehend in every department of the concern, upon which, and upon an efficient management, the prosperity of the company seemed mainly to depend. The report was signed, "William Venning, John Horler,[11] and William Clark."

When the report, which excited considerable astonishment amongst the shareholders, was concluded, several gentlemen requested that the auditors would enter into some detail of the extraordinary transactions to which it alluded.

Mr. Clark (having been called upon by name) rose amidst applause, and said he would endeavour to perform that duty to the best of his power, but he could not help expressing his surprise that the Directors, if they were conscious of having done no wrong, should have been so anxious to avoid inquiry, and the explanation which he would give to the meeting would perhaps make the matter intelligible. He would never attempt to screen men who, by their misconduct, had reduced the value of the property of the Company from 25*l*. to 7*l*. per share. The first thing he adverted to, was the 12,500*l*. which had been withheld by Mr. Wilks. He called it a fraudulent transaction, and said that it accounted for the non-conveyance of the titles to the estates in Wales. (Hear, hear.) In respect of the number of shares issued to the public, it appeared that there were 7,983 upon which the deposits and instalments had been paid into the hands of the bankers, and which formed the present capital of the company. 3,000 shares were reserved for the Directors, auditors, &c., originally, 900 of which had been appropriated, namely, 600 to Sir John Marjoribanks, 200 to Mr. Phillip Perring,[12] 100 to Mr. Gray,[13] the resident Director in Wales, and a few more to friends of the Directors, leaving about 2,000 still unappropriated, which if paid upon, would form an increased capital to the company of 50,000*l*.; and he hoped that as a minute had been made upon the share committee minute-book, of the number each particular Director and other officers was to take, which fixed the certainty of the appropriation, the shareholders would, if possible, compel the parties to pay upon them according to their engagement. (Hear, hear.) If they did not, it might happen that they would be, for the purpose of carrying on the affairs of the company, under the necessity of issuing those shares, which at their present price would produce only about 15,000*l*., and it would be the same thing as making the Directors a present of 35,000*l*. at the expense of the company. The next thing to observe upon was the sum of 1,114*l*. 7*s*. 6*d*., charged for the premiums, &c., upon shares purchased, and the net accounting for 1,713*l*. 15*s*. for premiums produced by the sale of shares, which latter sum, from the share committee minute-book, it appeared was divided amongst 13 of the Directors, who were to have 100*l*. each, and the balance of 413*l*. 15s. was paid to Mr. Wilks, who, finding the former auditors disapprove of such a transaction, drew four draughts upon his banker in their presence for 30*l*. each, which he presented to them as a bribe or hush-money; and he (Mr. Clark) was happy to say, that they had the virtue to reject the temptation with disdain. These draughts were afterwards sealed up in a brown paper parcel, and what became of them he would decline to state, in the absence of gentlemen who were not there to defend themselves. Mr. Clark here inquired whether any thing could be so dishonourable, so base, as for Directors of a joint stock company to charge losses to the company upon their own speculation in shares, and to put large profits into their pockets when other speculations of the same kind turned out profitable, at the same time charging to the company 294*l*. for Directors' attendance on committees held for the express purpose of this species of traffic. (Loud cries of "Shame," and cheers.) As for the 290*l*. loss by an inattention in the issuing of shares originally, it was too trifling to be noticed; but the mention might be calculated to weaken the effect of the strong facts to which he had alluded. This would account for the absence of the share committee minute-book. With regard to the other items of expenditure, he would first mention the expenses of management, which in the short period of eighteen months amounted to no less a sum than 7,959*l.* 8*s.* 6*d.* In this sum was included the amount paid to the Directors for their attendances. Mr. Clark said, that in the formation of a joint stock company, if Directors were governed by the feelings and liberality of gentlemen, they would give their time gratuitously, until the profits of the concern would afford them a remuneration (cheers); but here the ingenuity of the Directors was set to work, to ascertain by what contrivances then could put most money into their pockets. The deed of settlement provided, that there should be, at least, one board day in the week, which left them at liberty to assemble as often as they pleased; and they are not content with having four or five board days in the week, but they split and divide each day into two boards of Directors and six committees – namely, board of Directors, special board of Directors, committee of management, committee of accounts, instalment committee, dividend committee, and deed and rent-roll committee, (loud laughter), multiplying their fees by the variety of their transformation. (Cries of "shame, scandalous imposition.") He (Mr. Clark) would now show what the Directors had received, and what they would have been entitled to under the deed of settlement had their board-days been confined to two each week, which he considered ample for all the purposes of the company. In the space of 18 months Mr. Peter Moore had received –

For attendance the sum of			*By the deed he ought to have received*	
	£859	19	£283	10
–Barrett	507	3	218	8
–Kershaw	659	19	218	8
P. Perring	366	9	133	7
–Gray	307	19	120	15

Making, with the rest of the party, a total amount paid to them of 3,319*l.* 7*s*., instead of 1,232*l.* 14*s*., and a consequent overpayment of 2,680*l.* 13*s*. The meeting would say whether such conduct was to be endured, and decide whether, if the Directors did not refund the whole of that money, and make restitution of their ill-gotten gains in the traffic in shares bought and sold for the company, they would not proclaim themselves men devoid of all principle and honour. (Cheers.) The next item was in Mr. Wilks's law bills, which amounted in the whole to 3,514*l.*, besides 1,277*l.* 18*s*. 9*d.* for stamps – (shame, shame) – which presented a curious picture. The first of these bills for 12 months, amounted to upwards of 1,900*l.*, and amongst other extravagant and novel charges, contained the following: –

1824.	*MR. WILKS'S BILL.*	*£*	*s*	*d*
July 16.	Journey to, and attending at, Wales for several days, inspecting the works, and going fully into the particulars thereof, with a view of establishing an iron and coalmining company . .	105	0	0
	Paid expenses and chaise hire	67	0	0

1824.	*MR. WILKS'S BILL.*			£	*s.*	*d.*
Oct. 20.	Perusing four abstracts relating to tenements			21	0	0
30.	Making copies of abstracts of title for counsel			30	0	0
1825.						
Jan. 4.	Perusing and considering Mr. Preston's opinion	£ 2	2			
	Several subsequent attendances, and investigating the title	21	0	23	2	0
	Journey to and attending Messrs. Jones at Coed Tallon, with a view of purchasing the property, and establishing a joint stock company			105	0	0
	Paid expenses			67	0	0
	Drawing advertisement for the papers	£ 2	2			
	Making eight fair copies	2	2	4	4	0
	Drawing prospectus			5	0	0
	Engaged the whole day receiving tenders, for shares for self and six clerks.			10	10	0
18.	Attending at office answering inquiries			10	10	0
19.	The same			10	10	0
	Drawing letter requesting gentlemen to become Directors			1	0	0
	Twenty fair copies			5	0	0
	Filling-up, folding, and directing prospectusses			10	10	0
	Attending to take a suitable house in Broad-street for offices			5	5	0
	Many attendances on different persons.			10	10	0
March 1.	Attending deputation into Wales to inspect mines at Coed Tallon, &c.			52	10	0
	Travelling and other expenses of deputation, including the hire of a carriage			153	5	5
	Drawing report of deputation.			5	5	0
July 11.	Journey to Liverpool, and expenses.			83	17	6
1825.						
Feb.	Instructions for deed of settlement	£ 5	5			
	Drawing same	42	0			
	Fair copy	14	0			
14.	Engrossing deed on vellum	30	0			
	Parchment and duty.	30	0	121	5	0
	Making copies of deeds			20	0	0

[The reading of this bill caused as much laughter as indignation in the room.]

The next year's bill, which was of the same description, contained almost as many charges of one, two, and three guineas for attendances on the Board of Directors' committee, as they themselves had charged for attendances, from which it was inferred that it is necessary upon all occasions to take legal advice upon that subject. (A laugh.) The former account had never been checked or examined in any particular. It was an important fact, that upon applications being made by Mr. Wilks, two sums of money, one on the 8th of September, 1825, 655*l.* 18*s.* 9*d.*, the other on the 11th of April, 1826, 622*l.* were ordered, by the Directors to be paid to that gentleman, for stamps for the Coed Tallon deeds and the Llwyninion deeds,[14] he saying they were ready to be executed by Mr. Jones, which sums of money he appropriated to his own use, the stamps never having been paid for, and the deeds never having been executed to this day. (Shame, shame.) This (said Mr. Clark) and some other transactions of the same kind, in my opinion, bring Mr. Wilks's conduct within the statute of frauds of the 52d of George III., and subject him to the penalty of transportation. (Cheers.) Mr. Wilks was a holder of 280 shares, and upon being called upon to pay the third and fourth instalments, he gave his acceptance for 2,000*l.* to the company, which was not paid when it became due, and as he had possession of the title-deeds of all the estates, the Directors felt it prudent to renew his acceptance on condition of his delivering them up. This acceptance became due on the 13th instant, and was likewise dishonoured, and strange to say, the Directors in the mean time permitted Mr. Willks to sell out and transfer all his shares without paying the instalments due, and he was now their debtor in the above sum. This, Mr. Clark considered a piece of gross neglect and mismanagement on the part of the directors, to call it by no worse a name. In the arrangement made with Mr. Jones for the purchase of the Coed Tallon estate, he was to take 500 shares at par in part payment, and he gave directions to Mr. Wilks to pay the deposits into the bankers, amounting to 2,500*l.*, out of the first 10,000*l.* received from the company. When the second instalment was advertised to be paid by the public, the company discovered a much greater number of shares than corresponded with the receipts, which fact led to an inquiry. Mr. Wilks denied any knowledge as to the cause. It was ascertained, however, that he had sold Mr. Jones's 500 shares without his knowledge at a considerable premium, and appropriated the whole of the money to his own private use. Upon tracing the transactions to Mr. Wilks, through the medium of different brokers, and fixing him with the fraud, he said that such an occurrence might have happened in the multiplicity of his affairs, and refunded the money. (Loud laughter.) The expenses of establishing the company amounted to 7,550*l.*, embracing a most improvident and unjustifiable expenditure, as would be seen by the account laid before the meeting. For the establishment in Wales it was deemed necessary to purchase the residence of Colonel Wardle,[15] for the abode of Mr. Gray, the resident Director, for which the sum of 750*l.* was agreed to be paid to the Colonel, and his son and the company covenanted to lay out 2,500*l.* in repairs and additions; the whole amount which had been expended upon that place was about 5,000l. The sum of 750l. was given to Mr. Wilks for the express purpose of being paid over to Colonel Wardle and his son, the latter of whom only had been paid his moiety. The remainder had been applied by Mr. Wilks to his own private purposes. Mr. Gray, it appeared, engaged a farm of 40 acres of land, at a rental of 200l. per annum, without the sanction or even knowledge of the Company, and charged it in his accounts; and a resolution was lately come to, to allow him a salary of 600*l*. a year, making the whole expense of the resident Director a charge upon the company of about 1,500*l*. a-year. (Cries of "Scandalous" and other strong expressions of indignation.) The meeting were not to suppose from this picture that their affairs were in a hopeless state. On the contrary, they had an intrinsically valuable property in the mines themselves, which required only good and provident management to make them productive. The roots and the trunk of the tree were sound, and these locusts had devoured the honey, and lopped the tree of its branches. If any of the present Directors were unfit and incompetent to manage the affairs, the sooner they retired the better. It was a mistaken notion to suppose, as some of them had intimated, that an exposure of this sort would have the effect of lessening the value of the concern in the eyes of the public. It was always best to deal with openness and candour upon all occasions, and knowing the worst of the evil, the mind was the better satisfied and prepared to apply the remedy. He recommended the most rigid economy to be observed in every department, and the whole system to be remodelled, and then sat down in the midst of cheers.

Mr. Langslow, a Director, entered into a justification of the conduct of himself and brother Directors. They had always been most anxious to afford the fullest information to the auditors. With respect to the signing of the draughts for Mr. Wilks, at which meeting of the Directors he was present, he could assure the meeting that at that time he had no doubt Mr. Wilks deserved the utmost confidence. He was sure that had the hon. auditor (Mr. Clark) been in his place, he would have consented to have given the money to Mr. Wilks. (Mr. Clark shook his head.) It was a confidence, he was convinced, any individual similarly circumstanced would have placed in his solicitor. For, be it remembered, Mr. Wilks came to them, and said, that the deeds for the conveyance of the property would be immediately made out, at least as soon as the stamp duty was paid. The board of Directors, therefore, considered that as it was of the utmost importance to have the business settled without delay, they instantly drew a check for the money.

A Proprietor asked whether the hon. Director had not had some slight intimation of what might occur?

Mr. Langslow declared, upon his honour, that he had at the time no doubt as to the rectitude of the conduct of Mr. Wilks. With respect to the refusal of the minute-book, he would just say, that that was a book into which the auditors had no right at all to look; it was not a book of accounts; but at the same time, had the auditors gone into the company's office, they might have inspected it at any time. He had received a letter from Mr. Kershaw, in which he stated that he was unable, from business, to attend the present meeting, but should be glad, at another time, to give the proprietors all the information in his power. Now, Mr. Kershaw was one of the old Directors, and the sweeping accusation made by Mr. Clark was not altogether correct with respect to the original Directors. He was now more convinced than ever that the publication of the statement made to-day would have a most prejudicial effect on the company's affairs, and thought it would have been much better if the course he had previously recommended were adopted.

Mr. VENNING (one of the auditors) was sorry to say that they had the greatest difficulty in obtaining an inspection of the books. He had, in his official capacity, followed that course which strict honour dictated, and however much he had wished to spare those Directors whom he knew, he had been obliged strictly to adhere to the truth. As an instance of the total neglect of the Directors, he would state, that at one time not less than 60,000l. were allowed to remain in the banker's hands. Shortly after that period a check was drawn for 12,500l. in favour of Mr. Wilks, for the ostensible purpose of liquidating the debt due to Mr. Jones, the vendor of part of the property; but this money Mr. Wilks had kept himself, and the auditors adjourned their meetings from time to time, until they obtained from Mr. Wilks a proper acknowledgment that the money had been paid.

Mr. CLARK said, that Mr. Verbecke would probably give some information why the deeds were not duly executed.

Mr. VERBECKE,[16] the solicitor to the company, replied, that from what he knew of the matter, he was firmly persuaded that the sole cause why the deeds were not drawn up by Mr. Wilks, was, because he did not wish to give up the 12,500*l.* which he had received from the company.

Mr. CLARK said, that as it was probable that the proceedings would be published, it was necessary to state that the new Directors were not to be included in the accusations against the original Directors. He was sure that the former had used their utmost endeavours to bring the affairs of the Company into a wholesome state.

Mr. SELBY moved the following resolution: – "That a committee of the shareholders be appointed with the auditors, five of whom to be a quorum, consisting of the following proprietors: – Mr. W. Oakley, J. A. Valpy, J. Thomas, Robert Harris, jun., A. Favey, James Saunders, Joseph Wells, H. Turner, and R. Selby, to examine into the present state of the company's affairs, and to report to a general meeting, to be called by the committee, with all convenient despatch."

Mr. LANGSLOW said, that if this motion were carried, he would not continue a Director another hour. It was casting a reflection on the present directors, and he should, therefore, take his leave. If the proprietors did not place confidence in the directors, he thought they had all better resign.

A Proprietor. – We have no confidence in the Directors.

A scene of great confusion was here exhibited, in the midst of which the Chairman assured the proprietors that he would never preside there again. (Cries of "We are glad of it.") Mr. P. Moore declared that he had heard that day what he had never heard before. Ultimately, the motion was put and carried by an immense majority.

Mr. VERBECKE, jun., stated, that as the trusteeship of the company's property had become vacant by the resignation of Lord Palmerston,[17] and also that of Mr. P. Moore, he thought it would be expedient to propose gentlemen to fill up the vacancies.

It was then proposed and carried, that Mr. Turner, Mr. W. Davies, and Mr. Oakley, should become trustees.

Thanks were then voted to the auditors and chairman, and the meeting adjourned.

We have received the following letter from Mr. Wilks: –

To the Editor of the Times

Sir, – Having this day read in the *News*, the *Weekly Despatch*, and the *Observer*, reports of the proceedings at a meeting of the shareholders in this concern, held yesterday at the London Tavern, in which statements are made wholly false, and scandalously libellous relative to myself, I beg of you to insert this letter in your paper of Monday, in order that a report of the meeting, which will, doubtless, then appear, may, at the same time, be accompanied by this explanation.

First, as to the *News*. – In this paper it is stated, that "I bribed three of the Directors to hold their tongues by a donation of 500*l*. each." This statement is wholly untrue, and without any foundation whatever, and I challenge those who have made the charge to bring forward their proofs.

In the same paper it is alleged, that my bill amounted to nearly 4,000*l*., all of which has been paid almost without examination. This statement is also untrue, as the only bill which has been paid amounted to not quite 2,000*l*.; and although money has been paid by the Directors on account of another bill, yet such bill is under examination, and has been so for some months.

Secondly, as to the *Weekly Despatch*. – In that paper it is asserted, first, that I have drawn 1,200*l*. for stamps, and appropriated the money to my own use. This allegation is without foundation, since the money was appropriated as directed, and the deeds twice engrossed for execution, but owing to the resignation of Mr. Kershaw, as trustee, and now Lord Palmerston, the deeds must be a third time engrossed. Since my resignation of the office of solicitor in May last, and the re-engrossment of the deeds, I have not affixed the *ad valorem* stamps, but given the company credit for the amount. The other allegation in this paper is, that when the auditors commenced the examination of accounts, I offered them a check for 30*l*. each "as hush money." This statement is also without foundation. Many months ago, when Mr. Prater, Mr. Venning, Mr. Horlor, and Mr. Jackson Perring were auditors, I was instructed to pay to them the sum of 30*l*. each, being their proportion of the profit made on the sale of shares reserved for the benefit of the directors, auditors, and officers, and which, at the first audit, the auditors had not disapproved. In obedience to the instructions of the directors, I paid the amounts to the auditors, who made no objection at the time thereto; but I learned subsequently, that after some of the auditors had quarrelled with some of the directors, the auditors, with one exception, declined presenting the checks, and three out of the four were returned to me. This, then, is the charge of hush money which has been so falsely and wickedly made.

Thirdly, as to the *Observer*. – It is there stated, 1st, that the sum of 12,500*l.* was retained by me for a long time from Mr. Jones. This statement is false, as it was paid over directly, and a receipt soon after given by Mr. Jones to me for the amount, which receipt was required from me by the auditors, when I was out of town, but immediately on my arrival in town, I handed it to the Secretary. It is also alleged that I offered the sum of 413*l.* to the auditors, and that they rejected it. This also is untrue, and I must say Mr. Clark knew it to be so. The same charge as to the stamps, is also made in this paper, and needs not a separate refutation. The *Observer* further charges, that I am in debt to the company 2,500*l.*, and the individual who makes the statement is Mr. Clark, though I had previously, both in public, and by letter addressed to the auditors, proved the statement to be incorrect, as the company is indebted to me, instead of myself to the company.

As to the general allegations of Messrs. Wilks and Verbeke's bills being large in amount, I only observe, that I never professed to be what is called a cheap lawyer, nor to leave to the management of junior clerks and understrappers, business which if so managed might be cheaply, but would be sure to be badly executed.

I merely add, that before Mr. W. Clark became a shareholder, he was put in possession of every fact connected with the company, and especially relating to the shares, &c., and attended at a meeting of Directors to state, that he was perfectly satisfied with the company, its concerns and management; that he merely wished to invest some of his money in the company; and that he never would directly or indirectly, take any part in annoying or disturbing the directors or officers of the establishment. So much then for the accuracy, truth, honour, word, and character of Mr. Clark, the late clerk of Messrs. Timperon and Co.

I am, Sir, your most obedient servant.

August 27th, 1826. JOHN WILKS, Jun.

Notes

1 John Wilks Jun (1798–1846), who, after 1826, became known as "Bubble Wilks," was articled in his father's law firm in 1815. After publishing *A Christian Biographical Dictionary* and two other books between 1821 and 1823, he promoted companies in gas lighting, mining, and a fish market between 1823 and 1826. He leased three houses and led an opulent lifestyle until the failure of the WICMC exposed his fraudulent methods.

2 William Clark was a clerk in the London-based West India merchant house of Joseph Timperon, Joseph Dobinson, and William Clark, which he entered in 1795. His name was added to the firm in 1811, when a London partner retired, then dismissed in 1822. Over the next four years, Clark waged a campaign against Timperon, accusing him of embezzlement, and a pamphlet he published led to a libel conviction in 1826.

3 Peter Moore (1753–1828) was a radical Whig politician. See note to 1 (Drury Lane Theatre).

4 Robert Langslow (1790–1853) was a barrister who went on to be a judge in Ceylon.

5 William Venning was a Cheapside silk manufacturer and director of the East London Waterworks.

6 Coad Talon was an estate in Flintshire, just north of Wrexham County near the town of Mold.
7 Henry Francis Roper-Curzon, 14th Lord Teynham (1768–1842), was a retired British army colonel who succeeded to the peerage in 1824. He spoke regularly in the House of Lords on such issues as the coal trade, malt duties, Irish representation, corporation reform (which he favored), and the East India Company monopoly (which he opposed).
8 William Kershaw was deputy chairman of WICMC and also sat on the boards of the Cornwall and Devonshire Mining Company (also chaired by Peter Moore) and the Welsh Slate, Copper and Lead Mining Company.
9 John Marjoribanks (1763–1833) was an MP from 1812 to 1826, first for Bute and later for Berwick; he was also Provost of Edinburgh in 1814. His brothers included the chair of the East India Company and a partner in the private bank Coutts and Co.
10 Charles Danvers and Adolphus Kent were sugar refiners whose factory (since at least 1811) was in Rutland Place, London.
11 John Horler (also spelled Horlor) was an original WICMC auditor (with Venning), served in the same capacity for the British Annuity Company, and was a Middlesex County church warden.
12 Philip Perring was a merchant in Bishopsgate, London and a founding WICMC director.
13 John Gray was the WICMC's original "resident director" in Wales. He was a retired London physician who had prior experience supervising coal mines in Northumberland.
14 Llwyneinion is a small town near Wrexham in northern Wales near the English border.
15 Col. Gwyllym Lloyd Wardle (1761–1833) was born in Flintshire, Wales, and came into property in Caernarvonshire (in northwest Wales) when he married Ellen Parry (1766–1844) in 1792. He moved to Bath in 1804, where he ran a distillery and, between 1807 and 1812, and served in Parliament as a trenchant critic of the government. He retired to Tunbridge Wells on being voted out in 1812, then to Florence in 1815, where he remained until he died. Since Gray's residence was in or near Flintshire, it is likely that the property Wardle sold the WICMC had been inherited from his father and not his wife.
16 Frederick Verbeke was John Wilks's legal partner until they had a falling out in 1826 (prior to this meeting) over Wilks's refusal to hand over the company's share transfer book to a judge. Verbeke declared bankruptcy in 1827 and later founded the British Guiana Bank.
17 Henry John Temple, third Viscount Palmerston (1784–1865) served in Parliament from 1807 until his death with few interruptions, including two stints as Prime Minister between 1855 and 1865. Although his friendship with Wilks embroiled him in several bubble schemes in the 1820s, he escaped with his political reputation intact.

Editorial Headnote

National Provincial Bank (1834)

By the time the National Provincial Bank (NPB) held its first annual meeting in 1834, it had already been the talk of London for five years. The bank was the brainchild of Thomas Joplin (1790–1847), a timber merchant who became a full-time promoter of joint-stock banks in the early 1820s. He founded the London-based Provincial Bank of Ireland in 1824, which he managed until 1828. Under its "Scottish" system, the London office tightly supervised local boards in Irish towns, with the banks often staffed by clerks hired away from Scottish banks.[1] In 1829, four years before the Bank of England's charter was up for renewal, Joplin joined forces with London merchants to secure a provision in the new charter that would allow such banks to form within a 65-mile radius of the city, which prior charters had forbidden. By 1833, he was ready with a prospectus for a bank that would "spread its Branches in all directions . . . into agricultural as well as commercial districts." He assembled a powerful committee, including ten Members of Parliament, which raised £1 million in £100 shares and opened branches in more than 30 English towns by 1836. In contrast to his Irish bank, his original plan for the NPB was to structure it as a loose federation of provincial subsidiaries with local shareholders and directors.[2]

Although he was conspicuously absent at its first meeting, Joplin did publish a long pamphlet in January that stridently defended his original plan for the bank.[3] The main agenda item at the special meeting that followed concerned what one shareholder called a "party question"; namely, whether to go through with Joplin's "principle of local shareholders" (referred to as the "English" and—confusingly—the "Scottish" method in the meeting) or, instead, to copy the more top-down model that was practiced by the Provincial Bank of Ireland. Several speakers defended Joplin's original plan, including his hand-picked secretary, Thomas Lamie Murray. Others, including the director Oliver Farrer, worried that it would be too costly and would lack sufficient oversight. Although the meeting (and three additional "extraordinary general meetings" in ensuing months) decided in favor of Joplin's scheme, the directors abruptly reversed course at the NPB's second annual meeting in 1835, resulting in the swift departure of both Joplin and Murray.[4]

Joplin never returned to the spotlight during the final chapter of his life, although he did persist in badgering the NPB's directors with pamphlets and litigation. Murray went on to found the National Bank of Ireland, which he modeled on Joplin's first bank, then formed the National Loan Fund, which pioneered the practice of lending money on the security of customers' life insurance policies; its financial troubles led to Murray's ouster as National Bank chair in 1851.[5] The National Provincial, in contrast, grew steadily over the following decades after recruiting a new manager, Daniel Robertson, from the Union Bank of Scotland.

Its branch network grew to 128 offices by 1865, a tenth of all bank branches in England at the time, through a mixture of opening new buildings and acquiring smaller country banks. By 1914, it qualified as one of Britain's "big five" banks, with nearly 500 branches and almost £75 million in deposits. It remained in this position until 1970, when it combined with the London & Westminster Bank to form NatWest.[6]

Notes

1 Philip Ollerenshaw, *Banking in Nineteenth-Century Ireland: The Belfast Banks, 1825-1914* (Manchester: Manchester University Press, 1987), 17–22.
2 Maberly Phillips, *A History of Banks, Bankers, & Banking in Northumberland, Durham, and North Yorkshire* (London: Effingham Wilson, 1894), 313–315; Hartley Withers, *National Provincial Bank: 1833 to 1933* (London: National Provincial Bank, 1933), 32, 39–40, 45, 56; Timothy L. Alborn, *Conceiving Companies: Joint-Stock Politics in Victorian England* (London: Routledge, 1998), 110.
3 Thomas Joplin, *A Letter to the Directors of the National Provincial Bank of England* (London: James Ridgway and Sons, 1834).
4 Withers, *National Provincial Bank*, 44–51. Farrer is identified as the director in question by Withers, p. 35; his name was listed as Farrell in the *Morning Chronicle* and Ferrars in a *London Standard* report of the meeting,
5 Francis Watt, "Thomas Joplin," *Oxford Dictionary of National Biography Online*; Withers, *National Provincial Bank*, 50–52; Malcolm Dillon, *The History and Development of Banking in Ireland from the Earliest Times to the Present Day* (London: Effingham Wilson, 1889), 64–65; Timothy Alborn, *Regulated Lives: Life Insurance and British Society, 1800– 1914* (Toronto: University of Toronto Press, 2009), 204.
6 Lucy Newton and P.L. Cottrell, "Joint-Stock Banking in the English Provinces 1826–1857: To Branch or Not to Branch?" *Business and Economic History* 27 (1998), 124; Youssef Cassis, *City Bankers, 1890– 1914* (Cambridge: Cambridge University Press, 1994), 43–48. On Robertson see Withers, *National Provincial Bank*, 53–56.

4

NATIONAL PROVINCIAL BANK

Source: National Provincial Bank (1834), *Morning Chronicle*, 9 May 1834

PROVINCIAL BANK OF ENGLAND

The first Yearly General Meeting of the Provincial Bank of England was held yesterday in the London Tavern, at twelve o'clock, to receive the Report of the Directors.

A PROPRIETOR moved that Mr. Robinson, M.P.,[1] be appointed Chairman of the Meeting.

Another PROPRIETOR, whose name we could not learn, proposed that Mr. Halliburton, M.P.,[2] be called to the Chair.

Mr. HALLIBURTON felt gratified for the honour done him by the Gentleman who had proposed his name; but as there was so much difference of opinion among the Proprietors on certain points, he begged to decline being put in nomination. Mr. Robinson, he was sure, ought to be preferred to any Gentleman. He was certain that whoever should be elected Chairman would do full justice to every Gentleman who might address the Meeting.

A PROPRIETOR stated that an understanding had been come to among the Directors, that whoever was their Chairman should be the Chairman of the General Meeting. He therefore trusted that the Gentleman who had proposed, as an Amendment, that Mr. Halliburton take the Chair, would see the propriety of withdrawing that Amendment.

Colonel LEITH HAY, M.P.,[3] had suggested to the Directors, before coming into that room, that his friend Mr. Halliburton should be chosen Chairman; but as he found the general opinion among them to be, that in all the circumstances Mr. Robinson would make the best Chairman, he did not press the thing. Now, however, that Gentleman had duly proposed, as an Amendment, that Mr. Halliburton be appointed Chairman, he trusted that Gentleman would not withdraw his Amendment. He (Colonel Leith Hay) would support it.

A PROPRIETOR thought that the meeting was making the appointment of a Chairman quite a party question [cries of "no, no!"]. He knew little of either of the gentlemen proposed, but he had seen Mr. Robinson preside at a public meeting lately, and he must say, that no gentleman could have filled the office of Chairman more ably or impartially, or more to the satisfaction of the persons present.

DOI: 10.4324/9781003177715-5

Several Gentlemen here asked, whether there was not a standing clause in the deed of co-partnery, which stated, that the Chairman of the Directors must also be Chairman at the general meeting of the Proprietors?

Mr. MURRAY, the Secretary to the Company, said there was no such Clause.

The question was then put to the vote, whether Mr. Robinson or Mr. Halliburton should be Chairman, when there appeared a large majority for the latter gentleman.

The CHAIRMAN, after briefly stating the objects for which the meeting was called, then desired the Secretary to read the Report.

The Report, which is as follows, was accordingly read: –

"Although active steps were not taken to establish this Company until the month of April, 1833, yet its formation was contemplated in the year 1830.

"The Act of 7th Geo. IV. cap. 46, passed in 1826, permitted the formation of Joint Stock Banks at any place exceeding 65 miles from London. The Act of 1833, while it authorises the formation of banks of deposit within that range, excludes banks of issue beyond 65 miles, from carrying on business as bankers in the metropolis. The National Provincial Bank of England has therefore been established under the provisions of the Act of 1826.

"A National Banking Establishment had long been thought desirable, and the proposal of such an institution sanctioned by high authorities, as one which would afford a solidity to banking operations, concentrate the great sources of credit on which the success of banking must depend, and from the amount of its aggregate capital, affords a wider basis of security to the public than could be expected from private partnerships, however respectable, on the limited resources of local Joint Stock Banks.

"These were the views which led to the formation of the first Committee in 1830, and ultimately in the last year to the public announcement of a metropolitan establishment, by the Committee under whose auspices the Company has been formed.

"The Committee, on its formation, took immediate measures to ascertain the support the public was disposed to give the undertaking, and having selected respectable agents in different parts of the country, through whom inquiries as to their views might be fully answered, a Prospectus was issued at a Meeting of the Committee held on the 6th April, 1833.

"The Prospectus was inserted in all the leading newspapers in the kingdom, and numerous applications for Shares were the result.

"The applications having exceeded the number to be granted, the intention of the Committee to close the list on the 13th June was duly notified to the public. The whole number of Shares applied for amounted to 13,168; but those Shares reserved for the Directors' List not having been taken, the whole number of Shares assigned was 8,340. Out of this number the deposit of 5*l*. per cent. has been paid on 7,815 Shares, and the Deed of Settlement has been executed by 451 Proprietors, holding 7,464 Shares. Thus it would appear that 351 Shares, on which the deposit of 5*l*. per Share has been paid, yet remain to be registered.

"The preliminary steps succeeding, and the Company formed, the present Directors were nominated, and the preparation of the Deed of Copartnership commenced.

"A Deed of Copartnership, embracing operations of such extent and magnitude as the National Provincial Bank, necessarily involved mature deliberation. During the progress of the Deed of Settlement, however, questions of great importance arose as to the powers to be included in it. On this head great difference of opinion existed, and still continues. The effect of these discussions was to retard the completion of the Deed of Settlement, and it was not until September that it was finally engrossed, and ready for the signature of the Proprietors.

"About the beginning of October measures were taken by the Directors for the formation of Branches at Gloucester and Birmingham. A Branch at Gloucester was opened on the 1st of January, 1834. The opening of the Branch at Birmingham has been, in the first instance, delayed by the nature of the negociation, which, however, was at last abandoned. The probability of its completion induced the Directors, on the 20th of December last, from the large amount of capital required for that Branch, to make a call upon the proprietors for 10*l*. a share.

"The Directors have since taken extensive and most eligible premises in Birmingham, and preparations are actively making for the immediate opening of that Branch.

"At Brecon 192 shares have been subscribed. This town is well situated as regards the iron trade, and an agricultural district. A Branch was opened at that place on the 26th of March.

"There being every prospect of a Bank succeeding at Walsall, in Staffordshire, one was opened at that place on the 14th of April.

At Wotton-under-Edge strong and influential parties agreed to support a Branch of the National Provincial Bank of England, if established there. The Directors have announced their intention of opening a Branch at Wotton, and shares have been taken in that neighbourhood. A Manager has also been appointed, and a house engaged. The Directors will be enabled to open a Branch there immediately.

"At Boston, in Lincolnshire, and at Wisbech, it is the intention of the Directors to open Branches. In the former place, the preparations are so matured, that the Bank will open in the course of the present month. At the latter place, the difficulty of procuring suitable premises has been the only obstacle. It is, however, probable, the Branch will open at Wisbech in June.

"The call of 10*l*. per share remains unpaid on 1,217 shares.

"The arrangements for the London Office are in progress of completion, and a house, No. 50 and 51, Broad-street, has been taken at a moderate rental, and in every respect believed to be suited to the uses of the Company.

"The Directors refer the Proprietors to the item in the account of 433*l*. 6*s*. advanced to Mr. Joplin on account of expences in forming the Company previous to the 1st of April, 1833. They have also advanced on loan 2,250*l*. at 4 per cent. to the same gentleman, being the deposit and instalment on 150 shares held by him, and secured to the Company against the above advance.

"The Directors refer the Proprietors also to the annexed accounts, which exhibit the present state of the Company; by which it will be seen the amount of expences (advertising, law charges, travelling expences, salaries, &c.), up to the present day, do not exceed 3,358*l*. 8s., notwithstanding its extensive ramifications and enlarged objects.

THE NATIONAL PROVINCIAL BANK OF ENGLAND.

Dr.		£	*s.*	*d.*
Deposit of 5*l*. per Cent.	£39,075 0 0			
Instalment of 10*l*. per Cent.	62,470 0 0	101,545	0	0
Interest, &c.		1,516	11	4
		£103,061	11	4
Cr.				
Investment, cash at Banks, and advance to branches		97,017	17	4
Thomas Joplin, on his Shares		2,250	0	0
Advanced to Mr. Joplin for expences incurred in the formation of the Company previous to the 1st April, 1833		435	6	0
General expences		3,358	8	0
		£103,061	11	4"

Sir WILLIAM COSWAY[4] moved that the Report be adopted by the meeting, and that it be printed for circulation among the Proprietors. He congratulated the meeting on the unanimity of opinion and feeling which seemed to exist among the gentlemen present. The Report was not so satisfactory as, under all the circumstances, could have been wished; but he trusted that by next year the creditor side of the account would have a more favourable appearance.

Colonel LEITH HAY seconded the Motion of his friend, Sir W. Cosway.

Mr. STUART wished to impress on the Meeting, before they adopted the Report, that the adoption of it will confirm the advances made to Mr. Joplin.

The Motion was then put, that the Report should be adopted, when it was carried unanimously.

Sir WILLIAM COSWAY again congratulated the Meeting on the unanimity with which the Report was adopted. As the business of the Yearly General Meeting was now over, and as they were about to resolve themselves into a Special Meeting of the Proprietors, he begged to propose a vote of thanks to their Chairman for his able and impartial conduct that day.

The Motion having been unanimously carried,

The gentlemen present then resolved themselves into a Special Meeting of the Proprietors, to take into consideration a proposition for the establishment of Banks with local shareholders, deriving their profits or incurring their losses (as the case may be) solely from or at and by means of those banks, &c.

Sir WILLIAM COSWAY moved that Mr. Halliburton be Chairman of the Special Meeting.

Mr. JAMES, M.P.,[5] seconded the Motion, which was carried unanimously.

After the Secretary had read the Report of the Directors to the Special Meeting,

Colonel LEITH HAY rose and said, that having on a former occasion, as one of the Directors of this establishment, had to propose a Resolution connected with the principle of local shareholders, it was now his duty to move a Resolution to the same effect. As the Meeting were aware that a very considerable difference of opinion existed among the shareholders on the subject, it would be necessary for him, for his own satisfaction, and for the information of the gentlemen present, to make a few observations, and he could promise that his observations would be but few. It was satisfactory to him, as he knew it would be to the Meeting, that his observations would be of a conciliatory kind. The gentlemen who opposed the Resolution which he proposed, did so in an honourable spirit, and with much good temper. But, while he thus gave them every credit for good feeling in their opposition, he, and others who viewed the subject in the same light as himself, thought the Local Bank principle was a measure of vital importance to the Company [loud cheers]. He much regretted, on the one hand, the publications which had been put forth relative to the differences of opinion that existed among the Directors on this subject; though he was glad, on the other, they had been so, as those publications communicated general information on the subject. The gentlemen whom he (Colonel Leith Hay) had the honour to address, were so well qualified to decide on the point, that it would be improper in him to take up much of their time. He could only state, that an humble individual like himself might not be supposed to know much of the business part of the institution; but he might be permitted to say, that the active interest which he had taken in it from the first, led him to move a Resolution which, in his opinion, was essential to the interests of so great an establishment; for great it certainly ought to be, and would be, if the principle in question was adopted. If properly managed, the Provincial Bank of England would become one of the first and best establishments of the kind in the country [loud cheers]. He would only further say, that he should be sorry if he had done anything injurious to the interests of the establishment; but he conceived that what he had done was for its good, and he could never deviate from what appeared to him to be his duty, while he had the honour to fill the situation he now held [loud cheers]. The Secretary would read the Resolution.

A PROPRIETOR suggested, that as the question as to whether or not the Company could, in terms of its copartnery, act on the local bank principle, had been submitted to Mr. Brodie, it would be better, before the Resolution was read, or any opinion expressed upon it, that the meeting should have the case read to it which was submitted by Mr. Brodie, together with his answer.

The Secretary accordingly read the case and the answer.

Mr. MURRAY read the Resolution alluded to, which was as follows: – "Resolved, That with a view to the establishment of banks, with local shareholders deriving their profits or entering their losses, as the case may be, from such separate banks, a deed of copartnership be entered into on behalf of this Society, by any three of the Directors, to be specially appointed for that purpose by the Court of Directors, with subscribers for shares in any particular local bank, and that it be provided in the deed of copartnership that the local shareholders shall content themselves with such portion of the profits arising from their local banks as shall be agreed upon, and shall relinquish the other portion of such profits to the Metropolitan Bank; and that the shareholders of such local bank shall be guaranteed against any loss which such local bank may sustain beyond its own paid up capital, and that such guarantee be given by the metropolitan bank, and by every other local bank that may from time to time be associated therewith to the extent of the actual paid up capital in the shares in the metropolitan bank, and other local banks; and that, on the other hand, the metropolitan bank, and all the other local banks that may from time to time be associated therewith, shall be guaranteed against any loss which such metropolitan and other local banks, or any of them, may sustain beyond the amount of their respective paid up capitals, and that such guarantee be given by the shareholders in such local bank to the extent of the actual paid up capital in that bank, and that the Court of Directors of the metropolitan bank shall fix for the amount of the instalments to be from time to time paid up on the shares in such local banks to form the cash capital of that bank, and that any call for an instalment of the shares on such bank may be made either by the Court of Directors of the Metropolitan Bank in the same way as they are authorized in the deed of settlement to make calls on their own shareholders, or by such person or persons as the Court of Directors may adopt for that purpose. Further resolved, that in addition to the calls necessary to carry into effect the suggestions contained in the Resolutions, there shall be inserted in every such deed of copartnership, such further calls and provisions as the Court of Directors, under the advice of their Counsel, shall think proper."

Sir W. COSWAY rose to second the Resolution. He said that the opinion which had been read to the Meeting was merely a lawyer's opinion upon what was necessary to be done to enable the Company to carry the plan of local shareholders into execution. The subject had been so extensively canvassed, both in print and in conversation, that he had no doubt the proprietors, who had come from different parts of the country, had already formed an opinion upon the matter. From the first proceedings, in 1831, he had taken an active part in the formation of a Bank on the principles on which the present was proposed to be established – viz., the local shareholders' system. It might be said that they had no precedent; that was true. This plan was the extension of the Scotch system of banking to the wants, to the feelings, and, if he might so say, to the prejudices of England. What might be very sound in Scotland – he alluded to the cash credits – was not, it must be admitted very practicable in England. When the Scotch banks were established, one pound notes were in being, but that was no longer the case in England. The present plan was, therefore, adapted to the present state of English society. It was proposed to carry the principles of the Scotch system into England, on the foundation that Life Insurances were established.

It was sufficient to know that there was no sort of establishment in the country, the profits of which were so secure as those of Life Insurance Companies. It was well known that their profits were calculated on the average of lives, and he believed that same principle would be carried into this system of Country Banks which was then propounded to the Meeting. He had been asked what was this Local Shareholders' system, and how the local shareholders were to meet the capital required for the country? If the local shareholders subscribed one hundred thousand pounds, the Company would put down the same amount to meet their subscription. The Company being subscribers would give so much security that the utmost confidence would be placed in the Banks. In Birmingham, Worcester, and other great manufacturing towns, it was possible there might be a great excitement at some particular moment. There might be a tendency on the part of the Bank to over-trade. The London Directors would then step in, and give notice to draw the cord a little tighter, knowing the general state of the country, & how far it would be advisable to go. Sir William next alluded to the difference of opinion between the Directors of the Company on the subject of the proposed plan. Those who differed from him thought that the Irish system, as it was technically called, was preferable, because they had had the advantage of practice. That system had, however, been tried when Ireland was free, when the other Banks had failed, and when there was no competition. But in England the case at present was very different; they would have numerous Banks to contend with, and therefore it was necessary to have recourse to local Directors, whose advice and information, as well as local influence, would be of the utmost service. The Irish Provincial Bank had only 22 Branch Banks. [More]. Well, they might be 30, and that number was quite sufficient if they were to be effectively managed. But the grand principle of the local shareholders' system would be, that they could all establish 200 Branch Banks, because they would have local Directors to manage them. When the question whether the proposed plan should be adopted was decided, he trusted that the result would not be, that those Directors who were opposed to the plan, and whose great abilities he could not too highly praise, would not deem it necessary, as they had intimated, to retire. He hoped that the proprietors would still have continued to them the benefit of their services. The present was quite as much a national question as it was an individual one. He was of opinion that if the principle was carried out, it would become a great service to the country, and would in a great degree prevent the amasing fluctuations of property which had unhappily been too frequent. He must not omit to mention that the opinion of the Learned Counsel (Mr. Brodie) did by no means do away with the Branch system, as it was still in the power of the Directors to establish a Branch Bank where they pleased. What they called upon the Meeting to do was, to give the Directors power to carry out the principle of local shareholders where they deemed it advisable.

A PROPRIETOR: Are we to have any voice in the choice of Directors?

Sir W. COSWAY: The intention is this. Suppose the local shareholders' system to be established in Birmingham, and the Shareholders to elect a Board of

Directors, we can have only a negative on an individual. A *veto* must necessarilly be vested in us.

A PROPRIETOR: How is the London Board to know the state of the country business, and the manner in which it is being carried on?

Sir W. COSWAY: That will be done by inspection every half year, on the spot, and we shall also have a weekly report.

A PROPRIETOR: What actual controul shall we have? Can we prevent the issue of notes [oh! yes]?

A PROPRIETOR: What advantages will the local shareholders derive from our connection?

Sir W. COSWAY: The advantages they will derive will accrue from the great credit of the London Company, and whatever subscribed capital they pay, we shall give them a certain interest for it.

A PROPRIETOR: Suppose they increase their notes beyond a certain number, what controul can we have?

Sir W. COSWAY: In that case we should send down a London Director, who would say to the Local Directors, "you are going beyond the mark." In fact there will be a most absolute controul.

A PROPRIETOR: Should I be liable for the whole of my subscribed capital?

Sir W. COSWAY: Yes, beyond a doubt.

A PROPRIETOR: Is the capital which will be advanced to be applied to the working of the concerns?

The CHAIRMAN: The true spirit of banking is to have a large capital for banking, and to have in reserve the money received from individuals, putting it out to the best advantage. Twenty-five thousand pounds is to be subscribed in every one hundred thousand, and that amount which is subscribed in London will be kept in reserve for the local banks. The business of the Directors will be only to keep it in security. It will therefore be the same as if actually employed in the country.

Sir W. COSWAY: A reserve fund, in fact, to be used in case of necessity.

Mr. BARNES: The sum subscribed in London will be applicable only in the event of the local banks sustaining a loss.

Mr. BROWN, a proprietor, who stated that he had been much engaged in banking in the West of England, stated his opinion, that the profit proposed to be allowed to the local shareholders was too small, and that the plan would not be successful.

It was here stated that the Meeting was convened merely to discuss the principle, and not to go into the details of the plan.

A PROPRIETOR: But the principle is of no use if the details are impracticable.

Colonel HAY said the details had not been decided upon, and referred to that part of the Resolution which stated that the local shareholders "shall content themselves with such profits as *shall be agreed upon*."

A PROPRIETOR: I beg to ask whether in any emergency the portion of capital subscribed by us to the Country Banks would actually be employed by them? Would it be drawn out under any circumstances?

Sir W. COSWAY: Oh, yes.

Mr. FARRELL,[6] a Director, said he must express his satisfaction that the question had come before the Proprietors to receive their approbation, or the contrary. They were, however, under a complete misunderstanding as to the motives and the feelings of those who were denominated the Irish Directors. He was not aware, however, that those Directors had ever advocated the Irish system. They had conscientiously opposed the English system, but they had not attempted to do more than this. The question now came before the Proprietors, and he and those who acted with him were no longer irresponsible. It was his honest opinion that the present was a most dangerous measure. They were about to incur a most dangerous responsibility. They were about to engage in the setting up of Local Bank Shareholders, who were to trade upon credit instead of capital. If they established two or three hundred Local Banks, they must have two or three hundred partnership deeds; and who would be the gainers then? – The lawyers only. The very preparation of the deeds would take a great deal of money; and was it likely, that where two or three hundred partnership deeds were carried on, they would be without the blessings of 50 Chancery suits? He had no object to answer in objecting to the plan – he proposed it from conscientious motives. Suppose they went down to Liverpool, Birmingham, or any other large and wealthy town, and said to some of the leading men, "We have a proposal to make to you. We will lend you our credit to bank upon." What would be the answer? "Thank you, Gentlemen, we can carry on our own affairs very well; we can make use of our capital without you." They certainly might establish the Banks in poor counties, where their credit might be of service; but they must, in that case, take a very inferior description of persons as partners. In the great towns of this kingdom did they want credit? On the contrary, they said there – "We have plenty of capital. We only need an advantageous way of employing our capital ourselves." With regard to principle and details, if any principle did depend upon details, it was that of banking. Admit that the principle was advisable, then let them see also whether they could put it in practice or not. He would undertake to say that not one of his colleagues knew anything about the details of the plan. In conclusion he would say, if the proprietors were determined to adopt the plan, at all events give the most unlimited power to the Directors, and let them take the best means they could to do it [cheers].

Dr. ELMORE said he felt great regret at the intended retirement of those Directors whose opinions were adverse to the proposed measure; but at the same time he was fully aware that they could no longer act with the gentlemen who would remain. With regard to the Irish system, they had commenced with it, and what had it done for them? Three millions had been subscribed, and yet how few banks had been established. But, in fact, they could not establish any number under the Irish system. The present plan, in his opinion, combined the advantages of the two systems – the Scotch and the Irish [hear, hear!]. He thought it was the general feeling of the shareholders that the Directors should be allowed to do all they thought advisable for the execution of the proposed plan.

Mr. REMINGTON, a Director,[7] thought the measure would be dangerous to society and to the stability of the interests of the country at large. By the proposed measure the Society wanted a certain quantity of profits from the local shareholders, but what was to be given to them in return? Nothing at all.

Another DIRECTOR said he objected to the plan upon principle. They were not authorised, according to the prospectus of the Society, to enter into a new plan. He, and those who acted with him, washed their hands of it, and he was determined to resign his power into the hands of the Proprietors, as had been intimated to them in the circular which had been sent round.

Captain WARREN trusted that the question would now be put to the vote. The Proprietors had made up their minds upon it.

Colonel HAY begged to say a few words in reply. Mr. Farrell had spoken of the great expence of the partnership deeds. One general deed would answer the purpose – the rest would be copies. With respect to what he had said of the merchants and others in the great towns, he thought that his statements were not founded in fact. Was there no reciprocity in the security given to the country banks of the present great establishment in town? By having this security, would they not be able to extend their business in a way that no private joint stock bank could do? And would not the customers place additional confidence in them? If there was an obligation, it would be on the part of the local shareholders to the Company.

The CHAIRMAN, in putting the question, said, that if he and his friends had not been convinced of the soundness of the English system, they would not have recommended its adoption. He had remained in the direction for the last eight or ten months under the most unpleasant circumstances, solely from a sense of duty, and from a feeling for the shareholders. There were, in consequence of the division of opinion, constant sources of irritation; and the meetings of the Directors from day to day were occupied with disputes. When this question was decided, there would be unanimity amongst the Directors, and the affairs of the Society would of course be more efficiently managed.

The Resolution was then put to the vote, and carried almost unanimously.

A Resolution for altering and adding to the deed of settlement, in order to carry into effect the plan proposed, was then agreed to.

A Resolution enabling Proprietors residing at a distance from town to vote by proxy at the Meetings of the Society was also carried without any discussion.

It was then moved and seconded that the Meeting should a adopt a recommendation made by the Court of Directors, to the effect that the powers then vested in the Court of Directors relative to the appointment of additional Directors, and the filling up vacancies in the office of Directors, should be thenceforth vested in the general body of Proprietors.

Sir W. COSWAY said, that to carry out the principle which has been adopted, it was very necessary that the Directors should have the opportunity of meeting with gentlemen who would co-operate with them in the most effective manner. He therefore moved an Amendment to the effect, that the powers which the Directors now had of choosing additional Directors should be continued to them.

Dr. ELMORE seconded the Amendment.

Mr. FARRELL said that the Directors, who should be 24 in number, were only 19, and of these 10 were now about to retire. Under such circumstances, it was thought due to the Proprietors to leave the matter to their decision. Not the slightest slur was intended to be cast on the Directors who would remain.

The Amendment was then carried.

After a vote of thanks to the Chairman, the Meeting adjourned.

Notes

1 George Richard Robinson (1781–1850) was a partner in the London merchant house of Robinson, Brooking and Garland, which specialized in trading with Newfoundland, where Robinson spent his early adult life. A Liberal Tory MP for Worcester from 1826 to 1837 and for Poole from 1847 to 1850, he served as chairman of Lloyd's of London (1834–1850) and as a director in the British American Land Company.

2 Douglas Gordon-Hallyburton (1777–1841) was a Liberal MP for Forfarshire from 1832 to 1841. A retired army officer, he devoted himself to agricultural improvement after inheriting a large estate in Forfarshire.

3 Andrew Leith Hay (1785–1862) was born in Aberdeen, fought in the Napoleonic Wars, and was military secretary in Barbados from 1816 to 1819. After retiring from the army, he entered politics, representing Elgin as a Reform candidate from 1832 to 1838 and again from 1841 to 1847.

4 William Richard Cosway (1782–1834) was a Devonport baker's son who served as secretary to Rear-Admiral Collingwood at Trafalgar. He married a banker's daughter and became involved in politics, unsuccessfully standing as a Reform candidate for East Kent in 1832. An original director of the NPB when it formed in 1833, he died in a coach accident in June 1834, less than a month after taking a leading part at its first general meeting.

5 William James of Barrock Lodge (1791–1861) was a Carlisle landowner and a Radical MP, representing Carlisle from 1820 to 1836 and East Cumberland, from 1836 to 1847.

6 Oliver Farrer (1785–1866) was a Yorkshire barrister and landowner, who sat on the boards of several London banks, including the Provincial Bank of Ireland, which he chaired during the 1850s.

7 James G. Remington was a London merchant and ship owner specializing in the trade (including opium) with India and China and a member of the Royal Asiatic Society. From at least 1809 through 1836, he was a partner with William Crawford with an office in Broad Street.

Editorial Headnote

Eastern Counties Railway (1849)

The man of the hour at the Eastern Counties Railway (ECR) meeting on 28 February 1849 did not show up. George Hudson (1800–1871), "the Railway King," was halfway into a precipitous fall from grace when he put his vice chairman, David Waddington, in the awkward position of reading his letter *in absentia* to a crowd of angry shareholders. Twelve years earlier, Hudson had become chair of the York and North Midland Railway Company, and by 1844, he had consolidated other local lines to control track stretching from Birmingham to Newcastle. During the railway mania of 1845–47, Hudson promoted numerous companies, including the ECR, which he chaired from October 1845. When the stock market crashed in 1847, Hudson was exposed as having leveraged many of his companies with bank loans, leading to bankruptcy in some cases, and diminished dividends across the board. The call for a committee of inquiry into Hudson's activities that emerged from the ECR meeting, which a trade journal called a "bear garden display," joined similar calls at the Midland and the York, Newcastle & Berwick Railway. Later in 1849, the *Yorkshireman* would refer to the "repeated betrayals of Mr. Hudson by his truculent friends."[1]

The ECR, which formed in 1836 to provide service from London to Colchester, lurched from crisis to crisis before Hudson appeared on the scene. A series of fatal accidents and a glacial pace of track construction yielded minimal dividends over its first decade, which was marked by open hostility between the East Anglian landowners and Liverpool industrialists who sat on its board (revealingly, none of the named speakers at the 1849 meeting were from East Anglia). Although Hudson did extend its track miles and raised more than £9 million in new capital, he arguably made matters worse by paying dividends out of share capital in order to prop up the stock price. The committee's report in April 1849 revealed that Hudson had falsified accounts to show £353,459 in fictitious profits.[2] On the basis of this report, the directors ousted Hudson from the chair, replacing him with Waddington.[3] William Cash, who chaired the committee, raised eyebrows, since he was a director of a competing line. A pamphlet war ensued, in which partisans respectively lined up behind Waddington and Hudson.[4] As for Waddington, his tenure as Hudson's successor abruptly ended in 1856, when another shareholder committee ousted him amid allegations of still more financial irregularities. The troubled company limped along until 1862, when several competing lines in East Anglia convinced Parliament to approve an amalgamation under the new name of the Great Eastern Railway.[5]

Notes

1 Robert Beaumont, *The Railway King: A Biography of George Hudson* (London: Headline Publishing Group, 2002), 116–118; "Eastern Counties Railway," *Herapath's Journal* 3 March 1849.

2 Sean McCartney and A. J. Arnold, "George Hudson's Financial Reporting Practices: Putting the Eastern Counties Railway in Context," *Accounting, Business and Financial History* 10 (2000), 300–301, 309–312; Clive Hodges, *Cobbold and Kin: Life Stories from an East Anglian Family* (London: Boydell and Brewer, 2014), 16–21.

3 Beaumont, *The Railway King*, 122; *Eastern Counties Railway Company* (London: Thompson and Davidson, 1849).

4 "Eastern Counties Railway"; *To the Shareholders of the Eastern Counties Railway* (London: Nassau Steam Press, 1849); *Hudson versus Waddington* (London: Willoughby and Co., 1849).

5 Timothy L. Alborn, *Conceiving Companies: Joint-Stock Politics in Victorian England* (London: Routledge, 1998), 199; "Eastern Counties Railway Company," *Saturday Review* 15 December 1855; "The Eastern Counties Railway," *The Engineer* 18 July 1856; "Eastern Counties Railway (Now Great Eastern)," *Money Market Review* 27 September 1862.

5

EASTERN COUNTIES RAILWAY

Sources: Eastern Counties Railway (1849), *London Standard*, 1 March 1849; *Essex Standard*, 11 May 1849

London Standard, 1 March 1849

RAILWAY INTELLIGENCE

Eastern-Counties Railway

The half-yearly meeting of the proprietors of the above company was held yesterday at the London Tavern. The meeting was advertised to take place at one o'clock, but at half-past twelve not fewer than 400 or 500 shareholders were present. At the appointed time the area of the gallery of the large room of the tavern was densely crowded, not fewer than from 800 to 1000 persons having arrived.

A few minutes after one o'clock the directors, with Mr. Waddington,[1] the deputy chairman, at their head, entered the room. They were received with mingled groans, hisses, and cheers; but immediately the shareholders became aware that Mr. Hudson,[2] the chairman, was not present, they expressed their feelings by tremendous groaning and vociferous shouts of "Off, off." It was with such sounds ringing in his ears that

Mr. Waddington rose to address the proprietors. – He said, – I attend here before you to-day as a matter of duty (hissing and groaning.) I hope you will support me to-day in the discharge of that duty (cheers and hisses). If I had not thought proper to appear before you to-day you might then have said that I neglected to do that duty which I was bound, in honour to you, to discharge as deputy chairman, in the absence of your chairman; and therefore I claim from you that which you are bound to accord to every gentleman – not to condemn him unheard (cheers). I was exceedingly desirous, and so were my colleagues, that Mr. Hudson should have attended here this day (loud groans). The first intimation I received that he would not be present was on Monday morning last.

A Proprietor. – He is ashamed to come forward.

Another Proprietor. – Mr. Waddington is not to blame for it.

Mr. Waddington. – Do hear me patiently, gentlemen, if you please. I say I received a letter from Mr. Hudson on Monday morning last, and immediately on the receipt of it I convened a meeting of the directors resident in London. I read to them the letter which Mr. Hudson had forwarded to me, and we then agreed upon a letter that should be sent to him in answer to it. I requested that he would give me a reply, but he has not done so (groaning). Why he has not done so I cannot tell – I cannot account for it. It may be that Mr. Hudson is not at home (laughter, and hisses). I say, gentlemen, it may be that Mr. Hudson is not at home; but, at all events, his absence, and his not replying to the letter, have placed me in a very painful position in meeting you on this occasion; and I shall, in justice to myself, and, indeed, in justice also to you, take the opportunity of reading Mr. Hudson's letter to myself and my answer thereto (cheers), and I wish to say at the outset that in conducting the proceedings of to-day the directors who surround me and myself have only one desire – that you should know as much of the position of this concern as we know ourselves. The letter from Mr. Hudson to me is to this effect: –

"Newby Park, Thirsk, Feb. 25, 1849.

"My dear Sir, – As I feel I cannot go thoroughly along with you in reference to the steam-boat question, I have made up my mind not to attend the meeting on Wednesday next. I sincerely wish you well through it (laughter and hissing). I hope if any attack is made on me you will, if you can, defend me with reference to your company (cries of 'oh, oh'). I unfortunately hold a large stake, and bought at a very great price, and lose terribly by the concern; they invited us, they were in a ruined condition both as to stock and credit (loud cries of 'no, no'). I shall resign whenever it may suit you and the board. By not attending I shall avoid the Norfolk question, which I could not but throw over. – I am yours very truly,

(Signed)

"GEO. HUDSON."

(Laughter and hissing). I am sorry to have had to read this letter, because Mr. Hudson may think there are portions of it which should not be made public; but I feel, and the board feel, that under the circumstances we had no alternative (hear). The following is the answer I sent to Mr. Hudson: –

"London, Feb. 26, 1849.

"My dear Sir, – Upon receipt of your letter I convened a meeting of our directors residing in London, and read your letter to them. It leaves us all in considerable difficulty as to the best course to be pursued; but my impression is, that as the steam-boat matter is approved of in the report of the board, and as no vote on the Norfolk amalgamation will have to be taken at the meeting, it is difficult to explain your absence from the meeting on any ground stated in your letter (hear, hear). Besides which I read your letter as not wishing your opinion on these two matters to be brought forward, lest they should disturb the action of myself and the board at the meeting, as entertaining opposite opinions. It appears therefore to us, that as you have determined on resigning your seat, it would be better for you to do this previous to the meeting. Should you concur in this, and send me the resignation, to be at the board prior to the meeting, you can give such reasons reduced working expenses were very evident by an examination of the pay bills for the first four weeks after they commenced working the Norfolk line with the last four weeks' expenses. Such pay-bills showed that the working expenses had, in consequence of the continuous working of the traffic over both lines, been reduced at the rate of 370*l*. per week; and this decrease of expense had been effected without impairing the efficiency of the line, the staff of officers being most complete and the line in excellent order. The directors felt that as the traffic was paying a reduced dividend it was incumbent upon them to reduce the expenses as far as possible; but in doing this they were not diminishing the wages of the lower class of workmen in their employ. They were equalising rather than reducing wages. As to the maintenance of the permanent way, it had been said that they were keeping it up at a less cost than it could possibly be done for. The fact was that the line cost them for labour 76*l*. per mile only, and 23*l*. for materials, making the total cost 99*l*. per mile for labour and materials, which he believed would, looking at the nature of the traffic, the heavy engines, and the large amount of goods trade passing over it, stand a favourable comparison with any line in England. They would find by comparing the traffic of the present with that of the previous half-year that with 69 additional miles open the working expenses had increased 14,732*l*.; but, at the same time, that everything which could be charged against revenue had been so charged during the past half-year, and that, with the exception of half of the salary of their resident engineer, a great portion of whose time was occupied in attending to lines in the course of construction, the whole of the salaries paid to the secretary and other officers, as well as the whole of the directors' allowance, was charged to revenue. He was quite aware that he could not disguise, and it was evident that the shareholders could not disguise, as was evident from what had just transpired, that they were dissatisfied with the dividend of 5s. 6d. which had been recommended. He felt with them that the dividend was not so large as they could expect it to be; and he was exceedingly sorry that the directors had it not in their power to offer them a larger one; but was it not better to declare a dividend of 5s. 6d., honestly earned, than a dividend of 8s. not honestly earned? (hear, hear.) Was it not better that the directors should lay the naked truth before them at this moment, than be obliged to do so at some future time? (loud cries of "hear, hear," and much confusion.) He wished to bring the attention of the shareholders back to the time when he first appeared in that room at their half-yearly meeting, as he thought he ought in justice to himself to go a little into a personal history of his own, as to his connection with the railway. It was supposed that he was brought into the direction by those who had nothing to do with his becoming a member of the board. He begged to state that he was solicited by the directors to become chairman before Mr. Hudson was applied to; but the shareholders saw that gentleman, and having great confidence in his management prevailed on him to take that office. He (Mr. Waddington) conferred with Mr. Hudson, and stated that if the directors would give him the entire management of the traffic, and he (Mr. Hudson) would take what might be termed the political part of the management, he was prepared to work with him, but not otherwise. Mr.

Hudson conceded the point to him, and he became chairman of the traffic committee, and he was quite prepared to justify the course which that traffic committee had taken, as he could, he was satisfied, prove that their railway had been more efficiently managed than any other line running out of the metropolis. In reference to this point, he had made an examination as to the amount of their revenue for the corresponding six months three years ago. He was not speaking of predictions, nor of what any man had stated; but if they would look at the accounts they would see that it was impossible for them to attain that rate of dividend which had been predicted when the traffic of their line was in the course of development. He had nothing to do with that prediction. What he had to do with were facts and figures, and he found that at the time he was alluding to – viz., the 4th of January, 1846, the first half-year when he appeared there as deputy chairman, a dividend of 9s. per share was declared – and he wished particularly to point their attention to the statement, as it was a startling one – on 143,267 shares of 14*l*. 10s. each, and loans, and the Northern and Eastern proportion of capital, making a total of 3,587,352*l*., to which revenue was then made chargeable, there having been, during that period, a revenue obtained for five months upon the line from Bishop Stortford to Brandon, or upon 56 miles. On this no interest was payable out of revenue, the line being in the contractor's hands, as was usual, for 12 months after the opening. This was their starting point. They had at that period 141 miles opened and paid on a share capital, with the Northern and Eastern, and the bonded debt of 3,587,352*l*. only. He admitted this was a great error (hear, hear). He was free to admit that an error had been committed in paying a dividend of 9s., when for the previous half-year 3s. only had been paid. He must say that a 9s. dividend was the rock on which they had split. They had not brought forward as a charge against revenue the lines which had been opened during the preceding six months, and this had not been done on the ground that the traffic of such lines was not fully developed. That enabled them at the time to pay a dividend of 9s., they not having, as he had stated, charged the revenue account with the capital for constructing the 56 miles of line opened for five months, and the traffic over which had gone in payment of dividend. He admitted that in doing this a great mistake was committed. If they had brought forward the capital as it was expended, and charged it against the revenue account, they would not have had so large a fall in the dividend in one half-year. This system of keeping back large amounts until the traffic of the line has had time to develope itself, the directors now purposed to put a stop to. Hence they would find that with an addition of 83 miles open, 12 of which had been open for three months only, their capital had increased during the period to 289,096 shares of 20*l*. each, including the bonus, and making, with the Northern and Eastern[3] and the other guarantee stock and loans, a capital of 10,312,775*l*. now subject to a rent-charge, as compared with 3,587,352*l*. made chargeable on the 4th January, 1846, and showing an excess of 6,725,423*l*. added to the account on which they had to pay dividend or interest – that was as compared with this time three years. They would find that the gross traffic for the half-year ending 4th January, 1846, amounted to 173,166*l*., while for the half-year ending 4th January,

1849, after deducting the receipts of the Norfolk line, and taking the Eastern Counties line proper, it was 336,712*l.* – that was with only 83 additional miles open, with 12 of that number open but for three months of the period, and with a great portion of such additional mileage running through a barren district of country. He therefore must say this was strong evidence that their traffic had been managed successfully (hear). The payment of 5s. 6d. per share would leave a surplus of 14,000*l.* for depreciation. Railway companies had not arrived at correct data on the subject of depreciation, but they (the directors of the Eastern Counties) were endeavouring to do so. They did not know what the amount of depreciation might be, but they did know that they were relaying a certain amount of line between London and Stratford, the cost of which would come into the next half-year's account. The sum he had named had been kept as a reserve to meet such contingencies, and with a view to give stability to their property, and to arrest the downward course that appeared to be pressing on them. If the directors did not on this occasion present to the shareholders their property in those blooming colours in which it had been depicted to them from time to time, they at least presented it to them in the honest and naked truth. The chairman had stated to them at the last meeting that the remainder of the 6 per cent. shares should not be issued to the present moment. With the exception of some small portion those shares were in the company's hands. It was their intention not to issue the 6 per cent. stock, though they might realise a premium of 2*l.* per share.

A Proprietor wished to know how much of this stock they had in hand?

The Chairman said they held 3400 shares, that would be about 34,000*l.* He now came to the directors' report; and first, as to the agreement with the Norfolk line. They had an agreement to work it for seven years, giving the proprietors of that company equal profits with themselves, and they were in the meantime to apply to parliament for powers to amalgamate the two undertakings. The exact amount of traffic which had been earned by the Norfolk line proper for the last half-year was 60,879*l.*, which was, upon 47,666 shares of 20*l.* each, 5s. 8¾d. per share, after deducting the working expenses, including a mileage proportion of direction and management of head officers, which, if not debited to them, would show a return of 6s. 1d. per share for the Norfolk line. Thus far there was not any loss. An addition to the capital, however, would be made on the completion of the Fakenham line and Lowestoffe Harbour,[4] yet the traffic to the latter was far from being developed for want of a sufficient number of trucks. As to the question of amalgamation with the Norfolk Company, it was not necessary to go into it, as that matter would come before them prior to the bill going to a second reading in the House of Lords. The amount required for Lowestoffe Harbour was estimated at 24,000*l.* or 25,000*l.* He now had to refer to the Harwich line. It had been obtained by the Eastern Union Company,[5] and upon the line the Eastern Counties granted 4½ per cent. – that was on 153,000*l.* If the Harwich line were made, the distance to Ostend *via* the Eastern Counties would be 141 miles, while by the South-Eastern line *via* Dover it would be 153. After offering some observations on the unjust mode in which railway property is taxed to parish and other local rates, he besought the meeting to go calmly and closely into the questions before them, and endeavour to come to a conclusion that would do justice and credit to themselves (cheers). At the conclusion of his address the Chairman said he had just received a telegraphic answer to his letter to Mr. Hudson (hear). Mr. Hudson's answer was as follows: – "I had not an opportunity to reply yesterday, but will write tomorrow (laughter, and marks of disapprobation). Mr. Waddington may use his discretion as to the reason of my resignation. He is aware it was a measure I had long contemplated" (cries of "oh, oh").

A Proprietor asked Mr. Waddington if he had been aware of Mr. Hudson's intention to vacate the chair the last six months?

The Chairman had seen a letter – not one written to himself – in which Mr. Hudson intimated his intention to resign at the then coming board meeting. About six months ago Mr. Hudson saw him in London, and asked his opinion on the subject. He (Mr. Waddington) told him that as he (Mr. Hudson) had such extensive engagements, and could afford very little time to the concerns of the company, he would perhaps be consulting his own feelings if he retired. Mr. Hudson on that occasion told him he should not retire (hear). That was all the communication he had had with Mr. Hudson on the matter.

Mr. Nathan asked if the Eastern Counties had leased the Lowestoffe Harbour with the Norfolk line, as he was told the harbour would require 100,000*l.* to complete it? What authority had the Eastern Counties directors to amalgamate with the Norfolk line, when they knew the Stowmarket line to Norwich would soon be opened, and give them the Norfolk traffic, without additional cost to themselves? He should like to know what number of shares Mr. Hudson held, and on what terms it was proposed to amalgamate with the Newmarket line?

The Chairman repeated that the estimated expense of the Lowestoffe Harbour was 24,000*l.* or 25,000*l.* The Eastern Counties directors had received authority at a special meeting of proprietors to amalgamate with the Norfolk Company. As to the opening of the Stowmarket line, it was true that the line would bring the Norfolk traffic over the Eastern Counties line, but it would bring it over only 51 miles, from Colchester; whereas the directors desired to have it run over the 88 miles from Brandon (hear). Mr. Hudson held 625 shares, according to the register. As to the Newmarket line the decision of the matter was left to the shareholders.

Mr. Box moved "That a committee of shareholders be now appointed to make a strict and searching inquiry into the financial condition of the Eastern Counties Railway Company, taking into consideration the cost of construction per mile executed and to be executed, and the cost of the several stations" (loud cheers).

Mr. Price seconded the resolution. He was sorry Mr. Hudson had not shown today (loud cries of "hear"). He should really have liked to see that Mr. Hudson had sufficient brass in his composition to show his face (cheers).

A Proprietor suggested that no director should be reelected till the committee of shareholders made their report (loud cheers).

Mr. Serjeant Gaselee[6] was glad to hear the chairman say that all persons were to have a fair hearing, because when he (Mr. Gaselee) endeavoured, on a former occasion, to stop the directors in their mad career, he was not only hooted by the shareholders, just in the same way they had been hooting Mr. Waddington, but had been insulted by the chairman (Mr. Hudson) into the bargain.

A Proprietor. – That is quite true. You were insulted.

Mr. Serjeant Gaselee. – They must have a committee of inquiry (loud cheers). They must not be led away by the eloquence of the chairman. His advice was not to receive the absurd report of the directors, and not to do anything but appoint the committee (loud cheers).

After a very tumultuous discussion, during which Mr. Hudson's conduct as chairman of the company was frequently alluded to in very strong, but not very complimentary terms, and during which the chairman found it very difficult to obtain a hearing for the purpose of repelling some personal attacks upon himself.

Mr. Box modified his resolution in the following manner: – "That a committee of inquiry be appointed to inquire into all the affairs and accounts of the company, and report their opinion thereon to an adjourned meeting, and that the committee be at liberty to send for books, papers, and accounts, to examine any parties they think fit, and to employ such accountants as they may require" (loud cheers).

A Proprietor. – And that in the meantime the dividend be accepted (loud cries of "no, no").

The resolution for the appointment of a committee of shareholders was then put and carried amidst loud cheering.

A Proprietor called for three cheers, which were immediately given.

It was next decided that the committee should consist of nine, and that the members of it should each hold 50 shares.

Messrs. Christle, Cash, Sherman, Ellis, and Mayhew were appointed, and power was given them to select the remaining four members.

Mr. Fryer moved that the Norfolk bill should be withdrawn.

This motion led to a very noisy discussion. On a show of hands,

The Chairman said the numbers were nearly equal, but that he thought Mr. Fryer's motion was carried.

A poll was demanded on the question, and

The Chairman declared the meeting adjourned till nine o'clock this morning for the purpose of taking the votes.

Essex Standard, 11 May 1849

EASTERN COUNTIES' RAILWAY

The Adjourned Meeting

(*From our own Reporter*.)

The adjourned meeting of the shareholders of the above company to receive the report of the committee of investigation appointed at the last half-yearly meeting on the 28th of February, took place yesterday (Thursday), at the London Tavern, Bishopsgate Street.

The attendance of proprietors was extremely large; the immense apartment being nearly filled at least an hour before the time of meeting.

At one o'clock there was a call for the Directors; and the members of the committee, who first made their appearance, being mistaken for the Board, were greeted with hisses and uproar. On being recognized, these marks of disapprobation were replaced by cheers; but the uproar was revived with vigour a few seconds after, when the Directors entered the room.

Mr. Waddington, as Chairman of the Board, occupied the post of president.

The Chairman, on rising, was received with renewed clamour. He said he appeared there in fulfilment of the pledge he gave at the last meeting. (Interruption, and cries of "Where's the £2,000?") He would give them an explanation of that presently; he did not possess a craven heart, and he felt backed up in demanding a fair hearing for every one. (Cheers and uproar.) He was not going to make any lengthened observations; but he called upon them to conduct themselves as men feeling the interests of the undertaking. If they did not do so, they would be the sufferers, and not himself; but, with a most sincere desire that they should do all they could at the present juncture to promote their own interests, he appeared before them simply as the organ of order; and he, therefore, called upon them to listen quietly and calmly to the recital that would be laid before them. (Cheers.) His first duty was to call upon some member of the committee to introduce their own report; after which it would be his duty to offer such observations as he might think proper, leaving it to the meeting to take such course as they might think themselves justified in doing. (Hear and cheers.)

Mr. Cash,[7] the chairman of the committee, then rose amidst general cheering, with a few hisses. The report, he said, having been placed in the hands of all the proprietors, the reading of the document might be dispensed with on the present occasion. He should therefore proceed at once to move a resolution "That the report be received and adopted; and that the recommendations therein contained be carried out at the earliest convenience." ("No, no, yes, yes," and cheers.) He wished to give a brief explanation of a matter personal to himself, inasmuch as his name was mentioned in the House of Commons in connexion with an expenditure of £7,594..19, alleged to have been made by the Size Lane Committee. Although he was a member of that committee, he never knew of their receiving any money; he never had a halfpenny himself, and it never passed through his hands. (Applause.) Of course he was aware if there were expenses they must be borne by the Eastern Counties' Company; but the gentleman who solicited him to join the committee proved to him that the object in view was not only legitimate, but highly desirable for this company. He had only that morning got a statement of that expenditure, which he must say he was not prepared to defend; but the items of which he would read, and leave them to judge for themselves. He found those items to be as follow: –

Advertising per Mr. Thomas	£1,530	19	0
Paid to Mr. Phillips, Solicitor	1,619	0	0
Losses on Shares	3,400	0	0
Advertising per Messrs. Barker and Co.	340	0	0
Printing and other expenses	465	0	0
Further amounts paid as balance	231	0	0
	£7,594	19	0

(The announcement of the various sums elicited cries of "Oh, oh," and "shame.") He would now read over a summary of the recommendations which were embodied in the committee's report: – 1st, to approve of the amalgamation with the Norfolk Company – (No, no) – 2nd, that no dividend be paid at this time; 3rd, that the directors be reduced from 18 to 12 – eight for the Eastern Counties and four for the North Eastern Company – the latter to be paid no remuneration beyond the £1,000 a year secured under their own Act, and that the Eastern Counties' Railway Representatives be more efficiently remunerated than heretofore; 4th, that the capital account be closed as early as possible; 5th, that early care be taken to secure the services of a law clerk by salary; 6th, to consider the propriety of appointing professed accountants as auditors; 7th, that the committee be directed to pursue their inquiry as to the state of the capital account, and present the result at the next half-yearly meeting, or, if necessary, to call a special meeting; 8th and lastly, that stringent economy be practised in every department." (Loud cheers.). With regard to dividend (observed Mr. Cash), the committee considered it would be quite folly to attempt it this half year. For his own part, he did not know where the money was to come from, but perhaps the directors would be able to tell them. (Hear and laughter.) After remarking upon some of the other items, Mr. Cash concluded by moving the resolution which he had read.

Mr. Meek[8] seconded the resolution in a lengthened speech. He gave in the first instance a strong recommendation to the shareholders to confirm the Norfolk amalgamation;[9] indeed he believed it to be legally binding; but at any rate before they attempted to get rid of it they ought to have another committee; and so strongly did he feel on the subject that he should wish it to be composed of those who at the present felt the strongest opposition to the measure. He next spoke in deprecation of any dividend being declared this half-year, and then adverted to some of the facts brought out by the report. He spoke in strong condemnation of the circumstance that without any resolution of the Board of Directors, the sum of £2,000 – equal to twenty years' legal remuneration – had passed into the hands of one of those gentlemen (Mr. Waddington). Then, with regard to the sum of £7,594, that was about to form the subject of Parliamentary inquiry. The House of Commons had been told how that money was not spent; but he hoped that this house, from whose not overflowing treasury that money was taken, would have some better account to-day. The transaction with regard to the Wisbeach and St. Ives Railway[10] next came under condemnation; and the conduct of the directors was strongly remarked upon. With regard to future prospects, he believed if they would reject the bait held out by the directors of a proffered dividend, and select as directors men who had the courage to look difficulties in the face, and who would rigidly practice economy – in that event, he believed, he might promise them a return to a peaceful and healthy state, which, to his mind, would be cheaply bought even at the expense of the present strife. (The gentleman sat down amidst loud cheers.)

The CHAIRMAN rose to reply, but was for some time unable to obtain a hearing. He said he did not stand there for his own aggrandizement; he felt himself in a most painful position – (laughter) – because he had been called to the office of Chairman, which he had previously refused; and because he occupied the chair of one in whom they formerly placed confidence, which he regretted to say, from what had since taken place in their concerns, had resulted in large losses to the shareholders – (hear, hear, and "oh, oh,") – but he must state his belief, from the large stake which that gentleman held in the company, that he really felt the course he was pursuing would have placed them in a very different position from what they were now. (Hisses and confusion.) He would not attempt to shield himself by saying that he was not guilty, and laying all the blame upon the gentleman referred to. (Hear, hear.) It had now been proved that a great mistake was made by declaring a 9s. dividend in 1845, when it was quite evident it was not in Mr. Hudson's power, from the short period which he had been connected with the Eastern Counties' Railway, to know what had been the earnings of the line. ("Why did you allow it?" and disapprobation.) He would not take up their time by going through the various items which the committee had described as misplaced; they had been answered in the pamphlet which had been put forth in reply; but at the same time he was prepared to state, and to prove it by the documents which had been issued by the committee, that the earnings of the last half-year did warrant a dividend of 4s. per share. An honourable gentleman asked where the money was to come from. He knew not how the matter might have been affected by what had since taken place, but he could only say that it had been arranged. (Cries of "How? by borrowing.") Yes, it would have been borrowed; and if gentlemen thought that an undertaking like this could be carried on, and its credit maintained, without borrowing they, were much mistaken. (Hear, and "no, no.") It had been said that the dividend was held out as a bait; but he denied it altogether; the directors were bound to give them what it was thought the line had earned. (Hear, hear.) They had done so, and with all deference to the committee, to whom he had no wish to impute motives – ("oh, oh," and laughter) – but what reason did the committee give why a 4s. dividend should not be paid? Why, on account of the heavy depreciation, which had been put in their second report at £150 a mile, whereas in the first document it was only stated at £100; and, from all he could ascertain, the engineer, in giving the larger estimate, had mistaken the question asked him. After a further explanation of this point, as bearing upon the question of dividend, the Chairman said he would now go to a matter personal to himself, and he had to thank Mr. Cash for the kind tone of his observations throughout. He was sorry he could not say the same of Mr. Meek: generosity he did not expect, and he would not enter upon the question, whether at a business meeting like this the remarks of that honourable gentlemen were just; but he did question the policy of making such a meeting the medium for running down any man – be he chairman, director, or shareholder. (Hear, hear, cheers, and uproar.) As this would in probability be the last time he should have the honour of addressing them – (loud cheers) – he hoped they would grant him a few moments' patient hearing. He became a member of this Board on the 7th of October, 1845; the goods traffic at that time they would find yielded only £9 per mile per week; whereas the last return, notwithstanding the increased mileage into, he regretted to say, some very unprofitable districts, averaged about £22 per week; so that, in regard to traffic, he thought they would not say that that had suffered under his management. (Cheers.) From his first connexion to the present time, although for a long period his family lived 200 miles away, he had given almost daily attention to the affairs of the company, for which he received no remuneration whatever beyond what was paid to the other directors. (Hear, hear.) With regard to the item of £2,000 which had been referred to, he had only to say that on the 25th of June, 1847, when the committee met at Westminster, he was ordered out of the room with the secretary; the matter was discussed in his absence; he knew not the reasons which were given; he knew that the resolution was passed, and he knew that he received the money. (Laughter.) Why it was not reported to the directors and entered upon the Company's books he could not say, but for that he was not responsible. Much had been said as to its being charged to "extensions," but he believed the explanation of it was that given by Mr. Patterson to the committee, because it was placed to the account of extensions, the bills for which were then in Parliament. ("Oh, oh.") There was another point which had been dwelt upon by Mr. Meek, and he was not going to defend it further than this – that at the time the Wisbeach and St. Ives shares came in (and he had had no communication with Mr. Hudson on the subject since it was brought before the committee) it was his belief that Mr. Hudson thought as he did, that he was entitled to the money. (Laughter and "no, no.") He was quite prepared to take his share of the responsibility, and he had no objection to any committee they might choose to appoint; but during the investigation of any question affecting his personal character – (cries of "that's lost already") – he thought that he ought to be at liberty to question the witnesses, and to adduce such counter testimony as he might be able to bring forward. It had been alleged against him that he had granted passes to the Maldon voters; but, although persons had been put in communication with discarded servants of the company, the committee could get no evidence to support the charge. He could fearlessly say that he had never granted any, and he was not aware of one having been granted by any one else. He complained of an allusion in the report, with respect to the expenditure by the Size Lane Committee,[11] that he (Mr. Waddington) could not answer further questions without affecting his position in another place. He had given an answer to that in the House of Commons; but he asked the committee whether they did not come to a resolution that that passage should be expunged, and whether it was not afterwards inserted by the majority? That, he considered, was wrong: a man in his position had quite sufficient to answer for without having matters of that kind inserted, tending to cast upon him a slur which he ought not to bear. He should be sorry not to allude to any matter which might be thought to require explanation, but he did not remember any other point that need be alluded to. He did not flinch from the responsibility attaching to him during the 3 and a half years that he had devoted himself to their interests – (laughter) – he did not object to any committee they might wish to appoint, but he warned them that their property would suffer from continued agitation, and his advice was to select a Board in whom they had confidence; and let them report on the state of affairs without being harrassed by a committee from without. (Hear and cheers.)

Two amendments were subsequently moved, one condemnatory of the Norfolk Amalgamation, and the other in favour of the 4s. dividend proposed by the directors; but both met with a negative, and the committee's report was adopted by a large majority.

Upon the Norfolk question a poll was demanded, to commence that evening and continue on Friday and Saturday.

Resignation of the Directors

The CHAIRMAN said he had already told them that he had attended there to fulfil the pledge which he gave at the last meeting. Previous to the business of to-day, the Board came to the unanimous resolution of resigning – (loud cheers) – and he had now to announce that they only retained office till their successors were appointed.

The Chairman then vacated the chair, and left the room with his colleagues, amidst no very flattering noises and observations.

Mr. MEEK and Mr. CASH subsequently recommended the appointment of a Committee of 30 shareholders to assist in selecting a Board, and a resolution which had been prepared was read; but the latter gentleman was of opinion that as the meeting was legally at an end it could not be acted upon at present.

The meeting throughout was a scene of the greatest noise and confusion.

Notes

1 David Waddington (1810–1863), a Manchester iron founder, was vice-chairman of the Eastern Counties Railway from 1845 to 1849 and its chair from 1851 to 1856; he also chaired the boards of two smaller railways. He was a Conservative MP from 1847 to 1856; his first electoral victory, in Maldon (Essex), allegedly benefited from votes cast by employees who were working on an ECR branch line there.

2 George Hudson was apprenticed as a draper in York, then entered finance and politics after inheriting £30,000 from an uncle in 1827. He helped found the York Union Banking Company in 1833 and joined the reformed York city council in 1835. He served in Parliament from 1845 to 1857, then fled to France to avoid his creditors.

3 The Northern and Eastern Railway opened a line from Stratford to Bishop's Stortford and Hertford between 1840 and 1842, leasing this to the ECR in 1844.

4 Lowestoft Harbour, Suffolk, is the eastern-most point in England, 110 miles east of London.

5 The Eastern Union Railway opened in 1846 and connected Colchester with Norwich via Ipswich. The ECR took over operation of this line in 1854 and joined with it and other companies in 1862 to form the Great Eastern.

6 Stephen Gaselee (1807–1883), the son of a Common Pleas judge, was called to the bar in 1832 after graduating from Oxford; he was made a serjeant-at-law in 1840. He later served as Liberal MP for Portsmouth from 1865 to 1868. He was a longtime director of the London & Southwestern Railway and the Portsmouth & Ryde United Steam Packet Company, held shares in several other Portsmouth companies, and sat on the boards of the local hospital and grammar school.

7 William Cash (1792–1849) was a partner in a London wool warehouse and a director of the National Provident Institution.

8 George Meek, besides being on the ECR board, was director of the Cheltenham, Oxford & Brighton Railway and the London Joint Stock Bank and auditor of the General Fire & Life Assurance Company.

9 The Norfolk Amalgamation concerned the ECR's plans to operate the Norfolk Railway with extensions to Lowestoft, Dereham, and Fakenham. Under an agreement reached in 1848, the Norfolk became a holding company and ceded operation to the ECR.

10 The Wisbech, St. Ives and Cambridge Junction Railway first issued shares in 1845, a third of which were bought by the Eastern Counties Railway. It opened in 1847 and was purchased by the ECR in 1848.

11 The Size Lane Committee was so called because one of its members had an office in Size Lane, London. It was composed of members who held shares in both the ECR and the London & York Railway and formed in 1846 to advocate a merger between the two firms.

Editorial Headnote

Guinness and Company, Ltd. (1887)

Guinness went public toward the end of a period of explosive growth in British beer consumption. As overall growth in brewing slowed in the 1880s, raising capital to purchase pubs was one of the only ways to increase market share. Brewers tapped the stock market for this purpose, rather than banks or their own reserves, to benefit from rising overall share prices and to share the wealth with potential voters against a backdrop of temperance reform. Guinness was the first of 264 brewers that went public during a sustained boom between 1886 and 1900, and its £6 million IPO joined a total issue of £185 million in shares and bonds. The majority of such firms followed Guinness's strategy of retaining family control by raising most of their capital in non-voting preference shares and debentures.[1] This boom also brought concentration: whereas 200 firms, out of a total of 17,110, supplied 54.4% of Britain's beer in 1881, 50, out of a much smaller total of 3,846, supplied 48.8% in 1913. This severely diminished publicans' bargaining power and also inhibited competitive pricing.[2]

Guinness was a large Irish fish in this shrinking, mostly English pond. Founded in 1759 by Arthur Guinness (1725–1803) in Dublin, the firm switched from ale to porter in 1778. Business boomed in the first half of the nineteenth century under the direction of his son, Arthur Guinness II (1768–1855), who was exporting nearly two-thirds of his beer to England by the time he died.[3] When Edward Cecil Guinness (1847–1927) inherited the business in 1868, the brewery was producing 350,000 barrels of porter (and the stronger stout, which came to be eponymous with the company's name), more than any other Irish brewer. By the time Guinness went public in 1886, it brewed nearly 60% of all the beer consumed in Ireland and was the leading brewer in the British Isles. Edward was only 29 when he became sole proprietor in 1876, buying out his older brother Arthur's share. He resisted the trend of buying pubs, relying on Guinness's distinctive brand to sell it as a "guest beer" directly to publicans and bottlers by the cask.[4]

Despite its strong financial position, rising plant costs and excise taxes created cash-flow challenges that made incorporation seem like a wise course. To accomplish this, Guinness approached the head of Baring Brothers, Lord Revelstoke, who issued £2.5 million in ordinary shares, £2 million in preference shares, and £1.5 million in debenture stock in October 1886. This was the first time Barings (or any other British investment bank) had floated an IPO for a British firm, and it was marred by numerous miscues. The purchase offer prompted a rush for shares, which nearly doubled in price by early 1887, and within two years, three other leading British brewers – Allsopp, Whitbread, and Bass – had also incorporated. By the time the company held its second meeting in August 1887, Edward

Guinness chaired the board of directors and held a controlling stake in the firm, with 53% of its ordinary shares; Barings held another 25%, and the rest were widely dispersed. Mirroring the Guinness brothers' Unionist politics, the new company's board featured a mix of London bankers (including Herman Hoskier and George Grenfell Glyn) and Irish elites; most (but not all) of the latter took the Unionist side in the Home Rule debate. Its new secretary, Charles Theobald, was an Essex native who moved from the Bank of England's cashier's office to Guinness's new head office across town. In the pre-circulated annual report, the board paired a 14% dividend with substantial reserves; its share price, which had more than tripled by late 1888, rose by another 76% over the next decade. Well into the next century, Guinness outpaced the market, more than doubling its output of porter and stout from 1.6 million to 3.5 million barrels between 1886 and 1914 and increasing its UK market share in beer sales from 5.7% to 10.4%.[5]

Notes

1 K. H. Hawkins and C. L. Pass, *The Brewing Industry: A Study in Industrial Organization and Public Policy* (London: Heinemann, 1974); S. R. Dennison and Oliver MacDonagh, *Guinness 1886–1939: From Incorporation to the Second World War* (Cork: Cork University Press, 1998), 17, 34–35; Katherine Watson, "Banks and Industrial Finance: The Experience of Brewers, 1880–1913," *Economic History Review* 49 (1996): 58–81.

2 Katherine Watson, "The New Issue Market as a Source of Finance for the U.K. Brewing and Iron and Steel Industries, 1870–1913," in *The Evolution of Financial Institutions and Markets in Twentieth-Century Europe*, ed. Y. Cassis, G. Feldman, and U. Olsson (Aldershot: Scolar Press, 1995), 214–222.

3 Paul Townend, "Guinness," in *Alcohol and Temperance in Modern History: A Global Encyclopedia*, eds. J. S. Blocker, D. M. Fahey, and I. R. Tyrrell (Oxford: ABC CLIO, 2003), 202.

4 Dennison and MacDonagh, *Guinness 1886–1939*, 1–15; Bill Yenne, *Guinness: The 250-Year Quest for the Perfect Pint* (Hoboken: John Wiley and Sons, 2007), 62; Andy Bielenberg, "The Irish Brewing Industry and the Rise of Guinness, 1790–1914," in *The Dynamics of the Modern Brewing Industry*, ed. T. Gourvish and R. G. Wilson (London: Routledge, 1998), 90–106.

5 Dennison and MacDonagh, *Guinness 1886–1939*, 16–29, 37; Nigel Edward Morecraft, *The Origins of Asset Management from 1700 to 1960* (Cham: Palgrave Macmillan, 2017), 188; "Prospectuses: Their Theory and their Practice," *Bankers' Magazine* 68 (1899), 712.

6

GUINNESS AND COMPANY, LTD.

Source: Guinness and Company, Ltd. (1887), *Freeman's Journal*, 16 August 1887

GUINNESS AND COMPANY, LIMITED

HALF-YEARLY MEETING.
SPECIAL TELEGRAM.
(FROM OUR CORRESPONDENT.)

London, Monday.

To-day at twelve o'clock the ordinary general meeting of Arthur Guinness, Son, and Company, Limited, was held here in the Cannon street Hotel. Sir E C Guinness, Bart (chairman), presided.[1] There was a large attendance of directors and shareholders.

The Secretary (Mr. C Tiobald)[2] read the notice convening the meeting. The directors' report having been taken as read,

The Chairman, who was received with applause, said – Gentlemen, I rise to move the adoption of the report and accounts. They call, I think, for very few words of explanation from me. We have endeavoured to place before you a full and clear statement of our financial position, and I think you will agree with me that it is satisfactory. In February last I informed you that we were doing well, and that the prospects before us were good. It is very gratifying for me to be able to tell you that my anticipations have been fully realised. We have had much in our favour. The prices of materials have been exceptionally low, but you must permit me to warn you that we cannot always count upon a similar state of things (hear, hear.) In the brewing trade, where success depends to some extent upon uncertain factors, upon the clemency of the seasons and those apparently capricious laws which govern all trade, we must make provision for less favourable times, or it may be for extensions which an increase of business may necessitate. So far, however, as we can at present foresee, we have every prospect of a good barley harvest and of at least an average crop of hops. In February I pointed out that we felt it to be our duty to see to the creation of a substantial reserve fund. Under the circumstances this was, and is, our first care. We have, therefore, devoted a large proportion of our earnings to this object to the extent of £200,000, as you are aware; and the fact that we were practically free during the first quarter of the

DOI: 10.4324/9781003177715-7

company's existence from the payment of interest or dividend to the stockholders has enabled us to go, perhaps, further in this direction than would otherwise have been practicable. The creation of a depreciation fund has been decided upon, after careful consideration, as a prudent step; for, although we have not spared expense in maintaining our property and keeping our machinery of all sorts in thorough repair, as the figures in the profit and loss account show, we still considered that it would be right to provide for the inevitable waste, if I may be permitted the expression, of the fixed plant and buildings, the depreciation of other classes of property – locomotives, boats, &c – being provided for in the ordinary course when the stock is taken every quarter. As to the dividend and the bonus which we recommend to your approval, I trust that you are satisfied (hear, hear). It is, I know, not possible to satisfy everyone's aspirations, but, looking at all the circumstances, I think you will agree with me that we have done our best in the interest of *bona fide* investors (hear, hear), and although stockholders may have to forego present profit they have the satisfaction of feeling that the self-denial exercised in this respect to-day is the best possible insurance for the future (applause). I beg to move the adoption of the report and accounts (applause).

Mr. Hoskier[3] seconded the motion, which was carried unanimously.

Sir A Young[4] moved a vote of thanks to the chairman for his kindness in presiding at their meeting, and also to the chairman and directors for the admirable manner in which their interests had been considered. He offered his congratulations to the chairman and directors for the extremely successful result of all their exertions on their behalf (applause.)

Mr. W Quill, B L (Dublin)[5] seconded the motion. He had the honour of appearing there as the delegate and specially appointed representative of many Irish shareholders. Whatever their differences in political or religious views might be they were singularly unanimous and at one in the entire reliance on the integrity and financial ability of their distinguished countryman, Sir Edward Guinness (applause). Speaking in his representative capacity he felt justified in making a few observations on the present condition and future development of the splendid property which it was the good fortune of the shareholders to possess; and before doing so he might say that increasing business was the outcome of the unwearied industry, the provident forethought, the philanthropic management of that remarkable family, whose escutcheon was undimmed by a single slip, and whose representatives all men deemed worthy of the highest honour (hear, hear). Therefore, it appeared to him that the company had the advantage, although but nine months in existence, of being the heir and inheritor of great commercial skill, energy, and wisdom; and it would be their fault if they did not reap the advantages which would accrue from such a state of things (hear, hear). The statement of accounts presented should give unbounded satisfaction in Ireland, and must also commend itself to those present, because it was not only the record of great financial success in the past, but was pregnant with meaning for the future which was before them (hear, hear). The net profits not only showed a profit for the nine months equal to the entire annual profits of the private firm, but also showed that this vast result had been accomplished notwithstanding the fact that the quarter embracing the months of July, August, and September was the most lucrative quarter in the year. Everyone conversant with the business knew that the quarter now current was the great financial quarter of the year, and they might, therefore, look with greater confidence to the future when they knew the enormous profit which had been made did not include the most lucrative quarter of the year, whilst the success at their commencement was still more wonderful when they considered that it did not include this lucrative quarter. Even assuming that the business did not increase, on the figures placed before them by the board of directors, it would appear if the profits went on in the same ratio, and what was known to be the most lucrative quarter did not exceed the other quarters, they would make a handsome profit (hear). He hoped the company, under the presidency of Sir Edwd Guinness, might long continue to afford shareholders, both in England and Ireland, such evidences of its great prosperity (applause).

Mr. Stewart Wallace, Belfast,[6] supported the motion, and expressed his agreement with the observations which had been made by previous speakers. He thought it was worthy of note that notwithstanding the huge earnings of the company the directors' fees were so very moderate (hear, hear). That was a fact which was singularly favourable compared with other companies of which he unfortunately was a shareholder. Some time ago he was told that the excellence of the liquor provided by their company was owing to a secret possessed only by one person, and if that secret died out their success would be at an end (laughter). At the time this incident was related to him he was at a considerable distance from Dublin, but he immediately repaired to the city as a private detective (laughter). He instituted inquiries, and, as a result, he ascertained that there were no fewer than six brewers, some of them old, some of them middle-aged, and some of them young, and that, as a matter of fact, the secret was one of continuity, handed down from the old brewers to middle-aged brewers, and from the middle-aged to young brewers, so that they were not likely to be ruined by the death of one man (laughter, and hear, hear). He knew that use had been made of the statement that the secret was in the possession of one man to damage the shares, and he considered it right to let the truth be known (hear, hear).

The motion was then passed by acclamation.

Sir Edward Guinness, in returning thanks, assured the shareholders that it would always be the aim of the directors to maintain the prosperity of the company (applause).

The proceedings then terminated.

Notes

1 Edward Cecil Guinness (1847–1927) inherited his father Benjamin's brewery in 1868 along with his older brother Arthur, who focused on politics and became a Unionist peer in 1880. Edward bought out his brother's share in the brewery in 1876 for £680,000 and spent most of the 1880s running the firm, although he did dabble in

Dublin politics, eventually joining his brother in the peerage in 1891 as the Earl of Iveagh.

2 Charles Theobald (1860–1924) graduated from Tonbridge School in 1877, was in the chief cashier's office in the Bank of England from 1881–1886, then took over as secretary of Guinness, where he stayed until his early retirement in 1909 at age 49.

3 Herman Hoskier (1832–1904) was a merchant banker, born in Norway and raised in Denmark, who lived in Florence, Algiers, Alabama, New York, and Liverpool before settling in London in 1864. He was a partner in the private bank Brown Shipley from 1866 to 1880, then a director of the Union Bank of London from 1881 until his death. In 1886, he mainly worked at Guinness as its director in charge of finances. His close ties with Barings and Hambros, two of London's largest investment banks, rendered him an invaluable ally when Guinness went public in 1886.

4 Sir Allen William Young (1827–1915), son of a London solicitor, was a merchant navy officer and polar explorer, who was still sailing around the world as late as 1885. His connection to Guinness most likely derived from his family connection to Young and Co., a brewery based in South London.

5 Albert William Quill (1844–1908) was a Dublin barrister, an opponent of Irish Home Rule, an expert on Irish land law, and a translator of Tacitus.

6 John Stewart Wallace (1840–1910) was a Belfast native who lived in County Down. He was a contractor with American mining interests and a Liberal MP for Limehouse from 1892 to 1895. He was Vice-President of the Irish Protestant Home Rule Association, which formed in 1886 to defend Gladstone's home rule legislation.

Editorial Headnote

Great Western Railway (1891)

The Great Western Railway (GWR) had been running trains between London and Bristol for 50 years when it held its 111th half-yearly meeting at Paddington Station in February 1891.[1] Presided over by its long-time secretary and recently-promoted chair, Frederick Saunders, the meeting covered a broad range of issues that reflected railway companies' central role in the social and economic life of late-Victorian Britain. A Bath retiree complained that the GWR platform there was inaccessible to passengers with disabilities. More urgently, a recent collision near Taunton between a freight train and a passenger train, which left ten dead, stood as a reminder of the risks accompanying rail travel – and the liability often ascribed to the companies involved. A "country parson of West Somerset" had complained to *The Times* about "the miserably slipshod way things were managed" on the GWR, while a grand jury acquitted its signalman, George Rice, of negligent manslaughter on the grounds that the company shared blame for the accident.[2] Another issue raised at the meeting pitted the farmers and factory owners who shipped their goods by rail against the companies that charged them for this service. The GWR meeting took place on the heels of two new laws that called on railways to submit a revised set of maximum rates, then invited traders to air any objections before the Board of Trade. The chief architects of these laws, Courtney Boyle, Arthur Balfour, and Lord Stanley, had hoped they would resolve the ongoing tensions between the two interests, but instead, they prolonged disputes into the next century.[3]

Finally, railways also stood at the center of rising British labor unrest at the end of the nineteenth century, reaching a climax with a strike in 1900 on the Taff Vale line – which the GWR, in this meeting, debated purchasing. A preview of that strike occurred at Bute Dock in Cardiff, which began as a temporary work stoppage in August 1890 among railwaymen who worked for the Taff Vale, GWR, and other firms serving the dock, then turned into a more substantial strike among dockers and seamen by the end of the year.[4] Against the backdrop of this strike, the GWR shareholders' perspective on their company's labor force was both typical and revealing. First, they insisted that they knew better than Liberal MPs or their own workers what was best for their staff. Regarding politicians, Saunders chastised Francis Channing, who, three weeks earlier, had urged the House of Commons to inquire into the "social injustice" and safety risks associated with "the excessive hours of labour imposed on railwaymen."[5] Regarding workers, the paternalist attitudes on display at this meeting dated back to British railways' earliest years, in company towns and military-style hierarchies and uniforms – but such efforts were starting to fray around the edges by the 1890s.[6] The only dispute within the GWR, in this setting, was how best to confront the problem: by browbeating workers or appealing to the state to intervene. Ultimately, the state did intervene – but on the side of labor, when a Liberal-Labour alliance in 1906 passed the Trade Disputes Act, which shielded unions from liability in the event of a strike, and which ushered in a golden age for labor organization in Britain.[7]

Notes

1 In 1891, the GWR was also a year away from completing the elimination of its broad-gauge tracks, which, for decades, had set it apart from other British railways: Andrew Roden, *Great Western Railway: A History* (London: Aurum Press, 2010), 130–133.

2 F. H. Rich, *Great Western Railway* (London: Board of Trade, 1890); "The Railway Accident Near Taunton," *London Times* 13 November 1890; "The Taunton Railway Disaster," *Illustrated Police News* 29 November 1890.

3 Timothy L. Alborn, *Conceiving Companies: Joint-Stock Politics in Victorian England* (London: Routledge, 1998), 234–237.

4 M. J. Daunton, "Inter-Union Relations on the Waterfront: Cardiff, 1888–1910," *International Review of Social History* 22 (1977), 352–361; Michael J. Freeman, *Railways and the Victorian Imagination* (New Haven: Yale University Press, 1999), 173–194.

5 Quoted in Peter Nicholls, "Labour, Management, and Control: The Early Railway Industry in Britain," in *A Business and Labour History of Great Britain*, ed. Michael Richardson and Peter Nicholls (Houndmills: Palgrave Macmillan, 2011), 22.

6 Alborn, *Conceiving* Companies, 182–183, 245–247.

7 Geoffrey Alderman, "The Railway Companies and the Growth of Trade Unionism in the Late Nineteenth and Early Twentieth Centuries," *Historical Journal* 14 (1971): 129–152. The Trade Disputes Act reversed a punitive legal decision against the organizers of the Taff Vale strike.

7

GREAT WESTERN RAILWAY

Source: Great Western Railway (1891), *Supplement to the Railway Times*, 14 February 1891

GREAT WESTERN RAILWAY

The 111th half-yearly general meeting was held on Thursday, at the Paddington Station; Mr. FRED. G. SAUNDERS[1] presiding.

The SECRETARY (Mr. J. D. Higgins)[2] read the notice convening the meeting. The report and accounts were taken as read.

The CHAIRMAN said – Gentlemen, I have to move: –

"That the report of the directors, circulated among the proprietors, and now presented to the meeting, be received and adopted."

Before I go into the matters which are the subjects of that report, I hope you will allow me to say a word upon a matter which has scarcely been out of my mind during the last three months. I allude to the unfortunate accident which occurred at Norton Fitzwarren, and I desire to express the sympathy, which I am sure we all feel, with the unfortunate people who suffered on that occasion. I need not say that it was with a feeling of dismay and horror we received the news of that accident – the directors and officers alike. We did all we could to alleviate the sufferings of the poor people, and our superintendents and officers were on the spot almost immediately after the occurrence. Our own medical officers, too, who are gentlemen of great skill and ability, went down to assist in the matter, and they were ably assisted by the medical officers on the spot, who attended with kindly consideration and attention to the sufferers. It has been very gratifying to us to receive from several of the injured letters expressing their thankfulness for what we did for them, and I desire to acknowledge the receipt of other sympathetic letters which have been forwarded to me, because it is no little trial for the chairman of a great company like this that an accident of that kind should have happened. I will not say more on that subject at the present moment except this, that there were four separate inquiries held, and that throughout the whole of those inquiries there was not a suggestion made that there was any want of care or forethought in the regulations of the company, either as to the conduct of the traffic or the appliances by which it was carried on. Everything was apparently in perfect working order, and all the regulations were as complete as it was possible to make them. There was, of course, one little defect, and that was in the brain of the signalman,

DOI: 10.4324/9781003177715-8

for whom we must all feel. I don't want to say nasty things with reference to circumstances connected with that catastrophe, but it is a little hard upon those who are responsible for the affairs of this great company, that the newspapers on their own account and by the admission of correspondence into their columns, should try to increase the difficulties under which the directors and railways and their officers at present work. ("Hear, hear."). I was very much annoyed by the letter of one gentleman in particular, who calls himself a west country parson, and who thought fit to fix upon the chairman and the general manager the responsibility for that accident. I am told it would be undignified to refer more particularly to his communication, so I will only say that he does not state anything of his own knowledge, or make any suggestion by which the accident could have been avoided. He says that for months he – and I suppose the old women of his parish – had been predicting that the accident would happen, and therefore I imagine that he was more pleased than otherwise that his prophecy was fulfilled. He also says that the chairman should have been hanged, because by cutting down the men's wages, and keeping them at work for many hours at a time, he was responsible for the accident. Now, there is not a shadow of foundation for any of these assertions; and I think if that parson would only go home and try to practise a little more of that consideration for the feelings of others, which I dare say he preaches to his own congregation, he would do much better than writing anonymous letters to the newspapers. ("Hear, hear.")

If you will allow me, I will just go through the statement of figures in the accounts, and touch upon the more salient points. I don't think there is much to be said about the capital expenditure. The receipts on capital account amount to 463,000*l*., of which 316,000*l*. has been raised by the issue of 190,000*l*. of consolidated ordinary stock, and the premiums on stocks issued. The other items of the 463,000*l*. are represented not by increased capital, but by the substitutions we made when we took over the Witney and East Gloucestershire railways.[3] We took these over and one other little railway and their stocks, and that proceeding did not involve any increase of capital. The same may be said of the capital expenditure. It is shown as 743,000*l*., and that includes in addition to the lines I have mentioned the 100,000*l*, we paid for the abolition of the obligation we were under in connection with the Severn Navigation.[4] On the whole, I hope it has not been a disadvantageous bargain to us. Then as to the revenue account, I do not say that it is altogether disappointing, but it certainly is unsatisfactory. With increased earnings of 151,000*l*. we are obliged to come to you with an announcement that you must have a less dividend. That is not satisfactory, but the explanation is – increased expenses, increased wages, increased numbers of men, and additional materials, to which I will allude more in detail presently. As to the increased revenue arising from the different classes of traffic, I may say that in the third-class there is an increase of 115,000*l*. in money and 1,378,000 in the number of passengers. In the second-class there is a decrease of 20,000*l*. in money and 13,000 in numbers; and in the first-class there is a decrease of 1,700*l*, in money and 18,600 in the number carried. Although some people are anxious that the second-class should be abolished, I think as long as we carry more than 2 millions of second-class passengers in a half-year, and as long as those want accommodation in that class we must not shut them out of it. ("Hear, hear.") The receipts which we get from each class may be of interest to you. We get 4s. 1d. from each passenger in the first-class, 1s. 7d. from each in the second-class, and 1s. 0.777d. from each in the third. Then as to parcels, horses, and carriages there is an increase of 18,000*l*., which I think is not unsatisfactory. In mails there is a diminution of 84*l*.; in merchandise an increase of 3,600*l*.; in livestock an increase of 8,000*l*.; in minerals an increase of 25,000*l*.; and in dock and harbour dues a diminution of 2,756*l*. That arises almost entirely from the docks at Plymouth and local circumstances with which I need not trouble you. The canal traffic is down 700*l*.; rents of property are up 2,500*l*.; transfer fees are down 50*l*.; and mileage and demurrage of rolling stock are up 1,400*l*. The total result is 151,253*l*, increase. It may also interest you to know that the train mileage receipts per mile for passengers were 4s. 10.274d., against 4s. 10.339d. in 1889, or a decrease of .065d.; but we have rather a larger number of passenger train miles, and I do not think that is unsatisfactory. From goods trains we have earned 5s. 4:479d. per mile, against 5s. 5.888d., or a diminution of 1.409d. As regards expenditure, the maintenance of way and works increased 26,000*l*., and you may take it that about 7,000*l*. of that was increased wages. In locomotive power the expenses increased 70,000*l*., and of that 45,000*l*. is due to increased wages and materials and about 25,000*l*. to increased miles run. Carriage and wagon repairs show an increase of 8,200*l*.; traffic expenses have increased 40,800*l*., and 30,000*l*. of that is due to increased wages, and 5,000*l*. to the increased prices of materials. In general charges there is an increased expenditure of 3,592*l*., and about 1,500*l*. of that is due to telegraph charges, which seem inclined to rise. The law charges are up 2,400*l*., and if it had not been for the unfortunate Board of Trade inquiry those charges would have gone down. Of the 11,500*l*. law charges, nearly 5,000*l*. is due to the inquiry before the Board of Trade about two years ago. Parliamentary charges are down 5,600*l*., and that is satisfactory. Compensation for personal injury is up 8,800*l*., and compensation for damage and loss of goods bas increased 3,000*l*. Of course, a great deal of that is due to increased traffic. Rates and taxes are down 900*l*. That decrease is practically due to the contribution we get from the County Council. It is an application of money from the Imperial Exchequer in aid of local rates. Government duty is up 400*l*., and steamboat charges have increased 4,400*l*. The canal expenses are down 950*l*. The results per train mile for passengers and goods were 5s. 1.3d., compared with 5s. 2.07d. in 1889, and the expenses were 2s. 7.2d., compared with 2s. 6.4d. last year. The per-centage on traffic receipts was 51 per cent., as against 49 last year, so that practically it has increased nearly 2 per cent. Our receipts per mile per week have increased from 68*l*. 7s. 6d. to 70*l*. 9s. 10d. Upon the whole our working expenses do not compare unfavourably with those of other companies. Then our suspense accounts, that is the accident account, the fire insurance fund, the steamboat depreciation and insurance fund, and the reconstruction of viaducts and stations account all stand satisfactorily with the exception of the fire insurance fund. We had two bad fires – one at Liverpool (which cost us 6,200*l.*) and another at Dudley (which cost 2,700*l.*). We show a diminution in the balance of 1,500*l.*, but all the other funds have increased. The result is that the total revenue receipts amount to 4,657,000*l.*, and the total revenue expenditure amounts to 2,355,000*l.*, thus giving a balance of revenue account of 2,301,000*l.* After meeting prior charges, dividends on shares held by the company, debenture interest, &c., there is a balance remaining of 867,000*l.*, available for division amongst the ordinary shareholders, and we ask you to divide at the rate of 7¾ per cent. per annum, carrying forward a balance of 61,000*l.* to next account, as against 59,000*l.* in the corresponding period of last year. (Cheers.)

Upon the whole I am glad to find that that has been accepted as not an unsatisfactory result of the half-year's working, and I hope you will be content to adopt our recommendations. I don't know that there is anything in the report, as regards capital, that you will care to hear. In paragraph 5 we refer to the reconstruction of the viaducts between Hemerdon and Rattery, on the South Devon Railway, and the construction of the second tunnel at the latter place. I wish to point out that it is all in the direction of a discontinuance of our old friend the broad gauge and a substitution of the narrow gauge. If all goes well, in fifteen or eighteen months from this time, we hope to be able to carry out that arrangement. It is rather a blow to some of us who have been brought up as broad gauge men, and have rather an affection for it, but still it is inevitable, and the substitution of narrow gauge for broad gauge must come about. I hope when the change has been carried out we shall derive substantial advantages from the economies which will result from it. ("Hear, hear.") In paragraph 9 we tell you that we are providing an additional vessel of increased speed and capacity for the Channel Islands service. We provided three new vessels for that service about a year and a half ago, and our experience of them has been satisfactory on the whole. We have largely increased our traffic by means of them, but there is still a cry for larger steamers and better accommodation altogether, and we think the experience we have had justifies us in building another boat for that service. ("Hear, hear.") A new steam tender is also being built for the company for use at Plymouth. One of our boats there is getting old and obsolete, and there is a demand for a larger vessel and better accommodation.

With regard to the proceedings under the Railway and Canal Traffic Act I cannot say much more than what is set forth in the report, except that yesterday we received copies of the provisional orders which were prepared by the Board of Trade in respect of nine of the railway companies, and which were deposited in Parliament the day before yesterday. We have not had time to go through them yet. It is difficult to work out what they mean, but, as you know, Lord Balfour[6] and Mr. Courtenay Boyle[5] carried out an inquiry at enormous cost – I won't say and waste of time – and they heard witnesses for and against the railway companies. That inquiry resulted in a report by Lord Balfour and Mr. C. Boyle to the Board of Trade, and since then the Board of Trade have received deputations from almost every class of traders and freighters, who wish to induce the board to lower the rates which Lord Balfour and Mr. Boyle thought reasonable. We have also had opportunities from time to time of expressing our opinions before the Board of Trade upon some of the suggestions, but the result, I am afraid, is that, although Lord Balfour and Mr. Boyle had the benefit of holding an inquiry and examining witnesses in open court, the Board of Trade intend to cut down the rates and recommendations which Lord Balfour and Mr. Boyle thought after an exhaustive inquiry were fair and reasonable. I don't want to frighten you, but I think the action taken will involve another fight in the House of Lords, and, perhaps, a strong committee will be appointed to consider the question, and we shall have a repetition of the struggle we had at enormous cost before Lord Balfour and Mr. Boyle. But we shall know more about the effect of these provisional orders in a few days.

Then, as regards the Bills before Parliament, I shall allude to them when we come to the special meeting for their consideration, and I shall be happy to answer any detailed questions which any of the shareholders may wish to ask. The matters referred to in our own Bill are not of great importance, and I may say we do not propose to raise more capital than we have powers to raise now. ("Hear, hear.") Then the vote of the proprietors will be asked for an expenditure of 460,000*l*. Of that 120,000*l*. is for goods and ballast wagons, and 100,000*l*. for widening the line between Maidenhead and Didcot. The necessities of our traffic also require that we should introduce more sidings, and those are accommodations which will facilitate traffic and which, I hope, will in some sense reduce expenditure. But all these improvements involve a large amount of capital outlay. Fortunately we are able at this moment to raise our capital on pretty advantageous terms. ("Hear, hear.")

Then we refer in the report to the death of our old friend Mr. Basset.[7] He was an old South Wales man, and was introduced to us by our old friend Mr. Talbot.[8] He became a director in 1863, and he gave a great deal of useful service. ("Hear, hear.") We have elected in his place Mr. Heywood Lonsdale,[9] who for many years has been a large shareholder in the company. I had not the pleasure of his acquaintance until he became a director, but I shall be greatly disappointed if he does not prove himself to be a useful director, and a great acquisition to the board of this company. ("Hear, hear.") While speaking on this subject I think I ought to allude to the death of our old friend Mr. Thomas Adams.[10] He was a familiar figure here for a good many years. He was appointed on a committee of shareholders in 1863, and I fancy he thought the committee of shareholders made a great mistake in not recommending that he should form a portion of the new blood which was to invigorate the board. His rejection, I think, he attributed to our old friend Sir Spencer Walpole.[11] However, he always took a leading part in our general meetings, and gave us the benefit of a great deal of criticism. I don't know that it was always of the most useful kind, but criticism from the other side of the table helps to keep us in order. He was also fond of statistics, but the results he arrived at with his figures were not always correct. He died about three or four months ago.

Mr. BEAVIS[12] – I did not know it.

The CHAIRMAN – You might have assumed it from not seeing him here.

Mr. BEAVIS – I am very sorry to hear it.

The CHAIRMAN – Now I think I must say a word to you about the relations with our servants. There has been a great deal of criticism lately upon the relations which exist between railway companies and their employés, and I think it right that I should say a few words upon the subject, and at any rate that I should tell you pretty much how we stand with our men, and in what condition the men generally are. I do not want to have to make a long story on the subject; but it is a very important question. At the last meeting, I think, or the meeting before last, I told you tbat there were suggestions flying about as to dissatisfied men, and strikes, and all that sort of thing, and that I did not think very much of them upon the whole, as I thought our relations with our men, and particularly the older men in the service, were satisfactory, and I had no apprehension of any evil result. Well, the remarks I then made have been a good deal criticised, particularly by some of the agitators amongst the men in our service, and by men outside the service who care to encourage this sort of agitation. I adhere to all I said then, and, although there are still discussions and suggestions as to the strikes that have been going on in other parts of the country, and are still unfortunately in South Wales, I think on the whole we have got a united and satisfied set of men engaged in our service, and if they could only be let alone I am perfectly sure they would be perfectly happy. I very much deprecate the interference of mischievous agitators, some of them possessing the quality in which I am sorry to say I fail so much, the gift of the gab, and who lay before the young men in the service, who are more inclined to listen to them than their seniors, statements that they are going to get all sorts of benefits out of agitation. Of course we recognise, as all railway companies must, that a tendency exists throughout the country to increase the remuneration for labour, and particularly skilled labour. We can see that well enough, and the improved condition in which the company has been placed for the last two or three years has enabled us to meet the men as we think in a fair and liberal spirit. We wish always to deal with them, I won't say liberally, but fairly and considerately. If they have grievances they want remedied, they can to come before us and we listen to them. I am sure in the last half-year we have listened by the hour in our own board-room to deputations of men who come up to tell us not so much their own grievances as those of others, because whenever we ask a man what is his grievance he generally says, "I have not any grievance myself, but a friend of mine who lives somewhere else worked fourteen hours a day," or something frightful of that sort. (Laughter.) But as to the men themselves, we can scarcely find a man who has a real grievance of his own which he wants to thresh out. As far as we can do so we receive the men and listen to them, and I will undertake that no deputation which has come before us can say that it has not been kindly and considerately heard. In that respect there has been no deficiency on the part of the Great Western board or, I believe, the boards of other companies. The result of the consideration we have given to the men is chiefly to be seen in increased wages and to some extent in the reduction of the hours of work as regards signalmen particularly. The reduction of the hours of work, of course, means that a man does less work for the same result as to money value, and what we gave in this way in the course of last year by that process amounts to at least 100,000*l*. That is a substantial sum, and an amount so appreciable cannot be ignored altogether. The regularity with which our service has been worked is attributable in a large degree to the steadiness and efficiency of the staff who work under us. We like to appreciate and we think you gentlemen will support us in anything we can do to raise and keep up that feeling on the part of the staff, and if it is even at the expense, as to-day, of a 4 per cent. less dividend, you won't grudge it.

Then as to the tyrannical oppression under which it is said that railway men labour, you know the whole thing is gammon, and utter rubbish. I will tell you what the wages of our men are, for I would like you to judge by this criterion. We have an enormous staff of men in our employment, at any rate something like fifty thousand. As regards the number of men who voluntarily leave the service it is perfectly infinitesimal. You would not believe bow small is the number of men who ever go away from this horrid state of oppression of their own accord. This morning I received a return from the locomotive superintendent. We have 1,500 enginemen at Swindon and Wolverhampton and elsewhere, and, of course, the same number of firemen. Last year one man voluntarily left the service, and out of 1,500 that is not a very large per-centage, and taking the average of five years the number of engine-drivers who have voluntarily left the service is not more than one in 500. Of course, we have a large number of men employed at Swindon, many of them on piecework. We had a rolling mill – we have not got it now – and, of course, we have men in collieries and that sort of thing, but I do not call those permanent staff. Of course, those men must vary according to the work that has to be done, but in our regular staff of guards, porters, policemen, engine-drivers, and that class, regularly employed, it is an unknown thing for a man to be dismissed the service for want of employment; I mean, of course, men may be dismissed the service for irregularity or complaints of some kind or another, but nobody can point to a man who has been compelled to leave the service because we could not find him work. If our trade is dull a little, of course we do not want so many men; but we let them hang on, and in order that we may not be obliged to get rid of them we do not take new men on. Perhaps a man does not rise so rapidly in bad times as in good times, but as a matter of fact a man does not get dismissed the service. Such a state of things as that is known in few great commercial undertakings except railway companies. Other great employers of labour may fail, or other things may happen, and a man may have to get rid of half his staff. But no such thing happens in the service of a great railway company, and, judging by the number of men who are always waiting to join, it does not look as though the service was oppressive. I am bothered out of my life to make recommendations to the officers in respect of men whom I know they cannot find room for, and it is absurd on the face of it to suggest that the service is not an attractive one.

We have not yet been seriously troubled with strikes, but in the case of the unfortunate strikes which have occurred in Scotland,[13] where, by the way, the men are not half so well treated as ours are, what do you see? The moment they think the door is going to be shut against them they are eager to come back, and to place their necks again under the yoke of the men who are said to be crushing them to death. I repeat that it is absurd to suggest that there is anything in railway labour which is so extremely hard and oppressive. If the wealthy philanthropists and Church dignitaries who air their liberality in finding money for people on strike would withhold a little bit of that sympathy and not interfere in matters they cannot possibly understand, this being one of the most complicated questions one could have to do with, they would help to lessen the difficulty, and they would play less into the hands of the people whose dupes they unfortunately are. The only place on the Great Western system where there is any feeling of dissatisfaction at the present moment – I mean any general feeling, because individually no one is ever satisfied – is in South Wales, and there is certainly a feeling that the men in South Wales have been hardly treated. There has been a disorganisation of traffic in South Wales or something like it. There have been delays to trains and interference with the current of work, which of course involves long hours for the men.

We have received the men once upon the subject, and we shall hope to meet their wishes, and to some extent we have removed the causes of complaint, though I am not sure they are entirely removed. But we have not shut the door to further negotiation, and I hope before the thing is done with we shall be able to satisfy them that they have no very substantial grievances. The goods guards are the people who think they have been worst used, and no doubt if the goods trains have to be shunted into sidings to enable the passenger trains to pass, the detention and the bother to them is very great. We have met them in a large degree, and we have no other desire than to try and meet all the reasonable wishes of these men. So far as long hours are concerned, we have as much interest as other people in keeping down the hours of the men. We do not believe we can get the same attention from the man who has been at work fifteen or sixteen hours as from the man who works only nine or ten, and we would much prefer that the men should work an equal number of hours, and if a man works overhours it is not in our interest that it should be so. We should very much prefer that he should keep his hours within a reasonable amount of time, we getting the best energy we can out of him. But it is nonsense to talk about a man who is engaged for a great number of hours in our service as if his brain and muscles were employed the whole time. Take the case of an engineman upon a little branch railway. Perhaps he will only work some 60 miles or 70 miles [a] day, but it will take him twelve hours to do it, and for half the time the fellow is playing, or rather I won't say playing, but there is no strain upon his powers, and he is fit to work. I am sure I could work for hours and hours more than that without incurring any risk or danger to anybody by so doing.

The proprietors are aware of the strike that is now going on at the Bute Dock at Cardiff. It has not at present involved us in any substantial trouble. I hope it will not, but traffic has necessarily been disorganised lately, and a lot of innocent men at the collieries will be put out of work because gentlemen at Cardiff do not choose to allow the union men to associate with free labour on board ship. Except for that we have not up to the present moment been affected by the strike. I confess I have myself a very strong feeling about that iniquitous system of picketing and violence and intimidation which strikes at the root of the relations between employer and employed and seeks to prevent an honest man from earning his bread with the best power he possesses. I confess I have a strong feeling about it, but my friends about me say I must control my feelings, and that discretion is the better part of valour. Therefore I won't express myself as strongly as I would like to express myself to you to-day. An article appeared in the Times of Monday which, if you will allow me to read it to you, I think you will say is very much to the point. It is as follows:

The question raised at Cardiff is of the widest possible interest. It affects not only all employers of labour in this country; in a very real sense the whole country is concerned in it. The new unionism claims to extend everywhere and to dominate all departments of work. If it has its way it will put an end to free labour. To join its ranks, to agree to its rules, to contribute to its funds, and to yield a blind obedience to its chiefs will be made conditions, apart from which no one will be suffered to gain a living. It is a form of tyranny which workers and capitalists have a like interest in putting down. If it prevails, its result will be to place an excessive and arbitrary power in reckless and irresponsible hands, who will use it for their own ends, with small regard to the welfare of those who have intrusted them with it, and with small care for the permanent mischief which they will bring about. But we have no fear that it will prevail. It can claim one success, and it has sustained a dozen defeats since. At the great dock strike the public were hardly aware of what the question at issue really was. They gave their sympathy and their support freely and generously and thoughtlessly to a poor body of men who had genuine grievances to complain of. The leaders of the new unionism saw their opportunity, and availed themselves of it promptly and skilfully. They were successful against weak antagonists, but with no benefit in the end to those whose cause they professed to be championing. This, however, has been their first victory and their last. On several important occasions they have tried their strength against more formidable opponents, and have failed utterly and ignominiously. The great strike at the South Metropolitan Gasworks, and that on the Scotch railway lines, were well contested on both sides, and the result showed that the new unionism was powerless when it was met with firmness and determination. We shall look for the same lesson from the strike at the Bute Docks. The struggle may be short or it may be prolonged. It may be wide or narrow in its range. But if it is fought aright it will end in one way, in a defeat of the new unionism, and in a victory for free labour.[14] (Cheers.)

I want now to give an illustration of the wages of our men, and we begin our labour in various grades. In the locomotive department, for instance, we begin with lads at 7s. a week, who of course spoil tools and materials for about twelve months, and eventually get to be useful fellows. As to the permanent way men, their wages of course vary according to the district they are employed in. We are a commercial undertaking, and must be guided by commercial rules, but I may say that the wages of those men are fixed at a substantial advance on the wages paid in the agricultural districts through which the line passes, and we are able by that means to attract all the labour we require for that service. If a man gets to be a signalman he would start at 18s. or 19s. a week and go up to 28s. in the country or 30s. in London. In addition to his wages the signalman is entitled to a bonus of from 2*l*. to 5*l*. a year, according to the time he has been in the service, and that means certainly another 9d. or 2s. a week. He also has his clothes, which we contract to get supplied to us at as cheap a price as we can, and those we calculate are worth another ls. 2d. a week to him, and if he works on Sunday he gets overtime. When we reduce the number of hours in some of the boxes there are of course more men to do the work, and the Sunday duty does not come round so often, and it is now a grievance with some of the men that they cannot go on Sunday work, whereas it was formerly a grievance that they must go.

I am half afraid to speak about a passenger guard; but a passenger guard gets in fixed wages from 1*l*. ls. to 40s. a week. He gets his clothing, which we calculate at the rate of ls. 6d. a week, and gentlemen who travel about know pretty well what else he gets. It is a position which almost any of us might desire to attain. You cannot get a porter at Paddington to leave the station, and a number of men are always wanting to occupy that delightful position. Then as to goods guards who are no doubt worked a greater number of hours than the guards of passenger trains, theirs is a much rougher sort of work, and they are not always such highly accomplished gentlemen as the passenger guards are. They get from 22s. to 32s. in the country and 34s. 6d. in London, with the addition of clothes, which we estimate at another 1s. 3d. The hours of the goods guard are no doubt longer than those of the passenger guard, but he travels in a comfortable van provided with a fire, and he can make up his way bills with his feet on the stove. As regards the engine-driver beginning as a boy at 7s. a week, his wages go up to 64s. a week, and that is not bad pay, you know. In addition to that an engine-driver gets a bonus if he has no record against him of 10*l*. a year, or equal to 4s. a week. He also gets an overcoat, but that does not amount to much. You may take it that an engine-driver can rise to 68s. a week, and perhaps more sometimes, but that is only by running a larger number of miles and being employed a greater number of hours. A mechanic may earn from 40s. to 45s. per week, but a good deal of that is paid by piecework.

I have given you an outline of our scale of wages, and I maintain that it is large enough to attract people to our service in all districts of the country into which we go. I have shown that the proportion of people who leave us is infinitesimal, and as a matter of fact we never dismiss except for wrongdoing of some kind or another, and I think upon the whole you will agree that it is not a bad service. In addition to the wages every one of these men has three days' holiday in a year in respect of which no wages are deducted, and if a man wants to go away we give him a pass for himself and wife, and three or four children. From that they often derive substantial pleasure. I do not say it is money, but it is something they do not get elsewhere. We have also recently decided to give what we call "privilege" tickets to our servants, enabling them to travel at ¼d. a mile instead of !d., and I may tell you that at Swindon alone our servants availed themselves of the privilege last Friday to the number of 1,000. One of our officers was told that the value of the ticket was estimated at from 1s. to 2s. a week, as it enabled the servants to attend the markets.

We have throughout our service some 6,000 allotments, for which we make the holders pay a moderate price. We do not give them as a matter of right, but wherever we have got land available on the tops of the banks or the slopes of the railway near country stations we like to encourage a man to have an allotment. That is a substantial boon which men cannot get in any other service, and, of course, that does not apply to London, where there is no land to let out in allotment gardens. We have also a benefit fund to meet sickness, a superannuation fund, a fund for widows and orphans, and even if our men are not "in the funds" we help them if they come to grief in any way. There are many young men in the rural districts, such as permanent way men, whom we should like to have join, but who from some reason or another do not like to be obliged to contribute. Our contribution towards these funds amounts one way and another to 12,500*l.* a year, and a committee of our board is at this moment considering whether the system of benefits to the men can be extended. I think we see our way pretty clearly to starting a savings-bank fund, so that we may give our people facilities for putting their money into a savings-bank, and with us they may probably get a little more liberal treatment than they would out of the Chancellor of the Exchequer. I hope we may also be able to extend these benefits in other directions, but I must not anticipate in that way. At any rate we shall not put aside the consideration of these questions, which in some form or another are always pressing upon us.

The proprietors are aware that Mr. Channing[15] thought it his duty to bring forward a resolution in the House of Commons to the effect that the hours of labour imposed on railway men were an injustice to the men and a source of danger to the public. The division was rather a shave and the majority was not as large as it ought to have been, but does any one for one moment believe that Mr. Channing, or those gentlemen who went into the lobby with him, care one jot more or sympathise one bit more with the men than those who went into the other lobby, comprising as they did a number of railway directors, and do you think that any of these care one-tenth part as much for the men as we do? We know the value a good man is to us, and we are doing what we can to limit the hours of work and to make the service attractive and pleasing to him. I do not believe there is a shadow of a foundation for saying that any accident resulting from travelling by railway is attributable to long hours of work any more than to short hours of work. I do not think there is anything to prove it, and I would rather myself be in the hands of an experienced man even though he worked fourteen hours a day, than in the hands of one who had recently come into the service even though his hours were shorter. It was mentioned as a sort of justification for the resolution, that in the case of an accident on one of the northern lines the Board of Trade reported that the engine-driver had been at work for fourteen hours, or something of that kind, but it was denied that the accident had any reference to the number of hours the man was employed. In another case which was mentioned, where a man had been booked out fifteen hours, it turned out that he had three hours to take his train to Ramsgate, then he had nine hours to bathe, and three hours to bring his train back – (laughter) – and it is preposterous to quote cases of this kind as a reason for such a resolution.

When Sir Michael Hicks Beach[16] came to propound his resolution as to the terms of reference, the clause as to the hours of labour was struck out. A committee has been appointed and will sit. I have no doubt there will be lots of evidence to show that enginemen and goods guards are booked out for long hours, but that does not mean a continued strain where they are employed on little local lines, or where signalmen are employed on branch lines. The signalman has a cooking-stove in his cabin and all the most modern appliances for his comfort, and it is idle to say that men who are employed twelve hours are under an imposition which they are not able to bear. And I venture to say that if a man goes into his cabin and smokes his pipe he will do a great deal better than if he went into a public-house or gossiped about in different places. (Cheers.) A day or two ago the Times had a very successful article as to what might happen with this committee. Of course if the committee are going to report that railway directors are not fit to manage their affairs the proper thing would be for the Government to take over the railways. You cannot have conditional management of an intricate concern like this, and as between railway directors and the Board of Trade either the one or the other must take the responsibility. If the Government think they can take over and work the railways better than the directors can, for God's sake let them do it. I should be remarkably grateful to them, that is all I can say.

I think I am right in saying that railway companies move more in the light of day than any other public body in the country, certainly more than any private body. We do not do a thing that is not known to all the world. We live by the favour of the public, and we are obliged to make our passenger trains accommodating to the public, and to work our traffic to the best advantage of the public, and it is only by doing that we can get the favour of the public and the traffic that we want. We are bound to public opinion to the fullest possible extent. Thank God, I have not any constituents except you, gentlemen. But these gentlemen in the House of Commons who preach all this nonsense do it because they know they are talking to reporters. On the eve of a General Election they think that by pretending that they are sympathising with the large body of railway men they will get them to vote in one or the other interest. But my own impression is that the large and tried body of railway men are certainly not going to be humbugged by that sort of chaff, and I hope the gentlemen in the House of Commons who think they are going to catch the votes of railway men will be disappointed. That is all I can say. (Cheers.)

Viscount COBHAM[17] (deputy-chairman) seconded the resolution.

Mr. STROUD thought the shareholders should take some action to strengthen the hands of the directors in the present labour crisis, and show to the public that the policy which the board had pursued was confirmed by the shareholders generally of this company. ("Hear, hear.") He contended that the railway employés in various parts of the country were the dupes and victims of professional agitators, and be hoped that through the medium of the press the employés would be led to see that the railway service was a good one, and that it was not wise for the men to quarrel with their bread and butter. The chief agitators made a comfortable livelihood out of strikes, but what recompense did their dupes get from them when they threw up their constant employment and all the privileges they enjoyed as servants of the railway companies? ("Hear, hear.") In conclusion he proposed as a rider to the chairman's resolution the following:

"That this meeting of shareholders of the Great Western Railway Company expresses its entire approval of the course pursued by the directors respecting the recent and pending questions between them and their employés, and desires to assure the directors that they may rely on the loyal and earnest support of the whole body of the shareholders in a firm and sustained resistance to agitators, and in whatever may be necessary to maintain their perfect control over all branches of labour in the service."

Mr. WATSON seconded the proposition. He said he had recently returned from Scotland, where he had been a witness of the railway strikes there and the system of picketing which had been adopted. He could vouch for the accuracy of the chairman's statement that it was not the general body of railway servants who were dissatisfied with their position, and who brought about strikes, but it was some half-a-dozen professional agitators who came forward, and who lived by propagating dissension. In his opinion, the time had come when the Government should take action to thwart the professional agitators, for until they did so there would be no rest for the trades and industries of the country. ("Hear, hear.") Much credit was due to the Scotch companies and their officers for resisting the demands of the men, and also to the press for the just views they had promulgated in respect of the struggle which was now taking place between labour and capital. The chairman, in an exhaustive statement, had given the meeting details of the wages paid and the number of hours during which the principal employés were at work, and he would ask any one of common sense whether, according to the statement, it could be said that there was any injustice done to any of this company's servants? ("No.") Although there had been an increase of 300,000*l.* in the receipts, yet there was a reduction of ¼ per cent. in the dividend, and this was chiefly owing to the increased amount paid away in wages. He had never met with a railway servant who was prepared to say that he individually had a just grievance. Usually the answer given was that when a strike took place all had to go with the stream. He had confidence in the directors of this company that they would do justice to the men in their employ, as would all right-minded men, and he hoped the shareholders generally would give their unanimous support to the resolution which had been proposed by Mr. Stroud. ("Hear, hear.")

Mr. KING remarked that he sympathised entirely with the remarks made by the two previous speakers; nevertheless, if the meeting had confidence in the directors, he thought they might safely leave the management of the employés in the directors' hands without passing the resolution which had been suggested. ("Hear, hear.") He believed the chairman's interesting speech would be a great influence not only with the shareholders, but with the outside public, for it would show that the labour agitation was nothing but humbug. ("Hear, hear.") The men had sadly humbugged themselves, but the results to their wives and families were something fearful. Referring to the recent accident, on which the chairman had spoken very feelingly, he desired to know whether, the amount of compensation which the company would be called upon to pay would be very heavy or not. With regard to an increased charge of 17,000*l*. for locomotive engines, he wished to know whether that amount had been expended in improving the locomotives. They all knew that coal had greatly increased in price, but he was surprised to find in the accounts that the company were paying about 1,400*l*. a year more for water. Was that owing to increased consumption, or to an increased scale of charges?

Colonel VAUGHTON[18] complained of the unsuitable character of the station at Bath, and said that the numerous visitors who went to Bath to find relief from gout, sciatica, and rheumatism were compelled to go down, or to be carried down, thirty or forty steps. He had heard that one of the directors lived at Bath, and that he was an octogenarian. If such was the case he thought that the director in question ought to retire. (Laughter.)

Mr. GILES[19] called attention to the importance of the Taff Vale district and coalfields, and suggested that the board should enter into negotiations for the acquisition of the Taff Vale Railway[20] by fusion or otherwise. ("Hear, bear.")

The CHAIRMAN, in reply, said he could only promise that the suggestion by Mr. Giles as to the Taff Vale Railway should receive careful consideration by the board. The question of fusion was beset with difficulties and complications, as so many interests had to be considered. The relations with the Taff Vale directorate were of a friendly character, and the Great Western had endeavoured to avoid undue or unfair competition with the Taff Vale line; but unfortunately, several large interests would be involved in any scheme having for its object the fusion of the two companies. With regard to Bath station he deeply sympathised with the invalids who had to go up and down the stairs, but to improve the station it had been estimated that a sum of about 12,000*l*. would be involved. That was a large outlay, especially in view of the possibility of the company having some day to rebuild the station. As to the octogenarian director, he could only say that the gentleman in question was very useful in keeping the London directors well informed of what went on in the Bath district, and of the grievances of the public there. (Laughter.) The extra cost of water was chiefly in connection with water for locomotive purposes, and Paddington was responsible for a great deal of it.

The increased charge of 17,000*l*. in the locomotive department was for engines not yet put into stock. They were in course of building, and the board were looking forward to substituting new engines for some of the old ones when the broad gauge was entirely supplanted by the narrow gauge system. With regard to the railway accident, he did not wish to anticipate what the cost would be to the company, but he might say that the board had every desire to act with liberality, and they had charged the revenue of the half-year with 10,000*l*. for the accident without trenching at all upon the accident fund, which still remained at 50,000*l*. Up to the present time the board had not paid so much as 1,500*l*. in claims, but they had charged the revenue with 10,000*l*. to meet the claims which would, no doubt, be sent in, and he had little doubt that they would be all met without touching the existing accident fund. ("Hear, hear.") He was much obliged to Mr. Stroud and Mr. Watson for the support they had given to the policy of the board, but he thought it would be preferable not to tie the hands of the directors by passing any formal resolution, especially as the terms of it were generally acquiesced in by the meeting; He would suggest, therefore, that it should be withdrawn. ("Hear, hear.")

Mr. STROUD – Oh, certainly.

The rider to the resolution was then formally withdrawn, and the proposition by the CHAIRMAN for the adoption of the report and the accounts was carried unanimously.

The CHAIRMAN further moved:

"That dividends for the half-year ending December 31st last, at the rate of 5*l*. per centum per annum, be paid on the consolidated guaranteed and consolidated preference stocks of the company, and that a dividend for the same half-year on the consolidated ordinary stock be now declared at the rate of 7*l*. 15s. per centum per annum. That such dividends be paid on and after the 19th inst. to the proprietors who were registered at the closing of the transfer books on the 15th ult."

Viscount COBHAM seconded the resolution, which was also unanimously agreed to.

The CHAIRMAN moved:

"That the proposed expenditure set forth in paragraph 13 of the report be and the same is hereby sanctioned and approved."

Viscount COBHAM seconded the resolution, and it was carried *nem. con.*[21]

Mr. WATSON moved and Mr. PHILLIPS seconded:

"That the following directors now retiring by rotation be and they are hereby re-elected: – Frederick G. Saunders, Esq.; Viscount Cobham; Charles Gray Mott, Esq.; and William Henry Wills, Esq."

The resolution was unanimously agreed to.

In reply to Mr. Watson, who suggested an improvement in the train service from Southall to Willesden,

The CHAIRMAN said the consideration of the board would be given to the subject.

The meeting was then made special for the consideration of two Bills now before Parliament.

The CHAIRMAN proposed:

"That the Bill now submitted to the meeting, intituled 'A Bill for conferring further powers upon the Great Western Railway Company in respect of their own undertaking, and upon that company and the London and North Western Railway Company[22] in respect of undertakings in which they are jointly interested, and for other purposes,' be and the same is hereby approved, subject to such alterations therein as may be sanctioned by Parliament."

Viscount COBHAM seconded the resolution, which was carried *nem. con.*

The CHAIRMAN further moved:

"That the Bill now submitted to the meeting, intituled 'A Bill for conferring further powers upon the London and North Western Railway Company in relation to their own undertaking and other undertakings in which they are interested jointly with other companies, and also for conferring powers upon the Great Western Railway Company, the Central Wales and Carmarthen Junction Railway Company, the Harrow and Stanmore Railway Company, the North Staffordshire Railway Company,[23] and other railway companies, in relation to such other undertakings, and for conferring powers upon the London and North Western Railway Company and the Great Western Railway Company, with respect to the acquisition by those companies of the undertaking of the Central Wales and Carmarthen Junction Railway Company, and for other purposes,' be and the same is hereby approved, subject to such alterations therein as may be sanctioned by Parliament."

He explained that although the title of the Bill was a long one, yet it involved very little cost to the company, the chief matters, so far as they affected the Great Western, being certain alterations to roads on properties in which the company, with others, was jointly interested.

Viscount COBHAM seconded the resolution, and it was carried unanimously.

On the motion of Mr. Watson, a hearty vote of thanks was accorded to the chairman, directors, and officers of the company for their past services; and the CHAIRMAN having briefly acknowledged the same, the proceedings terminated.

Notes

1 Frederick G. Saunders (1820–1901) had been the GWR's secretary under Daniel Gooch (1816–1889), who was its chair from 1865 until his death. He joined the board in 1886 and took over from Gooch as chair in 1889, holding that post until 1895.

2 J. D. Higgins (1831–1892) joined the GWR in 1850 as a clerk, was named assistant secretary in 1860, and succeeded Saunders as secretary in 1886.

3 The Witney branch of the Oxford, Witney and Fairford Railway was constructed in 1861, and the East Gloucestershire Railway formed in 1864 to connect Witney with Fairford, though it did not open until 1873. The GWR operated both lines starting in 1873 and absorbed both in July 1890.

4 The Severn Navigation refers to the navigable sections of the River Severn (which flows through Gloucester into Monmouthshire), which were expanded through the construction of locks from Worcester to Tewksbury between 1843 and 1858.

5 Arthur James Balfour (1848–1930) was Secretary for Ireland under Lord Salisbury between 1887 and 1891, first lord of the Treasury from 1891 to 1902, then Prime Minster from 1902 to 1905. In Ireland he introduced a Light Railway Act (1889) and a congested districts board (1891).

6 Sir Courtenay Edmund Boyle (1845–1901) was appointed assistant secretary for the railway department of the Board of Trade in 1886. In this role he was instrumental in

the passage of the Railway and Canal Traffic Act (1888) and the Regulation of Railways Act (1889).

7 Richard Basset (1820–1891), GWR director from 1867 to 1891, lived in Newbury (Berkshire) on the GWR trunk line between Reading and Swindon.

8 Christopher Rice Mansel Talbot (1803–1890) was a Welsh landowner who built an ironworks on his estate near Swansea and was an MP for Glamorganshire from 1830 until his death. He joined the board of the GWR in 1863, when it acquired the South Wales Railway, which he had chaired.

9 Arthur Pemberton Heywood-Lonsdale (1835–1897) was a landowner, investor, and fox-hunting enthusiast who owned extensive property in Vancouver, Canada.

10 Thomas Adams was an active GWR shareholder from 1863 through 1891. He served as its auditor in the 1880s and on a committee that brought in a new slate of directors in 1863.

11 Spencer Horatio Walpole (1806–1898) was a successful barrister and entered Parliament in 1846 as a Conservative, serving until 1882.

12 Charles Beavis spoke at numerous railway shareholder meetings in the early 1890s, mainly to defend the abolition of second-class passenger fares. His campaign yielded results on some smaller lines, but he was generally written off as a crank.

13 Members of the Amalgamated Society of Railway Servants in Glasgow went on strike against the Caledonian and North British Railways in December 1890 for shorter hours, bringing Scottish rail travel to a standstill. The strike ended after six weeks with minimal gains for the workers.

14 Saunders is quoting the final paragraph of a three-paragraph editorial published in the *London Times*, 9 February 1891.

15 Francis Channing (1841–1926) was born in Cincinnati, Ohio, and became a naturalized British subject in 1883. He was Liberal MP for East Northamptonshire from 1885 through 1910.

16 Michael Hicks Beach (1837–1916) was President of the Board of Trade under Lord Salisbury from 1888 to 1892, where he worked with Courtenay Boyle on railway legislation.

17 Charles Lyttelton, Viscount Cobham (1842–1922), was a Liberal MP for East Worcestershire from 1868 to 1874, when he was elevated to the House of Lords. He became a GWR director in 1878 and became Deputy Chair in 1890, stepping down at the end of 1891 to take over as chair of the Railway and Canal Commission.

18 Theophilus Vaughton (1829–1905) was a lieutenant colonel in the Royal Marine Light Infantry, which he served from 1843 to 1873. After retiring, he moved to Bath in 1878 and was active in the town's affairs: he was a magistrate, trustee of its savings bank, and director of its electric lighting company and two local hospitals.

19 Richard W. Giles was a frequent critic of high first-class fares on the GWR and other lines, in pamphlets and letters to the editor and at shareholder meetings. He served on two different GWR reorganization committees in 1863 and 1867. He later served as an auditor for the GWR in 1893, with Saunders's support.

20 The Taff Vale Railway opened in 1840–41 to connect the iron and coal mines near Merthyr Tydfil with the Cardiff docks. It was absorbed by the GWR in 1922.

21 *Nemine contradicente* (unanimously).

22 On the London and North Western Railway (LNWR) see document 16 in this volume.

23 The Central Wales and Carmarthen Junction Railway Company formed in 1873 and was absorbed by the LNWR in 1891. The Harrow and Stanmore Railway was constructed in 1882 to connect Harrow to the Stanmore LNWR station two miles away; it was absorbed by the LNWR in 1899. The North Staffordshire Railway Company formed in 1845 and connected several towns in the Potteries district to the LNWR branch line; it lasted until 1923, when it joined the London, Midland, and Scottish Railway.

Editorial Headnote

Liverpool Union Bank (1891)

The directors of the Liverpool Union Bank informed their shareholders of two bankruptcies when they assembled in 1891: one local, one national, and both involving grain imports. The failure of Boumphrey and Co., "a well-known firm of corn-merchants in Liverpool," cost the bank £56,000 and occasioned an embarrassing admission of neglect on the directors' part.[1] After the failure of Baring Brothers in 1890 – owing mainly to unpaid loans by the Argentine government for railways and other public works but built on the South American grain trade – the Liverpool Union reported that it had pledged £100,000 to assist in a bailout, which helped to prevent the failure from metastasizing. Although its pledge represented a tiny fraction of the £15 million that British banks set aside for the bailout, it was typical among joint stock banks in casting its effort as a noble and necessary act.[2]

The Liverpool Union was one of seven joint-stock banks to form in Liverpool by 1843, more than any other British city including London.[3] Of these, the Bank of Liverpool nearly failed in 1857 and the Royal Bank of Liverpool stopped payment in 1867 in the midst of a topsy-turvy cotton market. Boundaries between bankers, brokers, speculators, and cotton and grain importers had long been blurred in Liverpool. Brokers were in the habit of borrowing from banks to front money for imports, relying on their personal reputation to secure the loan – in the Liverpool Union's case, up to £10,000 per loan.[4] Samuel Williamson, who joined Boumphrey and Co. in 1865 and was made partner in 1876, purchased "cargoes and parcels of wheat" with the bank's loans, then, instead of repaying them with the wheat sales, used these to pay off debts incurred from speculating on grain prices. In Joseph Boumphrey's words, Williamson was "bulling wheat and bearing corn" and cooked the books to hide his losses from his partner and the bank. By the time the Liverpool Union figured this out, Boumphrey and Co. owed it £58,000 (along with £4000 to other creditors), with assets estimated at under £2,000.[5]

Apart from acknowledging (and fending off mild criticism from shareholders regarding) the Boumphrey fiasco and bragging about the patriotic Barings pledge, the rest of the Liverpool Union meeting was business as usual. Directors retired and were re-elected; a new local branch on London Road – a central location a mile east of the Liverpool docks – was announced. As of 1890, the bank was still a thoroughly local concern: nearly all its directors were merchants, brokers, and shipowners from Liverpool, and although its chair, James Wilson, lived in Surrey, he had been a leading corn merchant in Liverpool prior to his retirement. Although the Liverpool Union survived the two-pronged crisis of 1890, it failed to survive the merger movement of the following decade: Lloyds would absorb it in 1900 on the way to becoming Britain's largest bank.[6]

Notes

1 *Birmingham Daily Post* 18 December 1890.
2 Timothy L. Alborn, *Conceiving Companies: Joint-stock Politics in Victorian England* (London: Routledge, 1998), 155–158.
3 *Post Office London Directory* (London: Frederic Kelly, 1843), 1534–1536; Iain S. Black, "Money, Information and Space: Banking in Early-nineteenth-century England and Wales," *Journal of Historical Geography* 21 (1995): 398–412.
4 Charles P. Kindleberger, *Economic Response: Comparative Studies in Trade, Finance, and Growth* (Cambridge, MA: Harvard University Press, 1978), 81–82; Jim Powell, *Losing the Thread: Cotton, Liverpool and the American Civil War* (Liverpool: Liverpool University Press, 2021), 158–162.
5 *Birmingham Daily Post* 1 January 1891; *Liverpool Mercury* 23 January 1891.
6 Kindleberger, *Economic* Response, 82; Youssef Cassis, "Management and Strategy in the English Joint Stock Banks 1890–1914," *Business History* 27 (1985), 302.

8

LIVERPOOL UNION BANK

Source: Liverpool Union Bank (1891), *Bankers', Insurance Managers', and Agents' Magazine* 51 (March 1891): 528–532.

LIVERPOOL UNION BANK, LIMITED

THE directors beg to submit the following report: – They greatly regret to have to communicate the loss of nearly £60,000, by fraudulent misappropriations of produce on the part of Samuel Williamson, corn factor, whose firm (Joseph Boumphrey and Co.) had been customers of the bank for seventeen years, and in whose honest fulfilment of strict brokers' engagements, in connection with legitimate import transactions, entire confidence had been placed. To provide at once for the whole amount due, the directors have transferred £30,000 from the contingent fund, the steady growth of which to a much larger sum, during many years' immunity from bad debts of any consequence, has been reported from time to time to the proprietors. The remainder, along with the ordinary losses of the year (under £500 in all), they have charged to the year's profits, which, from the active demand for money and the high rates of interest almost throughout, have been exceptionally good. While expressing their keen disappointment at a gross violation of trust having resulted in so serious a loss, the directors have had some satisfaction in being able promptly to meet it without reducing the published reserve fund of the bank or the dividend usually paid to the proprietors.

The profits for the year, after thus amply providing for all bad and doubtful debts, and deducting rebate on bills in hand at 5 per cent., are £108,315. 10s. 4d. The total expenses of management, including salaries, directors' and auditors' fees, the cost of painting and alterations, enlarging the head office, and all other charges, have been £24,282. 9s. 11d., leaving the nett profits, £84,033. 0s. 5d.; the undivided profits, brought forward from the previous year, were £17,811. 1s. 5d. – together, £101,844. 1s. 10d. From which have been deducted – Two half-yearly dividends (in July, 1890, and January, 1891), at the rate of 10 per cent. per annum, £60,000; bonus of 24 per cent. for the year, paid in January, 1891, £15,000; income-tax paid by the bank, £2,073. 9s.; and the directors have set aside to complete the new premises for London Road branch, £3,500, leaving as the balance of profits now carried forward, £21,270. 125. 10d. At the request of the Bank of England – whose prompt and public-spirited action in dealing with the difficulties of Messrs. Baring Brothers and Co. undoubtedly saved the country

DOI: 10.4324/9781003177715-9

from a disastrous panic – the directors concurred to the extent of £100,000 in the guarantee, terminable in three years, given by the leading banks in England and Scotland against possible ultimate loss (notwithstanding a large apparent surplus) in the gradual liquidation of the firm. The retiring directors are Mr. Brancker,[1] Mr. Holder[2] and Mr. McFerran. Mr. Brancker and Mr. Holder offer themselves for re-election, but the directors regret that Mr McFerran, having left the district, is unable to continue his services to the bank, and they recommend that Mr. George Holt,[3] of Messrs. Lamport and Holt, be elected in his room. The usual statement is annexed of the assets and liabilities of the bank, audited by Messrs. Harmood Banner and Son, chartered accountants.

JAMES WILSON, Chairman.[4]

Abstract General Balance-sheet at 31st December, 1890.

LIABILITIES.	
Capital subscribed, £3,000,000; of which in reserve liability, £2,400,000. Capital paid-up, £600,000; reserve fund, £365,000; dividend and bonus to be paid 13th January, 1891, £45,000; balance of profits carried forward, £21,270. 12s. 10d	£1,031,270 12 10
Due on current accounts, deposit accounts and receipts, etc., £2,752,232 16s. 2d.; acceptances by the bank and its London agents, against cash and securities, £838, 105. 4s. 10d.; credits outstanding, £77,687. 4s. 6d.; bills rediscounted, * £186,341. 14s. 9d	3,854, 367 0 3
	4,885,637 13 1
ASSETS.	
Bills discounted, £1,614,679. 18s. 7d.; less rebate on bills in hand at 5 per cent., £11,786. 10s. 1d	£1,602,893 8 6
Advances on current and loan accounts, including short loans on stocks	1,290,072 1 6
Cash on hand, with Bank of England, and with London bankers at call, £683,424. 18s.; Consols-New 24 per Cent., £225,000, held at 90, £202,500; due by London discount brokers (with security) at call or seven days' notice, and by country bank correspondents, £140.954 15s. 9d.	1,026,879 13 9
Liabilities of customers for acceptances and credits, per contra	915,792 9 4
Bank's business premises and let property	50,000 0 0
	4,885,637 13 1

* With the Bank of England, including the parliamentary composition agreement in lieu of a note issue

At the fifty-sixth annual meeting of the proprietors, held on 4th February, 1891, Mr. James Wilson, chairman of the board, presided. The notice of meeting was read by Mr. Warr[5] (of Messrs. Bateson, Warr and Bateson, the bank's solicitors), and the annual report by the directors, having been previously circulated, was taken as read. The chairman rose and said:

We meet you, gentlemen, for the first time for a long period with a disappointing result from our year's business. After a most prosperous eleven months, we had to face at the beginning of December a serious and particularly vexatious loss from fraudulent misappropriations of produce on the part of an old customer. The report in your hands is candid and explicit both about the amount and the circumstances. The firm were known to have only limited means, but they had good connections abroad, in Canada and the United States, and having been in the way of receiving consignments for many years to an amount which made our account active and profitable, they were considered worthy of trust for the ordinary facilities required to handle such consignments. Our friends in Liverpool know exactly what this means; but, for the sake of proprietors at a distance, it is perhaps important to make clear how far – and how far only – the bank did trust the firm. On every occasion when money was lent to them, the bank received into its own hands the documents giving right to the produce consigned. The ships having then arrived, these documents were delivered to the firm under the usual letters of pledge, and with the understanding that the produce, if not already sold to arrive, would be sold at an early date after landing, at the market credit of a month or so. Obviously, if borrowers under such circumstances are only honest, and after having sold the goods, will bring to the bank the money received in payment for them whenever it is so received, there is no risk, except from a fall in prices or from sales to bad buyers, both of which contingencies are not commonly of material account with people of fair capacity and experience.

Unfortunately, our borrower was not honest – or rather became dishonest, when involved in speculations – sold for prompt cash (which of course could not at the time be known to the bank) the goods with which his firm were entrusted, and applied the proceeds – which ought at once to have been handed to us – in settlement of losses in their speculations. Well, gentlemen, we are prepared for the criticisms – and we cannot complain of them – that the amount was too large, however justifiable the business, with a firm of such standing, and that we ought to have known of the speculations. In respect to the amount, there is this to be said, that the total was not for one consigner only, but was spread over seven or eight different Transatlantic accounts, the figures in each being within quite moderate and reasonable compass; while as regards the speculation, no one outside the firm's own office could have actual knowledge till the end came, that it was of dangerous amount, or on their own account, instead of on behalf of the good principals named from time to time in connection with it. Besides, while it is easy now, after the event, to see the mistake, it must not be forgotten that our loans were made not to assist speculation, but, in every case, against strict security, to work legitimate trade; that Williamson had been well known as a large customer for nearly twenty years; that all through these years, in good times and in bad, he had scrupulously kept his engagements to the bank; that he was respectably connected, and lived an inexpensive and entirely reputable life, with no sanctimonious profession, as has been alleged, of being better than his neighbours, but certainly with nothing whatever in his conduct or surroundings to suggest the suspicion that he was worse.

As a matter of fact, now that the books of the firm have been examined in bankruptcy, there was no dishonesty whatever, or mishandling of the bank's money, till about a year and a half ago, and till only a few months ago the sum misappropriated was comparatively small. The proprietors will accept my assurance that the account was worked with every danger carefully guarded against, except unfortunately this of wholesale dishonesty, and that the frauds were carried out with singular cleverness and effrontery. It will be noticed that we ascribe the entire blame to Williamson. He admitted this in writing, and the working of the account in the main confirmed it. We have accordingly taken criminal proceedings against him only. But, granting that his partner was, as he himself maintains, not in any way cognisant of the wrong-doing, he cannot at the least be acquitted of most blameworthy inattention to the affairs of his firm, and the directors have insisted that he shall submit to the examination and judgment of the Bankruptcy Court. (Hear, hear.)

I have gone thus in detail into this most painful case, from the feeling that you would not wish me to make too little of it. (Hear, hear.) But, on the other hand, I hope you will agree with me that we must equally avoid making too much. (Hear, hear.) We must not forget in a bad year the good years which have gone before it, and that we have had a most remarkable absence for many years of any losses worth naming. We greatly regret that the occasion has arisen for our first drawing on our inner reserve, but we had no hesitation in charging half of this exceptional loss to the fund which our long run of good fortune has enabled us to build up specially to provide for any such unforeseen disaster. We have accordingly paid our usual dividend and bonus; and I may say – anticipating the perhaps reasonable curiosity of our friends at this time – that, after deducting the £30,000 now required, a balance remains at the credit of our contingent funds very little short of £100,000 (hear, hear), without reckoning our margins in Consols or in our property accounts, while the published reserve fund is intact in addition at £365,000. (Applause.)

Gentlemen, the report has informed you that we joined in the guarantee to the Bank of England re Baring Brothers and Co. to the extent of £100,000. We had ourselves no direct interest in the liquidation, but we fully shared the view, already expressed by bank chairmen at recent meetings, that indirectly we might easily have become concerned, and that a reasonable share ought gratefully to be taken by us of the responsibility assumed for the public benefit in a grave crisis by the Bank of England and its able governor. (Hear, hear.) As most of you are aware, the governor's opinion has lately been quoted to the effect that no call is likely to be made upon the guarantors, but the liability must remain for some time, and as against it we have increased by a few thousand pounds the balance of undivided profits carried forward, the amount now being over £20,000. The items in our balance-sheet call for little special remark. Our acceptances, which are at their maximum about this date, are higher than last year by £200,000, the Baring difficulties having brought us new business, and also the unsettled condition of the American exchange and money market having required bank acceptances to be given against cotton shipments, where in ordinary years mercantile paper is freely taken. On the other side of the account, we shew a somewhat similar increase of money at call or short notice in London, our manager properly working with ample balances within easy reach in rather critical times. (Hear, hear.)

Our new building in London Road is now open for business. It is, thanks to Mr. Grayson, an ornament to the district, is central and comfortable, and we are already reaping advantage from it. We begin 1891 with low rates for money, but hope, notwithstanding, to have a fair year. And now, gentlemen, I have only one further remark. In room of our friend, Mr. McFerran, whose removal from Liverpool, and consequent loss to the board, we all much regret, we have secured the services as a director, subject to your approval, of Mr. George Holt, of Messrs. Lamport and Holt. (Hear, hear.) Mr. Holt needs no commendation from me. No man in Liverpool stands higher than he, and his firm and his family have been among our largest depositors and best customers for a very long time. I am glad to end my speech with what can give rise to nothing bnt the heartiest congratulation. (Applause.) I beg to move that the report, as circulated, be adopted. (Loud applause.)

Mr. Thomas Holder, deputy-chairman, in seconding the adoption of the report, said:- I can add very little to what has been so clearly put before you by the chairman. No doubt the chief thing that has been uppermost in your minds, for some weeks past, has been the great fraud on the bank, the particulars of which you fully know. I need scarcely remind the meeting that the foundation of all sound banking and mercantile transactions is honesty and integrity; if this basis is lacking, and has to give place to doubt and suspicion, then legitimate business becomes paralyzed and is rendered almost impossible. At the same time we know how liable bankers and others are to meet, when least expecting it, with deception and fraud. The only safeguard against such evil deeds is to do, what all prudent banking establishments do, make ample and timely provision, so that the shareholders may be protected, when such unfortunate contingencies occur. It is on these lines that the directors have conducted the business of the bank in past years, and I trust it will meet with your approval if they pursue the same policy in the future. It must to-day be matter of some congratulation to the proprietors to feel that so large a loss is not only of rare occurrence, but also, that it can be borne without impairing either the soundness or efficiency of the bank. (Hear, hear.) I am sure we all deeply sympathise with our worthy and esteemed manager in the great anxiety and annoyance to which he has been put by the frauds of a man of whom better things might have been expected. It is our bounden duty to acknowledge the valuable services of Mr. Henderson,[6] and give him full credit for the continued prosperity of the bank, notwithstanding the recent heavy loss. (Applause.)

Mr. John Temple remarked on the increase in the expenses; and with reference to the fraud, the circumstances of which had been so fully explained by the chairman, said that no board could be infallible; that while it was a very serious loss, there was no use crying over spilt milk; but that it was of real consequence to provide against any similar disaster in future. He did not himself understand about the hypothecations of produce, and comparing loans to brokers with other business, it was a noticeable drawback that the securities had to be delivered up for realization. This made it of importance that the amounts so dealt with should not be excessive. He gave every credit to the directors and manager for having done so well for the shareholders in past years. (Hear, hear.)

No other proprietor offering any remarks, the chairman, in reply to Mr. Temple, explained that the expenses this year included a considerable sum for enlarging and painting the head office, which would not again be required for some years. He doubted whether the class of risks by which the bank had now lost could be altogether avoided. The working of the business required a measure of trust in those with whom the bank dealt. At the same time Mr. Temple's suggestions would receive the careful consideration of the directors. The report was then unanimously adopted.

Mr. Fletcher Rogers[7] moved that Mr. John Brancker and Mr. Thomas Holder be reelected directors, and that Mr. George Holt be elected a director. If he were addressing a meeting composed solely of Liverpool men, he should content himself by merely mentioning these names, but as there were probably proprietors present from a distance, he should say that these three gentlemen had spent long, honourable and successful careers in various branches of commerce in Liverpool. One of them was an ex-mayor of the city; and two were members of the dock board, one being now its chairman. (Hear, hear.) He thought the bank fortunate in securing the services of men so eminent in trade. (Applause.) Mr. Charles J. Bushell[8] cordially seconded the motion, and it was carried unanimously.

Mr. Temple moved that "the thanks of the proprietors be given to the directors for their valuable services, and for their prompt concurrence in the guarantee given by the leading bankers of the kingdom to the Bank of England in connection with the liquidation of Messrs, Baring Bros. and Čo." He felt sure that every shareholder would entirely agree that the directors did in this matter what was best, not only for the bank's own interests, but for the country (hear, hear), and that their promptitude deserved the highest approval. Mr. Richard Nicholson seconded the motion, and gave great praise to the chairman for the clear and full account of the loss which had overtaken the bank. The year's business must in other respects have been remarkably satisfactory, and they had got out of a bad deception exceedingly well. (Hear, hear.) The resolution was carried unanimously; as was also the reappointment, on the motion of Mr. William Blain,[9] seconded by Mr. G. C Dobell,[10] of Messrs. Harmood Banner and Son[11] as auditors. The chairman, in moving the thanks of meeting to the manager, officers and clerks, said that nothing could be more satisfactory than the management of the bank under Mr. Henderson. (Hear, hear, and applause.) A mistake had been committed, but for that the directors and he himself were responsible equally with the manager. Mr. Herbert W. Hind,[12] in seconding the motion, assured Mr. Henderson and his staff that the shareholders had the most absolute confidence in their management. (Cheers.)

Mr. Henderson, who was received with hearty applause, thanked the meeting on behalf of his assistants and the staff generally. For himself he need scarcely say that this year their far too warm and kind reception was particularly welcome. He felt that for once at all events he had not deserved it, and he certainly could not allow the chairman to say that he and his colleagues were equally responsible for their grievous loss. He was most grateful to the directors for the consideration and support they had given him in what had been a most trying time – the only serious business trouble he had ever had. He earnestly hoped that so bitter an experience could occur only once in a lifetime, and that the bank had again entered on a long succession of good years, when it would be gradually forgotten. (Applause.)

Mr. Stanton Eddowes,[13] in moving a vote of thanks to the chairman, referred to the admirable and lucid explanation given of the bank's affairs. The cloud under which they were met was largely composed of regret at the personal annoyance to which the chairman and those associated with him had been put. (Applause.) It would be unwise if an isolated instance of misplaced trust, coming after a long spell of prosperity, should in the slightest degree impair the bank's confidence in the honour and integrity of its customers. (Hear, hear.) He hoped the chairman would be spared many years to preside over them, and to give to the bank the great benefit of his long experience. (Loud applause.)

Mr. James Smith heartily endorsed every word of Mr. Eddowes; and, the motion having been carried unanimously, the chairman thanked the meeting for their cordial acknowledgment of his services, regretted again the disappointment they had met with, and hoped that in future, as with rare exceptions in the past, they would have only a good account to submit of their year's results.

Notes

1 John Brancker (1818–1903), a prosperous Liverpool cotton merchant, entered the trade in 1842 after apprenticing with his father. He served on the Mersey Docks and Habour Board starting in 1870 and was its chair from 1890 to 1899.

2 Thomas Holder (died 1896) was a partner in Holder and Co., cotton brokers; also, deputy chair of the Queen Insurance Company, past Mayor of Liverpool (1883–1884), and longtime member of the Liverpool Cotton Brokers' Association.

3 George Holt was a partner in Lamport and Holt, Liverpool steamship owners.

4 James Wilson (1817–1891) was a Liverpool corn merchant who joined the board of the Liverpool Union Bank in 1864 and served as its chair for several years up to his death. He moved to Reigate, Surrey, after retiring in 1873, but remained active in the bank's affairs.

5 Augustus Frederick Warr (1847–1908) was a Liverpool solicitor specializing in commercial law and a Conservative MP for East Toxteth between 1895 and 1902.

6 William Gavin Henderson (1842–1901) worked as the assistant manager at the Bank of Scotland's London branch until he joined the Liverpool Union as its general manager in 1874.

7 Fletcher Rogers, director of Queen Insurance and cotton broker, joined the firm of Bourne, Latham and Rogers in 1847, which, in 1857, became Rogers and Calder. He was President of the Liverpool Cotton Brokers' Association in 1867 and also served on the town council.

8 Charles J. Bushell was a director of the Royal Insurance Company and Liverpool Mortgage Insurance Company, honorary treasurer of the Liverpool Diocesan Finance Association, and county magistrate for Wirral.
9 William Blain was a partner in William Blain and Sons, corn and flour merchants, Liverpool.
10 G. C. Dobell was a Liverpool merchant and warehouse keeper.
11 The Liverpool accounting firm of Harmood Banner and Sons dated back to 1805. John Sutherland Harmood-Banner (1847–1927), the founder's grandson, was a Conservative MP for Liverpool between 1905 and 1924.
12 Herbert W. Hind was a partner in the Liverpool merchant house of J. H. Hind and Co. and Director of the Queen insurance Company.
13 Stanton Eddowes was senior partner in a company described as "an old established firm of general merchants and London bankers' agents in Liverpool."

Editorial Headnote

Dunlop Pneumatic Tyre Company (1896)

A bicycle boom swept the USA and Europe in the mid-1890s, and with it, an explosion of new investment in cycle as well as pneumatic tire companies. In 1896 and 1897, cycle firms attracted £13.1 million in shares, while tire companies raised an additional £8.6 million, 86% of the total capitalization in these two sectors between 1882 and 1913. Leading the charge in tires was Dunlop, the brainchild of Harvey Du Cros (1846–1918). Born in Dublin, Du Cros began his business career at the Irish Commercial Travellers' Association and spent his spare time as an amateur cyclist, boxing champion, and rugby captain. In the late 1880s, while watching his sons taking part in a bicycle race, he took notice of the pneumatic tires that had recently been invented by the Belfast veterinarian John Boyd Dunlop and soon secured patents to manufacture and attach them to cycles.[1] He floated the Pneumatic Tyre and Booth's Cycle Agency Ltd in 1889, dispatching his six sons to market its tires abroad. In 1896, he sold the company, which had a capital of £260,000, for £3 million to a set of company speculators led by Ernest Hooley (1859–1947), although Du Cros and his son Arthur retained £400,000 in preference stock. Within three months, a second company had formed with a capital of £650,000 to purchase Du Cros's French subsidiary.[2]

Du Cros was the main speaker at his reconstituted company's first meeting, which rolled it out to its new English investors. Besides describing the "sea of clerical work" that going public entailed, he brushed aside concerns about the large number of titled directors on the new company's board – a trademark of firms floated by Hooley. In Dunlop's case, these included Earl de la Warr, the Duke of Somerset, and the Earl of Albemarle, whose social connections helped direct old London money to provincial producers. As well as the Dunlop IPOs in 1896, Hooley had arranged for the Raleigh, Singer, and Swift Cycle Companies to go public, pocketing £3.3 million in all and another £1.7 million from flotations in 1897–98 (including Bovril and Schweppe's), before abruptly declaring bankruptcy in 1899. A *Leeds Mercury* report hinted at fraud and blamed his bankruptcy on "extravagant payments . . . to titled and other persons" to sit on his companies' various boards. This would be the first of four such setbacks in his long and colored career, earning him the sobriquet "the splendid bankrupt."[3] Dunlop fared much better. A year after its 1896 meeting, the company reported nearly £1 million in profits, and by 1900, it had moved into automobile and airplane tires as well as golf balls. By 1930, this diversification strategy (which helped it survive a drastic decline in cycle sales after 1900) had turned it into Britain's eighth-largest company, with subsidiaries in Canada, Japan, and Australia as well as France and the US.[4]

Notes

1 A. E. Harrison, "The Competitiveness of the British Cycle Industry, 1890–1914," *Economic History Review* 22 (1969), 287–303; A. E. Harrison, "Joint-Stock Company Flotation in the Cycle, Motor-Vehicle and Related Industries, 1882–1914," *Business History* 23 (1981), 167; Shima Amini and Steven Toms, "Accessing Capital Markets: Aristocrats and New Share Issues in the British Bicycle Boom of the 1890s," *Business History* 60 (2018), 232–242; Martin Adeney, "(William) Harvey De Cros," *Oxford Dictionary of National Biography Online*.

2 *Morning Post* 11 May 1896.

3 Harrison, "Joint-Stock Company Flotation," 175; Amini and Toms, "Accessing Capital Markets," 240–248; "Mr. Hooley's Bankruptcy," *Leeds Mercury* 23 January 1899; Aylmer Vallance, *Very Private Enterprise: An Anatomy of Fraud and High Finance* (London: Thames and Hudson, 1955), 66–75.

4 *Glasgow Herald* 14 July 1897; Geoffrey Jones, "The Growth and Performance of British Multinational Firms before 1939: The Case of Dunlop," *Economic History Review* 37 (1984): 35–53.

9

DUNLOP PNEUMATIC TYRE COMPANY

Source: Dunlop Pneumatic Tyre Company (1896), *London Standard*, 29 August 1896

THE DUNLOP PNEUMATIC TYRE COMPANY

The first statutory meeting of the Shareholders of the Dunlop Pneumatic Tyre Company (Limited) was held yesterday, at Cannon-street Hotel, Mr. Harvey du Cros in the chair.

The Chairman said the object of a statutory meeting was to afford an opportunity for the Directors to make the acquaintance of the Shareholders, who were naturally anxious to see that the undertaking to which they had subscribed was in existence. The Company had just been formed, and the first duty of the Directors was to examine the property, although, of course, they were bound to make every inquiry that prudence suggested before accepting office. They had to report that, having taken over the responsibilities of this business, they found that every statement put forward in the prospectus was warranted. They had been working for three or four months, and had had ample opportunity of making themselves thoroughly acquainted with the business, and they had found that it was all that it was represented to be. The prospectus was an unusually full one, dealing with the assets and earnings up to a very recent period, and those earnings had been justly stated. Since the figures were made up the principal part of the cycling season had expired, and they had been in intimate touch with the most important part of the cycling year. He had nothing but excellent business to report. Everything that had been anticipated had been more than realised. He could tell them in a few words what had been accomplished since they took office. In London they had made very considerable developments. It had become necessary to quadruple their business premises in Clerkenwell-road in order to provide accommodation for their London business, and the Company had purchased out and out the entire block, about one-fourth of which they had previously occupied. At Coventry the principal manufacturing departure foreshadowed was in connection with the manufacture of rims. To enable the Company to do that in a thoroughly satisfactory way they thought proper to authorise a very great extension of the Coventry factory. For that purpose freehold ground had been acquired, and the buildings were now in progress. The Company already possessed an exceedingly fine factory there, but the effect of the alterations would be that it would be more

DOI: 10.4324/9781003177715-10

than doubled, and he had no hesitation in saying that there would not be a factory engaged in the same or kindred business to equal it in the world. An arrangement had been made to fill it with machinery which had been already acquired, and he felt satisfied that in December the Company would have in full working order the manufacture of rims, inflators, and valves, and that they would in future manipulate their own wires, thus gaining additional sources of income. It was found necessary at Coventry to take down a large number of dwellings of humble sort, and the Company, for the convenience of its *employés*, and to make provision for those who had been disturbed, had acquired a considerable freehold plot, on which it was proposed to erect immediately artisans' dwellings. This had a particular bearing upon a certain section of their Shareholders. The investment of the funds of the Company in freehold property and suitable buildings would offer a security of a very permanent character to the Debenture and Preference Shareholders in particular. Already they were enabled to form some idea of the business of the Company with regard to next season. It was generally known that this had been one of the most prosperous years in the cycling trade of this country. He was happy to be able to tell them that there were apparently no signs of any falling off, and, speaking from some experience, he had no hesitation in saying that next season would probably surpass, and certainly equal, the season that they had just enjoyed. Another matter that referred particularly to the Shareholders was the transaction that had just been carried out successfully on behalf of the Company in the sale of the Company's interest in the French Dunlop Company, by which they received a very large sum in cash. He could assure them that judicious use would be made of the funds thus placed at their disposal in excess of the capital with which they commenced. Another pleasant matter in connection with the French business, which though in a measure out of their hands, always had a very immediate bearing on their business, was that the legal experts in France, after a troublesome law suit extending over three years, had reported favourably in the interest of that Company, and that all their principal opponents in France were declared to be nonsuited. That required the confirmation of the Courts, and this their advisers had no doubt would come rapidly. He could also congratulate them on the recent decisions in the Chancery Court in the matter of the Clincher patents, of which they were held to be the sole proprietors. They would remember that the prospectus contained a very strong counsel's opinion that the patents held by them practically ruled the tyre trade. The gist of his remarks would convey to them that that opinion had been upheld by two eminent Judges in the Chancery Division. In the last few months the Company had come under the rule of a new set of Directors. They had already fully acquainted themselves with the details of the business. On the Board of the old Company from its foundation nothing but good feeling prevailed; no decision had been the subject of a disputed resolution. The Board was always unanimous, and the entire policy of the Company from start to finish was one of perfect accord. In their short experience of three or four months there was the same promise of harmony, the Directors working with each other in complete concord.

Mr. MULLIGAN asked whether the whole capital had been subscribed; and, if so, why had the Board not applied for a settlement on the Stock Exchange?

The CHAIRMAN said the whole capital was subscribed many times over, and application had been made to the Stock Exchange for a settlement.

The meeting then became an extraordinary one for the purpose of approving certain alterations in the Articles of Association required by the Stock Exchange.

The CHAIRMAN moved the adoption of the alterations, and asked a Shareholder to second the motion.

Mr. HOLFORD asked whether these alterations were the sole cause of the delay in the settlement.

The CHAIRMAN said they had nothing to do with it.

Mr. HOLFORD. – Will the Chairman enlighten us as to the delay in the settlement?

The CHAIRMAN asked a Shareholder to second the motion.

Mr. CROCKER, another Shareholder. – Before the business is proceeded with the question should be answered.

The CHAIRMAN did not think that there had been any delay; he was not aware of any. (A VOICE: "Three months.") They could not easily find a parallel for the magnitude of their Company. The Directors, in allotting the Shares, endeavoured to deal as fairly as they possibly could with the applicants, and the consequence was that there was an enormous distribution. They would be greatly astonished if he told them the number of Shareholders. The clerical work resolved itself into this, that the ledgers of the Company had been multiplied to an unusual extent to facilitate operations. They would understand that only a certain number of persons could manage the share register. They had provided a large number of ledgers, and a staff which worked all day, and this was replaced by a staff which worked all night. Under the circumstances he thought he must say that there was no delay. It was merely the difficulty of dealing with such an enormous volume of clerical work. He had never, in any of the undertakings that he had been associated with, seen anything like it.

A SHAREHOLDER. – What letter have you arrived at?

The CHAIRMAN said he could not exactly tell them that, but they had made great progress, and the certificates were very nearly complete, bar the balancing. He could tell them at once if he could speak of the reconciliation, but that was a very large undertaking, and he would not like to do it. The answer to the question was that there was really no delay, and he did not know any quicker way of dealing with the register and ledgers than that which he had indicated.

Mr. CROCKER. – Do you know that this is a matter of public comment in the newspapers, who say that larger Companies have been dealt with more promptly?

The CHAIRMAN said he did not know that larger Companies had been dealt with more promptly. He would like some Shareholder to make some suggestion in place of their working night and day, and if he could tell them anything better they would be glad to try it. He did not know of anything better.

A SHAREHOLDER. – We ask if there is any other cause for the delay except the clerical work.

The CHAIRMAN. – No; there is no other cause (hear, hear). I do not think the alterations in the articles will affect the settlement at all.

A SHAREHOLDER. – Are we to expect a settlement next month?

The CHAIRMAN. – That is in the hands of the Stock Exchange. We shall be ready.

A SHAREHOLDER. – How long ago did you apply?

The CHAIRMAN. – About twelve days. We applied as soon as we saw land. We were wading through a sea of clerical work, and when we saw land within measurable distance we informed the Stock Exchange of the date on which we should be ready.

Mr. HOLFORD. – There are rumours going about the City that the Directors have taken a great many Shares, and more than they are able to pay for; that is why I asked the question.

The CHAIRMAN. – I am very much obliged to you for your candour. I do not know that the Directors want to boast about their financial position, but I may tell you that there is no ground for the rumour.

Mr. HOLFORD. – I only tell you what the rumour is.

The CHAIRMAN (drily) – Thank you (laughter). And now, gentlemen, as you are smiling, I will ask some one to second the resolution.

Mr. T. THOMPSON seconded the motion, which was agreed to, and the meeting concluded with a vote of thanks to the Chairman.

Editorial Headnote

Casualty Insurance Company (1906)

Accidents joined life, fire, and marine risks as a focus of British insurance after 1850, with threats associated with rail travel driving the market. Companies typically specialized in a single type of risk through the end of the century: besides train-related injuries, these included boiler explosions, broken windows, and workplace injuries.[1] Legislation that permitted parties to sue for damages often prompted company formation. The Railway Passengers Assurance Company, which held 40% of the accident market share in 1885, was one of 13 companies to form within five years of the passage of the Accident Compensation Act of 1846, and the Workman's Compensation Acts of 1897 and 1906 also occasioned waves of new insurers.[2] The Casualty Insurance Company, which formed in 1905, expanded from railways into the new motor-car and bicycle market and also covered against illness, offering "CASH DOWN immediately on the contraction of any Sickness, in addition to Weekly Compensation."[3] At its inaugural annual meeting in 1906, it announced the appointment of more than 2000 agents and the establishment of six provincial branches under the supervision of a seasoned managing director, F. J. Lee-Smith, and a chairman, R. J. Price, who had most of the firm's bases covered: he was a surgeon, barrister, and Liberal MP.

During the decade before World War One, composite insurance offices gobbled up many of the most successful accident insurers. The Commercial Union absorbed five such firms between 1900 and 1912, including what was at the time the market leader, Ocean Accident; the North British and Mercantile absorbed the Railway Passengers in 1910. Such firms, which had typically started out decades earlier selling fire and/or life insurance, slotted accident coverage into a divisional structure that offered "one-stop shopping" to their customers.[4] The arrival of such major players in the market squeezed new firms, and in 1909 – three years after its optimistic first general meeting – the Casualty Insurance Company closed its doors. It had tried to expand its geographical reach through a new share issue in 1908, and when that failed, it sold its business to a composite office, the Glasgow Assurance Corporation.[5]

Notes

1 H.A.L. Cockerell and Edwin Green, *The British Insurance Business: A Guide to its History and Records* (Sheffield: Sheffield Academic Press, 1994), 123–188; Oliver M. Westall, "Entrepreneurship and Product Innovation in British General Insurance, 1840–1914," in *Entrepreneurship, Networks and Modern Business*, ed. J. Brown and M. B. Rose (Manchester: Manchester University Press, 1993), 193, 199.

2 *Post Magazine* 47 (1886), 514; Cornelius Walford, *Insurance Cyclopaedia* (London: Layton, 1871–1880), 1: 7; Barry Supple, *The Royal Exchange Assurance: A History of British Insurance 1720–1970* (Cambridge: Cambridge University Press, 1970), 228–231.

3 *Post Magazine* 67 (1906): 213.

4 Cockerell and Green, *The British Insurance Business*, 170; Harold E. Raynes, *A History of British Insurance* (London: Sir Isaac Pitman & Sons, 1948), 374; Clive Trebilcock, *Phoenix Assurance and the Development of British Insurance* (Cambridge: Cambridge University Press, 1999), 2: 108–110, 126.

5 "Casualty Insurance Company, Limited," *Post Magazine* 69 (1908): 518; "Casualty Insurance Company (Limited)," *London Times* 4 March 1909.

10

CASUALTY INSURANCE COMPANY

Source: Casualty Insurance Company (1906), *Post Magazine and Insurance Monitor*, 24 March 1906

CASUALTY INSURANCE COMPANY, LIMITED

The first annual general meeting of the shareholders of the above Company was held at the Company's offices, 7, Waterloo Place, London, S. W., on Wednesday last, Mr. R. J. Price,[1] M. P., Chairman of the Board, presiding. The following report and accounts were submitted:

Directors' Report

The directors have much pleasure in submitting their first annual report on the business of the Company, together with the certified accounts for the period ending 31st December, 1905.

The Company was registered on the 18th February, 1904, and the certificate entitling it to commence business was issued on the 20th April following, but of course some little time necessarily elapsed before active work was begun.

As originally intended the operations of the Company have been confined to Personal Accident and Sickness Insurance, and the directors consider that the amount of business obtained in the short period since the Company started is highly satisfactory.

The directors have adopted a safe and prudent course by the re-insurance of a moiety of the larger fatal risks, a precaution which they feel sure will meet with the approval of the shareholders.

The results during the period covered by the accounts are as follows:

Accounts for the period ending 31*st December*, 1905.

REVENUE ACCOUNT.

	£ s. d.		£	s.	d.
Premiums, less re-insurances	10,030 4 4	Claims paid and outstanding	2,925	9	4
Transfer fees.	0 10 0	Commissions paid and outstanding and reserve for cancelments	2,004	4	3

DOI: 10.4324/9781003177715-11

(Continued)

REVENUE ACCOUNT.

	£ s. d.		£ s. d.
		Expenses of management . .	3,584 7 7
		Balance, subject to unexpired risks	1,516 13 2
	£10,030 14 4		£10,030 14 4

BALANCE SHEET.

	£ s. d.		£ s. d.
Authorised capital. .	£60,000 0 0	Cash at bank and in hand . .	2,029 14 8
Subscribed capital: 2,705 shares at £5 each	13,525 0 0	Agents' balances and outstanding premiums (less reserve for cancelments)	1,471 15 6
		Sundry debtors	18 0 3
Called and paid-up £1 per share.	2,705 0 0	Office furniture	152 0 0
Paid in advance of calls	1,850 0 0	Preliminary and organisation account	3,198 1 10
Sundry creditors. . .	797 19 1		
Balance of revenue account, subject to unexpired risks . . .	1,516 13 2		
	£6,869 12 3		£6,869 12 3

Premium income (after deducting re-insurance premiums), £10,030 4s. 4d.; claims paid (including a liberal estimate for those notified but not settled), £2,925 9s. 4d., say 29 per cent.; expenses of management, £3,584 7s. 7d., say 35 per cent.

The credit balance is £1,516 13s. 2d., which the directors propose to carry forward. In this connection it may be mentioned that a considerable proportion of the risks represented by the premium income has entirely run off. This proportion is increased by the fact that many of the policies are half-yearly ones, and consequently only those half-yearly policies which were issued after June, 1905, were current at December 31st.

The preliminary and organisation expenses, including the opening and equipping of the branches and the establishment of an agency organisation, amount to £3,198 1s. 10d., which is, in the opinion of the directors, a moderate amount when what has been accomplished is taken into consideration.

Branches have been opened in Aberdeen, Birmingham, Glasgow, Leeds, Liverpool, and Manchester, and over 2,000 agents appointed throughout the United Kingdom.

The directors are happy to think that the results achieved have surpassed expectations, and that the Company has already attained a recognised position in the insurance world.

The auditors, Messrs. Martin, Farlow & Co.,[2] retire and offer themselves for re-election.

The CHAIRMAN, in the course of his remarks, said the shareholders would see that the Company was fitly and comfortably housed; the offices were very suitable for carrying on their business, the situation was good, and he hoped it would not be very long before they had outgrown their present accommodation. The report before the shareholders was one which the Board considered satisfactory. They had only been in active operation for 18 months up to 31st December last, and during that period they had transacted what he believed was a record business for a new company of the kind – that was to say, for sickness and accident insurance only. For the twelve months ending June they secured £6,000 premium income, and from June to December another £4,000. They had adhered to their plan of transacting exclusively sickness and accident business, and so far as be knew they intended to adhere to it. It was a safer and more reliable business than many other forms of insurance. They knew their risks and could calculate them, and with a comparatively small capital they felt it was safer as regards the shareholders' interests than if they were to launch out into other directions. At the same time, they extended their personal accident business further than was done by any other company, namely, to all sickness and all accidents as applied to all risks of all occupations. They made no exceptions, although, of course, their terms were considerably higher in some instances than for first-class risks. As regards their accounts, the claims were equal to 29 per cent. of the premium income, which should be regarded as quite satisfactory. Their expenses of management were 35 per cent., which was a reasonable charge for management in the first year of a company, when it had to make its business and when its percentage was charged upon a comparatively small income. As their income grew the percentage would materially decrease. Their rates of commission were normal. The percentage to premium income, including every sort of commission – overriding and branch commissions, which were sometimes, he understood, charged to salary account – was about 18 per cent., and there was another 2 per cent. reserve for possible cancelments. Allowing a sum of £3,198 for preliminary and organization expenses – the bulk of that, of course, being charged to organization and a comparatively small amount to preliminary expenses, the organization outlay being, in fact, a capital item really representing their good-will – they showed a balance of £1,516. As they were aware, amongst their business that day was not included the declaration of a dividend. The Board felt sure that the shareholders would agree that before they began to pay dividends they must make their position absolutely secure. He thought the amount put down to organization was really represented by good-will, and that if it should happen that they had to dispose of the business they would be able to obtain considerably more than that figure. They wanted to build themselves up and become a really strong company. They had their competitors, and the usual criticism was that they were a small company; but their ability to meet their risks was ample, and the fact that a very large percentage of their customers renewed their insurances with them when the time came round showed that they were satisfied. The number who dropped out was extraordinarily small – only 4½ per cent. – which certainly showed they had not come across any company offering them better terms or better security. The policy of the Board was not a policy of cutting down the expenses as far as they possibly could. Their own remuneration was of a very modest character, and he hoped it was going to grow as the Company grew. They wanted to make it stable and strong, and then he saw no reason why it should not grow, as other companies had grown, from small to large. He did not suppose they would ever rival the gigantic figures which he saw pasted up in some of the railway carriages in which he travelled, but he thought they would have no reason to regret the day when they became shareholders of the *Casualty*. He moved the adoption of the report and accounts.

Sir Henry Hibbert[3] seconded the motion, which was carried unanimously.

In reply to a question by a shareholder, the Chairman said they were not anxious to issue further shares at par, because they regarded them as worth more. At the same time, they might do so in the case of new shareholders who were likely to bring business to the Company.

The auditors, Messrs. Martin, Farlow and Co., were unanimously re-elected.

The Chairman proposed a vote of thanks and appreciation to the managing director and officials of the Company. In Mr. Lee-Smith,[4] he said, they had a man of great industry and extraordinary ingenuity. He (the speaker) believed that although their Company was not a large one they had been pioneers in personal accident insurance and had started several new movements in which other companies had been compelled to follow their lead. With Mr. Lee-Smith he was going to couple the rest of the staff. It had been a year of new business, of increasing business, and of enormous enquiries. This entailed a very large amount of detailed work in the office, carried on at first in small and inconvenient premises; and their success was largely due to the ability and unremitting care of their managing director and staff.

Mr. G. I. Boon[5] seconded the motion. He thought the amount of business got together during the 18 months was really remarkable, as it was entirely confined to personal accident and sickness insurance. So far as the expense of getting it was concerned, it was necessary to expend money for that purpose. Fire and life companies were beginning to transact accident insurance, and the first thing they did was to go to personal accident business, because it was a paying business, a clean business, they knew what their risks were, and the premiums for any particular benefit or combination of benefits could be calculated fairly well. He thought the claim ratio of the Company showed that, whatever people might say about the benefits being too great, their statements had been belied by the Company's experience. No doubt the benefits were good, and that to a great extent enabled them to retain their business. He knew from past experience that 20 to 25 per cent. was not thought a big lapse ratio. Of course, nobody could expect a dividend in the first year, but where care was exercised the expense ratio went down and gradually got to such a point as enabled a good surplus to be secured during the year.

The motion having been carried unanimously, the Managing Director and Secretary, Mr. F. J. LEE-SMITH, acknowledged it on behalf of himself and the staff. He had, he said, received the very greatest support, consideration and sympathy from the directors, and the assistance of a loyal and capable staff. He was satisfied that there was no man in the service of the Company, whether at the head office or branches, but had worked with zest and energy, knowing perfectly well that he had got something to work for and would get the reward which his capabilities and energies deserved and warranted. He had cut out of a paper the following extract from a saying of Sir Hiram Maxim:[6] "No enterprise whatsoever, no matter how self-evident its benefits may be, can be carried out in England without encountering the most severe and determined opposition." It struck him that that was very applicable to all new undertakings. They had certainly encountered opposition in competition, principally on the ground that they were young and small and could not afford to pay the benefits they offered against the premiums charged. They did not deny that the Company was young: they had all been young once. They did not deny that they were small; but when they spoke of smallness they must consider the comparative position. He could mention some offices with huge funds whose indemnity from an actuarial standpoint was no better than their own. The man in the street did not readily understand that, and when they had this question to contend with they had always endeavoured rather to encourage the view that they were giving too much, and persuade the enquirer to take the advantages offered and reconsider the matter at the end of twelve months. They had always made a special practice of paying claims promptly. One or more of the directors attended at the office three or four days a week, and frequently payment was made on the very day the statement of claim was received. When they paid a claim they always asked the claimant to express his satisfaction, and when they paid all that was asked he could not very well refuse to do so. But they received some extraordinary claims occasionally. In one case a woman wrote in great distress that her husband had been killed through being thrown out of a cab, and asked them to send her the insurance money. She wrote at some distance from her home address, and they discovered that her husband was still living and well. In another case they issued one of their small policies as recently as this year, and in February the policyholder wrote sending back his policy, stating that the children were laid up with measles and that he would be glad to know what the Company could do for them. And in still another case a woman, some two or three weeks after taking out a policy, wrote that she had made an awful mistake; her policy should have been in the name of her husband, who was now laid up with typhoid, and she hoped they would transfer and pay the claim. He (the speaker) would take the opportunity of conveying the expression of the thanks of the shareholders, not only to the head office staff but to their branches, and he was sure it would be very highly appreciated.

A vote of thanks to the Board concluded the proceedings.

Notes

1 Robert John Price (1854–1926), Liberal MP for East Norfolk from 1892 to 1918, was both a surgeon (from 1876) and a barrister (from 1883) and, in 1909, was referred to as a "surgeon and company director" in *Guy's Hospital Gazette*.

2 Martin, Farlow and Co. was a London accounting firm with an office in King Street, Cheapside. Its senior partner, James Martin (1861–1935), was Secretary of the Society of Accountants and Auditors in 1906 and, later, its president; he was knighted in 1919 for his work advising the government during the war. The firm's junior partner, Arthur King-Farlow (1860–1935), was a fellow of the Institute of Chartered Accountants and an avid golfer.

3 Henry Hibbert (1850–1927) was a Conservative politician and proponent of adult education and MP for his hometown of Chorley from 1913 to 1918. He chaired the Lancashire County Council and Education Committee in the early 1900s.

4 Before landing at Casualty Insurance in 1904, F. J. Lee-Smith managed numerous insurance companies, including the Globe Plate Glass, Globe General, Universal Plate Glass, Credit Assurance & Guarantee, and the New York-based Preferred Accident. He served as the latter firm's London manager between 1901 and 1904, after building the Credit Assurance's Canadian and American business.

5 Gerald I. Boon, who spoke as a shareholder at the Casualty Insurance meeting, spent the 1890s in Melbourne, first as actuary for the Australian Alliance Assurance Company and then as a freelance actuary and accountant. Back in London, he was successively Assistant Secretary of the Law Accident Insurance Society, General Manager of the United Legal Indemnity Insurance Society, and Secretary of the Omnium Insurance Corporation and the City Equitable Fire Insurance Company.

6 Sir Hiram Stevens Maxim (1840–1916), born in rural Maine in the US, moved to London in 1884 and soon became famous for his eponymous Maxim machine gun.

Part 2

POLITICAL COMPANIES

Editorial Headnote

Bank of England (1797–98)

Before the nineteenth century, which inaugurated an explosion of column space in newspapers and industry-specific trade journals, few shareholder meetings attracted attention in the press. Exceptions included large and politically vital chartered companies such as the East India Company and Bank of England. And no company was more newsworthy in 1797 than the Bank, which, for five years, had occupied the eye of the storm in Prime Minister William Pitt's efforts to finance Britain's war against France. The war depleted the Bank's reserves from £7 million to £2 million by the end of 1796; the following February, after a rumored French invasion and the failure of several private banks, they declined by another £1 million. Its directors and Pitt's cabinet agreed that it should be relieved of the legal obligation to redeem its paper money with gold. Though everyone assumed this would be a temporary measure, the Bank Restriction Act remained in force until 1819, and Britain would not return to the gold standard until 1821. Restriction arguably enabled the Bank to circulate a sufficient (many claimed overabundant) supply of notes to keep the British economy humming while still supplying more than £6 million in temporary loans to the state each year.[1]

Among the most interested parties during the Bank's tumultuous decades after 1790 were its nearly 2500 voting shareholders, who met regularly over the course of 1797 and 1798 to discuss the company's affairs. Many of the issues raised at these meetings would continue to appear in the widening public debate over the Bank's actions in subsequent decades, including its right to issue notes in denominations less than £5, the continuing extent of its loans to the government (and the government's ability to repay its debts), and the right of Parliament – or indeed its own shareholders – to inspect the company's accounts. On the last point – publicity of accounts – little is known about the two shareholders who led this charge. Mr. Durand might have been John Durand (1750–1809), who held Bank stock at his death and had been Superintendent of the Philanthropic Society in St. George Fields since 1792.[2] We know more about the MP Alexander Allardyce (1743–1801), an Aberdeen-born slave trader who entered politics a decade after returning from Jamaica in 1780. He supplemented his speech in December 1797 with a lengthy "Address to the Proprictors" the same month, then returned to the attack four years later, shortly before his death. Although his calls for publicity would be repeated three decades later by more a new wave of public-spirited reformers, Allardyce's goals were mainly selfish: he suspected the Bank's directors of hoarding reserves or donating money to "soup kitchens and other charities," instead of paying them out as dividends.[3]

As 1797 dragged on, another recurring theme was the continued renewal of the suspension of payments – which shareholders greeted with mild surprise, since the Bank's gold reserves had, after all, rebounded to over £4 million by August. By 1798, however, suspension was already starting to become the new normal, and in a meeting called on 6 February, the agenda instead concerned a £200,000 donation of the Bank's "surplus money" for the "defence of the country, and for the preservation of its free and valuable constitution." (This was a sequel to the so-called "loyalty loan" of 1796, to which the Bank and several individual directors had contributed £1.5 million).[4] Although some speakers questioned the legality of a such a corporate donation, most vied with each other to defend the war effort in the most patriotic tones they could muster.

The list of speakers at this meeting provides a representative cross-section of the Bank's officers, shareholders, and directors at the time, who played a variety of prominent roles in its turbulent war decades. Joseph Kaye, its solicitor, spearheaded the prosecution of forgeries of the Bank's voluminous paper currency, sending dozens of forgers to their deaths.[5] William Lushington and John Anderson were leading London merchants who supported Pitt as MPs during his final years as Prime Minister, while the merchant Henry Smith, a future Bank director, was active in the army reserve and volunteer militias for most of his adult life.[6] Samuel Thornton, who chaired the meeting as deputy governor, was 20 years into a 53-year tenure as a Bank director and was a Tory mainstay in Parliament from 1784 until 1818. The Huguenot scion Samuel Bosanquet provided the Bank's perspective at a series of Parliamentary hearings in the late 1790s. For both men, finance was a family affair. Thornton's cousin Geoffrey was a fellow Bank director, his brother Henry was a leading expert on British monetary policy, and Bosanquet's cousin Jacob was a longtime director of the East India Company[7]

Notes

1 David Kynaston, *Till Time's Last Stand: A History of the Bank of England 1694–2013* (London: Bloomsbury, 2017), 77–93; Michael J. Bordo and Eugene N. White. "A Tale of Two Currencies: British and French Finance During the Napoleonic Wars," *Journal of Economic History* 51 (1991): 303–316.

2 "Obituary," *Gentleman's Magazine* 105 (1809), 93–94; *The Names and Description of Proprietors of Unclaimed Dividends of Bank Stock* (London: Joseph Walsh, 1815), 440.

3 John Clapham, *The Bank of England: A History* (Cambridge: Cambridge University Press, 1966), 2: 40–41; David R. Fisher, "Andrew Allardyce," *History of Parliament Online*. On later calls for publicity see Timothy L. Alborn, *Conceiving Companies: Joint-Stock Politics in Victorian England* (London: Routledge, 1998), 63–71.

4 Clapham, *The Bank of England*, 1: 272–288; Kynaston, *Till Time's Last Stand*, 81.

5 Randall McGowen, "Managing the Gallows: The Bank of England and the Death Penalty, 1797–1821," *Law and History Review* 25 (2007): 241–282.

6 R. G. Thorne, "William Lushington" and "John William Anderson," *History of Parliament Online*; "Henry Smith," *Gentleman's Magazine* 140 (1826), 471.

7 Michael Reed, "Samuel Thornton," *Dictionary of National Biography Online*; Kynaston, *Till Time's Last Stand*, 84–85; Gillian Darley, *John Soane: An Accidental Romantic* (New Haven: Yale University Press, 1999), 71.

11

BANK OF ENGLAND

Sources: Bank of England (1797–98), *London Times*, 3, 24 and 31 March, 23 June, and 18 November 1797; and 7 February 1798; also *London Chronicle*, 26 March 1797; and *Star and Evening Advertiser*, 16 December 1797.

London Times, 3 March, 1797

THE BANK MEETING

The GOVERNOR[1] opened the business by reading the late Order of Council, and by informing the Proprietors of the conduct of the Directors in complying with it. He said, that perceiving there was an extraordinary drain of cash from the Bank, in consequence of the general alarm that was gone abroad, a Committee had waited on the Minister to acquaint him of the circumstance, that he might advise such measures as he thought proper. The Directors did not wish that the whole responsibility should remain with them. He hoped the Court would approve of their conduct.

Mr. *Harman*[2] moved the Thanks of the Court to the Directors; approving of their conduct in complying with the late Order of Council.

A resolution to this effect being read, Mr. *Dawes*,[3] a Barrister, said, that before such a resolution passed, he thought the Proprietors should be better informed. He understood that the Directors had first applied to Government to stop – (a cry of No, no.)

A *Director* said, that this had not been stated. The Committee had only informed the Minister, of the great demands that continued pressing on them.

Mr. *Dawes* proceeded – and begged to be informed, whether the Minister was to have any interference in the concerns of the Bank. Hitherto, the Bank was restrained from issuing notes above a certain amount; was the Bank now to issue to what amount the Directors pleased? Was there to be no check over them now, when they only paid notes for money? He thought there ought to be a controul over them, that no suspicion of their conduct might arise.

Mr. *Durand* thought it proper to call the Gentleman to order, as he had, in his opinion, entirely wandered from the question before the Court. He requested the resolution might be read, and he then asked what possible connection there was between it and the propositions suggested by the last speaker? This was no time for quibble. The Court of Proprietors would, he was convinced, act like Englishmen to increase the public credit, and save the country; and he trusted that a Banknote would soon appear like a bar of gold.

DOI: 10.4324/9781003177715-13

The resolution was then put and unanimously carried.

The question of adjournment being called for,

The *Governor* observed, that as the measure of instituting an enquiry into the affairs of the Bank was at that moment under the consideration of Parliament, the Court of Directors had nothing more to offer to the Proprietors, unless some specific proposition should be made on the part of the general Court.

Mr. *Cater* moved the question of Adjournment, and thought that the General Court would readily depend upon any further communication being made to them by the Governor and Directors.

Mr. *Durand* objected to the Adjournment, and moved the following resolution: – "That the Governor and Directors of the Bank of England are entitled to the confidence of the Public, and to the gratitude of this Court, for the faithful discharge of their duties to the public in general, and to the Proprietors in particular."

Mr. *Harman* submitted it to the consideration of Gentlemen, whether the first resolution was not quite sufficient? and whether proceeding to a farther length, might not call in question the sincerity of it.

Mr. *Sansom*[4] declared he was perfectly satisfied with the declaration of the Bank, that they were fully competent to meet every demand; without referring the inspection of their accounts to a Select Committee of the House of Commons. Such an enquiry might create suspicion, whereas, in his opinion, the Committee of Inspection ought to be composed of Proprietors; who, undoubtedly, were better qualified to carry on the proposed examination than Members of the House of Commons.

Mr. *Bosanquet*,[5] a Director, observed, that since a Gentleman had brought forward a motion of thanks to the Governor and Court of Directors, he begged leave, in their name, to decline such thanks, as the motion was grounded on nothing more than a general confidence in them. The business of enquiry was then before the House of Commons, and the Court of Directors did not think proper to interfere in a measure which they clearly conceived to be a matter of state. In consequence of the alarm which had taken place, and the drain of specie that followed the alarm, the Court of Directors thought proper to acquaint the Minister with the circumstance, who was unquestionably better informed on the subject of public affairs, and of the probability of future prospects. It would have been presumption in the Governor and Directors to have judged for themselves, and to have pointed out to his Majesty's Ministers any particular line of conduct. They had merely laid before Ministers the situation of the Bank, and that proceeding produced the Order of Council to which they readily submitted. It was not for them to decide on the legality of an order, which in the course of twenty-four hours after they received it, was to be taken into the consideration of Parliament. – "*I have the satisfaction to assure you, Gentlemen*" said Mr. BOSANQUET, "*that the state of the* BANK *is* AFFLUENT *and* PROSPEROUS; *that its surplus is very great; and I have no doubt but we shall very shortly see this restriction taken off, and Bank-notes once more exchanged for money.*"

After some remarks from Mr. *Waddington* and Mr. *Durand*,

Mr. *Thornton*,[6] one of the Directors, thought it necessary to observe, that the Governor and Court of Directors had not applied for a guarantee to Parliament; but if Parliament judged the guarantee necessary, they would not give it without previous examination.

The question of Adjournment was then put and carried.

London Times, March 24, 1797

London, March 24

Yesterday there was a Meeting of the Proprietors of BANK STOCK, to declare the half yearly dividend of 3l. 10s. per Cent. which being proposed by the Governor, was carried unanimously.

The GOVERNOR then informed the Court, that a new LOAN was in agitation, and would probably be concluded in the course of the ensuing week, which would enable Government to pay a part of its debt due to the Bank of England; and he had no scruple in declaring, that the sum so to be repaid, would amount to SEVEN MILLIONS sterling. He said the Bank had refused to pay any more Treasury Bills which might be drawn on it, without having a deposit; that a balance of 190,000l. was now in hand to defray the Bills payable at the Bank; and that when this sum was gone, the Bank would pay no more without farther supplies.

A *Proprietor*, whose name we could not learn, proposed, "that the Directors should have the power of using their own judgement in regard to the extension of their discounts, without being under the controul of Parliament or the Executive Government."

This motion was soon disposed of by the previous question, as it was thought to be nugatory, the Directors having already such a right.

Mr. DURAND made some observations on the state of the Bank and of public credit; he considered that the present disasters were principally to be attributed to the immense advances made to Government, which had lately been accustomed to have too much interference with the Bank. He advised that a resolution should be passed to preclude the Bank Directors from ever having it in their power to advance beyond a certain sum to Government without the consent of the Proprietors. He wished that Government had no authority over the Bank; and that the Directors should not be under Ministerial influence. He moved – "That the Directors be desired to lay before a General Court, the amount of the debt due to the Bank by Government;" which was agreed to, and the Court immediately broke up.

London Chronicle, March 26, 1797 (same meeting)

COURT OF PROPRIETORS OF THE BANK.

Yesterday a Court of Proprietors was held at the Bank to declare the dividend. The Governor moved that three and a-half per cent. be the half yearly dividend.

Mr. Allardyce desired the bye-law to be read, directing a Committee to be appointed to inquire into the circumstances of the Corporation previous to each half-yearly dividend, and he desired to know if this had been complied with at this most critical period.

Mr. Sansom said that by letters laid, on the table of the House of Commons, he saw that the Company had made advances to Government to the amount of near 10,000,000l. He desired to know whether an application had been made to the Ministers for the repayment of these advances, which the public understood to have occasioned all the present distress of the Company.

The Governor said, that they had not failed all along to make representations to Ministers of the injurious operation on their concerns the incessant advances necessarily had; every effort to impress this truth had been used. He was happy, however, to state to the General Court, that a Loan was now in train of negociation, and that Ministers had expressly declared their intention that a considerable part of their advances should be repaid out of the Loan. Another part, that which had been made on the security of the Land and Malt, was daily coming in. The Loan was in considerable forwardness; he had reason to believe that the negociation would be concluded next week; and a considerable part of their advances – indeed he might state the amount – *seven millions of their advances would be repaid* – a circumstance that would materially ease the Company.

Mr. Allardyce was glad to hear this from the Chair; but by a paper which he held in his hand, he saw that between the 25th February and the 9th of March, they had advanced a further sum, to the amount of several hundred thousand pounds; now it was of little avail to be repaid in a Loan, if these advances were to continue. He desired to know, therefore, whether these advances were also to be repaid, and whether further advances were to be restrained.

The Governor said, it was understood that the advances made since the 25th February, were also to be repaid, and that advances were not to be made to the same amount in future.

Mr. Durand moved, that no power had a right to interfere with the private management of their affairs.

Mr. Harman moved the previous question on this motion, and, on a shew of hands, only one hand or two was held up for it.

London Times 31 March 1797

THE BANK MEETING

Yesterday a Special Court of Proprietors was held at the Bank, to receive a proposition made by the CHANCELLOR OF THE EXCHEQUER to the Governor and Deputy Governor, for a temporary advance of 600,000l.

The *Governor* informed the Meeting, that he had received a Letter from the Chancellor of the Exchequer, requesting a Loan of 600,000l. on the credit of Exchequer Bills, which should be repaid out of the first receipts of a new Loan about to be made. The Governor thought this Letter of that importance as to make it necessary to convene a Court. – The Letter was read, and is nearly as follows: –

Downing-street, 17th March.

"SIR,

"I feel myself under the disagreeable necessity of informing you, that in consequence of the Committee for enquiring into the Finances of the Country not having been yet able to make their report, I have not been able to fix any precise time for the arrangement of the ensuing Loan. This week and the last, there have been very urgent demands on Government; for which, under the difficulty of extending the circulation of Exchequer Bills, there is no certain means of providing. It would therefore be of the highest importance to the public service if you would take the sense of the Proprietors on advancing 600,000l, on the conditions that the first installments of the new Loan should be applied to the repayment of this sum: I have this day proposed an exception in a Clause in a Bill now before the House for this purpose, which I trust will be fully satisfactory to the Court.

"I have honour to be, &c.

"W. PITT.[7]

"*To the Hon. Governor of the Bank.*"

The Governor then observed, that the Court of Directors had not thought themselves justified in acceding to this proposition, without the special approbation of the Proprietors. The Court, however, thought, that in consideration of all the circumstances of the case, it was expedient to accede to the Ministers proposition.

Mr. *Hoare*[8] said he was not qualified to meet the question without further information. He wished the Court to consider whether this measure would not rather prevent the restoration of public credit. Were the Court of Directors certain that no part of this money was to go out of the country. If he had not some such assurance from the Directors, he would not consent to the proposition.

Mr. *Allardice*, in a low tone of voice, moved, "That the Court do agree with Mr. PITT's proposition for a Loan of 600,000l."

Mr. *Durand* considered this question as the most important ever agitated. He could not make up his mind on this question, until he was told whether Ministers could not find out some mode of borrowing the money on the accustomed mode of Exchequer Bills, instead of coming to the Bank, which was already in such advance. If Exchequer Bills had been brought to market, there would have been no necessity of coming here. The Public were better able to bear the loss of the discount than the Proprietors. He must however know, whether the Bank, by lending this sum, would not be obliged to limit its discounts to the Merchants.

The *Governor* declared, that the time of the advance was too short to operate in such a way.

Mr. *Durand* said he was satisfied with this answer. He hoped, however, that the Court would not be called on again for any further advances.

The motion for lending 600,000l. to Government was then put and carried with only five dissentient voices.

London Times 23 June 1797

MEETING AT THE BANK

Yesterday there was a Court of Proprietors at the Bank of England, to receive the report of the Directors respecting the correspondence which has lately passed on the propriety of the Bank being still restricted from payments in specie.

Mr. PITT's letter to the Governor and Deputy Governor, dated the 12th inst. was read, in which he acquainted them of its being his intention to propose to Parliament the further duration of the Bill, empowering them to suspend payments in specie, unless he should hear of something which might lead him to alter such intention.

To this letter the GOVERNOR and DEPUTY GOVERNOR returned for answer, that the Court of Directors consented to his proposition, but wished that a Clause might be introduced into the new Bill, allowing them to pay in specie within a limited time, should they deem it expedient so to do. In consequence of this desire, a Clause had been introduced into the last Bill, which enables them to make their payments in specie.

Mr. DURAND asked whether any part of the monies owing to the Bank by Government had been repaid. The GOVERNOR replied, that an allotment had been made out of each payment of the last Loan for the repayment of the whole of the debt; that part had been already received, and in the course of the year the whole debt of 5,500,000l. would be repaid, besides 1,200,000l. lent on the Land and Malt Taxes, 500,000l. lent on Exchequer Bills, and other advances, making on the whole 8,100,000l. sterling.

A *Member* hoped that if any future application for a Loan from the MINISTER to the Bank should be made, the Court would take the sense of the Proprietors on it. The Governor said that no recent application of such a nature had been received.

A short conversation ensued, on which however no motion was made. Mr. HEYWOOD thought the salary of the Court of Directors was too inconsiderable for their attention, and the trust reposed in them, and said he should, at some future time, submit a resolution for the increase of it. Mr. DURAND said, he was sure if such a proposition was made, the Directors would be the first to negative it. – Adjourned.

London Times, 18 November 1797.

THE BANK MEETING

Yesterday a Court of Proprietors was held at the BANK; and we have particular satisfaction in announcing the proceedings that passed.

Mr. Raikes,[9] the Chairman, acquainted the Proprietors, that he and the Deputy Governor had had an interview on the preceding day with Mr. Pitt, and had also deposited with the Secret Committee of the House of Commons a Statement of the Affairs of the Bank, which he should also lay before the Proprietors. The result of this Statement was as follows: –

The Bank had in Cash, Bullion, and other Securities – Seventeen Millions Sterling and a Fraction.

Due to the Bank from Government, Four Millions and a Fraction.

The Debts of the Bank were – Eleven Millions of outstanding Notes – besides Six Millions of other Demands on it.

The nett Balance in favour of the Bank, independent of the Government Stock which it held, was – *Three Millions, Eight Hundred and Thirty-nine Thousand Pounds Sterling.*

Mr. Raikes then informed the Court, that the Minister had proposed to extend the further limitation of time when the Bank should resume its payments in specie; that it was not necessary for him to judge of the urgency of political motives which might render such a step adviseable; but he had the pleasure to inform the Court, that the Bank was in such a state of affluence, as to be ready to pay all the demands on it in specie, whenever called upon.

The consent of the Proprietors was then asked for advancing the amount of the Land and Malt Tax to Government, amounting to 2,750,000l. – which was unanimously agreed to.

The business of the Meeting being over, Mr. Hoare represented to the Directors the great inconvenience arising from the present scarcity of Silver; and was informed that a coinage was in agitation.

A Proprietor again recommended that the Salaries of the Bank Directors should be raised; but was told by the Chairman, that the Directors begged leave to decline any such recommendation at present.

The Meeting then adjourned, highly satisfied at the communications made by the Chairman.

Star and Evening Advertiser 16 December 1797

BANK OF ENGLAND

A GENERAL COURT of PROPRIETORS was held on Thursday the 14th of December, when the Governor informed the Court, that it had been called out of respect to an Honourable Member who he saw present, who at the last General Court had given notice, that at the next General Court he would move for some Accounts, and that this was likewise one of the General Quarterly Courts of the Corporation.

Mr. Allardyce rose, and prefaced his motion by complaining of the short notice which had been given of the time of holding this Court, which was only in the Royal Gazette, a paper not in general circulation, of Saturday the 9th, and in the Daily Papers of Tuesday the 12th. He was, however, happy in seeing a very full Court.

He then made the following motion, which was seconded: – "That there be laid before this Court, An Account of the Charge of managing the Business of the Governor and Company of the Bank of England; An Account of the Expence of Building; and, An Account of all the other Expences incurred by the Governor and Company from the 10th day of October, 1787, to the 10th of October 1797, distinguishing the different years, and the particulars under their respective heads."

Mr. Allardyce added, that if it could be made [to] appear that the production of these Accounts would do any harm, or that his motion called for any secret that ought to be concealed, that he would readily withdraw it; he thought it afforded the Directors an opportunity of refuting the rumours which were in circulation with respect to the expence of building, many of which he believed to be unfounded.

Mr. Hoare said, he thought that the motion, at the present moment, was inexpedient. He allowed that the Proprietors had a right to call upon the Directors for Accounts relative to the affairs of the Company; that this was not the time to make any additional dividend; but that when peace returned, he would be one of the first to propose it. He would therefore move the previous question.

Mr. Allardyce observed, that the Honourable Member had deviated from the question before the Court; that it was true he had given notice of a motion he should make at a future Court, for an Account of the State and Condition of the Company, and that a Dividend of all the Profits should be made Half-yearly; but that the motions were perfectly independent of one another, and ought to be argued separately.

Mr. Durand gave credit to the Mover for his abilities and talents, and for the information he had received from the Address he had published to the Proprietors, but agreed with Mr. Hoare in the present inexpediency of the motion,

The previous question was accordingly put, and the motion negatived by a considerable majority.

London Times, 7 February 1798

BANK OF ENGLAND

Yesterday a very full Court of Proprietors was held at the Bank, to consider of a Voluntary Contribution to the State. The meeting was called at the requisition of the following Gentlemen: –

JOHN WILLIAM ANDERSON,[10] Lord Mayor.

Henry Smith, Esq.
J. J. Angerstein, Esq.
William Curtis, Esq.
Richard Down, Esq.

THOMAS EVERETT, Esq.
ALEX. BAXTER, Esq.
P. AGUSSIZ, Esq.
THOMAS BROWN, Esq.
ROBERT WILLIAMS, Esq.

The Chair was taken a little after 12 o'clock by Mr. THORNTON, who stated to the Court that the purpose for which it was then called, was to consider of the propriety of voting a Voluntary Contribution for the service of Government. He then desired the requisition signed by nine Proprietors, for calling the present meeting, to be read; which being done,

Mr. *Forster* said, it was not his wish to throw any embarrassments in the way of the proceedings of the Court, so as to prevent it from contributing to the exigencies of the State. But he desired that it might first be ascertained whether the Bank, as a Corporation, had a right to give away any money, and whether the surplus money remaining in its possession was not the property of the Proprietors individually. Suppose the Corporation was to be dissolved; to whom then did that money belong?

Mr. *Thornton* said, that in order to clear up any difficulty which might arise in the mind of any Gentleman on this subject, directions had been given for the attendance of Counsel, who were expected every moment to arrive: but the Solicitor of the Bank, who was then present, would state his opinion as to the objections that had been advanced.

Mr. *Kaye*,[11] the Solicitor, stated it as his opinion, that the Corporation of the Bank had the power to dispose of any surplus money in its possession; and he then read an extract from the charter, which stated, that a General Court of Proprietors could determine on all matters relating to the Corporation. After some more desultory conversation,

Mr. *Smith*[12] observing that there was no question before the Court, said, he rose to offer a motion on the subject for which it had been called. He then entered into the necessity of using every exertion to repel the threatened attacks of an inveterate enemy, whose object it was to overturn the Government, and destroy the importance and even the very existence of this country. If any Gentleman entertained a doubt as to the enemies' views, and the manner in which they would be carried into effect, should they prove successful against Great Britain, let them look to the present degraded and subjugated situation of Holland; let them look to the treatment which Venice had received – that of being given over to one of the most despotic Governments in Europe. Who could tell but that some such fate might befall this country, if she became a prey to that implacable nation, that had long envied her greatness as well as her liberty. As he was sure that the example set to the country that day would be productive of the most important benefits, he would move – "that the General Court of Proprietors do, in its corporate capacity, subscribe the sum of ______ to the books now open at the Bank for receiving Voluntary Subscriptions."

This motion being seconded, and put from the Chair,

Mr. *Foster* again rose, to state his objection to the power which the Court had to vote such a sum.

Mr. *Bosanquet* would not say any thing upon the expediency or necessity of the present measure, convinced as he was that every Gentleman entertained but one opinion on that subject. He rose, however, to contend that the Court had a right to dispose of, in any manner it thought fit, the surplus money remaining in the Bank, after the Proprietors were paid. This was evident from the charter, a part of which Gentlemen had heard read; and nothing could be more clear than the right which people had of disposing of that money which was their own.

Mr. *Foster* said, that the Proprietors who assembled there, might give away their own money if they chose; but they had not the power of voting the money of those Proprietors who were absent, which must be the case if the Court subscribed in its corporate capacity.

Mr. *Bosanquet* replied, that every act of the majority of any Corporation was binding on the remainder of its Members, whether they were present or not.

Mr. Alderman *Lushington*[13] supported the opinion of the last speaker, as to the right the majority of a General Court had of voting money for the public service. To bring the question nearer to every Gentleman's feelings, he would suppose there was a violent insurrection in the City of London; who then had a right of voting money to defend the Bank? The General Court of Proprietors certainly. But he would ask whether there was not a motive still greater which called for their contributions? – That of preserving the venerable Constitution of this country – of preserving its political and commercial importance, and defending themselves from inevitable ruin, which must be the consequence of supineness and indifference. The prosperity of Great-Britain had been an object of envy to the ancient Monarchy of France, as well as to her still more tyrannical Democracy. That envy had encreased to such a pitch, that nothing could satisfy the enemy but our utter destruction. It was with these views they carried on their system of dissimulation during the late Negociation; and abruptly broke it off after they could dissemble no longer. What were the individuals who enjoyed any thing in this country to expect, if they did not cordially unite in defending their liberty and their property? Was it not incumbent on every man who valued either to contribute a large share of what he possessed, in order that the remainder might be preserved? But it was not to be expected that individuals could take the lead with any considerable effect in the business of contribution. In a country where so many factions existed; where there was such a difference in opinion it was natural to suppose that numbers of people would keep back their subscriptions because some discontented individual in their neighbourhood refused to give any. It was therefore from Corporate Bodies that every thing was at first to be expected, and the contributions of individuals would afterwards follow. Not to make great exertions at this moment, would be no less than inviting the enemy to come and take possession of the country. As many allusions had lately been made to the smallness of the sum subscribed by a certain Great Personage, he thought it necessary to observe, that after all the expences of the Civil List were paid, his Majesty had no more than 60,000l. a year – a sum barely sufficient to answer all those benevolent purposes to which his Majesty was so eminently disposed. When therefore it was considered that the sum he had subscribed was one-third of his income which he had any power over, and that the same was to be continued during the war, he hoped those invidious objections that had been made would be effectually removed. He said he would most cordially second and support the motion that had been made, because, if carried, it would set an example of liberality to the whole kingdom, which would produce the happiest effects, by lessening the new Assessments, as no more than 15 millions was to be raised in all.

Mr. *Hunter* rose to move, that the sum to be subscribed should amount to *Two Hundred Thousand Pounds*. This motion was received with shouts of applause, and several voices cried out, "*Half a Million – Half a Million*."

Mr. *Kemble* said, he rose to express his hearty approbation of the motion, as well as of the sum which had been proposed, and wished it was greater. For his part, he had but a small share of Bank Stock, and that he had not been long in the possession of. But if the whole of his property was in Bank Stock, he would chearfully support any motion that went even to give away the greater part of it for the service and defence of the country, and for the preservation of its free and valuable Constitution. He was happy to have it in his power to inform the Meeting, that a general spirit was spreading through the country, and that numbers were animated with a desire to come forward in its support. He would relate one instance of loyalty which occurred within the last three or four days: He had received a letter from a Frenchman, (who kept a large school) containing 50l. which he desired might be subscribed at the Bank in his name. This Gentleman said, he loved England better than his own country, and he would do his utmost to defend the one against the attacks of the other. As a proof of the public spirit and loyalty of the rising generation, he would relate a circumstance of which this French Gentleman informed him: He had called all his Scholars together, who amounted to near ninety in number: "My lads, (said he) I have subscribed 50l. towards carrying on the war for the defence of this country; and I have called you together to ask whether you are willing to subscribe any thing." They all emptied their pockets immediately of all the money they had, and the whole of their contributions amounted to near 20l. After these and other instances, no doubt could be entertained, but that Subscriptions would flow in in abundance.

Mr. *Thornton* observed, that if any Gentleman doubted of the power of that Court to grant money, they might wait until Mr. *Pigott* should arrive, who was expected every moment; and he would then give his opinion as Counsel to the Bank.

There was immediately a cry of "*No! – No!*"

Mr. *Thornton* then adverted to what had fallen from an Hon. Alderman concerning the contribution made by his Majesty. Upon that subject, he had it in his power to state as a fact, that 60,000l. a year was all the disposable property possessed by his Majesty in this country; and that he did not derive any other disposable property from any other country. He then suggested the propriety, in point of form, of altering the motion in the following manner: – "That the General Court of Proprietors do give directions to the Governor of the Bank of England to subscribe the sum of 200,000l. out of the surplus money belonging to the Bank, in its corporate capacity, to the Books now lying open at the Bank for receiving Voluntary Contributions."

This motion was put and carried unanimously. After which the Court adjourned.

Notes

1 Daniel Giles (1725–1800) was Governor of the Bank of England from 1795 to 1797. He amassed a fortune close to £200,000, which was (according to one obituary) "realized chiefly during the present war, by the loans to government, and by his speculations in the funds."

2 Jeremiah Harman (1764–1844) was a Bank of England director from 1794 to 1827 and its governor from 1816 to 1818. He was a partner in the London firm of Harman, Hoare, and Co., founded by his father to trade in Lisbon and later Russia.

3 Possibly Manessah Dawes (died 1829), who was admitted to the bar in 1776 but had ceased to practice law by the 1780s. He was best known for his poetry and political writing; his Whig tendencies in the latter would be consistent with the stance exhibited in this meeting.

4 Most likely the London private banker Philip Sansom, who formed the partnership of Harcourt, Blake, Postlethwaite and Tanner in 1791, which became Sansom, Blake and Postethwaite in 1801, with offices in Lombard Street.

5 Samuel Bosanquet (1744–1804) was Governor of the Bank of England from 1791 to 1793 and remained on its board until his death. He belonged to a powerful Huguenot merchant dynasty, and his family ties won him directorships at both the Bank and the Levant Company.

6 Samuel Thornton (1754–1838) was Deputy Governor of the Bank of England from 1797 to 1799 and Governor from 1799 to 1801. In 1790, he succeeded his father as a prominent Baltic merchant based in Hull, and besides his leading role at the Bank, was governor of the Russia Company from 1810 until his death.

7 William Pitt (1759–1806) was Britain's Prime Minister between 1783 and 1801 and again from 1804 until his death. Following the outbreak of war against France in 1792, Pitt raised close to £300 million in public debt and more than £200 million in new taxes and played a central role in ongoing negotiations with the Bank of England over its role in supporting the war effort.

8 Possibly Peter Richard Hoare (1772–1849), a partner in Hoare's Bank, London, and Bank of England shareholder, who published a pamphlet critical of the Bank in 1811.

9 Thomas Raikes (1741–1813) was Deputy Governor of the Bank of England from 1795 to 1797 and succeeded Giles as Governor in 1797. A London merchant, he counted William Wilberforce and William Pitt among his friends.

10 John William Anderson (1736–1813) was Lord Mayor of London in 1797 and 1798, an alderman from 1789 to 1813, a Tory Member of Parliament for the City of London from 1793 to 1806, and a baronet from 1798. The son of a British merchant in Danzig, he set up shop as an "agent and commissary for the city of Danzig" in London in 1777 and continued as a Baltic merchant up to 1811.

11 Joseph Kaye (1756–1840), with his partner John Winter, was the Bank of England's solicitor, later joined by James Freshfield. This team of solicitors was responsible for prosecuting more than 2000 forgers between 1797 and 1821, leading to the execution of more than 200 of them.

12 Henry Smith (1741–1826) was a junior partner with the Huguenot merchant Philip Devisme and active in the Honorable Artillery Company in the 1780s and the Camberwell Volunteer Corps. after 1800.

13 William Lushington (1747–1823) made his fortune in India as an East India Company servant, and on returning to London, became a partner in the Cornhill banking firm of Boldero, Adey, Lushington and Boldero. He was a London alderman from 1795 to 1799 and, as a Tory Member of Parliament from 1795 to 1802, was a strong supporter of Pitt.

Editorial Headnote

Imperial Brazilian Mining Company (1841)

Compared to other Latin American mining regions that attracted British investment during the 1825 stock market bubble, Brazil provided an exceptional share of winning gambles. The metal, in this case, was gold, the production of which British companies hoped to revive from the eighteenth-century boom years, when Brazil provided Britain with enough to form the basis of its currency. After declaring independence from Portugal in 1822, Brazil actively promoted British investment, and two firms emerged as durable stakeholders in the reopened Brazilian mining sector: the Imperial British Mining Company (IBMC), which received concessions in 1824 to work the abandoned Gongo Soco mine; and the St. John d'el Rey, which formed in 1830 and mined two adjacent lodes. Together, the two companies extracted more than 25,000 kg of gold between 1825 and 1850 (a third of Brazil's total output), enough to assist in a moderate revival in the country's mining fortunes. Although profitable enough, they attracted the wrong sort of publicity owing to their labor practices. As of 1840, British mining companies in Brazil owned around 2000 slaves; after 1845, they adapted to a new law banning expatriates from owning slaves by renting them from neighboring plantations. From early on, these firms broadcast their efforts "to ameliorate and soften" the condition of the slaves who worked for them – although this claim did little to appease abolitionists in Britain, including some of their own shareholders.[1]

In 1840, a small group of IBMC shareholders, led by wealthy Bristol Quakers, commenced a vocal but unsuccessful campaign to end their company's reliance on slave labor. The timing of their protest coincided with the firm's departure from its promise of gradual emancipation, following the appointment of George Duval as its chief commissioner in Brazil in 1835. They began by publishing an exposé of "the Frightful Horrors of Modern Slavery" by a former IBMC clerk, F. A. Kentish, which prompted a response from the company's solicitors that was published in the *Anti-Slavery Reporter*, an organ of the British and Foreign Anti-Slavery Society. The following May, they circulated a report to IBMC shareholders ahead of a special general meeting, in which they renewed their complaints. Distancing themselves from Kentish's charges, they relied, instead, on new testimony from a superintendent, H. L. Bayly, who had worked under Duval, and from his prior supervisor, J. M. A. Skerrett, whose reforms had since been reversed. The Bristol grocer George Thomas, who led the charge at the meeting, supplemented these testimonials with historical evidence that immediate emancipation had proven more effective where it had been tried than the gradual methods that the IBMC had borrowed from other West Indian colonies. After Thomas concluded with a heartfelt appeal to Christianity, the Jewish financier Isaac Goldsmid responded with a lengthy defense of the company's gradual approach. The response to the abolitionists' efforts at the meeting was mixed, at best. Although their fellow shareholders unanimously rejected their call for immediate emancipation, a few press outlets did offer support. Besides receiving a detailed report in the *Anti-Slavery Reporter*, the *Morning Chronicle* praised the "Seven Champions" who spoke at the meeting, and the *Odd Fellow* printed a letter from Kentish praising the proceedings under the title "The Humanity-Mongers." Most other papers, however, provided fewer details and focused instead on their overwhelming defeat at the hands of their fellow shareholders.[2]

Notes

1 This paragraph is based on Timothy Alborn, *All That Glittered: Britain's Most Precious Metal from Adam Smith to the Gold Rush* (New York: Oxford University Press, 2019). 163–166.

2 Joseph Kelly, "The Problem of Anti-Slavery in the Age of Capital: Britain and Transatlantic Slavery, c. 1833–1888" (University of Liverpool Ph.D. dissertation, 2018), 203–254; "The Humanity-Mongers: Brazil Sugar and Brazil Gold," *Odd Fellow*, 19 June 1841.

12

IMPERIAL BRAZILIAN MINING COMPANY

Source: Imperial Brazilian Mining Company (1841), *Anti-Slavery Reporter*, 2 June 1841

IMPERIAL BRAZILIAN MINING COMPANY

A GENERAL MEETING of the Proprietary of this Company was held at the London Tavern, at one o'clock, on Thursday, the 13th of May, 1841; Joshua Walker, Esq.,[1] in the Chair.

The attendance was unusually large, in consequence of the following Address having been circulated among the shareholders: –

"TO THE SHAREHOLDERS OF THE IMPERIAL BRAZILIAN MINING COMPANY.

"Having, unknowingly in the first instance, become shareholders in a Mining Company which employs slave-labour, we deeply feel the responsibility which devolves upon us, and upon all who have an interest in companies similarly situated. Thus impressed, allow us to call attention to the painful fact, that you, with ourselves, are slave-holders, and to present to you some information and reflections in connexion with the subject.

"We may observe, that the Brazilian Mining Company claims about 413 slaves, of whom about 168 are men, about 114 are women, and 131 are children; and, in addition, there are forty slaves hired by contract for a period of two years. Allow us to remind you, that the slaves which are thus owned or hired are the victims or descendants of those who were obtained by cruel wars carried on in Africa, in many instances waged for the very purpose of procuring captives for sale, or have been procured in other ways no less inconsistent with humanity and religion. This is the origin of the slavery the Imperial Brazilian Mining Company is countenancing.

"We not only object in the strongest manner to the way in which this unrighteous species of property is acquired, but to the system of slavery, as in itself unjust and necessarily cruel. We cannot but regard such a system as in direct opposition to the righteous law of God, and to the merciful principles of the gospel.

"Entertaining these views of the essential character of slavery, we must strongly deprecate the countenance of it by the Imperial Brazilian Mining Company

DOI: 10.4324/9781003177715-14

under any circumstances. We have, however, thought it our duty to make some inquiry as to the particular situation of the slaves held by the Company; and we regret, that, upon several important points on which we have sought information, we have either not been able to obtain it, or that which we have obtained is of the most unsatisfactory character: for instance, the nature, extent, and effect of the punishments inflicted on the slaves is not known to our Directors – only one return of such punishments appears to have been sent home, and that several years since! And, with respect to the education of the slaves, it appears to have been abandoned in deference to the feelings and wishes of the slave holders in the vicinity!

"We will not dwell upon the statements which have been made of cruelties perpetrated by some of the servants of the company, when separated thousands of miles from the Directors± – some of which, however, we believe to be too true; we would rather call your attention to the circumstance, that the slavery which is thus sanctioned by the Imperial Brazilian Mining Company is a system by which millions of human beings are subjected to a debasing, cruel, and in many instances, life-destroying bondage – a system which fosters, both on the part of the slave and his oppressor, a fearful amount of immorality, and neglect of religious obligations.

"It must also be ever borne in mind, that, as slavery originated in the enormous iniquity of the slave-trade, so it continually fosters this evil which exists to an enormous extent in the Brazils, in despite of laws for its abolition; the number of its annual victims is calculated at 60,000! With a knowledge of these facts, can you withhold your most strenuous exertions to remove from your character the reproach of being a slaveholder, and from your conscience the guilt of being implicated in a crime so fatally and extensively destructive to human happiness, and to the advancement of civilization and religion?

"The directors have, in accordance with our earnest request, resolved, to make the general meeting of the proprietary on the 13th of 5th mo. (May) special, for the consideration of the propriety of emancipating the slaves, and providing for the security of their future freedom; we, therefore, respectfully but earnestly call upon our brother shareholders to attend that meeting, or entrust their proxies to the friends of this righteous cause; and we trust they will be so deeply impressed with the necessity of this step, that they will freely offer their assistance to accomplish it and let all bear in mind the precept of our Holy Redeemer, 'Therefore, all things whatsoever ye would that men should do to you, do ye even so to them.' Should the company perform that act of justice which is sought at their hands, we entertain the hope that it would in no small degree promote the righteous cause of emancipation in Brazil, and in other parts of the world.

"For ourselves, we feel it a solemn duty to protest against the employment of slave-labour by the Imperial Brazilian Mining Company and express our determination to use our most earnest exertions to prevent its continuance, whenever an opportunity is afforded.

Signed

"EDWARD HARRIS, London.
"GEORGE THOMAS, Bristol[2]
"EDWARD THOMAS, Bristol
"JOSEPH FRY, Bristol[3]
"FRANCIS FRY, Bristol
"RICHARD FRY, Bristol
"HENRY TUCKETT, London.[4]

"Any communication on the subject may be addressed to Henry Tuckett, at No. 7, South-street, Finsbury.
"London, 4th mo. 26th, 1841."

The CHAIRMAN opened the business of the meeting by reading the report of the Directors.

Mr. GIBSON,[5] the treasurer of the Company, read the statement of accounts.

The CHAIRMAN then said. – As our time advances rapidly, and the report has been a very long one, I will proceed at once to the usual business of the day. The resolution which I have to propose is, "That the report and statement of accounts now read be received and adopted, and that the same, together with the appendix, be printed, at the discretion of the directors, for the use of the proprietors."

Mr. GEORGE THOMAS. – I suppose that the adoption of that report would not preclude me from making the motion which the requisition has given notice of.

Mr. GIBSON – O! certainly it would.

Mr. THOMAS. – In that case I must move an amendment to that report, and the amendment which I propose is as follows: – "That measures be taken immediately to emancipate the slaves held by this company, and to secure to them their future freedom." It is very nearly in the words of the requisition. I shall move that as an amendment, if I am to be precluded from moving it in any other shape. I observe that, in the report delivered by the directors, they have stated that the gentlemen who have signed the requisition have been shareholders for a number of years; that various reports have been sent out, in which it has been stated that slaves were employed by the company, and that they conceive that that fact is incompatible with the declaration of the requisitionists, that they were ignorant that slaves were employed in these mines. But I beg leave to state to the directors, that we do not say that we were at a late time ignorant of the fact, but "unknowingly in the first instance;" and I would put it to this meeting, how it is possible for any member of this association to be acquainted with that fact, till he actually becomes a member of the association. There is no such thing as a report sent to a person before he buys the shares; and therefore how is he to know that? I think this is a complete answer to that point. However, I do state for myself, and I believe I may state for my friends, that we were ignorant, entirely ignorant, in the first instance, of these mines being worked by slaves. (Cries of Oh! oh!).

I can only say for myself, gentlemen may believe me, or not believe me, as they please, that I did suppose that these mines were worked entirely by British miners, because I had an opportunity of seeing that Cornish miners were sent out. Immediately after discovering that we were so circumstanced, (it was with great regret that we discovered it) we did, through our friend Samuel Waring,[6] who was, I believe, well acquainted with many of the directors, make efforts to get an alteration made, or ameliorations carried into effect for the benefit of the slaves. Those ameliorations have been alluded to in the report of the directors which has been read this morning; and we do not mean to call in question the statement that some ameliorations have been carried into effect by the directors. If I mistake not, a resolution was passed in 1830 to emancipate the children, and I believe, in 1833, provision was made for their education. Then, besides that, there was a resolution, or at least an instruction – I believe I gathered so much from the report – an instruction to the chief commissioner, that he might, under certain conditions, liberate a certain number of adults yearly, not exceeding ten.

Now the ground of our calling this meeting is, that we were satisfied at that time with the steps taken by the directors to ameliorate the condition of the negro population; but, from certain documents which have been printed – we disclaim those of Mr. Kentish[7] entirely, that individual being actuated by mercenary motives, and we agree in what the directors say upon that point. But, if the directors are to bring forward evidence to support their report, namely, that of the officers of the company, surely those who have signed the requisition have an equal right to appeal to documents issued by those very gentlemen (I mean Mr Bayly[8] and Colonel Skerrett),[9] to show that the directors have gone in a retrograde course, rather than forward. That is one point which has made the gentlemen who have signed the requisition uncomfortable; that the original intentions of the directors, instead of being carried out, have been either relaxed or given up. In order to show that, I shall read to this meeting certain documents, signed by the two gentlemen who have been so largely quoted in the report today. The first is signed, "H. L. Bayly."

A PROPRIETOR. – What is the date, pray?

Mr. THOMAS. – It is dated the 16th of November, 1840. I will first state, that the Directors having identified the statements of Mr. Bayly, I need not produce proofs of it. In this letter, which is dated the 16th of November, 1840. –

A PROPRIETOR. – From whence?

Mr. THOMAS. – Rathfarnham, county of Dublin. In this letter he says, "Women, when pregnant, do not work for two months previous to their confinement; they remain all day in a large shed, taking care of the younger children (this was the regular rule); and formerly they went to hospital a month or more before they expected to be confined. I am sorry, however, to say, that the system had been altered after the departure of Dr. Collier,[10] when they were prohibited from going to hospital till they were in daily expectation of being confined, and, in one instance, a woman was confined in her own house; this was owing to her not having been admitted into hospital when her time for so doing had arrived. Late regulations prohibited the slaves from remaining in hospital, unless they were severely ill. Numbers have informed me that they could not work on account of illness, and that, when they went to hospital, they were told they were not ill, and they must go back to their work. I immediately, when they appeared to me to be ill, sent them back to hospital, and this in many instances several times; when they were, with few exceptions, again sent back to me. When this failed, I had no alternative left but to keep them in the wine shed, where several were obliged to remain for many days, quite incapable of doing any work. Here they were exposed to the draught of an open shed, where children were playing and making a noise all the day. This gave me great pain; and, after I had remonstrated with the doctor, I was driven to the painful alternative of reporting the matter officially in writing, but I am sorry to say, without effect – which made me feel that I was not properly supported, and made me desirous of quitting the service. The injurious result this had generally, together with the severe regulations adopted in the hospital, made me acquainted with many cases amongst the blacks of persons severely ill, which they would rather endure than subject themselves to the treatment they met with in hospital, or to be told they were only skulking. A long correspondence took place between Mr. Duval and myself on this subject, but I am sorry to say it ended like most other things, without redress, which determined me to give it up, which I did in disgust."

A PROPRIETOR. – Who is this person?

Mr. THOMAS. – The late Superintendent of the Gongo Soco slaves.

A PROPRIETOR. – Did he retire, or was he discharged?

The CHAIRMAN. – He retired in consequence of ill health.

Mr. THOMAS. – I will also read to you another extract, in order to show that the Directors recognise the statements of this gentleman; it is from a letter signed J. C. and H. Freshfield,[11] and addressed to the editor of the *Anti-Slavery Reporter*, October 21st, 1840. "The Directors, some months since, extracted from a letter of your correspondent, the principal charges which appear to be reiterated, nearly verbatim, in your paper; and we now transmit to you these, with the replies they received from a gentleman who had the charge of the blacks on their establishment for seven years, from 1832 to 1839, and who, having left the service of the association, had no inducement to represent any facts otherwise than as they really existed." I read this in order to show that the Directors identify themselves with this gentleman, and that he was a servant of the company.

Then as to the stop put to emancipation, he states this: "I have always regretted the stop put to emancipation by Mr. Duval, of course with the sanction of the board, as having had the very worst possible effect. The emulation it created to obtain that greatest of all boons to this unfortunate class of persons, and the success which attended the experiment was, at one period, beyond the expectations of the most sanguine – nothing could surpass it; their conduct was the admiration of every one possessing a heart to appreciate it. This continued till after the arrival of Mr. Duval, when he informed me he would not free any more, because it had been found not to answer. Because, truly, three or four out of fifteen had behaved ill after his arrival in Gongo, the remaining 288 were therefore to suffer perpetual slavery on their account! Surely it would be expecting too much, to suppose that a man brought up in slavery and in ignorance could change his nature in a day.

What I saw of emancipation in Gongo answered my utmost expectations; many were the appeals to me, why it was not to continue; and I am confident that, from the hour I was obliged to make Mr. Duval's sentiments known to them, they never were the same. There were many at that time who ought to have had, and did expect their freedom; and I am prepared at this moment with the names of a dozen, at least, who would now be enjoying that blessing, had Mr. Avaline[12] lived to avail himself of the consent obtained from the board by his predecessor. About five months after the arrival of Mr. Duval at Gongo, the slaves became so careless and indifferent" – now mark the effects gentlemen – "and crime gradually increased to so serious an extent, in consequence of an altered and new system attempted by him, that I was obliged to represent very strongly to Mr. Duval, that, unless some prompt means were put in force to stop it, I could not possibly answer for the consequences; and I begged to assure him, I would not remain longer in the service of the association than to the expiration of my then engagement, 10th of January, 1837. Soon after this, an order was issued, in which the entire charge of the slaves was handed over to me, and which remained in force up to the time of my departure."

Now, that is one of the facts which I have to bring forward, to show that, in the opinion of this gentleman, the directors, instead of carrying out those good intentions which they formed in 1830 and 1833, were taking a retrograde motion. Now, from the same authority, though not from the same individual, but from the authority quoted by the directors in their report, I have from another late officer of the company information which fully bears me out in saying, that such was the state of the case at least if the documents themselves are to be depended upon. This is from Colonel Skerrett, dated January 8th, 1841, from Ireland. "I shall confine myself to what I know or heard from the latter part of 1829 to 1835 inclusive, during which I positively deny, in the most unqualified terms, that a single sentiment was ever expressed by the directors, either verbally or in their letters, publicly or privately, collectively or individually, that did not manifest the most perfect humanity and unsparing liberality towards the negros of the company." I beg to say, that nobody wishes to deny this statement; all that we want is that they should carry out their own views at that time, and carry them a little further. "And if they did not go quite so far with me in the last act of bounty (strongly as I urged it) I was myself sensible of the obstacles that opposed it, in the customs and prejudices of Brazil, and the guardianship of those interests over which they presided; nor could I flatter myself that no considerations, no representations, and no views, but those of their commissioner, would find favour in the calm deliberations of a distant board, subject to be misled by plausible, ignorant, or designing parties. I was therefore satisfied with the permission humanely and generously granted, to proceed in the experiment already commenced in 1833 at my own risk, trusting to its ultimate extension in proportion to its success. Before I received the appointment of commissioner in 1829, my sentiments were investigated respecting the treatment of slaves. I fully expressed my disgust at what I had witnessed at the Cape of Good Hope, and stated fairly that I had brought the subject before the commissioners of inquiry in that colony, &c. &c. If the directors of the Imperial Brazilian Mining Company did not approve of this, why did they elect me? But, so far from differing with me on the subject – "

A PROPRIETOR. – I beg pardon for the interruption; but perhaps you will have the goodness to say, whether what you are reading from is circulated through the country?

Mr. THOMAS. – Yes.

A PROPRIETOR. – Have you any objection to mention the name of it?

Mr. THOMAS. – The *Anti-Slavery Reporter*, of January 13th, 1841. "They assured me that their commissioner would be encouraged to use every exertion for the civilization and comfort of the negros, that the amelioration of their condition was only a preliminary to education and every improvement of which they were susceptible, that *every child born on the property was to be actually free from its birth*; and they allowed me to infer, that, on our success and my future reports, would depend that which I looked forward to with the deepest anxiety, the blessing of emancipation, at least to the deserving. With this understanding I arrived at Gongo Soco. The slaves presented a better and more healthy appearance than those I had previously met with; it was evident that the company had not limited the expenses of this part of the establishment, but it was equally so that it required the eye of an active and honourable man to protect them. The contractor for their meat was dismissed for fraud, and a new system of messing them adopted, which insured regularity and abundance of excellent food. That they had not acquired the Portuguese language sufficiently, was the cause assigned by the paid Padre for their total ignorance of the worship of the country; and Sunday with them was passed in dancing, and occasionally in riot, till put down, with indiscriminate violence, as a boasted exploit. An appeal to their reason, accompanied with encouraging promise of reward, was adopted, and found to be quite sufficient; and the strictest orders were issued against any sort of ill-treatment by the English. Their motley and fantastic appearance was represented to the board, and uniform and respectable clothing recommended – the directors sent out forthwith a most liberal supply for both sexes: their bedding was that common to the lower orders in all warm climates, and never was complained of. Medals for good conduct were next suggested; they were as promptly provided, and the comfort, emulation, and good order of this little colony soon became the theme of general observation.

"But I could not carry out my object entirely to my satisfaction, until the arrival of Mr. Bayly. Under that gentleman's zealous superintendency, I no longer apprehended secret violence, either on the part of the miners or the feitors (native overseers, frequently very worthless characters). From the commencement of his guardianship, the improvement in their condition became more rapid; the negros responded to his exertions, they felt that they could not any longer be ill-treated without my knowledge, or with impunity; and that, although their testimony might be rejected in a Brazilian court, in the jurisdiction to which they were then subjected it was respected. It would be absurd to suppose, that from three to four hundred human beings were to be at once released from all liability to punishment or restraint. It is enough, therefore, to say, that, within the period embraced in this statement, there was not a tenth part of the crime or penalty I have witnessed through life amongst the same number of Europeans, nor was there a single instance." –

A PROPRIETOR. – Really, Mr. Chairman, I beg to speak to the point of order. If this gentleman is reading from published documents, I should like to know how much time he means to occupy. Everything we have heard yet is in favour of what the Directors have already told us; and as many gentlemen, who are quite averse to that gentleman's principles, are leaving the room, I think it is only fair that he should tell us how much time he means to occupy.

Mr. THOMAS. – I should think ten minutes would be ample. The fact is, I have nothing to found my case upon but these documents. I have no access to the books of the company, and therefore cannot see what there is there. "It is enough, therefore, to say, that, within the period embraced in this statement, there was not a tenth part of the crime or penalty I have witnessed through life, amongst the same number of Europeans, nor was there a single instance of hasty or severe coercion – the profligacy of ruffians, and its lamented effects, were not chargeable to a management instituted for the prevention or punishment of brutality, and the protection of the weak. Such was the principle on which Mr. Bayly acted during my residence at Gongo, and his feelings were at least rewarded by the devoted gratitude and affection of the poor blacks. The deaths (vide 15th report of the company) decreased. The casualties of 1826-27-28-29, and 30, amounted to more than a hundred, for the succeeding eighteen months only to one; and at length, such was the excellent conduct of the negros that I felt justified in urging the board to sanction the emancipation of the most deserving." Now that is one of the points to which I wish particularly to call your attention; that the board did agree to a certain number of adults being emancipated year after year, and I believe it cannot be said, that they still go on with that practice.

Mr. GIBSON. – Will you allow me to say, that we were never asked to do it. We proposed it.

Mr. THOMAS. – "I, in fact, had commenced the experiment, and soon after received permission to proceed in it, at the limited rate of ten per annum. This long promised boon was attended with the happiest results. Those who were freed (and they were, with one exception, in the full prime of youth) became, if possible, more zealous in their duties and attachment, generously remaining on very trifling wages" – bear that in mind – "generously remaining on very trifling wages, rather than leave their benefactors, though they were qualified, either as tradesmen or labourers, to obtain the highest elsewhere. They were likewise actuated by a generous desire to encourage the emancipation of their comrades, continuance of that conduct by which they had secured their own. Such was the grateful and noble return of these admirable people" – to work for less wages than they could get elsewhere. "In what country was it ever surpassed? No assumption of superiority was for one moment visible, no symptoms of pride; in all things they were modest, grateful, and obedient, advancing in respectability to the hour of my departure, an hour I shall not easily forget. Is it then extraordinary that I find it difficult to believe their very natures could have altered, that they who for a year-and-a-half proved zealous and affectionate servants, could suddenly by an opposite course, have justified the retraction of a blessing to which all had been permitted to aspire?"

Now I think that I have shown you that the directors have gone backwards, if this report is to be depended upon; and I have nothing else to appeal to, but that which I see printed. "A blessing, my humble instrumentality in which was the principal solace of my arduous position for so many years, and I am confident at that time sincerely participated by all the directors. Their word once passed, it was received by the negros as an irrevocable decree. On the faith of it (I cannot shrink from the avowal) they worked under a delusion, which, although never designed, was, in its bitter effects, not less fatal to their confidence in that high character established for their masters, and which can only be restored by a discharge of the debt contracted on their written authority. Not sixteen, but seventy-three slaves would now have been emancipated, fifty-seven of whom are at this moment still subject to the evils of bondage, and who would, I am confident, have been all voluntary labourers in the company's service, had faith been kept with them, and the system of superintendence remained unchanged. I am entirely ignorant of the cause of their heart-rending disappointment, or whether the children (many of them are now from twelve to fourteen years old) have been either educated, or made acquainted with their freedom. But I must, in the latter case, candidly state the difficulty of the board, as to the proper moment for promulgating this happy intelligence, unless the parents likewise were to enjoy the same blessing. All the best affections of their nature might otherwise have been outraged; and it was on this account that I considered it, not only prudent, but humane, to leave the infant part of this establishment, nearly six years younger than at present, in ignorance of the blessing they were then incompetent to appreciate, but of which they might have availed themselves in a manner highly prejudicial to the comfort and authority of their less fortunate parents."

I will now just allude to a subject which I brought before the directors about three years ago. I then recommended the directors to take precisely the same line of conduct which I recommend to them now. In a private letter, which I addressed to the directors, I recommended the emancipation of the negros at that time, and stated my unwillingness, and that I should not, unless they assented to the proposition, to receive any future dividends from the company. And I explain this, that may not appear to be at all inconsistent; because, although I have not received those dividends, it would appear as though my agents had done so for me. My agents, Messrs. Foster and Braithwaite have received them, (a laugh,) gentlemen before they laugh, will just understand that I have not received them for my own benefit, but that I have paid over the amount received for those dividends to the Anti-Slavery Society. Now I think I have shown clearly, that certain promises which were made through the officers of the company have not been fulfilled. The expectation was certainly held out, that ten at least of the adults belonging to the company should be released every year, and Colonel Skerrett says, that if that had been carried into effect, there would have been seventy-three persons at this moment enjoying their freedom. I think I have, as a shareholder, a right to complain that the directors have not carried out their own views; but, if they had, I should not feel, under present circumstances satisfied with that. If I were to read some other things, it would be seen by the same evidence, (I believe given to the company themselves,) that flogging exists at the mines in Brazil.

A PROPRIETOR. – Not of females, I think.

Mr. THOMAS. – Not of females, but of males; and I think from the same testimony it appears, that 100 lashes is the highest amount.

A PROPRIETOR. – He states that five-and-twenty lashes given in the army, are equal in severity to 100 in Brazil.

Mr. THOMAS. – This is from the same letter that I have quoted before. "Whenever it was necessary to punish, they were always sent to hospital after it, where they remained in general but a few minutes; the number of lashes never exceeded 100, nor did they ever amount to that, but in two or three instances, all the time I was there. The cat-o'-nine-tails is much the same as that used in the army, but not so severe."

A PROPRIETOR. – You remember, Sir, the medical man stated, that 100 lashes given there was not so severe a punishment as five-and-twenty given here.

Mr. THOMAS. – Very well, I have no objection to admit that it is so stated. But I would also state, for the information of the proprietors, that the directors have only received one account of the punishments inflicted upon negros. I understand that to be a declaration they have made to a friend of mine.

Mr. GIBSON. – It is a mistake.

Mr. TUCKETT (to Mr. Gibson). – You remember that I asked for a statement, and the reply was, it had not been received for many years.

A PROPRIETOR. – If the gentleman is going for any specific point, he had better state it. If he only means to say that certain recommendations have not been attended to, I dare say the directors will be happy to investigate that point; but, if he means to come to the general subject of emancipation, he would do well to state it; because, whether flogging has been excessive in one instance, or the terms have not been properly observed in another, becomes quite another consideration. Let him go upon the broad question, whether emancipation is to be carried out or not; that is the point submitted for our discussion this day. It is not whether the directors, in the flogging which has been inflicted, have or have not exceeded a certain point of severity. Let us only know the point he is drawing our attention to.

Mr. THOMAS. – I am going to refer to that point, but I think it is of great importance to state to the meeting, that the resolutions formed many years ago have been rather relaxed than carried out.

A PROPRIETOR. – Then ask the directors to strengthen them.

Mr. THOMAS. – My argument tends to show that there is no safety in any scheme but entire emancipation; because, if you are satisfied today that the directors will do what is right, and they go next year from their resolution formed to-day, what reliance can you place upon the resolutions of the directors? I think you will see clearly from the letters of Colonel Skerrett and Mr. Bayly, that the alteration of the system has produced disobedient conduct in the negro population, and that so long as those ameliorations were carried on, the behaviour of the people was better. Now, I mean to say, that as a matter of sound policy, it is better for us to emancipate the negros than to keep them in a state of bondage; because you have proof from your own accounts, that they actually behaved better in a state of freedom, and were willing to work for less wages than they could get from other persons. What can more strongly show that it is consistent with sound policy to emancipate these negros? Now, we have proof, we have strong proof, that it would be the wisest course to grant the whole boon. In order to show that, I will bring forward the case of Antigua. Antigua is the only island, which I am aware of, that did not adopt the apprenticeship, or the gradual system of emancipation, but proceeded immediately to grant emancipation. What has been the effect of that? Why, that the whole island has doubled the amount of produce since the act of emancipation, and the planters themselves declare that the whole of the compensation granted to them by the act of emancipation, was clear profit. Why can we not suppose, that, if we adopted the same liberal policy, it would be attended with the same results? I say it would.

A PROPRIETOR. – Different kingdoms, sir.

Mr. THOMAS. – That makes no difference. A certain line of conduct will produce certain consequences. Then, when we come to consider that this country, England, has condemned the system; that it is contrary to the laws of this country to hold slave property, why should we, sitting in this room, be in a different position from our fellow countrymen? Why should we avail ourselves of the situation in which we are placed, to refuse to do that which our own country has done as a country?

A PROPRIETOR. – We are subject to the government.

Mr. THOMAS. – We have a right to deal with our own property, though we are subject to the government. The minister of Brazil has said that nothing stands in the way of emancipation, that the laws afford a facility for it, rather than otherwise, so that argument will not avail. The laws of England consider the holding of slave property as felony.* Why should we put ourselves in such a position? I do not conceive that a number of gentlemen assembled as English merchants, which I suppose most of the gentlemen present are, would like to put themselves in a different position from all their countrymen, simply because they have it in their power to do so; but that they would be regulated and governed in their public conduct by the same rule as those who live under English laws and English government. But now I come to another and more important reason, namely, that, in a religious point of view, we are called upon to grant emancipation. We do – I suppose we all do, profess christianity. If so, we have no right to hold a fellow creature in bondage, whatever we may consider expedient. There is an inalienable right to freedom in every man. The Creator has created all men alike. He has created all nations of one blood, and therefore they have all equal rights in his sight. And we are commanded to do justly, and to love mercy, and to walk humbly with our God; if we do so, we certainly cannot be owners of slave property. If we would do justly, we must put them in the same position as ourselves. I am sure no man would think, if I had the power to take the chairman this morning, and convert him into a slave, and should exercise that power, that that would be doing justly. And I don't know that we have any greater right to do so in the case of these poor creatures. It is a mere exercise of power, which does not only a deal of mischief to those who are under its influence, but to those who exercise it. I believe the effect upon those who exercise it, is quite as bad as upon those who are subject to it, and that it does in a great measure harden their feelings. If you are not desirous to act upon the principle, "do unto others, as you would be done by," then I don't know that I have any hope of your voting for this resolution; but I do submit that you ought to do so as a company of professing christians. Having now, as I think, very fairly brought the matter before the present meeting, I conceive that the responsibility of holding these people in bondage will rest with those who support the system. I believe that there is a certain amount of guilt attached to our maintaining the position which we occupy. I think we have too long suffered this question to remain where it is, and that we ought, as Englishmen, to take some steps upon it.

The CHAIRMAN. – There is one point, gentlemen, upon which I wish to make a remark, and I will not take up more than a minute of your time. Colonel Skerrett received his orders from the board. Now he was sent out in 1833. He tried the system in 1834, and came away in 1835; consequently he could not have been long enough there to know the effect of it. The effect we learned from Mr. Duval, and upon that ground we proceeded. We are told we have been going back. We did not withdraw our order till the system had been tried, and was proved to have failed; nor have we ever withdrawn it. With regard to flogging, we sent out some time ago unconditional orders to put a stop to it entirely.

Mr. GOLDSMID.[13] – I should not trouble this meeting –

Mr. R. FRY. – I think in common courtesy, the Chairman should allow the resolution to be seconded.

Mr. GOLDSMID. – I beg your pardon, I am sure.

Mr. E. HARRIS. – I beg to second the motion.

The CHAIRMAN. – The amendment which has been proposed is as follows: – "That measures be taken immediately to emancipate the slaves held by this company, and to secure to them their future freedom."

Mr. GOLDSMID. – Before that amendment is put, I only beg leave to say a very few words on this occasion. Having taken a very active part in the formation of this company, I beg leave just to say a few words. There is no person who entertains more respect than I do for the humane feeling which dictated this. There is no person who respects that body of men, (the Society of Friends) more sincerely and affectionately than I do. I have been connected with them from the earliest period of my life. I was connected with them in various committees on a variety of subjects, and followed their steps as much as I could, both upon the subject of prison discipline, and the punishment of death; and therefore I blindly (almost blindly) would have been ready, if I were not placed in the situation in which I now stand, to have admitted their proposition. But I have been a director ever since the formation of the company; and, holding that position, I must say that I widely differ from them on this subject. When this company was originally formed, I considered that it would not be wise to employ slaves, and the consequence was, that I was doubtful whether it ought to be entertained. But I consulted an excellent friend of mine, Mr. Joseph Fry,[14] and I am sure I cannot mention that name without mentioning in connexion with it that most amiable woman, Mrs. Fry, to say that all the acts of her life were devoted to philanthropy and kindness and he never would have joined in an undertaking of this kind – no money could have tempted him – if it had not been for the performance of a great work. Great moral good was performed, by setting an example of good conduct in the management of slaves in the midst of a large population. Now, how was that accomplished? Not by violence, but by an attempt to improve their condition. Now that condition could only be improved by example. Consider how widely different this is from colonies where the whole body are to be emancipated. Consider that here is a million and a half of slaves; and we have a handful; and that it is only by kind treatment that we have induced those around us to follow that example. Can it be doubted, after the statements made by various persons unconnected with the company, and after the statements used by the gentleman, who tells you frankly that he has nothing to support the proposition but his humane feelings, except the testimony of Colonel Skerrett and Mr. Bayly – the greater portion of that tells, I am sure they themselves would say, tells in favour of us? – If there have been any aberrations from the right course, it has been only in consequence of a difference of opinion having existed between Colonel Skerrett and his successor. The whole question turns upon that. You have one of two courses to pursue. Either to emancipate your slaves, and, in consequence, to create dissatisfaction and disgust in the minds of those around – perhaps the probability is, that they would be either kidnapped or absorbed into the slave population; or to take them away altogether. Do not you destroy the moral effect which we anticipated at the commencement of this establishment, by taking away the example? What hope can there be ever after, of inducing the Brazilians to follow the bright example which this company may set? What have they to follow but the example which you set? As far as I am personally concerned, it is of very little consequence what is done; I have only 75 shares, which is about £400; and I would give ten times that amount, if we could but induce the Brazilians, which is the great object and desire that I believe we all have, to emancipate their slaves. Their emancipation is to be expected and hoped for, by the slow process of convincing them that they should do good to their fellow men, by the example which we shall set them, not by the untimely and hurried efforts made by the friends of humanity to deprive them of that example. Under these circumstances, I am quite sure that the humane gentlemen themselves will see the wisdom of withdrawing their amendment, in order to make it a unanimous feeling that we should leave the directors themselves, their minds, their own intentions, their hearts devoted to ameliorating the condition of the slaves.

If they were to see what unfortunately they have not seen of late years, that the condition of the older blacks would be improved by emancipation, depend upon it the directors would emancipate them. But, as to the children, what better could you expect than that, at the age of twenty-one, they have pledged themselves that they shall be emancipated? How could they better instruct and teach those around them, than by the example of good conduct set by these children? I am quite sure that the directors have done the utmost in their power, that, if there have been these changes, it has not been their fault; and that they were not stimulated by the inducements of their friends here to urge them forward, but by their own feelings. Under these circumstances I do hope that my friends – I am sure they will allow me to call them so – no man feels more disposed to call them so, or to lend himself to their good works; but I trust that they will give their support and confidence to the directors, and, instead of finding fault with what we have done, strengthen our hands. The gentleman has stated that the government of Brazil gives every facility to emancipation. I think we have a letter in our possession, which would show very distinctly that the Brazilian government have not moved either one way or the other, that they have not at all interfered with emancipation, and have expressed no opinion; but it must be for the gentlemen themselves to determine, whether they can desire to see the emancipation of two or three hundred men in the midst of a slave population of a million and a half. There is one important circumstance mentioned in the report, which is, that we have so kindly treated our slaves, that a number of persons have come to us in order to be taken into our service. Under these circumstances, I hope and trust that the gentleman will withdraw his motion.

Mr. R. FRY. – Considering the long report which has been read, I trust I may be allowed to address you for five minutes. I was one of those who signed and circulated the address. My name is Richard Fry. I live in Bristol. I mention that to show that I am not the gentleman who has been alluded to by Isaac L. Goldsmid. I respond, I am sure, to the name he gave me, a friend; and I wish to return it to him. I wish to call every man my brother, and my friend. I wish to say something in explanation of the introductory part of the address, which states that, when we became proprietors we did not know that there were slaves employed by this company. When I first became a proprietor of these mines, I was of the age of twenty-one, and was engaged in a mercantile counting-house in this city. One morning by post I received a transfer of the shares; my kind father made me a present of certain shares in this company. I knew nothing about the company, about mines in Brazil, or mines in Cornwall: whether they were worked by blacks or whites; and therefore, gentlemen, for myself, what I state is perfectly true. I did not know that these mines were worked by slaves. I trust, gentlemen, that you will believe me for myself.

A PROPRIETOR. – Ten years ago?

Mr. FRY. – I think it is twelve. (Here considerable impatience was manifested by several proprietors). Be patient, gentlemen, we gave the chairman a very fair hearing. I must throw myself upon the chairman.

A PROPRIETOR. – I hope the gentleman will consider the time of the meeting, and compress his observations.

Mr. FRY. – So I will; but we are assembled for an important purpose. I wish to do my duty, and to throw the responsibility off my own shoulders, and on yours. I hope you will take it. Mr. Goldsmid has spoken of the propriety of setting a good example, by treating our slaves well. I fully agree with him, that, inasmuch as you treat your slaves well, you set a good example; but, if we do to them as we should be done by, should we not set them a much better example? (A voice, "No, you would do much harm.") No, gentlemen, we should be then doing to others as we would be done by. (Cries of "question.")

The CHAIRMAN. – We will not keep you more than a few minutes.

Mr. FRY. – If I did, I maintain that I have a full right to keep you as long as I please.

A PROPRIETOR. – We cannot stay any longer; you positively said that you would only detain us five minutes.

The CHAIRMAN. – It really is, gentlemen, a matter of such vital importance that this question should be set at rest to-day, and with, as I believe it will be, an overwhelming majority, that I should be sorry indeed if you were to go away; because I should be sorry to see a small majority. I think it would be tantamount to a disapproval of our conduct.

Mr. FRY. – If you will have the goodness to listen to me, I will keep my promise. A gentleman spoke of kidnapping; if you observe the words of the resolution, we provide for that by saying, "secure to the slaves their future freedom." With regard to the policy of the thing, I believe it is always the best policy to do that which is right, to do to others as we would be done by, and that will secure to us prosperity. I hope that every gentleman present will lay it to his conscience, before he gives his vote, whether he believes that he is acting up to the precepts of the New Testament.

A PROPRIETOR. – You must submit youself to the powers that be.

Mr. FRY. – Yes; your own power is to liberate these slaves. I am much obliged to you for listening to me.

A PROPRIETOR. – Will the gentleman allow me to ask him a question? Has he, or has he not, sold any of his shares, since he became a proprietor?

Mr. FRY. – I have not.

A PROPRIETOR. – Why not?

Mr. FRY. – Because I will keep them, to endeavour to use any power or influence which I have to set at liberty the slaves. That is the motive by which we are all influenced. I have held these shares when I could have sold them at a considerable profit, but I kept them for that purpose.

Mr. GRAY. – The gentleman who proposed the motion, said, that he considered his statement was confirmed. He copiously referred to a publication which I never saw before. In some parts of that quotation he did great justice to Colonel Skerrett. I should certainly not object to their dealing as they please with other people's property. It is quite clear, as Mr. Goldsmid has said, that, if you were to emancipate the slaves, they would only fall into worse hands, and that they would exchange a state of comparative happiness for one of great hardship. I was really surprised at the statement made by a gentleman to the meeting, that he was perfectly ignorant of the mode of carrying on mining in Brazil. I did suppose, that the Society of Friends, who were very anxious to acquire knowledge, must have read some history of Brazil, and, if so, must have come to the conviction that the laborious part of the work was carried on by slaves. Abstractedly, I am as great an enemy to slavery as any man can be; but I think it is the bounden duty of every person, before he votes for the emancipation, to consider, whether it will be a benefit to those who are emancipated. I quite agree that the course recommended by the gentleman is dictated by the humanest feelings; but, if their advice is adopted, it must end in the complete destruction of the property. Mr. Macaulay,[15] the other night, stated, with much force and propriety, that it was the bounden duty of this country to suppress slavery in its own dominions; but that we have no right to interfere with the internal slavery of other countries. If the society for the suppression of slavery would subscribe to buy the property, I am quite ready to give up my share to them. There is no analogy between the case of Antigua and Brazil. The gentleman said, that cultivation in Antigua had gone on since the emancipation much more successfully than it did before; but, in the first instance, they were compensated for the value of their slaves. I say, compensate me, and take the slaves.

A PROPRIETOR (to Mr. Thomas). – You have made strong allusions to those slaves who have been emancipated by the instructions of the directors. Pray, sir, have you any account how many of those men that were liberated turned out well, and how many badly? Because it is very likely, and very possible, that the whole ten per year that were emancipated (and as you say there would by this time be 70) would be bad. I think it is desirable to know whether the older slaves were entirely good after they were emancipated. There can be no doubt as to the propriety of emancipating children, when they arrive at the age of twenty-one.

Mr. THOMAS. – I think I may be allowed to say a few words in reply.

A PROPRIETOR. – I only ask, have you any statement of that kind?

THE CHAIRMAN (to Mr. Thomas). – Have you any such statement?

A PROPRIETOR. – From what I can understand, they have generally turned out badly.

Mr. THOMAS. – Why? Simply because of disappointment; their just expectations not being realised, and that which was promised being withheld, that was the reason. Colonel Skerrett and Mr. Bayly both say so distinctly. (Cries of chair, chair.) I would just say in reply to the gentlemen who are opposed to us, that honesty is the best policy, and that we cannot without being dishonest retain these people in slavery against their will. (Cries of "question"). The Chairman here intimated that, as Mr. Thomas was the mover of an amendment, he had no right of reply.

The CHAIRMAN then put the amendment and called upon those who were in favour of it to signify the same by holding up their bands. Seven hands only were held up for the amendment. The Chairman then put the original resolution, which was carried.

*By the Consolidated Slave-trade Act of 1824, the purchase, or any participation in the purchase of a slave, by a British subject, is felony.[16]

Notes

1 Joshua Walker (1786–1862) was the founding chairman of the IBMC and remained in that position into the 1850s. He was also a director of the Sheffield & Rotherham Bank from the 1820s until 1862, a director of the London & Westminster Bank from 1847 to 1862, and a Conservative MP from 1818 until 1829. With his brother, he inherited his family's iron and lead manufacturing business.

2 George Thomas (1791–1869) was a wholesale grocer from Bristol; he and his brother Edward (1789–1849) were also involved in two local gas-lighting companies. He was active in the Bristol Chamber of Commerce and the Bristol General Hospital and was a town councilor from 1835 through 1852. Edward Thomas, an active temperance reformer, left £120,000 (mostly to George), including a fortune in canal shares. Both were lifelong abolitionists and devout Quakers.

3 Joseph Storrs Fry (1769–1835) married Ann Allen (1764–1829) in 1794 and took over his father's chocolate business the following year. After his business partner died in 1822, he changed the firm's name from Fry and Hunt to J. S. Fry and Sons; his three sons, Joseph (1795–1879), Francis (1803–1886), and Richard (1807–1878), became junior partners in what was by that time Britain's largest chocolate manufacturer. Francis took a leading role in its management after his father's death and also sat on the board of five railways, Bristol's waterworks, and Bristol's philosophical society and subscription library. He was also active in the British and Foreign Bible Society and in anti-slavery causes.

4 Henry Tuckett, Quaker physician and cousin of the abolitionist Thomas Hodgkin, was the first Treasurer of the British and Foreign Aborigines' Protection Society. He was also active in the British and Foreign Anti-Slavery Society and the British and Foreign School Society.

5 Thomas Gibson was a founding IBMC director and became its chair in the 1850s.

6 Samuel Waring was a Bristol shipping agent in the 1820s and 1830s who remitted IBMC funds to its agent in Brazil, Edward Oxenford, in 1830.

7 F. A. Kentish was a former IBMA clerk who assisted George Thomas's efforts to expose the company's labor practices.

8 H. L. Bayly was a superintendent of the IBMC mine in Gongo Soco under George Duval; he moved to Rathfarnham, a Dublin suburb, after leaving the company's service.

9 Lieut. Col. J. M. A. Skerrett was a former director of the IBMC and its chief commissioner in Brazil from 1830 to 1835. An early historian of the company reported that his "judicious military discipline" had "kept the mine 'in apple-pie order,'" but he returned to England when the company refused his demand for a raise in salary from £2000 to £3000 per year.

10 Richard Collier joined the IBMC in 1833 as an assistant surgeon and remained there through 1837.

11 James William Freshfield (1801–1857), Charles Kaye Freshfield (1808–1891), and Henry Ray Freshfield (1814–1895) became partners in their father J. J. W.'s law firm between 1825 and 1839, working from an office adjacent to the Bank of England. Besides the Bank and the IBMA, the Freshfields represented Royal Exchange Assurance and several prominent aristocratic families.

12 Thomas Avaline replaced Skerret as interim commissioner in 1835 but died within a few weeks of assuming this role.

13 Sir Isaac Lyon Goldsmid (1778–1859) was a stockbroker who was involved in the promotion or direction of numerous railway and dock companies in Britain, Portugal, Turkey, and Brazil, amassing more than £1 million by the time of his death. He was also a patron of University College, London, and worked on behalf of Jewish political emancipation and prison reform.

14 Goldsmid is referring to Joseph Fry (1777–1861), a Quaker banker and tea dealer who lived in London, and his wife Elizabeth (1780–1845), with whom he worked on prison reform. Fry was a cousin of Joseph Storrs Fry, whose three sons attended this meeting.

15 This refers to speech by Thomas Babington Macaulay in Parliament in May 1841, in which he defended the removal of sugar duties against the abolitionist argument that it would promote slavery in Brazil.

16 The Act to Amend and Consolidate the Laws relating to the Abolition of the Slave Trade (5 Geo. 4, c. 113), which passed in 1824, clarified provisions in the 1807 Abolition Act and a subsequent Privy Council order in 1808.

Editorial Headnote

New Zealand Company (1846)

The several colonial land companies that sprang up during the second quarter of the nineteenth century illustrated more clearly than any other case how closely intertwined the corporate form could be with British politics. Following the success of the Canada Company and the British American Land Company, which respectively formed to colonize Lower and Upper Canada (present-day Quebec and Ontario) in 1825 and 1832, company promoters set their eyes on New Zealand.[1] The project passed through many stops and starts, including aborted flotations in 1825 and 1837, and after it finally secured a charter in 1840, land companies passed out of Parliamentary favor. On assuming office in 1841, the Liberal Tory Prime Minister Robert Peel tried to balance the rights of the Māori who resided in New Zealand with those of more than 13,000 British settlers, and he viewed the Company as an impediment to his efforts. By 1846, the New Zealand Company was deep in debt and still lacked secure title to the land it had sold to emigrants. Meanwhile, the Māori spent the 1840s either wrangling with a new Land Commission, which had been established by the Waitangi Treaty of 1840 to compensate for loss of property, or, increasingly, waging war on settlers and colonial officials alike.[2]

In its account of the meeting, *The Morning Post* provided a longer summary of the report, as read by its secretary, T. C. Harrington, than was included in the *London Times* report printed below. It described how the directors had spent the previous six months lobbying William Gladstone, who had taken over as Peel's colonial secretary in December 1845, to "restore confidence in the company's powers . . . to enable them to resume the functions assigned to them by their charter." The report paired this with impatience at George Grey, who had arrived in New Zealand as its new governor with the intention of "subject[ing] the native tribes to the same laws which bound the colonists." It was too late for that, Harrington assured the shareholders, since previous governors' policies had induced the Māori "to despise the power of the white man, to doubt his promises, to laugh at his threats . . . and only to tolerate his presence." He concluded by imploring Peel to "substitut[e] a policy of peace with the natives for the state of war which must continue if the attempt to subject the dense native population to British authority and law should be pursued."[3]

Turning from foreign policy to the company's balance sheet, Harrington proposed dissolution on the grounds that it had spent its £300,000 in paid-up capital as well as the settlers' "purchase money in lands," with no hope of success. As a *Times* editorial opined a few days later: "Bankrupt thus in fortune, frustrated in all their endeavours, and increasingly opposed by a jealous and implacable enemy," delaying dissolution "could only lead them into further expense, and plunge them in a more irretrievable ruin." The editorial fully took the company's side in this dispute, calling it New Zealand's "firm and constant friend," which had "fostered its earliest years, and with watchful care has attended its declining state."[4] Neither the *Times* nor any speakers at the meeting mentioned the right of the Māori to their land, which had been the whole premise of Peel's New Zealand policy.

Peel's defeat as Prime Minister in 1846 briefly breathed new life into the company's hopes. His successor, Lord John Russell, had granted the Company its charter in 1841; the new colonial secretary, Earl Grey (1802–1894 – no relation to George Grey), had been a keen supporter of state-sponsored emigration, and his under-secretary was Benjamin Hawes, a Company director. Within months, the Company secured a £236,000 loan from Russell's ministry, which it used to establish a new settlement in Canterbury on the South Island, and hatched a new scheme to cede control of the North Island to the colonial office and keep the South Island to itself. With little in the way of new land sales by 1850, Grey commenced a drawn-out process of recovering his loan from the Company's paid-up capital. Finally, after a final Parliamentary committee attributed its losses to "rashness and maladministration," it wound up in 1858, leaving in its wake thriving white settlements in Wellington, Nelson, and Otago and a legacy of racial violence and disharmony that would persist for generations.[5]

Notes

1 Cheryl Wahl, "The Business of Settlement: Land Companies and Colonization in the British Empire, ca 1800–1850" (Ph.D. dissertation, City University of New York, 2010), 18–82, 130–134.

2 Wahl, "The Business of Settlement," 135–181; Edward Wakefield, *The Hand-Book for New Zealand* (London: John W. Parker, 1848), 473; James Belich, *The New Zealand Wars and the Victorian Interpretation of Racial Conflict* (Auckland: University of Auckland Press, 2015), 15–72.

3 "The New Zealand Company – Proposed Dissolution," *Morning Post* 30 May 1846.

4 "The New Zealand Company – Proposed Dissolution"; *London Times* 2 June 1846.

5 Patricia Burns, *Fatal Success: A History of the New Zealand* Company (Auckland: Heinemann Reed, 1989), 286–300.

13

NEW ZEALAND COMPANY

Source: New Zealand Company (1846), *London Times*, 30 May 1846

NEW ZEALAND COMPANY

The annual meeting of this company was held yesterday, at 1 o'clock, at the company's offices, Broad-street-buildings, to receive the report of the directors upon the expediency of winding up the affairs of the company. There was a numerous attendance of the directors and proprietors. Viscount Ingestre,[1] M.P., chairman of the Court of Directors, presided.

The CHAIRMAN said the directors felt unabated interest in the magnificent colony of New Zealand; and, if the company were supported by the Government, it would become one of the most important parts of the globe.

The Secretary[2] then read the 20th report of the directors, which complained of the refusal of the Government to legislate upon the affairs of the island until despatches were received from Governor Grey.[3] This the directors considered to be an indefinite postponement, by which a whole year would be lost. "If," the report stated, "the present session should close without the repeal of the act 3 and 4 Victoria, cap. 62,[4] so far as concerned the present despotic government of New Zealand, and the passing of an act authorizing the Crown to grant a charter of government on the old English model, we shall despair of good government for New Zealand." The subscribed capital of 300,000*l*. was expended or mortgaged. A further sum of 300,000*l*. had been expended, which had been paid to the company by settlers as the purchase-money of lands, not an acre of which had yet been obtained. For this great outlay there was no property to show. On the faith of the promise of a loan of 100,000*l*. from the Government the company had obtained a loan from their bankers, which maintained their establishments here and in the settlements. The directors, therefore, recommended the abandonment of the enterprise, and that compensation should be claimed for the losses incurred, in the event of the session closing without such a legislative measure as the directors deemed indispensable.

Mr. AGLIONBY,[5] M.P., moved that the report be received and adopted. The directors had one faint hope, that they might yet obtain redress during the present session, and to that hope they still clung. But if the session passed over without something being done, the directors had nothing to propose, and the proprietors

DOI: 10.4324/9781003177715-15

must, as honourable men, abandon their enterprise. They would only embarrass the settlers and get further into debt by going on. The proprietors had no object but that of the public good in carrying out this undertaking; their object had been to acquire one of the best colonies in the world for the enterprise *of* Englishmen, and to carry the blessings of civilization and Christianity to the natives. The meeting scarcely knew the painful scenes which the directors had to witness from settlers who returned to this country, or the painful letters they received from settlers in the colony who could not obtain a title to their land. They had reason to expect when they parted with their land that they would obtain a title to it, but at this moment they had not done so, the conditional grant offered to them being a mockery of justice. (Hear, hear.) [The hon. member then read an extract from the twelfth report, describing the proceedings in the Court of Land Claims,[6] and the vexatious delay in obtaining awards, owing to the constitution of the court.] When an award was made in favour of the company by Mr. Spain,[7] they only obtained a grant that was valueless; for where the natives happened to have driven off the settlers their "cultivations" would be excepted under the grant in question. Mr. Spain said of the land so awarded that the company had well paid for it, and they ought to have it. In the only case in which the company had got full justice from the Court of Land Claims, viz., in an award in their favour of 60,000 acres at New Plymouth, the governor[8] had refused to confirm the award. Since Mr. Gladstone[9] had entered upon office as Colonial Secretary the company had been in communication with him. They had laid before him a point which did not require to be delayed until the arrival of despatches from Governor Grey – namely, that of a representative system of good government to the company's settlers, which ought to be granted. It was for the proprietors to determine whether the directors had acted wisely in obtaining the power to wind up the affairs of the company. (Cheers.) The pecuniary interests of the proprietors were not an ingredient to be neglected, and if they failed now the directors trusted that after years would do justice to them. He still believed that New Zealand would become what her warmest well-wishers desired.

Mr. C. Buller[10] said, that having taken an active part in Parliament respecting the company's affairs (cheers), he had been asked by the directors to offer a few remarks upon the important report now laid before the meeting. He did hope that the struggle of the New Zealand Company with an adverse Government had come to a satisfactory end last session. It had been admitted that the debates on the subject had disclosed a tale of mismanagement on the part of successive Governments which was the cause of the difficulties of that once thriving settlement. He had hoped that reparation to the company would have been at once made. Nothing could be more satisfactory than the assurances received from the right hon. baronet at the head of the Government during the debates, and he trusted that Government would at once have proceeded to act upon their promises. It was, therefore, with deep mortification he had given his assent to the report, but the course recommended in it was the only course that, as men of honour and sagacity, they could pursue. It was discouraging to have to battle with the Government, and still more to face those whose insidious opposition was at the bottom of the treatment they had experienced. (Cheers.) But now, having gained every triumph, having it admitted that the remedy they recommended was the right one, they had still produced no vivid and vital effect in action. The disasters of New Zealand were not to be repaired by admissions, but by acts – acts which it was in the power of the Government to do. The directors were told that Her Majesty's Government would do nothing to relieve them until they received reports from Governor Grey. He wished that those who made them that answer could be aware of the state in which the colonies were, and would remain, until a satisfactory decision was given. Every moment was fraught with mischief, evil, and despair to thousands of their countrymen. The debate of last session had produced a revival of hope in the breasts of the colonists, but now some of the best and most valuable settlers were deserting the colony. Every vessel that arrived from the colony contained some of the best of its settlers, who wisely tried to save what little property they had left, by quitting the scene in which they had lost so much. (Cheers.) The condition of the labourers in the colony was deplorable; some had obtained temporary employment, others had gone to the neighbouring colonies. But, if such were the state of the labourers, what must be the condition of those who had paid for the lands which they now saw in the possession of the savages? The weight of colonial misgovernment had fallen upon those who had purchased land. They had seen the titles to their lands withheld; they had been compelled to dance attendance at the office of some official in the colony; and after all they were still doomed to disappointment. He regretted to see his learned friend Mr. Halswell[11] present, who had been one of the first settlers in Wellington. His main object in going to New Zealand had been to do good to the natives, and it was deplorable to see a gentleman obliged, through the mismanagement of the British Government, to abandon the country in which he had hoped to pass his life. He had spoken of the colonists out in New Zealand; but what should be say of the intended colonists who remained at home? He observed a gentleman there (Captain Cargill),[12] who was one of a colony started three years ago, under the auspices of the Free Church of Scotland, which consisted of labourers, shopkeepers, and farmers, who were prepared to quit the country. They had abandoned their occupations, and transferred the investment of their capital; and, after all, they were not able to go out of the country. They had, first no guarantee of their land when they got there; and, secondly, no guarantee could be given them that they would enjoy free institutions. What was it the company wanted? A title to the land which they had purchased, and fairly purchased, and institutions under which Englishmen could live. The caprices, vagaries, and follies of its governors justified him in asserting that the despotic Government of New Zealand had been as stupid as it was mischievous. The question between the company and the Government was a great question, which concerned every colony in the empire. Why should Englishmen when they went to a colony be subjected to a despotic Government, and be considered enemies, and not friends to the state? They ought to lose no rights by extending our empire over the ocean, and the notion to the contrary was a revolting notion, which had its rise in our convict colonies. The directors asked that Government should do for the free and intelligent settlers of New Zealand what James I. and II. and Charles I. and II. did for the Englishmen of their day, viz., that they should carry with them the rights of self-taxation and self-government. (Cheers.) He claimed for every colony as well as for New Zealand, that they should revert to the sound practice of their ancestors, and enable every free and intelligent man to vote on all matters affecting the good of the community. Who were the persons usually sent out as governors of our colonies, and intrusted with almost arbitrary power? – captains of men-of-war, colonels of regiments, old generals who had passed the period of service, gentlemen who had tried to make their way in Parliament, and had not been able. (A laugh.) The bowing and scraping which such persons were the object of in their new title of "your Excellency" was enough to turn the heads of the wisest and best men that ever lived. The Legislative Councils had as little claim to public confidence as the governors. The company required a total alteration in our relations with the natives, and a total abandonment of the foolish way in which the Government had acted. He admitted that the opinion of the directors had changed as to the policy to be pursued towards the natives. They had recommended at first the colonization of all the natives, believing that it would be practicable. The company's settlers lived in happy relations with the natives until the Government came among them, and disturbed those relations. He asserted that the impolitic course of the Government had alone produced that sanguinary war in the north of New Zealand which had arrested the improvement of the colony. The scene of those disasters was where the missionary system had had full scope, where the treaty of Waitangi was made, and where Governor Fitzroy had established what relations he pleased with the natives. And there had grown up a war, which, unless it were put a stop to, would put an end to the colonization of the island. He thought they ought to abandon the hope of colonizing the north of New Zealand. The natives should be left in possession of those districts, and the company and the Government should confine their attention to the settlements of Europeans, and to prevent contact between the natives and the Europeans. If the Government persisted in conquering the native tribes by military force, it must be followed by the utter extermination of the weaker race. Government were now employing one part of the natives to cut the throats of the others. They ought to give up the attempt to plant our colony where the natives were thickest, and ought not to attempt to impose their laws upon the natives. If nothing were to be done for the colonies for another year, he advised the directors to give up the attempt to carry on the government and the affairs of the colony, to throw the responsibility upon the Ministry, and to quit the field of action, from which they had been driven by injustice and impolicy. (Cheers.) The directors were told, that the objects they had in view would be accomplished by the instructions last sent out to Governor Grey. He doubted this, and thought the company ought to have an act of Parliament securing to the colony a representative government. A general reform of the system by which the colonies were governed was what was wanted, and until the colonies made common cause together their interests would continue to suffer. When Mr. Ewart,[13] the other evening, brought forward a motion exhibiting the grossest instance of mismanagement in the case of Van Diemen's Land, the house was counted out. Only 27 members were present on a motion affecting the very existence and well-being of a colony. If all the interests of the colonies were brought to bear on this subject, success would be certain, for never in a better cause did men appeal to the sympathies of all wise and right-thinking persons. (Cheers.)

Mr. CLARKE wished to know in what position a dissentient proprietor would be placed, and what compensation would be due to the company from the Government if they took the company's land. Four years ago, he had paid down money, which he could ill afford to lose, for land which he understood was guaranteed, and now his title was, he feared, little better than a waste sheet of paper.

Dr. BOWRING[14] thought the directors had done right in throwing the responsibility upon the Government, and he hoped that Parliament would feel bound to protect the shareholders against loss. He seconded the motion, that the report be received and adopted.

The noble Chairman having been compelled to leave the meeting shortly after the commencement of the proceedings,

Mr. AGLIONBY, who took the chair, in reply to the first question of Mr. Clarke, said the voice of the majority would bind the meeting. He hoped he would not press for an answer upon the other point.

After a few words from other proprietors in support of the resolution, the chairman put the motion, which was passed unanimously amidst applause. The retiring directors and auditors were then re-elected, and after a vote of thanks to the directors for the skill and ability with which they had conducted the affairs of the company, the meeting broke up.

Notes

1 Henry Chetwynd-Talbot (1803–1868) was known as Viscount Ingestre from 1826 until 1849, when he became the 18th Earl of Salisbury. He was a Conservative MP who represented Staffordshire from 1837 until 1849, when he joined the House of Lords.

2 Thomas Cudbert Harrington (1798–1863) was born in Calcutta and in 1820 moved to Australia, where he became a landowner and public servant. After moving to London in 1842, he became secretary of the New Zealand Company, remaining in the position until the Company dissolved ten years later.

3 George Grey (1812–1898) was governor of New Zealand from 1845 to 1853 and again from 1861 to 1868 after serving as governor of the Cape Colony. He later served as New Zealand's Prime Minister from 1877 to 1879.

4 This act, passed in August 1840, revised and extended through 1841 an earlier act passed in 1828 "to provide for the administration of justice in New South Wales and Van Diemen's Land." Section 2 of the 1840 act enabled the formation as "a separate colony . . . any islands which are now or which hereafter may be comprised within or be dependencies of . . . New South Wales," which included New Zealand, owing to a law passed in the previous June. Although New Zealand received a charter under this act in 1841, the New Zealand Company took issue with its adequacy in matters of land title and efficient governance.

5 Henry Aglionby Aglionby (1790–1854) received his MA from Cambridge and became a barrister in 1816. He represented Cockermouth as a Liberal MP from 1832 until his death.

6 This refers to a commission that the Colonial Office attached to its agreement with the New Zealand Company in November 1840, not the more general Land Commission that had been set up under the Waitangi Treaty earlier that year.

7 William Spain (1803–1876), a merchant's son from the Isle of Wight, was a solicitor who promoted New Zealand colonization in the 1830s. In 1841, Lord John Russell appointed him to investigate all land claims in New Zealand, but on arrival, the then-governor, William Hobson, limited him to those involving the New Zealand Company. Spain awarded all but two claims to the Company, but the new governor, Robert Fitzroy, only granted two of these owing to Māori resistance – though most others did eventually pass to British settlers. In 1845, Spain moved to Australia, where he practiced law and held political office through 1861.

8 Robert Fitzroy (1805–1864) was appointed Governor of New Zealand in 1843. He frequently ruled against the New Zealand Company and its settlers in land disputes with the Māori and also faced challenges in quelling violence on the North Island; both factors led to his recall in 1845. In 1835, he had commanded the *Beagle*, on which Charles Darwin sailed around the world.

9 William Gladstone (1809–1898) was Britain's Prime Minster in 1868–74, 1880–86, and 1892–94. He briefly served as Colonial Minister under Robert Peel from December 1845 until Peel's ministry fell in June 1846.

10 Charles Buller (1806–1848) was born in Calcutta, where his father was an Indian civil servant. Buller succeeded his father as MP for West Looe, Cornwall, then represented Liskeard from 1832 until his death. He was an early advocate of Edward Gibbon Wakefield's plans for systematic colonization, was a director of the South Australian Association, and drafted the New Zealand Company's charter in 1840.

11 Edmund Storr Halswell (1790–1874) was a London barrister who traveled to Wellington on behalf of the New Zealand Company in 1841. After serving there as a judge and commissioner of Māori reserves, he returned to England in 1845.

12 William Cargill (1784–1860) led an expedition of Scottish settlers to Otago Province in 1847, sponsored by the Scottish Free Kirk, an Evangelical sect that had broken with the Presbyterians in 1843. The expedition was delayed for four years owing to lack of promised financial support from the New Zealand Company. Cargill served as the province's first superintendent from 1853 to 1859 and was a member of the New Zealand Parliament, representing Dunedin, from 1855 to 1859.

13 William Ewart (1798–1869) was a Liberal MP who called on Parliament in 1846 to abolish transportation and end the policy of sending convicts to Van Diemen's Land.

14 John Bowring (1792–1872) was a merchant, travel writer, and diplomat who represented Bolton as a free-trade MP between 1841 and 1848, then acted as an ambassador in Canton and Hong Kong through 1859.

Editorial Headnote

East India Company (1857)

When the East India Company (EIC) held its quarterly general court in December 1857 at its head office in Leadenhall Street, a little over six months had passed since the Indian Rebellion sent shock waves through the British Empire. Less than eight months later, the Government of India Act would transfer Indian rule from the Company to the British Crown. Under these circumstances, the first part of the meeting was predictable enough, with the sober announcement of pensions to a retired major general and to widows of two other officers who had died during the rebellion. The second part was dominated by a proposal by W. S. Jones, a retired law clerk, to pay for deputies from Indian universities to reside in London and "inform the proprietors as to the wishes and complaints of the people of India." Before several shareholders rose to quash the motion – including a long speech by the chairman, Ross Mangles, who insisted that the recent events were a mutiny and not an insurrection – Jones found an ally in Malcolm Lewin, a Unitarian judge who had served in Madras, then became a vocal critic of Company rule and Indian missionaries.[1]

Jones and Lewin were classic examples of the shareholder gadfly, a figure that was coming into its own in the early Victorian era. Between 1848 and 1858, they spoke (often in tandem) at close to 50 EIC shareholder meetings, rarely missing an opportunity to vent on such varied issues as colonial judges and jails, the "opium question," the Madras army, the governor of Sindh, Haileybury College, the confiscation of princely estates in Punjab, and numerous procedural questions (Jones's sole official capacity at the Company was on its bye-laws committee). Their ability to speak so frequently mainly resulted from Company rules entitling anyone holding at least £500 worth of shares to do so, but also reflected a lack of competition from other speakers.[2] When they could be bothered, EIC shareholders periodically exerted major influence on Company affairs: their votes helped open India to missionaries and British imports in 1813, then ended the Company's monopoly on Anglo-Chinese trade in 1833. Also, dating back to the seventeenth century and persisting until the onset of civil service reform in 1853, shareholders industriously secured patronage from their elected directors on behalf of friends and relatives. This was a special boon in the EIC, which was uniquely tolerant of "private trading" by its servants in India.[3]

Jones and Lewin's harangue against Company rule in India was not an isolated incident in the 1850s. Among EIC shareholders, the Radical MP Joseph Hume and the journalist James Silk Buckingham often joined them in criticizing its policies. Numerous other critics of Britain's presence in India gained a larger, if less influential, audience than its cantankerous shareholders: these included

John Bruce Norton, a lawyer who remained in Madras after Lewin had left; the Chartist Ernest Jones; and Karl Marx, who chronicled the Indian Rebellion for the *New York Tribune*.[4] A more consequential chorus arose after 1857: leading this charge were John Bright and Richard Cobden, fresh from their defeat of the Corn Laws a decade earlier. Against them, Company directors and officials (including, famously, John Stuart Mill) offered a weak and ineffectual defense, leading to the transfer of the Company's governing powers to the Colonial Office within a year. Its sole consolation prize was what Mill called "a really independent Council," a 15-person advisory committee that met regularly at Leadenhall Street and sported seven members – including two of the speakers at the December 1857 meeting – selected by former Company directors. This limped along until 1874, at which point the last vestiges of the Company ended.[5]

Notes

1 On Jones, see *Gentleman's Magazine* 212 (1862), 515. On Lewin see Robert Eric Frykenberg, "Modern Education in South India, 1784–1854: Its Roots and Its Role as a Vehicle of Integration under Company Raj," *American Historical Review* 91 (1986), 60; Zoe Laidlaw, "'Justice to India – Prosperity to England – Freedom to the Slave! Humanitarian and Moral Reform Campaigns on India, Aborigines and American Slavery," *Journal of the Royal Asiatic* Society 22 (2012), 322.

2 Frank H. H. King and Sara Joynes, *Survey Our Empire! Robert Montgomery Martin . . . A Bio-Bibliography* (Hong Kong: Centre of Asian Studies, 1979), 65.

3 Timothy L. Alborn, *Conceiving Companies: Joint-Stock Politics in Victorian England* (London: Routledge, 1998), 21–43; H. V. Bowen, *The Business of Empire: The East India Company and Imperial Britain, 1756–1833* (Cambridge: Cambridge University Press, 2006), 84–117; Emily Erikson, *Between Monopoly and Free Trade: The English East India Company, 1660–1757* (Princeton: Princeton University Press, 2014).

4 *Debates at the East India House* (London: privately printed, 1858); Margarita Barns, *The Indian Press: A History of the Growth of Public Opinion in India* (London: G. Allen and Unwin, 1940); Priyamvada Gopal, *Insurgent Empire: Anticolonial Resistance and British Dissent* (London: Verso, 2019), 41–82.

5 Alborn, *Conceiving Companies*, 44–51; Margaret Makepeace, *The East India Company's London Workers: Management of the Warehouse Labourers, 1800–1858* (Woodbridge: Boydell Press, 2010), 191.

14

EAST INDIA COMPANY

Source: East India Company (1857), *Allen's Indian Mail* 15 (1857), 933–936 (December 27)

EAST-INDIA HOUSE

A Quarterly General Court of the East-India Company was held at their house in Leadenhall-street, on Wednesday, the 23rd of December, 1857.

Mr. R. D. Mangles,[1] M.P., Chairman of the Court of Directors, in the chair.

The minutes of the last Court were read.

The Chairman. – I have to inform the Court that the warrants for the half-yearly dividend on the East-India Company's Stock are ready for delivery, and will be paid on the 16th January next.

The Chairman. – I have to inform the proprietors that this Court has been made special for the purpose of submitting for confirmation the resolutions of the general court on the 16th instant, approving the resolutions of the Court of Directors on the 2nd instant, granting to Major-General Sir Archdale Wilson,[2] Bart., G.C.B., an annuity of 1,000*l*.; and to Lady Neill,[3] the widow of the late Brigadier-General Neill; and to Mrs. Nicholson,[4] the mother of the late Brigadier-General John Nicholson, special pensions of 500*l*. per annum respectively, in addition to the allowances to which they are entitled under the regulations.

The Secretary[5] having read the resolutions,

The Chairman said: – I have now to move that this Court do confirm the resolution granting to Major-General Sir Archdale Wilson, Bart., K.C.B., an annuity of 1,000*l*.

Sir F. Currie[6] (Deputy Chairman). – I beg to second the motion.

The motion was put and agreed to unanimously.

The Chairman. – I now move that the resolution granting a pension of 500*l*. a year to Lady Neill and Mrs. Nicholson respectively be confirmed.

Sir F. Currie. – I second the motion.

Mr. Lewin.[7] – I will state my reasons why I think the resolution should be rejected. I consider that 500*l*. a year is not sufficient for a lady on whom the Queen bas conferred the honour of the order of the Bath. To sustain that rank, an increased expense is necessarily incurred. It should also be remembered that Lady Neill has nine children; and although some of them are said to be provided for, after a certain time, as cadets, still, in the mean time, they have to be supported

DOI: 10.4324/9781003177715-16

and educated, and how is Lady Neill, with 500*l*. a year, to educate those children so as to enable them to pass the necessary examinations before entering the army?

The resolution was then confirmed.

REPRESENTATION OF INDIA

Mr. Jones.[8] – I ask that the Secretary do read the motion of which I have given notice.

The Secretary then read the following:

"That it is due to the advancing intelligence of the people of India that a deputy from each university in the several presidencies be maintained at the public expense in this country, with a view to inform the proprietors as to the wishes and complaints of the people of India."

Mr. Jones. – I think it cannot fail to have occurred to this Court that since these sad events have taken place in India no debate has been had and no observations have been made in the Court with reference to those transactions. I think it would be very desirable that we should hear to-day the opinions of the Court of Directors in reference to the causes of these disasters, and to the future conduct which the Government of India should pursue. It is said that the sepoys are entirely separated from the general population, and that this is only a sepoy mutiny. Now, in looking through the proceedings of Parliament, and on referring to the petitions that have been presented, I find a large amount of discontent existing among the people of India, which I think answers the question, what is the cause of this outbreak? The Rev. Dr. Duff,[9] of Calcutta, is opposed to your opinion. He states, in a letter to the Rev. Dr. Tweedie, that the people are decidedly in favour of the sepoys, and adds, that "after escaping from the murderous hands of the mutineers, British gentlemen and ladies have, in particular instances, experienced kindness at the hands of the common villagers, but that in a far greater number of instances they have experienced quite the reverse." I think there is sufficient to account for these mutinies, and to prove that, instead of the sepoys being the originators of them, they have been acted upon by the people. One of the chief causes of discontent, I believe, is to be found in the alteration which has been made in the law of inheritance by the Indian Government. A petition from the Hindoo committee at Calcutta,[10] which was sent over here in 1850, contained a clause in which the petitioners almost predicted what would shortly happen. That clause ran thus: – "Should this inroad upon their religion be allowed by your Honourable Court, your memorialists expect no outbreak at. present – no present disturbance; but they expect and they would not do their duty as loyal subjects of the British crown it they did not candidly state their belief – that if this odious attack on the Hindoo religion shall become law, her Majesty will have eighty millions of Hindoo subjects in India dissatisfied and discontented." With respect to the law of inheritance in India, it appears to be built upon these grounds. The Hindoo acquires the possession of property, not for his present personal comfort, as we do in this country, but for the safety of his soul in a future state. When he dies, not having power to will his property away, it necessarily falls into the hands of his son, either by lineal right, or by adoption; by whom it is held as a sacred trust that he should perform certain periodical ceremonies to secure the soul's repose of him who had first acquired it. It was also a rule of Hindoo law, and as a consequence of the law of inheritance, that if the party failed to fulfil the trust, he should be deprived of the property, and that some other descendant should take the property, and perform the services. Now what have you done? You have said to the Hindoo – You shall inherit the property of your ancestor, but you shall not inherit it with those obligations, for the very purpose of your performing which your ancestor acquired it.

By our refusing to recognize the law of adoption, which is part of the law of transmission of property, we have absorbed the territories of the native princes into our own dominions; and if there be any truth in Lord Ellenborough's[11] allegation, that the sepoys felt an interest in the compliments paid to the native princes, surely the converse must be true, and that discontent must exist in the minds of the sepoys, when injury was inflicted upon the native princes. Not content with having injured the native princes and dishonoured the Hindoo religion, Lord Dalhousie[12] disgraced Sir Charles Napier,[13] the best friend the sepoys ever had. But the crowning evil of all is the annexation of that very territory in whose capital our troops have so long been pent up, but from which they are now at last so happily relieved.[14] Still, I do not lay the whole blame of these transactions upon Lord Dalhousie, for he has been but the tool in the hands of higher powers. The noble lord was sent out to India in 1848; but in the preceding year, 1847, Sir Robert Peel[15] declared that there was a principle at work between ourselves and Asiatic nations that forbade us to apply the same rules in our intercourse with them as we should apply to the nations of Europe. Such was the statement made by the leading man of his day; and Lord Dalhousie only carried out the idea embodied in that statement of Sir Robert Peel.

But what have been the results of our occupation of India? We have, during the tenure of our rule, especially during the last twenty years, been diffusing European notions among them; we have introduced our European education, both English and vernacular: English at the presidencies and the vernacular in the provinces. We have 23,000 scholars in the Government schools, and 75,000 in the missionary schools. One hundred thousand are thus every five years supplied to Indian society, charged with European notions. Can we expect that they shall be content with their position? Must not European learning give European principles? What constitutes the spur to exertion among yourselves? Is it not that last infirmity of noble minds, the attainment of honour? Are they less sensitive than you? In your despatch you speak of the great advantages to result, morally and commercially, from the establishment of universities in India. What is the great stimulus to learning, but advancement? If you give them representative power, you will quicken their zeal for learning. I have heard that at the last examination at University College prizes were carried off by the natives of India in several departments; and that to the successful competitor in the department of zoology, the Professor bore the flattering testimony: – "Not merely, sir, are you the best and most successful man of the year, but the most intelligent pupil we have ever had."

It may be said that in the more subtle development of the intellect the Hindoos are equal to ourselves, but that in the practical ends of life they are far our inferiors. But those Hindoos who have most advanced themselves have done so in those very branches of practical knowledge considered the most useful to mankind. It was the textile fabrics of India, the elements of colour, and the beauty of design which produced the most effect on the manufactures of his country. And what is the state of the press in India? I find that there are published in Calcutta alone seven daily papers, three bi-weekly, eleven weekly, five bi-monthly, eight monthly periodicals, nine quarterly, and eight yearly; a larger issue than Edinburgh, Dublin, or any city but London can exhibit. There is evidence enough to show that a strong anxiety exists in the minds of the natives of India to know the truth. These are proofs that it is not safe for us to neglect this growing desire for self-government. Our own universities send members to Parliament in consideration that they are able to instruct the people upon those questions which are necessary to be under stood for the nation's welfare. Now, I think that the proprietors of this Court greatly need instruction, and I am of opinion that the instruction they require could not be conveyed to them in a more effectual form than by the personal presence of men from India who shall be deputed from each university in the several presidencies in that country. I am also of opinion that the position of those gentlemen should be made a lucrative one, and that they should be made members of the Direction. What we want, is to draw closer the bonds which unite England with India. This must be done by recognizing the new features of Indian society. The reliance of England henceforth must be on her army primarily, but eventually on her Anglo-Indian population whom we have raised up in that country. The hon. proprietor concluded by moving his resolution.

Mr. Lewin. – I rise to second the motion, but I do not agree with all its details. I should be sorry to express my dissent from any motion which would have the effect of introducing the representative system in India; but I do not approve that those men should be paid, because it would sacrifice their independence. This mutiny has been nothing more than a crisis which was certain to come at last, as the natural result of the oppression of the people, and of the annexation of the territories of the native princes. A more gross and scandalous act of injustice was never imputable to the British Government than the annexation of Oude. At the same time, you have kept the natives in a state of subjection and degradation. You do not allow them to attain stations of eminence. It is true, in Bengal you permit them to be judges in suits to a certain amount; but still you do not place them on an equality with Europeans. This must create a most rankling spirit against us. Also I agree with the hon. mover as to the ignorance of members of Parliament on matters relating to India. There is a degree of ignorance on Indian affairs among members of Parliament which has not only astonished but has almost disgusted me. If you had been as independent as you are able, and as independent as you are encroaching, I believe you would never have been threatened with loss of power. For, however desirable it may be to get rid of the double government, I do not think it is desirable to get rid of you. I think there is more honesty to be found here than can be found at the West-end. I am glad to say so; and I only regret that you have not been more independent. If you had, you would have been upheld by the public, and the Government would never have dared to attack you.

Mr. Mackenzie.[16] – I rise to oppose the motion, because I believe that nothing could more speedily bring your Indian empire to a calamitous end. The natives of India ought to be much indebted to Mr. Jones for his speech in their favour; but if it were translated into the vernacular and transmitted to them, they would merely look upon it as nonsense. Whatever the future form of the government of India may be, the first duty is to give ample protection to life and property, cheap, speedy, and efficient justice, a good police, and a guarantee to the people of their ancient rights and customs; but they must not be put into situations of trust and of importance, which, with their present ignorance, prejudices, and immorality, they are totally unfitted for. There is scarcely a native employé in all India but is open to corruption; and the higher the salary they receive, the greater is the bribe they demand.

Mr. Clark.[17] – I am desirous to make a few observations upon this subject, because I look at the question in a different aspect from that which the hon. mover has taken of it. I believe that he deals in fiction, and not in fact. But I would ask this single question, what would become of India if we were at this moment to withdraw ourselves from it? Why, there would be one scene of carnage throughout the length and breadth of India; there would be no civilized government, but the strongest would get off the best. In wielding the government of a country like India, it is impossible to be always right; but if there is a large per-centage of good to India, then, in my opinion, that is good government. The general result has been that, when you have deposed princes, you have protected the people and ameliorated their condition. The people have never enjoyed the protection of property, but have always been obliged to bury their money in order to secure it from plunder by their rulers.

The Chairman. – I do not propose to follow the hon. gentleman who has brought forward this motion through all the details of his very able and eloquent speech. There is one single point to which I wish more particularly to allude, and that is, whether the recent melancholy events have been the result of an insurrection, or merely of a military mutiny. Now both the mover and the seconder of the motion jumped at once to the conclusion that it was an insurrection of the people, and that the sepoys had merely been the instruments of the people. This certainly is contrary to the general belief; but the hon. mover has referred to certain petitions which had been presented to the House of Commons, in which it was stated that discontent prevailed among the people of India. I suppose he referred more especially to a petition presented to the House of Commons in 1850. To that petition the missionaries expressed their belief that a strong feeling of discontent existed among the people of Bengal, and also their fear that the rankling feeling of dissatisfaction with the government would display itself in an insurrectionary movement, and that the people would at last be driven by that feeling into the commission of outrage and violence.

Now, what are the facts of the case? Why, that with the exception of certain tribes who have led a predatory life from generation to generation, and who always plunder wherever they can, from one end of India to the other there has been no rising of the people. In Bengal many of the stations were totally defenceless, and a vast number of them have had no sepoys at all for several years. At these stations there is no other force to overawe the people than the weak police establishment; yet neither at Chittagong nor Dacca has there been any rising of the people. A partial insurrection occurred at Patna; but, with that exception, there has been no rising of the people whatever. In the province of Behar, where the people are a military, manly, self-reliant race, and from which many of the sepoys have been drawn, two remarkable facts occurred which are worthy of notice in considering the question whether it is an insurrection of the people or of the military. At the time the sepoys mutinied at Patna, the civil authorities of the two districts of which Chuppra and Mozufferpoor[18] are the capitals, were ordered by the resident commissioner to leave those stations and come to the capital of the province, Patna. The civil authorities at once retired in obedience to orders; and what was the result? So far from the people showing any hostility to the government, or acting by themselves in an insurrectionary manner, at Chuppra a Mahomedan gentleman took the command of the station, and assumed the protection of the town and the direction of the populace; and there was not only no rising of the people, but when the civil servants returned to the station and resumed their position, that gentleman and the people acting under his orders handed back to the authorities the treasury safe, the gaol safe, and the town safe and in perfect order. Does that look like a feeling of hostility on the part of the people against the Government of India? Is that any evidence on their part that they desire a change? Again, at Mozufferpoor, a small party of twelve irregular cavalry, who had mutinied and murdered their commanding officer, Major Holmes,[19] attempted to plunder the treasury, but were driven back by the police. They next made an attempt to plunder the town, but were again driven back by the police and inhabitants, who rose and resisted instead of aiding the mutineers. And then at Mozufferpoor, as at Chuppra, when the government authorities returned, they found the treasury intact, the prisoners in the gaol all safe, and the population of the town as peaceable and quiet as when they left it.

Look again at the state of things at Hyderabad, in the Deccan. Up to the latest advices it was in the most perfect state of order, and there was every appearance of good faith being observed towards us on the part of the native ruler. As an illustration of this, I will mention the following incident: – A short time ago a Mahomedan preacher was engaged in delivering a sermon in the principal mosque at Hyderabad. The sermon was upon the ordinary points of the Mahomedan faith; but whilst it was being delivered, a Mussulman fanatic in the congregation rose and exclaimed – "Oh! it is all nonsense. This is not the sort of advice to give us at such a time. The only thing to be preached at this moment is a crusade against the unbeliever" – meaning the British Government. The preacher rebuked the man, and told him he was mistaken in applying the term "unbelievers" to English Christians, who were believers in one God as Mussulmans were. The man continuing his attempts to incite the people to violence, the preacher took the opportunity of desiring a friend to give notice of what was passing to Salar-jung,[20] the minister, who at once hastened down to the mosque, arrested the fanatic, and carried him off to prison. Does that show any feeling of hostility towards the English Government? Up to this time Salar-jung has kept the city and province perfectly quiet, and the contingent force which is maintained at Hyderabad has acted with the utmost fidelity, and with the greatest success against the mutineers. The same has taken place on the part of the Mahratta chiefs. Scindia[21] and Holkar[22] – and eminently Holkar – have proved themselves in every instance our faithful friends. I ask whether these facts do not prove beyond question or doubt that the movement is a movement only of the sepoys – a military mutiny, and not an insurrection of the people?

By the last mail from India I received a letter from Sir John Lawrence,[23] in which that eminent individual expresses his most decided opinion that the movement was a purely military movement on the part of the sepoys, instigated by their believing that they were masters of the position, and that the power of India was in their hands. He also used this expression, that they had the feeling of the Prætorian guards of ancient Rome, and seemed to think they might give away the empire. This view of the matter I believe to be the correct one, and to be justified by the facts of the case, by the way in which especially the districts around Delhi have settled down into a state of order, and paid their revenue without irregularity or deduction; for directly the mutineers were driven out of the city, the inhabitants returned spontaneously and most gladly to order under the British Government.

The attempt to work out a representative system of government has, I believe, failed in every country in the world, except, perhaps, where the people are of Anglo-Saxon descent. What we have seen in France, in Spain, and in other countries, is certainly not calculated to induce us to believe that the people of India are fit for representative institutions. But supposing they were, is the best mode for carrying out the principle, and for enabling the people of India to make known their wishes and complaints to this country, that of giving to them representatives to be chosen from the Indian universities? Supposing the gentlemen of England, the iron-masters of Staffordshire, the copper-miners of Wales, the stocking manufacturers of Nottingham, the crape-manufacturers of Norwich, the bankers and merchants of London, in such a case, wished to make known their wants and complaints to Government, would they select their representatives from the universities of Oxford and Cambridge to make those wishes and complaints known? What do the inhabitants of Calcuita, Madras, and Bombay know of the general wishes, wants, and complaints of the people of those presidencies? Just about as much as the members from the universities of Oxford and Cambridge would be supposed to know about all those wants and interests I have mentioned. Therefore I do not think that either the people of India are fitted for a representative government, or if they were, that the members of the Indian universities are qualified to represent them. For these reasons I am obliged to oppose the motion.

Mr. Helps.[24] – I should like to make one or two observations before the close of this debate. I entirely agree with you that the hon. proposer of this motion has not proposed a feasible scheme for the end he has in view. But I don't think there is any parallel between the universities of this country and those of India. It is necessary that India should be represented by persons acquainted with Indian subjects, the Indian language, and also with the English language. I presume that that is the principal reason that has induced the hon. mover to propose that representatives from the Indian universities should come among us. Again, I agree with the mover that it is of the greatest importance that sound, accurate knowledge of India should be found in this Court. How is that to be secured? Why, by electing members into your hon. body who have had long experience of Indian affairs. That appears to me a much more natural way of obtaining an accurate knowledge of Indian affairs than the adoption of the motion. The only specific wrong of which the proprietor has represented the people of India to complain is this, that we have altered a most iniquitous law of inheritance. (Hear, bear.) Not very long ago it was the law applicable to the descent of landed property in Ireland, that real property was forfeited by the profession of the Roman Catholic religion. That law has since been repealed. That is precisely analogous to the principle on which the Indian Government has acted. They have said that no man shall suffer in his property by reason of his professing that which he believes to be religious truth. This is the only thing with which you are charged. But two or three days ago there was a fact communicated to us by the Times,[25] of which you have taken no notice whatever. (Hear, bear.) If that statement be founded in fact, I am afraid the motion of the hon. proprietor comes a little too late, and that our days are already numbered. (Hear, bear.) I would therefore respectfully ask you what has passed, so far as it is fit to be revealed, between the Government and yourselves, with regard to the abolition of what is called the double government of India? (Cheers.)

The Chairman. – I expected that this question would be put to me; but if it had not, I should have felt it my duty to state the facts to which it relates. I have to inform the Court that the deputy chairman and myself saw Lord Palmerston,[26] by appointment, on Saturday morning last, and that his lordship then communicated to us that it is the intention of her Majesty's Government to propose to Parliament, when it meets again at the beginning of next year, a bill for the purpose of placing the government of the Queen's East-Indian dominions under the direct authority of the Crown. (Loud cries of Hear.)

Mr. Jones rose to reply, when

Mr. Serjeant Gaselee[27] rose and said: – We have heard one eloquent speech; I hope we shall not have another. But the whole thing is perfectly ludicrous; and therefore I beg to suggest that before the Crown disposes of us, let us do the thing properly – dispose of ourselves, and take up our hats and be off. (Laughter.)

Mr. Jones. – I shall not detain you five minutes. It is supposed that this Court will very quickly be dissolved; but what the prime minister has threatened to do may nevertheless not be done, The Government have long threatened to reform the corporation of London; but that corporation has hitherto been strong enough to baffle the Government, and I hope it will continue so. I hope all corporate institutions will successfully resist the centralizing power, and that they will assist in giving to the population of India an opportunity of entering into your corporation. I hope that the same principle by which you upset Fox[28] when he attempted to destroy you, will upset Palmerston when he shall make a similar attempt. It has been suggested to me that I should withdraw my motion; and seeing what is the feeling of the Court, I will leave it to your consideration.

The Chairman. – Do you withdraw it?

Mr. Jones. – Yes.

The motion was accordingly withdrawn.

Mr. Lewin. – I wish the secretary to read the words of my motion.

The Secretary then read the following:

"That the disasters that have lately occurred in our Indian territories have been owing to a want of foresight on the part of the Indian Government, and to a neglect of the means which were at hand to control them. That to the supineness and apathy of the Home Gorernment of India is attributable the want of timely military aid, which it was in its power to supply by means of steam-vessels, which would bare arrested the slaughter of our troops and countrymen, and averted the danger which now threatened the garrison of Lucknow."

Mr. Lewin. – I will detain the Court but a very few minutes. My first proposition is, that the Government of Bengal knew perfectly the menaces that had been thrown out long before the outrages were committed, and that they were warned of what was about to come to pass. So early as the 8th of February, General Hearsey[29] stated that all the sepoys at Calcutta had been tampered with. On the 11th of February, the Government were informed that they were on a mine. Notwithstanding all these warnings, no troops were sent out from this country to India till the 28th of July, and then about 400 troops were sent in a sailing-vessel – the *Robert Lowe*.[30] About this time, Mr. Colvin,[31] the Lieutenant-Governor of the North-Western Provinces, a man who highly distinguished himself at the commencement of this outbreak, issued a proclamation. You have been since disposed to annul that proclamation; and yet, on the 8th of July, 1857, it met with your entire approval.

The Chairman. – That was his first proclamation: it was not the proclamation.

Mr. Lewin. – I am very glad to hear it.

Mr. Helps. – Do not go on to blame the Court now that they are going out. (A laugh.)

Mr. Lewin.- I cannot help it; they have brought it all on themselves. (Laughter.). Without detaining the Court further, I beg to move the resolution.

The Chairman. – Is the motion seconded?

Mr. Jones.- – I will second the motion for the purpose of hearing any observation the Chairman may have to offer.

The Chairman. – The only observation I shall make is to put the question.

The motion was then put and negatived.

BULLION SENT TO INDIA

The Chairman. – I have had a question put to me by Mr. Mackenzie, who wishes to know what is the amount of silver bullion sent to India by the East-India Company between the 1st of August and the 5th of December, and on what terms that bullion has been raised. I beg to state that the amount of bullion conveyed to India, at the urgent requisition of the Government of India, between the dates specified, is 752,701*l*., which was purchased at various prices – namely, 61½d., 61⅞d., 59¾d., and 59⅞d., per ounce. The bullion was purchased in the market.

Mr. Mackenzie said, nothing could be more injudicious than raising a loan in this country at 6 per cent. when they bad an open loan in India at 5 per cent. As the interest of money in India was always much higher than in this country, to give 6 per cent. here would at once prevent any chance of getting any money in India to meet the Government requirements. He begged to ask whether 6 per cent. was not given by the Government?

The Chairman. – The money was raised for the general purposes of India at 6 per cent.

Mr. Mackenzie. – Whatever money is required for India ought to be raised in India alone.

The Chairman. – The money has been raised at as cheap a rate as it could be got. An urgent requisition was made to us, and we should have betrayed our trust towards the Government of India if we had neglected to comply with that requisition. They wanted the money to enable them to carry on the operations of the Government, and also to carry on the war, and it was our bounden duty to comply with their request. (Hear, hear.)

"THE DOUBLE GOVERNMENT"

Mr. Serjeant Gaselee. – Is it the intention of the Court of Directors to appoint an early day to take into consideration the gracious message of the prime minister? (Laughter.)

The Chairman.-I only received this letter this morning, and the matter has not yet come under the consideration of the Court.

LORD DALHOUSIE'S PENSION

The Chairman. – Mr. Lewin has just handed to me a notice of motion for the next Court, and which I shall read to the Court: "That it is expedient to reconsider the grounds upon which an annuity of 5,000*l*. has been granted to the Marquis of Dalhousie, and to inquire whether the insurrection now raging in India is not attributable mainly to the measures of that noble lord." Now, I decline to receive a notice of such a motion; and I do so upon the ground that the annuity to Lord Dalhousie having been granted under all the forms required by Act of Parliament, we have no power to cancel that grant. I shall put it to the Court, therefore, whether I ought to receive the notice or not.

Mr. Serjeant Gaselee. – I cannot but express my disgust at the pension having been granted; but since it has been granted, I should feel a reluctance to discuss it again, and rather leave it to the delicacy of the noble marquis.

Mr. Lewin. – I have no wish to attack Lord Dalhousie, nor any wish to take the pension from him. So far from it, I give Lord Dalhousie great credit for what he has done in India. I wish to God he had been there during the last six months. But I say the grounds on which the grant was made are wrong; and my opinion is that many of the estates which were taken from the native princes should be given back to them.

The Chairman. – I move that this notice of motion be not received.

Mr. Lewin. – On what ground?

The Chairman. – I think it would stultify the Court to receive a notice of a motion which we have no right to entertain. Lord Dalhousie has as much right to the pension as he has to his estate.

Mr. Serjeant Gaselee. – I enter my protest against that doctrine.

Mr. Jones. – I move as an amendment that the question be submitted to the law officers of the East-India Company, whether this Court has power to entertain the motion.

Mr. Serjeani Gaselee. – I shall second the amendment, because I doubt whether the Court has power to reject the notice.

Mr. Lewin. – I consider the conduct of the chairman is an act of despotism. It is too late, perhaps, to stand up for the independence of the Court; still it is a case in which the independence of the Court is involved.

Mr. Prinsep.[32] – The hon. gentleman wishes not to touch the pension, but to consider the grounds upon which it was granted. Now, suppose an Act of Parliament was passed, and an hon. member gave notice that he would move its reconsideration, but that he did not intend to impugn the Act itself, but only the grounds on which it was passed, would any such motion be entertained by Parliament? We should be putting ourselves in an absurd position, if we were to allow any such notice of motion to be published.

The Chairman. With regard to the amendment, I beg to say that this Court is quite competent to judge of its own proceedings. The hon. gentleman says I wish to act in an arbitrary manner, and that my conduct is an act of despotism; if it is, it is a despotism which belongs to all authorities.

The question was then put, and it was decided that the notice of motion should not be received.

Notes

1 Ross Donnelly Mangles (1801–1877) attended East India College and worked as a civil servant in Calcutta from 1820 to 1839. Back in England, he was a Whig MP for Guildford from 1841 to 1858, where he defended the EIC's harsh taxation policies on Malthusian grounds. He joined the EIC board in 1847 and became its chair in 1857, and after the company was abolished, he sat on the Council for India through 1866.

2 Major-General Archdale Wilson (1803–1874) served in India from 1819 until 1858 and was promoted to Major-General in July 1857. He commanded an attack that recaptured Delhi in September 1857 during the Indian Rebellion.

3 Isabella Neill (1816–1875) was the daughter of a Bengal colonel and wife of James George Smith Neill (1810–1857), a brigadier-general during the Rebellion who was killed in Lucknow in September 1857. Besides receiving a pension from the EIC, Isabella Neill was made a baroness in honor of her husband's military service.

4 Clara Hogg Nicholson (1789–1874) was the widow of the Dublin physician Alexander Nicholson (died 1830) and mother of Brig. Gen. John Nicholson, who was Deputy Commissioner in Peshawar and killed in Delhi in September 1857 during the Indian Rebellion. She moved to Delgany, in County Wicklow, after her husband's death.

5 James Cosmo Melvill (1791–1861) entered EIC service as a clerk in 1808, became its chief auditor in 1824, financial secretary in 1834, and served as its chief secretary from 1834 until his retirement in 1858.

6 Frederick Currie (1799–1875) attended East India College and worked as a civil servant and judge in India from 1818 to 1844. As foreign secretary to India (1844–47), he helped negotiate treaties following the First Anglo-Sikh War. He joined the EIC's board in 1854, a year after returning to England, and was its final chairman in 1858.

7 Malcolm Lewin (1797–1869) was a judge who served in Madras between 1837 and 1848. After returning to England, he became a Council member of the Ethnological Society of London in 1850 and a committee member of the Aborigines' Protection Society in 1856. He had been an EIC shareholder since before he left for Madras.

8 William Samuel Jones (1780–1862) was Master of the Court of Queen's Bench Crown Office in Temple Bar into the 1840s; in 1850, he testified to Parliament on administering oaths of allegiance. He was a director of the Equitable Assurance Office from 1855 through 1861.

9 Alexander Duff (1806–1878) was a Presbyterian missionary in India who founded what is now the Scottish Church College in Calcutta and helped found the University of Calcutta. He served in India from 1830 to 1849. Duff's *The Indian Rebellion: Its Causes and Results* was serially published in 1857–58 in the form of 25 letters to William King Tweedie (1803–1863), who was the Convener of the Foreign Mission Committee of the Free Church of Scotland between 1848 and 1862. The quote is from Letter IX, which he wrote on 26 August 1857.

10 The "Memorial of the Hindoo Inhabitants of Bengal and its Dependencies," signed in 1850 by 14,000 Hindus and addressed to the EIC, called for the repeal of a law that prohibited discrimination against Christian converts, including in matters of inheritance.

11 Edward Law, first Earl of Ellenborough (1790–1871), was Governor-General of India between 1842 and 1844 (prior to being created Earl) and became first Lord of the Admiralty under Robert Peel in 1846.

12 James Ramsay, first Marquis of Dalhousie (1812–1860), was a Conservative MP in 1837 and joined the House of Lords in 1838 on his father's death. Robert Peel appointed him Vice-President of the Board of Trade in 1843, then Lord John Russell appointed him Governor-General of India in 1848, a position he held until 1856.

13 Charles Napier (1782–1853) served in Bombay between 1840 and 1851 as a military commander and briefly as its governor in 1849. He resigned his commission after

dissenting from Dalhousie's policy of raiding (and sometimes burning) villages in the princely states on India's northwest frontier for failure to pay taxes.

14 In February 1856, Lord Dalhousie annexed the princely state of Oudh, in present-day Uttar Pradesh, after its nawab refused to pledge loyalty to EIC rule. The move, which was rushed and unpopular, was a contributing factor in the Indian Rebellion.

15 Robert Peel (1788–1850) was Britain's Prime Minister in 1834–35 and 1841–46. The reference alluded to has not been found, but he was no longer Prime Minister (though still in Parliament) when he was alleged to have said it.

16 Holt Mackenzie (1787–1876) departed for India in 1807 as an EIC clerk and remained there until 1831, where he played an important role in tax reform. In England, he sat on the Board of Control from 1831 to 1834 and later served on the Privy Council.

17 Matthew Clark was an EIC shareholder who spoke regularly at its meetings and served on its bye-laws committee.

18 Chuppra (present-day Chopra) is in the Uttar Dinajpur district of western Bengal and Mozufferpoor (present-day Muzaffarpur) is in Behar, near the border of Nepal.

19 James Garner Homes (ca 1819–1857) commanded the 12th Regiment of Bengal Irregular Cavalry. He and his wife were murdered during the Indian Rebellion on 23 July 1857 in Segowlie, Bengal.

20 Mir Turab Ali Khan, Salar Jung I (1829–1883) was the dewan (or prime minister) of Hyderabad from 1853 until his death and assisted the British in suppressing the Indian Rebellion.

21 Jayajirao Scindia (1835–1886) was maharaja of Gawlior (in present-day Madhya Pradesh, in central India) from 1843 until his death. While still a boy, he was installed with British assistance after the previous maharaja died without an heir. He reluctantly supported the British against the rebels in 1857.

22 Tukojirao Holkar II (1835–1886), born Shrimant Yukaji Jaswant Holkar, was maharaja of Indore (in present-day Madhya Pradesh) from 1844 until his death. He assumed full governing powers in 1852 and sided with Britain during the 1857 Rebellion.

23 John Laird Mair Lawrence (1811–1879) entered the Bengal Civil Service in 1829 and rose to become Chief Commissioner of the Punjab in 1852, after forging close ties to Lord Dalhousie. In this capacity, he played a leading role in marshalling Sikh and Muslim allies during Britain's efforts to put down the Indian Rebellion. He later served as Indian Viceroy from 1864 to 1868.

24 Besides being an EIC director, Thomas Williams Helps (1802–1887) sat on the board of the Eastern Counties Railway. His brother was the essayist Arthur Helps.

25 This is apparently a reference to a report in the *Times* (18 December 1857) of a public meeting, spearheaded by the Radical MP John Roebuck and the Chartist Ernest Jones, that petitioned Parliament to establish "for India a responsible form of Government in the name of the Crown."

26 Henry John Temple, third Viscount Palmerston (1784–1865), was British Prime Minister between 1855 and 1858, then again, after 16 months, between 1859 and 1865.

27 Stephen Gaselee (1807–1883): see note to 5 (Eastern Counties Railway) for more details.

28 In 1783, Charles Fox, serving as Prime Minister in coalition with Lord North, proposed transferring the government of India to a Parliamentary commission. The defeat of this bill in the House of Lords led to the downfall of the coalition.

29 General John Bennett Hearsey (1793–1865) was in command of the division stationed at Barrackpore in Bihar in March 1857, when his troops in the Bengal Native Infantry famously refused to use the musket cartridges that had been assigned to them – an incident that is often viewed as sparking the Indian Rebellion.

30 The *Robert Lowe*, named after the British statesman Robert Lowe (1811–1892), was a screw-assisted sailing ship that was first deployed in 1854 to transport British troops to the Crimean War, then later used for troop transport in India.

31 John Russell Colvin (1807–1857), born in Calcutta, was Lieutenant-Governor of the North-Western Provinces from 1853 to 1857, when he died of cholera during the Indian Rebellion. Lewin was most likely referring to Colvin's proclamation on 25 May to troops in Gawlior; it is unclear which proclamation Mangles was referring to in his response.

32 Henry Thoby Prinsep (1792–1878) attended East India College and traveled widely while in the Company's civil service between 1809 and 1843, focusing on legal affairs and working closely with Mackenzie on land reform. He was elected as an EIC director in 1850 and was an active participant in its meetings. In 1858, he joined the new Council of India, where he remained until 1874 and frequently dissented from official policy there.

Editorial Headnote

British South Africa Company (1898)

Cecil Rhodes (1853–1902) was the star of the show when he took the podium at the British South Africa Company's general meeting in April 1898 – and it was a spectacular show, with an "overflowing" crowd of spectators and extensive press coverage. Rhodes treated his audience to sharp critiques of the company's opponents and would-be regulators at home and abroad, paired with descriptions of the company's past and future efforts to settle the territory that had recently been renamed Rhodesia in his honor.[1] He had first set foot in South Africa in 1871 and soon struck it rich in the Kimberley diamond mines. After a failed attempt to cash in on the Witwatersrand gold rush of 1886, Rhodes set his sights on settling Matabeleland to the north and secured a charter for the BSAC for that purpose in 1889. A year later, he was elected Prime Minister of the Cape Colony, where he remained in power until 1896, when his defense of Leander Jameson's bungled raid on the Transvaal Republic forced his resignation. The Matabele War later that year, which persisted into 1897 and pitted the BSAC against its territory's indigenous Ndebele people, also cost him his position as the company's managing director; and although he did preserve its charter, this came with government oversight in the form of a British resident commissioner in Bulawayo. The shareholder meeting in 1898 reversed this string of misfortunes, restoring Rhodes as Chairman, but success was brief. Within two years, he was mired in the throes of the Anglo-Boer War, which erupted in October 1899 and lasted until a few months after his premature death in 1902.[2]

Before Rhodes could speak at the meeting, he needed to be restored as a director. This task, as well as the reelection of other directors and an overview of the Company's history – not to mention crowd control – fell on the acting chair, the Duke of Abercorn, and his fellow director Earl Grey, who had recently returned to London after serving as Rhodesia's administrator during the Ndebele uprising. Besides briefly mentioning the Jameson Raid, Abercorn and Grey glossed over the devastating rinderpest epidemic that had spread to Rhodesia just as the Ndebele were taking up arms against the BSAC.[3] They also touched on the newly appointed oversight commission, the initiation of a settler-elected Council, "the condition of the native population in Rhodesia," railway construction, and mining prospects. Rhodes concluded the meeting with a rousing speech, detailing the implications of "changing . . . a barbarous territory into a civilized State," extolling the benefits of imperialism against "little Englanders," and insisting that indigenous Africans viewed him as a savior, not an oppressor. Abercorn's assessment that 1898 was a "turning point" was correct regarding South Africa but less so regarding the BSAC. After Rhodes's death, its steep administrative costs prevented it from declaring a dividend for two decades, until a new agreement with the British government in 1924 permitted it to collect copper mining royalties in Northern Rhodesia (present-day Zambia). This soon reversed its fortunes, and it remained an extremely lucrative investment until 1964, when Zambian independence led to its dissolution the following year.[4]

Notes

1 Janette Rutterford discusses this meeting in "The Shareholder Voice: British and American Accents, 1890–1965," *Enterprise and Society* 13 (2012), 131, 143.

2 Shula Marks and Stanley Trapido, "Cecil John Rhodes," *Oxford Dictionary of National Biography Online*. On Rhodes and the BSAC see John S. Galbraith, *Crown and Charter: The Early Years of the British South Africa Company* (Berkeley: University of California Press, 1974).

3 See Pule Phoofolo, "Epidemics and Revolutions: The Rinderpest Epidemic in Late-Nineteenth Century Southern Africa," *Past & Present* 138 (1993): 112–143.

4 L. J. Butler, *Copper Empire: Mining and the Colonial State in Northern Rhodesia, c. 1930–64* (Houndmills: Palgrave Macmillan, 2007).

15

BRITISH SOUTH AFRICA COMPANY

Source: British South Africa Company (1898), *Morning Post*, 22 April 1898

BRITISH SOUTH AFRICA COMPANY

Crowded and Enthusiastic Meeting

The ordinary general meeting of the British South Africa Company was held yesterday in the Great Hall of the Cannon-street Hotel, under the presidency of the Duke of Abercorn,[1] the Chairman of the Company.

The meeting was of an unprecedented character, and for hours prior to the time fixed for the commencement of the proceedings (noon) the shareholders began to assemble at the Hotel, the first arrivals being at about 9.30 a.m. By eleven o'clock the hall was filled to overflowing, on the floor and in the galleries; while the wide stone mantelpieces and other points of vantage were also invaded by venturesome shareholders. The arrangements for the accommodation of the Press were of an excellent description. By 11.15 a.m. the main staircase leading to the hall was blocked and the words passed down: "Hall full." Every inch of standing room was occupied, and it required all the tact and energy of Inspector Mackenzie, of the City Police, and a staff of constables to stem the incoming tide. From time to time as representatives of evening papers and others left the meeting they were besieged with inquiries from the excited crowd, kept back by a double cordon of police: "Is the meeting over? Is Rhodes speaking? Is there any room?" The proceedings lasted just over two hours, and at the close the gathering of shareholders still waiting without to glean particulars was of very considerable dimensions.

The Board of Directors, on entering the room, were loudly cheered. The opening remarks of the Chairman were punctuated by the uproar from without of the mass of shareholders blocking the corridors and staircases who were unable to obtain admittance.

The Chairman's Speech

The CHAIRMAN said: Ladies and Gentlemen, – Before we proceed with the business of the meeting I desire to express our great regret at the inconvenience that you are experiencing to-day in consequence of inadequate accommodation. You

DOI: 10.4324/9781003177715-17

are fortunate in being able to get into the hall, but I may tell you that there are hundreds of shareholders down below who are not in such a favourable position – (hear, hear) – and who are unable to obtain entrance. (Voices: Adjourn the meeting.). You may not be aware that we have nearly 35,000 registered shareholders, and in addition there are many holders of share warrants to bearer. It is manifest that no hall, either in London or elsewhere, could be found that would provide sufficient accommodation for so large a constituency. (Voices: Albert Hall.)[2] We considered carefully numerous suggestions, and came to the conclusion that it would be better to adhere to precedent and hold the meeting in the City of London – (hear, hear) – and therefore we have asked you to meet us here, the largest available hall east of Temple Bar. We shall be expeditious, so that your discomfort may be reduced as far as practicable. (A Voice: We are in no hurry.)

The Past Two Years

Much has happened during the last two years, and I desire to express our obligations for the continuous support we have received from you during the anxious and arduous period that has elapsed since our last annual general meeting, which was held so far back as January, 1895. In February, 1896, we issued our report and the accounts of the Company to the 31st of March, 1895, but as these accounts could not be passed at the meeting held in 1896, it is necessary to ask you to pass and adopt the report and accounts to the 31st of March, 1895, as well as those recently issued, which cover the periods to the 31st of March, 1896, and the 31st of March, 1897. It is right I should mention, though I need not do so at any great length, the untoward events in the closing days of 1895 and the first days of 1896. You are doubtless familiar with the evidence given before the Select Committee appointed by the House of Commons to investigate and report on the subject of the incursion of Dr. Jameson[3] into the Transvaal. I shall not, therefore, trouble you with any details. I will only say that I and the colleagues whom you see around me have thought it our duty to remain at the helm – (loud cheers) – and we have throughout readily acted in consultation and accord with Mr. Cecil Rhodes – (renewed cheers) – who is recognised on all hands as the founder of this Company – (hear, hear) – and from whom Rhodesia takes its name. As you will have seen, the Company has been refunded amounts expended by its officials in connection with the Transvaal incident, and when accounts now under consideration are adjusted further payments will be made. On the subject of the rinderpest and the native rebellion, to speak in chronological order, I can add nothing to the exhaustive statement already issued by the Company. When, in March, 1896, Lord Grey,[4] on short notice, and at a sacrifice which we must all acknowledge, accepted the post of Administrator and sailed for South Africa the horizon was clear. Before he could reach Buluwayo[5] the native rebellion, which followed close on the outbreak of rinderpest, had assumed serious proportions. Undeterred by any thought of danger, Lord Grey proceeded with all despatch to Buluwayo, and from the date of his arrival there until his return to England, nearly a year and a half later, he was untiring in his services to the country, and was ever at his post both in Buluwayo during the height of the rebellion in Matabeleland, and subsequently at Salisbury when the Mashonas followed the example of the Matabele and revolted. With a modesty and spirit which you will all appreciate Lord Grey, being a party to the reports recently issued to you, declined to allow any reference to be made in these reports to himself and to the work he has performed, but I and my colleagues, who are conscious of the services he has rendered and the untiring zeal for the interests of the Company that has actuated his motives, desire here to record our appreciation and thanks. (Loud applause.) Since Lord Grey returned to England he has been unceasing in his efforts for the Company's welfare. He has been in almost daily attendance at the Company's offices, and has been ever accessible to those who have sought his assistance and advice not only in business affairs directly concerning the Company, but in matters with which he became familiar during his residence in Rhodesia.

Progress of the Company

Gentlemen, I trust we are not too sanguine in believing that we have arrived at a turning point in the fortunes of the Company. As the result of negotiations between her Majesty's Government and your Board, a scheme has been prepared for the future administration of Southern Rhodesia which, while conferring extended authority on the Administrator, will introduce into the Council members elected by the settlers. Under this scheme the Imperial Government, acting through the High Commissioner, and the Board of Directors, acting through its Administrator, retain adequate control, while the Board is left with more time to develop and superintend the commercial resources of the country. These changes, however, do not involve a contribution from the Imperial Exchequer of any funds towards the government and settlement of Rhodesia. Shareholders and settlers alike – (interruption; A Voice: Mr. Chairman, I am sent here by 3,000 shareholders to ask you to adjourn the meeting) – will therefore recognise the justice of the repayment to the Company of these initial expenses, the results of which must benefit the country for all future time. (A Voice: What are you going to do about the shareholders downstairs?) When the country possesses full responsible government, and takes its place as one of the self-governing Colonies of the Empire, such portion of these expenses as has not been met from administrative revenue will be treated as a capital charge on the country, in other words as the public debt of the Colony. (Hear, hear.) As will be gathered from the report, the Directors recommend that the scheme embodied in the Government proposals should be accepted, and though the adoption of the report may fairly be considered as including the sanction of the Government proposals, yet we are advised that it will be better to submit an express resolution to you on this subject. Some remarks have been made in the public journals and elsewhere on the condition of the native population in Rhodesia. We believe that the regulations we have prepared, and which are now under the consideration of her Majesty's Government, will both protect and benefit the natives. They are based on the lines of the well-known Glen Grey Act[6] of the Cape Colony, but with provisions added giving salaried Indunas[7] limited control. By no stretch of imagination can these regulations, which aim at conferring privileges on the natives who have earned labour certificates, be regarded as restricting the rights of individual freedom. We have a good deal of business to do, and there are other speakers to follow. I do not propose to trouble you by any detailed references to the full accounts before you of the development of the country by the increase in the railroads and telegraphs, but I must congratulate you on the opening of the Bechuanaland Railway[8] to Buluwayo – (continued interruption and disturbance at back of the hall, shareholders forcing their way into the meeting) – and the financial success which has already attended that Company. The returns for February last are equal to the average of the preceding three months. All material for construction was carried practically at cost price, and the returns have not been thereby inflated. We may look to a continuance of the present returns, which are more than double the amount required for payment of the debenture interest guaranteed by this Company. A Stock Exchange quotation for the Bechuanaland Debentures will be granted in a few weeks. The line from Beira to the boundary between our territories and the Portuguese sphere – a little East of New Umtali – has been completed and opened for traffic. A separate Company, the Mashonaland Railway Company, has been established for the construction of a railway from Umtali to Salisbury, the requisite funds having been raised by the issue of Debentures of the Railway Company, the interest on which is guaranteed by this Company. The railway to Salisbury is to be opened in about a year. We do not anticipate that your Company will be called on to make any payment under the guarantees for either the Bechuanaland or Mashonaland Railways; the revenues will, it is estimated, more than meet working expenses and pay the Debenture interest.

Mineral Wealth of the Country

With regard to the minerals, as to the work done, we have so far naturally been dependent for information on the various prospectors, companies, syndicates, and other groups that have, under our mining laws, commenced the development of the mineral resources of the country. We are confident that gold exists in the country and in payable quantities, and, as you will see, we think the time has come when the Company may fairly be expected to take a more active part in the development of these resources to which it is entitled on joint account with prospectors and others under the Mineral Law. You will understand that there is no departure from the policy that has been consistently maintained by the Board, but there no doubt will be instances where, for the due protection of this Company's interests, it may be necessary for the Directors to embark capital for special developments; but I desire to issue a word of warning, lest sanguine hopes should be raised that the Company is henceforth going indiscriminately to find working capital for prospectors. That is not so. The Board will only in exceptional instances, and under the best available expert advice, advance moneys for development purposes and for working properties before they are producing gold at a profit. It is for this and the general purposes of the Company, including the deficit during the interval, which I believe will now be short, before the administrative revenue is sufficient to meet the expenditure, that we are proposing an increase in the capital of the Company. With reference to statements that have been circulated since this announcement was made public, I desire to emphasise the fact that it is only during the present month that the Board, after anxious and careful consideration, has determined to recommend this course. It is proposed to now issue 250,000 shares, being one-sixth of the new capital we ask your authority to create. We trust these will readily be subscribed for *pro ratâ* by the present shareholders at £2 per share. It is intended to retain the remaining 1,250,000 shares for issue hereafter from time to time as and when opportunity occurs for meeting the exceptional cases to which I have already referred, when it may be expedient to find money for development and such-like purposes. On these occasions the shares will, of course, in the first place, be offered *pro ratâ* to the shareholders. As I mentioned, the resolution authorising the increase of capital will have to be submitted at an extraordinary general meeting, which will be held as soon as our present meeting is over, but I have thought it better to give the needed explanations now, so that the extraordinary meeting may be purely formal, and not be an additional demand on your time. On the accounts I need not detain you. The balance-sheet is full, and I trust readily understood. The Administrative revenue for the year ending March 31, 1896, exceeded expenditure, and though this condition was not followed in the year ending March 31, 1897, in consequence of the heavy expenses connected with the rebellion and the rinderpest, we have every reason to think that the experience of the year to March 31, 1896, will shortly be repeated. You will learn with satisfaction that the revenue for the year ending March 31, 1898, is the highest reached since the incorporation of the Company.

Constitution of the Board

I now propose to say a few words with reference to the constitution of the Board. You are aware that the new scheme, to which I have already made reference, leaves to the shareholders the election of the entire Board. The provision in the Charter constituting Life Directors is to be abrogated, and the Government do not propose to act on the provision enabling it to appoint an Official Director. The Royal Charter appointed the Duke of Fife,[9] Lord Grey, and myself Life Directors. The Duke of Fife has, to our regret, resigned. Some time must necessarily elapse before the new scheme can be officially completed, as we must have a supplementary Charter, and there will be a new Order by her Majesty in Council. Lord Grey and myself have therefore thought it right that shareholders should at once have the opportunity that will be given on the completion of these documents, and we have resigned our seats as Directors in order that you may determine by your votes whether we retain your confidence and you desire our re-election. Should you do so, our services will continue at your disposal. Lord Gifford and Mr. George Cawston,[10] who have been our colleagues from the outset, retire as usual under the existing provisions of the deed of settlement. They offer themselves for re-election, and I have no doubt you will desire that they should continue in office. Lord Farquhar,[11] I regret to say, resigned his seat as Director at the same time as did the Duke of Fife. We have received notices that a resolution will be submitted proposing the election of Mr. Cecil Rhodes – (cheers) – and of Mr. Alfred Beit[12] – (cheers) – I should perhaps say the re-election of these gentlemen – and also proposing the election of Mr. Rochfort Maguire,[13] who has sat with us in London as Mr. Rhodes's alternate. Ladies and gentlemen, I heartily concur in the proposal to re-elect Mr. Rhodes. I have already referred to the incidents of 1895 and 1896. Mr. Rhodes has admitted his mistake, the only one, so far as I am aware, that he has made during his now long career in Africa, in the furtherance of his enlightened schemes for the Federation, under Imperial auspices, of the South African States. Need I remind you that everyone makes mistakes in this world? Every man in this hall has done so at some time in his life. (A Voice: You have in not having a larger room.) It has been said by a great Statesman, not of this country, but of a country speaking the English language, that a man who has never made a mistake has never made anything else. You must remember, on the other hand, the successes which Mr. Rhodes has achieved, and that if it had not been for the energy, the foresight, and, I may add, the generosity displayed by him, that enormous extent of territory which has now been added to the British Empire would without doubt have been in the possession of some other country. We derived so much advantage from the assistance of Mr. Maguire when sitting at our Board as alternate in London for Mr. Rhodes that we shall cordially welcome him as a Director in his own right on his election to-day. Since our report was issued, I have, with very great regret, received an intimation from Mr. Beit of his inability to rejoin the Board at the present juncture. This decision has been taken, not out of consideration for his private interests, but in deference to advice which he has felt unable to disregard, as to obligations arising out of his fiduciary relations in connection with important and varied interests in the Transvaal, which it is his duty to safeguard. Mr. Beit has thus been reluctantly compelled to sacrifice his personal inclinations, and I feel sure that you will both appreciate and respect his motives. Mr. Beit has requested me to say that he retains the deepest interest in the welfare of the Company, and, as evidence of his confidence in its future, and of his desire to co-operate in the settlement and development of our territories, he is prepared to guarantee free of charge, and in the face of the present war difficulties, half the proposed issue of 250,000 shares at £2 per share, and he renews the pledge, given when he resigned his seat in July, 1896, to place his energies and influence at the disposal of the Board. I and my colleagues feel it impossible to urge Mr. Beit to reconsider his decision, but trust that in a not distant future it may be possible for him to resume his seat at the Board. We entirely appreciate Mr. Beit's motive and his generosity in offering the guarantee. It is in accordance with the liberal and public-spirited action that has actuated him in everything connected with this Company, and I heartily thank him. But I am glad to think there is no reason to suppose that the shareholders will not readily respond to our appeal for further capital. Our deed of settlement provides that the number of Directors shall not be less than seven, and we propose therefore that the Board of Directors shall this afternoon, acting under the powers vested in it by the deed of settlement, appoint Sir Sidney Shippard,[14] K.C.M.G., a Director of this Company. (Cheers.) Sir Sidney Shippard is well known in South Africa, where he has a long record of service under the Imperial authorities, his last appointment being that of Deputy Commissioner for Bechuanaland. We are convinced that we shall have as our new colleague a gentleman of energy, ability, and great Colonial experience, and we thank him for on so short a notice undertaking the responsibilities of office. I will not detain you longer. The resolution which I am about to propose will be seconded by Lord Grey, who will be able to confirm from his personal experiences in Rhodesia the sanguine expectations which we still hold as to the future of the country. In our darkest hours, as well as in the brightest times, we have consistently maintained our confidence in the great enterprise, in furtharance of which her Majesty, so recently as less than ten years since, was graciously pleased to grant us her Royal Charter. (Cheers.) As soon as the resolution required to approve and adopt the reports and accounts has been passed we shall proceed to the election of Directors, immediately after which Mr. Rhodes will, I hope, join us at this Board and address you. I now beg to move: "That the reports and accounts of the Company to March 31, 1895, March 31, 1896, and March 31, 1897, be and the same are hereby approved and adopted." (Loud applause).

Earl Grey, who was warmly received, said: In rising to second the resolution proposed by the President, I am glad to have the opportunity of expressing my personal gratitude to all the officials of the Company, and also to the settlers of Rhodesia – including the Mayor of Buluwayo,[15] whom I am glad to see on the platform to-day – for the ungrudging assistance given to me during the whole period of my administration. Their friendly co-operation and support in great measure removed the burden of my responsibilities and have left in my memory the pleasantest recollections. I also wish to convey my thanks to the Imperial officers, to the officials of the Cape and Natal Governments, and to the Volunteers from England, South Africa, and Australia, who contributed so materially to the suppression of the rebellion. (Cheers.) Thanks to the heartiness of their support, and to your wise liberality in voting the supplies necessary to enable the Company to overcome its difficulties and to secure the extension of the railways, Mashonaland and Matabeleland have got through their troubles, and we may now, I think, confidently look forward to a period of peace, active commercial development, and steadily increasing prosperity. I am aware that the detractors of Rhodesia have been busy, but that is not necessarily an unhopeful sign. Detraction, like the measles, is an infantile affliction which every healthy young community has to suffer. We are told that our railways won't carry, that the materials don't exist, that the soil won't grow crops, and that the officials of the Company and the settlers are the most infamous and disreputable of mankind. Having lived in Rhodesia for nearly

18 months, and having been a daily witness of the unanimous and extraordinary confidence of the settlers in the future of their country, I am honestly indifferent as to the pessimistic forecasts of enemies and unbelievers. Because we cannot show more the country is condemned. When I think of the difficulties we have had to encounter I am amazed that we can show so much. People who indulge in these impatient criticisms cannot have realised the conditions. When I was in Rhodesia the cost of transport from Umtali to Salisbury at one time reached 2s. 6d. a pound, and so recently as last September was still nearly 1s. 6d. These figures supply an answer to the charge of little development. Here in England you can send parcels up to 11lb. from one end of the United Kingdom to the other for 1s., practically a penny per pound. Imagine what your position would be if, in addition to the home cost and ocean and railway freights over 8,000 miles, you had to pay on every article you consume transport rates from rail-head alone from 12 to 18 times as high as those charged for Parcel Post. That has been our position in Rhodesia since 1895. The fall in prices due to the extension of the railways has already completely altered the whole situation, and I am satisfied, from what I personally know of the country and its inhabitants, that before the close of the present year Rhodesia will show results more than sufficient to justify your faith in its future. Of that I am convinced. I am therefore indifferent to the accusations which have been made against the character of the country, but I feel more indignation than I can express at the wanton and groundless charges that have been so freely levelled against both the Administration and the settlers. I have no hesitation in saying that no Colony founded during the last 100 years can show so large a proportion of well-educated and well-conducted men as Rhodesia can to-day, and those who know the country will agree with me when I say that the tone of the community reflects the traditions of the best English Public Schools. It is impossible for me to say more. In every country bad characters are to be found, and Rhodesia is no exception; but I am in a position to state that where crime has been brought to the knowledge of the Administration every effort has been made to secure its punishment, and that offences of white men against natives have been treated with especial severity. In illustration I may quote recent cases where one man who had defrauded natives by representing himself to be a Native Commissioner was sentenced to six years' imprisonment with hard labour, and another who had violated a native girl to nine years. I have taken a great personal interest in the Native Question, and I am confident that when the regulations which are still under the consideration of her Majesty's Government are proclaimed it will be admitted that they are well calculated to enable a white and black population to live side by side as a civilised community. The proposals of her Majesty's Government have my warm approval. The control of the Crown, if properly exercised, should be both a safeguard and an assistance to the Company; but I cannot too earnestly state my conviction that the control, to be beneficial, must be exercised by men who, like Sir Alfred Milner,[16] combine with culture and wide experience the authority which comes from local knowledge and personal observation. (Applause.) Enthusiasts 8,000 miles away, however well-meaning they may be, cannot possibly

have a sufficiently complete understanding of the points at issue to justify their overriding the decisions of men on the spot. There are many important questions referred to in the report, such as the effect of the new Constitution upon the future of the country, and the policy of the Company in regard to the development and protection of your interests, as to which I should have been glad to have addressed you, but I think that I shall best consult your convenience by leaving these matters to be dealt with by Mr. Rhodes, who I am happy to think will, by your votes, immediately resume his rightful position on your Board. (Applause.) I have the honour to second the resolution.

Earl GREY then proposed that the Duke of Abercorn be re-elected a Director of the Company and Lord GIFFORD seconded the resolution, which was carried.

The CHAIRMAN proposed that Earl Grey be re-elected a Director of the Company and Mr. CAWSTON seconded the resolution, which was carried.

The CHAIRMAN proposed that Lord Gifford be re-elected a Director of the Company and Earl GREY seconded the resolution, which was carried.

The CHAIRMAN proposed that Mr. George Cawston be re-elected a Director of the Company and Earl GREY seconded the resolution, which was carried.

Mr. WESTON JARVIS[17] proposed the election of the Right Hon. Cecil J. Rhodes as a Director of the Company.

The CHAIRMAN seconded the motion, which was at once carried, as was also a furthur resolution electing Mr. Rochfort Maguire as a Director of the Company.

Mr. Rhodes's Address

Mr. CECIL RHODES (who was received with loud and prolonged cheers) said that he thanked the shareholders for having re-elected him as a Director of the Company. In accepting the position he recognised the responsibility which it represented. Her Majesty's Government had said that as they had become a commercial Company they had no objection to the course which they had now adopted, and he felt the confidence that the shareholders had shown in him by re-electing him to the Board, and he knew the obligation that the acceptance of that election meant. It would be only right for him to state that day their situation in connection with that Company, and he could state it more clearly now after a residence of 18 months in the country which the shareholders of that Company had added to the Empire. (Cheers.) He said fairly the shareholders of that Company, because ideas were all very well, but he recognised fully and clearly that the successful carrying out of those ideas was due first of all to the 8,000 gentlemen and now the 35,000 or 40,000 who had subscribed the capital towards the carrying out of the same. (A Voice: And you.) There were two matters on which he had to speak on that occasion, one was the dealing with the money which they had spent in the development and conquest of the country which they had named after him. That money had been referred to, he believed, by Lord Grey as being £10,000,000, and his Lordship would pardon him if he corrected that statement, and said that it was only about £6,000,000 with the Debenture debt. Now, the view that he took about that money, and he was speaking to two audiences – the shareholders present there that day and the people in the country – was that when the country became a self-governing State, just like another State in South Africa, then the money expended in the conquest and development of it should become a Debenture debt of the country – (hear, hear) – and a share of it should be borne by the people who came after them. He compared the early history of their territory with the early history of Australia, which when annexed in the first instance was said to be hopeless, but which now had 4,000,000 of inhabitants and a trade of about £100,000,000 a year. The people who were to come into their country in the future must bear the cost of the development of it, and the changing of a barbarous territory into a civilised State. (A Voice: Quite right.) He considered that it was only right that that should be so.

A Self-Governing State

They were sliding from a Chartered Administration to a Self-Governing State, and whenever the people chose to take on the full responsibilities of Self-Government they must take over the debt incurred in the development of the country – (hear, hear) – and he felt sure that they would do so. (Hear, hear). They were now in an intermediate state: they had got what was called a Semi-responsible Government. They had a Government of elective representation, like Natal and Griqualand West[18] in South Africa and perhaps many other Colonies in other parts of the world. That was their second stage following Crown Administration, because in this case the Charter must be regarded as taking the place of the Crown. They were therefore, as he had said, in their second stage of existence with an elective representation, they keeping the majority of the votes because, as they were responsible for the expenditure, they were entitled to the right of veto. It was only fair and right that those who paid for the music should set the tune, In this second stage there was a Council of four elective representatives, and there were five representing the Company. When the country became a fully Self-Governing State and took over the entire responsibility of government the first thing to be done would be to bring about a balance of revenue and expenditure. The wish for Self-Government was the essence of Englishmen. (Hear, hear.) The trouble in the Transvaal was that they were treated as slaves, and they would not have it.[19] (Loud cheers.) They would have their rights. (Hear, hear.) The English were the most uncomfortable people in the world. They insisted on their rights – (hear, hear) – and they would never stop until they got them. (Cheers.) That was the great characteristic of the nation. (Applause.) Well, with reference to the territory which they had annexed, they had the power of veto on the question of expenditure. The first step would be the balancing of the revenue and the expenditure, and he had little doubt but that they would be able to do that. He would suggest, now that he had been re-elected a Director, that they should join the Customs Union of the Cape Colony,[20] which would give them about £100,000 a year, and then he would next suggest the reduction of the police expenditure. Now that they had two railways he did not see the need for 1,000 white police and 300 native police. Cape Colony, with 1,000,000 natives, had only 800 police. There were other questions also in this connection, Excise, &c., which he would not go into on that occasion. He looked to see a balance of revenue and expenditure arrived at within 15 months' time.

Condition of the Country

Proceeding to refer to the country itself and its climate, he said that there was no truth whatever in the detractions that had been made. It had been asserted that white men could not live there, which was untrue, because it was not a tropical climate, but one where white men could live and marry and bring up white children. He firmly believed that these people would adopt Self-Government, and that they would readily assent to return to this Company, in the shape of debenture debt, the amount of money which had been expended in the acquisition and development of the country. There could be no doubt that it was only fair that they should be entitled to receive back the sums expended from time to time in the conversion of a barbaric territory into a civilised community. (Applause.) Well, he had done with that point. He now turned to the question of minerals, and their interest in the minerals which were discovered in their territory. He had not lost any faith about the minerals. (Hear, hear.) He believed in their existence, but he had always been extremely anxious that no one should gamble in their shares. He felt that they would get a fair return for their money expended, and he did not want them to gamble on the Stock Exchange in these shares, and thereby, by increasing the price now, discount the future. (Hear, hear.) He believed in the mineralised condition of the country. He noted that there were 16,000 holders of not exceeding 25 shares, which showed a great belief in the prospects of the development of that territory, apart from its commercial value. At the same time he did not want to see any gambling in the shares. (Hear, hear.) He did not wish to sound pessimistic in what he was saying, because he was really optimistic, and he felt a sure and certain belief in the future of the country and the great mineral resources it possessed. (Cheers.) During his residence there for the last year and a half he had been able to personally learn a great deal about it. There was a huge area – he only knew the area South of the Zambesi – of land, and no less than 157,000 claims had been registered, which meant that human beings had gone out there and had found gold quartz – quartz impregnated with gold – which was a good evidence of the mineral wealth of the territory. (Cheers.) They had now got the railways, and he knew that in May one or two batteries would be started. He could not believe that the whole of the experts and engineers of high position and great experience interested in the various claims there were telling deliberate untruths as to the mineralised condition of the different properties in which they were interested. (Hear, hear.) There had been plenty of detractors about. They had been told that the whole place was a swamp, and that no one could live there. That had been proved to be false, for the white men could live and thrive there.

They had been told that the place was hopeless, yet ten thousand white people were resident there. The detractors had attacked them on the minerals, and said that these were non-existent. That had been disproved. They had said there was no gold, and it had been proved that there was gold, and then there was only one thing left for the opponents to say, and they said that there was no payable gold. (Laughter.) There were plenty of people in South Africa who wanted to see the Company damned. There were plenty of people there who got up every morning not wishing to see their Hinterland a success, but to see it a failure. Every possible report that they could get hold of to its discredit was a matter of delight to them. He asked the meeting to conceive the possibility of having a valuable territory just at the back of you and half the community desiring that it should turn out a failure. They had been told that the country was a bad one, but that was not so; it was far from the truth, for the country was a very good one. (Hear, hear.) Lobengula[21] was the greatest chief in South Africa, and he took the best of the country, after going many miles before he stopped there. In his (the speaker's) opinion it was a rich country, highly mineralised and payably mineralised. (Applause.)

The Future of Rhodesia

He had every faith and belief in the future of Rhodesia. A great deal had been said about the share which the Company took in the Vendor's Scrip in connection with the minerals in the country, and it was stated that it was an unfair share, and one quite without precedent. With regard to the unfairness of the question, he would divide the question into three points, and lay each before the meeting. In the first place he would deal with the prospector, who very often started out with only a donkey and a pan, and he made the first discovery of the gold. In every other country in the world the law was that he was entitled to one claim, on which he had to pay a monthly license, and he was very often obliged to part with that claim before any results were obtained. In the case of the Company the prospector was allowed to take up two blocks of 10 claims each, in which the Company had a half interest, and on those claims he had to pay nothing in the shape of rent. Many prospectors had told him that that arrangement was a much better and a much fairer one to them. (Hear, hear.) The next person who had to deal with the matter was the capitalist who purchased the property from the prospector, who, of course, knew exactly what he was buying and paid accordingly, while the Government retained an interest in it. He maintained that the Government made the gold available by its administration, and they ought to, and should, take an interest in it. So they would see that the prospector received a considerable advantage in having a larger number of claims and not having to pay a license. The speculator knew exactly what he was buying, and the public who subscribed the capital knew that the Scrip belonged to the man who purchased the mine and to the Government. He was sure when the country became self-governing there would be no objection to the Company maintaining its interest and acting as it had done heretofore. He felt sure that the meeting would now begin to see that they were not only adding another province to the Empire but also that they would get a full return for the money which they had so liberally expended. (Applause.) The Board had had one difficulty lately, and that was in connection with some of the reefs which they had no doubt were extremely good, and would when worked be payable. Those who had possession of those reefs had approached the Company asking the Board to reduce their interest in the properties, as they said that if they did not do so it would be impossible for them to get the capital subscribed by the public. The Directors had to consider that it was necessary to produce the gold in order to convince the public that the country contained gold in payable quantities, and so they reduced the holding of the Company in some cases in order to get the batteries erected and work commenced. They now asked the shareholders, however, to give them power to raise some money, so that when any such proposal was made to them they might say in reply that they would not reduce their interest in the Scrip, but they would, if they approved of the property, raise a portion of the working capital. (Applause.) The proprietors might say that that would be a very great risk, as a number of improper properties might be assisted by the Company, but in reply to that he would say that the Company would appoint two or three able mining engineers who would carefully examine any property brought forward, not for a day or so but for about a month's working, and the Board would act on their advice. He thought, therefore, that the shareholders could safely leave the matter in the hands of the Board. (Hear, hear.) He had now pointed out how the money placed in the hands of the Directors had been expended on the development of the country, and shown how the Company held a share in the mineral wealth. He had alluded to the mineral wealth of that vast area, and he certainly thought that the interest which they held in it was worth keeping – (hear, hear) – but he urged them not to go and over gamble the shares. He had shown them what they had subscribed and how it had been spent, and he was of the opinion that in his lifetime he would return a good interest on that money – (loud applause) – but he hated to read the list and see how people had gambled the Shares up without any warranty, for they had dealt with the prospective value of the undertaking, and not with the present. (Hear, hear.)

Extension of Railways

He now wished to proceed to show them how marvellously they had succeeded in the development of the country. When they remembered that the railway to Buluwayo, which cost about £2,000,000 for 600 miles, was paying about £12,000 per month, or in excess of the 5 per cent. interest on its cost, he thought they would recognise that that was a most satisfactory and encouraging feature for the future development of the country. (Hear, hear.) He did not propose that the shareholders of the Company should be asked to obligate themselves for any further development in that direction, but he thought it was a practicable and possible scheme that the line should be further extended to the shore of Lake Tanganyika,[22] for they were responsible for the government of the North as well as the South. He would not, however, ask the Chartered Company to subscribe more capital, and he considered that they had plenty to do with what they possessed. The English people had received a vast area of territory, for which they had not paid a single shilling. It had cost them nothing, and had only given the Little Englanders an opportunity of indulging in every class of adverse criticism, without any cost whatever to the country, and having regard to that fact he had approached the Government and placed the position before them as a Director of the Bechuanaland Railway, and not as one having any connection with the Chartered Company – (hear, hear, and laughter) – and asked them if they would give any assistance towards the extension of that line. The cost would be about £2,000,000, and he asked in the most moderate way. He said that the Government had at last awakened to the fact that it was the trade of the world which kept England what it was, and it was always necessary to do all that was possible to extend that trade. A large tract of country had been added to the Empire, and he asked their assistance in its further development. He said that if he tried to borrow the money it would cost 5 per cent., while if the Government borrowed it for him they would be able to raise it at 3 per cent. (Hear, hear.) He wanted £2,000,000 for the extension of the line, and in one case it meant £100,000, in the other £60,000, and he asked the Government to help them to get it at the cheaper rate by backing their promisory note. He thought that the Chartered Company could give a guarantee, and the British Government could come behind that. He reminded the Government that they were responsible for the effective occupation of the country under the Berlin Treaty,[23] and urged them to give assistance in raising the money. If they were nervous of raising the whole sum at once, to raise it for building one hundred miles at a time, and so satisfy themselves that the line would pay. He asked the shareholders if they thought that the Government would do what they asked. (A Voice: Yes.) He did not know. It depended so much on the people. If the public took to the idea the Government would agree; if they did not, they would not consent to do it. If they got to Tanganyika, got the railway down from Uganda to join them, and got Kitchener to come down from Khartoum, what would be the position? (Loud applause.) It was no imaginative position; it was a practical question. The telegraph was regarded as imagination when he first brought the subject forward. This was a practical question and a practical position, and there was no reason why the Government should not assist them. By the Treaty of Berlin the Government was obliged to be in effective occupation, and if Sir William Harcourt[24] thought that the Company must eventually fail, surely it was better that they should extend the railway to Tanganyika first, as that was the best means of effective occupation. (Loud applause.) He thought that perhaps the Government might say: "If you act with care and caution we will give this guarantee, and so help you to raise the money at the cheaper rate." (Hear, hear.) He did not ask them for any money, only for the guarantee. It was the best thing they could do in order to add to the trade of the country. He remembered that some time ago he spoke of the Little Englanders, and the position which they held with regard to the Colonies, saying that immediately the Colonies became self-supporting they put prohibitive duties in the way of the Mother Country, and treated her as they would a foreign nation. The Chartered Company proposed to her Majesty's Government that in the constitution of the Company should be placed a clause to the effect that the duty on all British goods into Rhodesia should not exceed the Cape tariff, and that would be securing for England the whole of the trade of the country. Some people said that there was a scent of Protection in that and they were Freetraders, and some discussion arose as to whether the word "British" or "imported" should be used, but eventually the Government agreed to the suggestion that the duty on all British goods should not exceed the Cape tariff. In the meanwhile the tariff had come down, so that it meant that the whole trade of that vast area was practically assured for England. (Loud applause.) People were becoming more and more alive to the necessity of extending the trade of England in all parts of the world. Protective tariffs had been set up by foreign nations in order to keep British trade away, and England must take any part of the world she could get in order to still keep up and increase her trade. She must take anything that was left, and he was sorry that there was so very little. (Hear, hear, and laughter.) The working man had found that to keep her position England must have the trade of the world, and if the trade were shut down he was done for. Tariffs had been put against England to keep her from gaining the whole of the trade of the world, and the working man knew it, and that was why the Little Englander was out of it. (Loud applause.)

Disappearance of "The Little Englander"

Everyone was an Imperialist now, even the Radicals, for they had discovered that the public had that feeling and they must have it too or they would never get in. (Hear, hear.) He used to be very amused at the questions in the House of Commons with regard to the Chartered Company. How much had the Chartered Company paid towards the war? and the answer was: The whole of it; an answer that caused much dismal anger to the Little Englander. Now the Little Englander was gone, and he had asked the Government for their help, and he hoped they would give it. The two objections which they had were that it was unusual and that Mr. Rhodes was connected with it – (laughter) – but still they would do their best. There was one other point on which he wished to touch before concluding, and that was the stories which had been circulated to the effect that he was cruel to the natives. The best answer to that was the action of the natives themselves. When trouble came the natives gathered round, and settled around him, and it was not to be supposed that they would do that if he were something of a horror or a bogey to them, nor was it to be supposed that he would trust his skin among them unless he knew how he would be treated. (Hear, hear.) He had just received a telegram saying that 10,000 Fingoes[25] were going into their country to settle, and that was the best answer that he could give to such stories. It was a want of knowledge of the facts that started such rumours, but unfortunately Exeter Hall[26] had also taken it up. He was, however, prepared to take any member of Exeter Hall through South Africa, and let him see for himself what the natives thought of the matter. (Applause.) In conclusion, the speaker said that the country had done very well, and he had done very well in his connection with that country; but the picture would not be complete if he did not say, now that he was again responsible for their affairs, that upon the lines he had sketched out with regard to the future of the Company it would fall to him and his co-Directors to offer the shareholders an ample return upon the money which they had expended, and he had not the slighest doubt about it. (Loud and prolonged cheers.)

The CHAIRMAN then proposed: "That the proposals in regard to the future exercise of its administrative powers by this Company, the subject of the correspondence forming Appendix A to the Directors' report to the shareholders, dated April 7, 1898, be and the same are hereby approved, and the Board of Directors authorised to carry them into effect."

Earl GREY seconded the resolution, which was carried.

An extraordinary general meeting followed, when the CHAIRMAN proposed: "That the capital of Company be increased to £5,000,000 by the creation of 1,500,000 new shares of £1 each."

Earl GREY seconded the resolution, which was carried, and a vote of thanks to the Chairman for presiding closed the meeting.

Notes

1 James Hamilton, second Duke of Abercorn (1838–1913), was a Conservative MP for Donegal from 1860 to 1880 and joined the House of Lords on his father's death in 1885. After the collapse of Home Rule in 1886, he played a major role in forging and sustaining a 20-year alliance between Conservatives and Liberal Unionists, especially in Ulster. South Africa was his only other main interest beyond Ireland: a large shareholder in the BSAC, he agreed to chair its board during the brief interval between 1896 and 1898 when political crises stripped Cecil Rhodes of that position.

2 The Royal Albert Hall opened in 1871 in South Kensington, with a seating capacity of 7000 (later reduced to 5500 owing to more stringent fire regulations).

3 At the tail end of 1895, Leander Starr Jameson (1853–1917), who had played a central role in Rhodes's acquisition of territory in Matabeleland in the previous five years, led 500 BSAC police officers from Rhodesia into the South African Republic in a failed effort to incite an uprising by British expatriates who were working there.

4 Albert Henry George, fourth Earl Grey (1851–1917 – succeeding his uncle as Earl in 1896) was a Liberal MP from 1880 to1886, when he broke with Gladstone over Home Rule. He belonged to Joseph Chamberlain's South Africa Committee in the 1880s, which opposed granting a charter to the BSAC, but Rhodes won him over and he sat on its board from 1889 until 1904, when he became Governor-General of Canada. A keen admirer of Rhodes, Grey was complicit in the Jameson Raid and used his connections with Chamberlain to garner government support of the ensuing hostilities.

5 Bulawayo was Rhodesia's second-largest white-settled town, located 250 miles southwest of the capital city Salisbury.

6 The Glen Grey Act, which was passed by the Cape Colony Parliament in 1894 (while Rhodes was Prime Minister), replaced communal with individual land tenure and introduced a tax that forced many Xhosa residents to work as wage-laborers in farms, factories, and mines.

7 Induna is a Zulu and Ndebele title meaning officer or civil servant.

8 The BSAC began constructing the Bechuanaland Railway soon after it received its charter, extending rail service north from Kimberley through Bechuanaland (present-day Botswana), reaching Bulawayo in 1897. A second railway connected Bulawayo to Salisbury in 1899.

9 Alexander Duff (1849–1912) succeeded his father (the fifth Earl of Fife) as the first Duke of Fife in 1879. He was a founding "life director" of the BSAC but resigned in 1896 following the Jameson Raid.

10 Frederick Gifford (1849–1911) and George Cawston (1851–1918) formed the Bechuanaland Exploration Company in 1888, which Rhodes's BSAC absorbed the following year. Gifford was a military man who had fought in the Asante War (1874) and served as Colonial Secretary in West Australia and Gibraltar between 1880 and 1888; Cawston was a lawyer and stockbroker. Both joined the BSAC's board in 1889 and were the prime movers in calling for Rhodes's resignation from the board following the Jameson Raid in 1896. Cawston resigned after Rhodes resumed his seat in 1898, turning his sights to China, but Gifford remained on the board until his death.

11 Horace Brand Farquhar (1844–1922), raised to the peerage in 1898, was a wealthy and powerful London merchant and banker. A friend and financial advisor to the Duke of Fife, he joined the BSAC's board in 1889 but resigned in 1896, following the Jameson Raid.

12 Alfred Beit (1853–1906) was a Hamburg-born merchant who joined Rhodes on the De Beers board shortly after arriving in Kimberley in 1882. He soon became a naturalized British subject and close friends with Rhodes and was an original BSAC director when it formed in 1889. His role in the Jameson raid led him to resign his directorship in 1897.

13 James Rochfort Maguire (1855–1925) befriended Rhodes while at Oxford in the 1870s, and he followed Rhodes to South Africa, where he served as Secretary to the Cape Colony's deputy governor in the 1880s. He helped Rhodes win concessions in Matabeleland in 1888, subscribed £18,000 in BSAC shares when it formed the following year, and acted as Rhodes's "first alternate director" until 1902.

14 Sir Sidney Shippard (1837–1902) moved to Cape Town in 1867 and, in 1873, became Attorney General in the diamond district of Griqualand West, where he aggressively defended British land rights against indigenous African claims. He soon became close friends with Rhodes, following him to Oxford in 1878, then returning to South Africa as a colonial administrator in Bechuanaland. Rhodes invited him to join the BSAC board in 1898 to reward his assistance in mending fences following the Jameson Raid.

15 Isidore Hirschler was Bulawayo's first mayor, serving from November 1897 to August 1898. A former Austrian cavalry officer, he fought in the Ndebele War and was later the founding chair of the Wareleigh Development Company in Rhodesia in 1902.

16 Alfred Milner (1854–1925) served as Governor of the Cape Colony and High Commissioner for Southern Africa from 1897 to 1901 and played an important role in British imperial politics during the two decades after the Second Boer War.

17 Alexander Weston Jarvis (1855–1939) was a banker with close ties to Rhodesia, a Conservative MP for King's Lynn (1886–92), and an army officer who fought as a volunteer in the Matabele Uprising and would later serve in the Boer War and World War One.

18 Natal was a British colony in southeastern Africa from 1843 until 1910, when it became part of the Union of South Africa. Griqualand West, in central South Africa, became a British colony in 1873 with Kimberley as its capital, then was annexed by Cape Colony in 1880.

19 Rhodes is here referring to the Uitlanders – British workers in the South African Republic who lacked full political rights.

20 The Cape Colony Customs Union originally paired the Cape Colony with the Orange Free State in 1889. Although Natal joined in 1898, the Boer War prevented Rhodesia

from joining until 1903, when the renamed Southern African Customs Union included Transvaal and Southern Rhodesia.

21 Lobengula Khumalo (1845–1894), the second king of the Ndebele, gave concessions to the BSAC in 1889, but relations soured in 1893, resulting in the first of two wars between his subjects and the company.

22 Lake Tanganyika runs north-south from the northeastern corner of present-day Zambia, along the northwestern border of Tanzania, to Burundi. Rhodes had hoped to use the lake as a connector in his "Cape to Cairo" railway scheme, but Germany thwarted this plan.

23 The Treaty of Berlin was signed in July 1878 between Austria-Hungary, France, Germany, Great Britain, Italy, Russia, and the Ottoman Empire, establishing colonial borders in Africa.

24 Sir William Harcourt (1827–1904) was a lawyer and Liberal MP who served as Home Secretary and Chancellor of the Exchequer under Gladstone. As leader of the Liberal opposition after 1898, he emerged as a vocal critic of the Conservative Party's efforts during the Second Anglo-Boer War.

25 While Prime Minister of the Cape Colony, Rhodes enlisted the Fengu people as mercenaries in various frontier wars, including the Ndebele wars of 1893 and 1896. A month after this meeting, Rhodes made good on his promise to provide land in Southern Rhodesia to thousands of "loyal and progressive" Fengu settlers from the Cape.

26 Exeter Hall in Central London was a public meeting hall and was derisively referred to by critics of humanitarian reform as shorthand for such movements.

Part 3

MERGERS AND ACQUISITIONS

Editorial Headnote

London and North Western Railway (1846)

The first half-yearly meeting of the London and North Western Railway (LNWR) in 1846 followed the merger of the London & Birmingham (LBR) with the Manchester & Birmingham and the Grand Junction, which had absorbed the Liverpool & Manchester (LMR) the previous year and connected Birmingham to rail service between those two cities. The main speaker at the meeting, the banker George Carr Glyn, was a towering influence on early British railway development. He had chaired the LBR since 1837 and was founding chair from 1842 of the Railway Clearing House, which sorted out the complex accounting challenge of customers traveling on several different routes with a single ticket.[1] The LNWR's joint secretaries, Henry Booth and Richard Creed, who both spoke at the meeting, had respectively steered the LMR and LBR through their formative years. Besides being the LMR's treasurer and general manager, Booth helped develop the boiler used in its first locomotives.[2] Finally, the new company's report referred to Robert Stephenson and Joseph Locke, two of the most prominent engineers in the British railway scene; Stephenson had gained celebrity status in 1830 by designing the "Rocket" locomotive that was used on the LMR's maiden run. Both supervised railway and bridge construction around the world into the 1850s, turning Britain into a model for international rail transit.[3]

The LNWR merger – as well as George Hudson's creation of the Midland Railway from four local companies – took place at the height of the "railway mania" of 1845–47, which attracted £83 million in new investment before the stock market spectacularly crashed in 1847.[4] The companies that survived the crash, including the LNWR and other well-capitalized firms, responded by closing ranks. Glyn and his new general manager at the LNWR, Mark Huish (who had previously managed the Grand Junction), led this movement, negotiating treaties that reduced price competition and organizing annual conferences among goods managers at the Railway Clearing House. Such efforts informally extended the logic of concentration that the merger movement of the 1840s had set in motion. Glyn and others also responded to the crash by entering politics *en masse*: it was not an accident that Glyn, Stephenson, and Locke all entered Parliament in 1847. Later in the century, when their collusive pricing policies yielded lobbying activity by farmers and merchants, this political influence would pay dividends in the form of railway-friendly legislation.[5]

Notes

1 Timothy L. Alborn, *Conceiving Companies: Joint-Stock Politics in Victorian England* (London" Routledge, 1998), 178; Philip Bagwell, *The Railway Clearing House in the British Economy 1842–1922* (London: Allen and Unwin, 1968). The

Manchester & Birmingham Railway formed in 1840 and connected Manchester with Crewe, contracting with the Grand Junction to provide service to Birmingham.

2 A. H. John, *A Liverpool Merchant House: Being the History of Alfred Booth and Company 1863–1958* (London: Routledge, 1959). 19; "Richard Creed," *Monthly Railway Record* 1 (1847), 729.

3 Anthony Burton, *Joseph Locke: Civil Engineer and Railway Builder, 1805–1860* (Barnsley: Pen & Sword Transport, 2017); Michael Robbins, *George and Robert Stephenson* (Oxford: Oxford University Press, 1965).

4 E. G. Barnes, *The Rise of the Midland Railway 1844–1874* (London: Allen and Unwin, 1966); G. R. Hawke and M. C. Reed, "Railway Capital in the United Kingdom in the Nineteenth Century," *Economic History Review* 22 (1969), 270.

5 Alborn, *Conceiving Companies*, 198–199, 228–237.

16

LONDON AND NORTH WESTERN RAILWAY

Source: London and North Western Railway (1846), *Herapath's Journal and Railway Magazine*, 8 August 1846

LONDON AND NORTH WESTERN RAILWAY

The First Half-yearly Meeting of the Shareholders in this Company, since the passing of the Act amalgamating the London and Birmingham Grand Junction and Liverpool and Manchester Companies, was held yesterday, at the Euston Hotel, Euston-square; G. C. Glyn,[1] Esq., in the chair.

Mr. Creed,[2] the Secretary, read the advertisement convening the meeting.

The CHAIRMAN said: Gentlemen, from the notice which has just been read to you, as well as the usual course of our commencing business, you will perceive that we are now about to hold the first meeting of the London and North Western Railway Company. It is to us a matter of extreme satisfaction to see you convened together, under our recently passed Act of Parliament, under that title; for although my colleague and myself have always received much gratification in meeting the Proprietors of the London and Birmingham Company, and have also left that concern, under its old name, in such a prosperous state; nevertheless, it is a matter of extreme gratification to us to find that the great measure we have advocated for some time past, has at last received the Royal Assent. (Hear.) I am sure no words are necessary in this room upon that subject. The approval which that measure has, from time to time, received by the Proprietary at both ends of the line, and at Manchester, speaks their wishes upon the subject. In fact, I may say, that it almost eventually arises as a matter of course; and certainly as regards the Grand Junction Company, the only wonder, perhaps, which can be expressed is this, that it did not take place at an earlier period. It was originally the intention of the Proprietors of both those undertakings to carry on the concern conjointly; but we all know the difficulties which at the commencement of those two great undertakings the Directors and the Proprietors experienced in being able even to carry on, divided as they were, those two great undertakings. It is impossible for us yet to represent to you the full effects which, both as regards your own interest and that of the public at large, we hope may be derived from the fact of the amalgamation itself. We shall not forget that we have great interests to deal with in the position we now occupy – that, both as regards the wants of Liverpool, Manchester, and the other towns under our care, it is our

DOI: 10.4324/9781003177715-19

duty to carry out, to the fullest possible extent, the advantages that we have already brought before the Legislature as likely to result from the amalgamation. But, gentlemen, it is only right to state, that finding as we do three separate and large bodies acting, I may say, on three different systems, it would be rash and unwise for us to move immediately, and too quickly, in re-adjusting the mode in which hereafter the whole may be carried on. We do look in many respects for important results from that which we have undertaken. Gentlemen, it is not only a source of great gratification to have this measure carried out in its full extent; but individually and personally on the part of my colleagues, I do not hesitate to say, that we have the greatest possible satisfaction in finding ourselves now so closely connected with those to whom we must ever look up as the great promoters and movers in all railway projects, to whom, in fact, the merit of having carried the system out principally belongs, during the time when I may almost say the first proposition with regard to railways was met with scorn and sneering; when Parliament was against them: when the public were incredulous as regarded the results; nevertheless, the honourable gentleman who sits near me proceeded to carry out that great undertaking with which he was associated, and which I may say led to the Liverpool and Manchester Railway. I do not hesitate to say, that I feel I am occupying improperly the chair upon this occasion in the presence of my honourable friend, Mr. Lawrence,[3] who was one of the earliest Promoters, one of those most strenuous advocates for this scheme, and who was mainly instrumental at the time in carrying forward the Liverpool and Manchester line itself. (Cheers.) Gentlemen, it is rumoured – I can scarcely believe it, and I allude to it only as a rumour, – that the Companies which hitherto have been successful in their results, are likely soon to be brought under the notice of Parliament, with a view of showing to the public the enormous profits, as they are called, which are supposed to have been derived by some of the Railway Companies. Gentlemen, it is not in this room, or in the presence of the Proprietors of the Liverpool and Manchester, or the Grand Junction, or the Manchester and Birmingham, that we can deny the existence of large profits; but, we say, that those profits were fairly earned; we say that we undertook a very great experiment, and we have undertaken it successfully; and with regard particularly to the London and Birmingham, I state here publicly and openly, that as regards the creation of new shares, – which is the point upon which we are likely, I understand, to be commented upon publicly – that when we were forced by the great increase of our outlay, by the estimates far exceeding the anticipation which was originally made, when we were driven to Parliament to ask for renewed power of raising money for the purpose of completing the London and Birmingham works, the subject underwent a long investigation before the Committee of the House of Commons appointed on that particular Bill; and the result was, that we were ordered to allocate the shares with our Proprietors at par. It was an act of justice, and it was equally an act of policy. We asked no new privileges; we asked nothing that was likely to increase the traffic. Our calculation of traffic was founded on the same footing as it had been from the first; but it was not a very pleasant thing to the Proprietors in those days, which were very dark days in the money-market, to be called on to double their capital, or nearly so, to carry out the original intention of the Legislature. To whom was the benefit, if any benefit should arise from that creation, to be given? Can there be a doubt that those who invested their money in the first instance were the only proper parties to receive the benefit, if there was any contingent benefit in it? What were the circumstances at the time? If the share had not been offered to the Proprietors at that moment, the result would have been that probably the undertaking would have lingered. The money-market in the year to which I refer was in a state of the greatest possible gloom; and if it had not been for the untiring energy of the Proprietors of the London and Birmingham Company, year after year would have passed without our being able to find the necessary funds for its completion. (Applause.) I think it is rather hard when a great experiment has been successfully carried out, that we should now be called upon to state an account of those profits which are not the profits of individuals, but they are profits circulated over the whole country, because the shares of the London and Birmingham Railway and the others are changing hands from day to day. It is an invidious thing to hold us up as having sacked (if I may use the expression) such large profits. (Hear, hear.) Gentlemen, I am anxious not to occupy your time unnecessarily upon this occasion; and as the Report is of some considerable length, I would much rather refer you to that for the further investigation concerning our proceedings. But it will be expected of me, I think, that I should say one or two words about those different projects that we have, from time to time, submitted to your approval, and which we subsequently brought before Parliament. Our success in Parliament this year has been of a very chequered character. As far as the London and Birmingham was concerned – I need not enter into the question as regards the other, because the Grand Junction have carried every Bill they had in Parliament – with regard to the London and Birmingham, we have lost several very important measures. We have lost, during the inquiry of this Session, the whole of those which we designated to you as the Warwickshire lines; but, which is the worst part of the case, our opponents have carried the Birmingham and Oxford. With regard to the other measures, we have, I think, been generally successful as regards them. They are not of very great importance in themselves. We have lost the St. Albans and Luton line, a line that may or may not be renewed, as our adversaries lost their Bill. We have withdrawn the Newport Valley line, and one or two smaller things; but on the whole I think we come out fortified in our position, if I may say so, by our proceedings in Parliament. But during the discussions which have gone on in the present session, we cannot conceal from ourselves the fact, that if we look to the South Western Railway Company, we find the Direct Portsmouth line carried against them. If we look to the Norfolk line we find competition encouraged in that quarter, we find the London and York Bill carried. We find in Scotland also the principle of competition laid down; and we find in our case, also, the Oxford and Birmingham carried against us; and also, although the Bill is not yet carried, we hear the principle of competition announced as one that ought to be carried out on another line as regards the Exeter line. Therefore we must assume, that the principle of competition is one which during this Session of Parliament has been very considerably adopted. We have not altered our views the least on the general merits. We believe, that if the Legislature had exercised a wise discretion, they would have taken up the doctrine so ably laid down by the Board of Trade, and would have encouraged, under proper regulations existing railways, rather than promote the dangerous, and I believe impolitic, inexpedient, and futile principle of competition in railway property (Cheers.) But, gentlemen, competition we must be prepared to meet, and if we had no other argument whatever, for having originally pressed on you the amalgamation with the Company with whom we are so happily united, we would urge that from what has been carried in this session, your property is rendered infinitely more safe by the fact of the amalgamation with the Companies which are now connected together, having been matured and carried. (Hear, hear.) Gentlemen, we are in a position to carry on competition, and any Company that commences competition against us, must commence with this fact – a very large reduction on existing rates! I may say, that, although some are equally low with us, there is only one Company in the neighbourhood of London whose rates are as low as our own. (Hear.) Gentlemen, the passing of these several Bills, of course, will require an addition to your capital; and when I mention that, I think it is only right that I should point out to the Proprietors that many of the Bills we have secured this session are Bills more of a protective character than those for which we can look for any new or large returns. We have been obliged to carry Bills for the improvement of our stations at Liverpool, Manchester, and London. Upon that I can scarcely hold out to you any new return. The same remark applies to several of the Bills which the Grand Junction have been successful in obtaining. I mention this (and I must be expressly understood to speak only in an individual character, and I do not wish to commit my colleagues to the opinion I am about to utter) because I think, when the creation of this stock has taken place, and these works are finished, that it will be almost impossible for us, unless extraordinary circumstances shall intervene, to keep up on the whole of our capital the existing dividend. It has been the purpose of the London and Birmingham Directors never to conceal anything from their Proprietary. It is right therefore that in these early days I should make you acquainted with my own individual opinion. It will be some time before the new Company can be brought into operation; and it is impossible with the spring, the industry, and the enterprise of this country, to tell what the intervening time may produce. Many of my colleagues are most sanguine, that with the great increase we propose to you, we may keep up our present dividend. That is not my opinion; and my opinion I state to you in my individual capacity. (Hear.) Gentlemen, I will not mention to you (because it would only forestall the Report and the resolutions) the mode in which we propose to create the new capital. We mean to propose an immediate creation of

London and North Western stock. I will not occupy your attention many more minutes; I am quite sure you will be anxious to hear that which is the authentic document; namely, the Report of your Directors: but I cannot resist upon this, the first occasion of meeting you under our new name, alluding to a vote for which we shall ask your sanction. It is, I may say, a debt of gratitude which we owe, and have long owed, to both our engineers. We have the advantage of having secured for the Amalgamated Company, the services both of Mr. Robert Stephenson[4] and Mr. Locke:[5] a combination of talent of which we may be justly proud. They have, as you are all well aware, saved the two Companies for a long time past: and although the amount which we propose to you cannot be considered as at all a compensation, or worthy of the merit with which we view them, still I think, that if you receive with approbation the resolution which will be tendered to you, with regard to those two distinguished individuals, the compliment being unexpected by them, it will be received with the greatest satisfaction. We mean to propose, for your sanction, before this meeting closes, that a testimonial of some shape or other to the value, in each case, of £1,000, should be offered to Mr. Robert Stephenson and Mr. Locke by the Proprietors of this Company. (Hear, hear, and applause.) Having made these remarks, I will now request Mr. Booth to read the Report; and if there are any other points upon which you require any explanation which it is in my power to give, it will be a source of satisfaction to me to be able to give it.

Mr. BOOTH,[6] the Secretary of the late Manchester and Liverpool Company, said: I am obliged to the Chairman for this introduction to my new Proprietary. I will now proceed to read the

Report

The Directors are happy to report, that the Act "to consolidate the London and Birmingham, Grand Junction, and Manchester and Birmingham Railway Companies," received the Royal Assent on the 16th of July last. In meeting, for the first time, the Shareholders of the London and North-Western Company, the Directors have great pleasure in being able to inform them, that the traffic for the half-year, on the three lines which are now under the control of the Amalgamated Company, exceeds considerably in each case that of the corresponding six months of last year, and that this observation applies to the three divisions in which railway traffic is usually classed: namely – coaching, merchandise, and coals. But while an increased traffic on all the lines indicates the prosperous state of the concern, the Proprietors will recollect that from the larger amount of capital entitled to dividend, owing to fresh calls paid up, and to other circumstances, a larger sum is now required to pay the same rate of dividend: while, at the same time, the six months just ended constitute the least productive half-year. It will consequently be necessary to encroach, to some extent, on the reserve fund which the Proprietors allowed the Directors to lay by, after providing for the last dividend.

	£	s.	d.
By the accounts which will be laid before the meeting, it appears that the nett proceeds of the amalgamated concern for the six months are	543,929	4	4
To which must be added the surplus fund, amounting to	166,105	12	3
Making an available balance of	£710,034	16	7

The Directors recommend a dividend of 4 per cent. on the Manchester and Birmingham capital of £1,440,600, in conformity with the provisions of the Act	57,600	0	0
And of £5 per £100 share on the remaining capital	549,789	3	0
Which together will amount to	£507,389	3	0
And leaving a balance of	£102,643	13	7

to be carried forward as a surplus fund to the next half-year's account.

The Directors will now beg leave to state to the Proprietors the result of their proceedings in Parliament in the session which is about to close. It will be seen that the extent of new works contemplated at the commencement of the session has been very much curtailed. The Acts obtained this session for new lines are as follows, with the estimated capital required to carry them into effect: –

London and Birmingham –		
Easton extension, £150,000; Birmingham extension, £350,000; Stour Valley line, £300,000; Weedon and Northampton, £125,000; Rugby and Stamford £500,000; Rugby and Leamington, £135,000; Leamington extension, £85,000		1,645,000
Grand Junction –		
Huyton and Ashton, &c., £1,150,000; Huyton and Warrington, £180,000; South Staffordshire, £187,500; Showhill and Portobello, £100,000		1,617,500
Trent Valley	about	1,400,000
Manchester and Birmingham		25,000
Giving a grand total		£4,687,500

The Directors have taken into their consideration, the most expedient mode of providing the requisite capital for carrying into effect these several works; and in conformity with the powers granted by the Legislature for the purpose they propose a creation of £25 shares to the extent of £4,687,500, being the amount of capital required as above stated, and that one new share of £25 be allotted to the owner of every £100 share or £100 stock. But in order that this new creation may press as little injuriously as possible on the existing stock, it is proposed, in the first instance, that a call of £2 per share shall be paid, which shall not be entitled to interest or dividend until a further call is made. Second, that the remaining calls shall be as follows: – £5 per share in July, 1848; £5 in July, 1849: £5 in July, 1839; £5 in July,

1851; and the remaining £3 in July, 1852. Such calls being entitled to dividend at the rate of 4 per cent. from the date when they severally become due, till the whole amount be called, after which the holders of the New Quarter Shares will receive dividends rateably with the general Stock of the Company. Should the foregoing scheme obtain the sanction of the meeting, resolutions will be submitted to carry the same into effect. In reference to the general management of the London and North Western Railway it is obvious that much advantage may be expected from uniformity of system and concentration of authority, on all matters of general policy or mutual arrangement – while at the same time the Directors will be anxious to obviate as far as possible in regard to the northern division, whether in reference to Shareholders or the public, any inconvenience which might be apprehended from the principal office being in London. It is hoped, that the Liverpool and Manchester offices will afford such information, and answer all such purposes of a central office, as may be required by the locality. Transfers for registration, or certificates for endorsement, if left at the Liverpool or Manchester office, will be considered as delivered to the Company; and the transmission of documents, to and from London, being effected in the night, it is hoped that very little delay or inconvenience will be experienced. The Proprietors may be aware that the Grand Junction Company, prior to the amalgamation, entered into an agreement in conjunction with the Manchester and Leeds Company, for the leasing, in perpetuity, of the North Union Railway. This agreement is now confirmed by Act of Parliament; and during the last six months the North Union line has been worked conjointly with the lessee Companies. This engagement of lease was undertaken by the Grand Junction Company on grounds of general policy, and with a view to the promotion of the great north and south traffic, with the risk of some temporary loss in the working of the North Union Line. The Directors are happy to report that the traffic of the line has considerably increased, since it has been under the direct management of the lessee Companies, as compared with what it was in the hands of the common carrier, arising principally from the change of system in the carriage of goods. They have reason to expect, therefore, not only that their general anticipation of benefit to the north and south traffic will be realised, but that this result will be accomplished without loss on the North Union lease considered by itself. The Directors are glad of this opportunity of acknowledging the long and valuable services of the Principal Engineers of the two divisions of the railway – Robert Stephenson, Esq., and Jos. Locke, Esq.; and they are persuaded the Proprietors will join them in this feeling. They propose, accordingly, that two sums of 1,000 guineas each be appropriated to providing suitable testimonials for this object. At the first General Meeting of the London and North-Western Company, the Directors are anxious to express the high sense which they entertain of the confidence which for many years they have experienced from the Proprietors, while members of the several Directions, now united into one Board. They are sensible of the extended responsibility which devolves on them, in entering on the duties of to large an undertaking, whether contemplating their obligations in reference to the Shareholders, or to the public. They will endeavour to justify the trust hitherto reposed in them.

STATEMENT of the CAPITAL ACCOUNT. 30th of June, 1846.

Receipts.

	Jan. 1, to June 30, 1846.			*Total, 30th June.*		
	£	*s.*	*d.*	£	*s.*	*d.*
Stock in land and works, including stations, tunnels, bridges, permanent way, wharfs, warehouses, and all incidental expenses	322,314	6	7	11,665,001	13	1
Carrying stock, viz.: –						
Locomotive engines, carriages, wagons, &c	160,927	9	4	1,012,377	2	5
Estate of the Company, in lands and buildings yielding rent	17,874	19	0	212,621	14	0
Total main lines	701,116	14	11	13,090,000	9	6
Subsidiary lines, viz.: –						
Warwick and Leamington	381	16	11	141,377	9	4
Northampton and Peterborough	159,075	18	7	666,449	8	1
Aylesbury	10,916	18	1	51,714	7	8
West London	4,500	12	4	60,448	12	4
Chester and Holyhead	100,000	0	0	400,000	0	0
Lancaster and Carlisle	75,514	6	8	326,837	19	5
Trent Valley	718,880	0	8	589,231	6	7
Bedford and Bletchley	73,474	8	7	79,874	8	7
Dunstable	1,012	13	7	1,507	12	1
Caledonian	10,570	11	8	35,831	8	4
Macclesfield	27,436	16	1	166,540	2	2
South Junction and Altringham	402	17	1	20,000	7	1
Ashton branch	4,238	14	7	6,332	16	11
Manchester, Buxton, and Matlock	415	17	11	21,363	7	11
Bollington branch	220	19	2	220	19	2

Lines for which Bills are pending: – Buckinghamshire, Rugby, and Stamford, Birmingham, Wolverhampton and Stour Valley, Rugby, Lexington, and Warwick, South Staffordshire, Liverpool, Preston, and Manchester, Southport, and York and Cartisle	284,857	16	1	388,666	1	3
	2,164,267	3	7	16,327,526	16	5
Expenditure						
	Jan. 1, to June 30, 1840.			*Total, 50th June.*		
	£	*s.*	*d.*	£	*s.*	*d.*
Consolidated stock	161,432	10	0	7,566,360	11	6
London & Birmingham						
£32 shares	555,196	13	5	974,041	6	5
£25 do.	14	0	0	109,343	17	3
£20 do.	2,190	3	3	136,661	15	4
Grand Junction –						
£40 shares	23,736	1	10	71,918	6	1
£12 10s. do.	139,234	16	10	249,193	0	0
Manchester & Birming.						
£40 shares	220	0	0	1,195,330	0	0
£10A do.	814	0	0	118,136	0	0
£10a do.	101,898	0	0	223,934	0	0
£10c do.	2,189	0	0	67,750	0	0
				10,712,910	16	7
Loans on debentures	1,327,313	4	5	3,326,750	2	2
Loan notes				4,000	0	0
Loans in account with Proprietors,	£131,612	5	10			
Less paid off,	94,208	6	3			
	2,318,235	10	1			
Less paid off as above	94,248	6	2			
	2,224,035	3	10	16,311,061	18	4
Balances				16,461	11	1
				16,327,526	16	5

STATEMENT of the REVENUE ACCOUNT. Half-year ending 30th June, 1846.

Expenditure.	£	*s.*	*d.*
Maintenance of way and stations	45,276	2	8
Locomotive power:			
Wages of engineers, enginemen, firemen, repairs, and cost of material, £76,917 7s. 11d.: Coke, £42,576 1s.	119,493	8	11
Police charges	15,013	7	3
Coach traffic charges:			
Salaries, wages, stationery, tickets, and carriage repairs	74,863	18	6
Merchandise traffic charges:			
Salaries, wages, and repairs of wagons	65,544	11	3
Compensation for accidents and losses	934	3	7
Stores Department charges	876	1	6
General charges:			
Including secretary's, accountants', audit, transfer, and superintendent's department, clearing house, and other expenses, not classed	21,980	11	9
Schools at Wolverton and Crewe, including town expenses	637	12	10
	£344,624	18	3
Parish rates and taxes, £21,425 8s. 3d.: Duty on passenger traffic, £24,582 12s. 5d.	46,008	0	8
Aylesbury Railway – Rent	582	10	0
Interest on loans	76,125	9	11
Balance	534,929	4	4
	£1,002,270	3	2
Receipts.	£	*s.*	*d.*
Traffic. viz.:			
Coaching, £611,696 14s. 8d.; Horses, carriages, and dogs, £18,715 19s. 3d.: Parcels, £44,827 19s.	675,196	12	11
Merchandise, £261,677 12s. 11d.: Live stock, £30,275 0s. 7d.; Coal, £14,267 12s. 8d.	306,220	6	2
	£981,416	19	1
Interest on Cash balance, £10,352 0s. 6d.; Rent of land and buildings, £10,501 3s. 7d.	20,853	4	1
	£1,002,270	3	2

GENERAL BALANCE SHEET, 30th June, 1846.

Receipts.	£	s.	d.
Balance of Revenue Account, 31st Dec. last	£719,064	4	6
Less Dividend ordered at General Meeting in Feb. and March last	532,253	12	3
	166,105	12	3
Balance of Revenue Account at this date, £534,929 4s. 4d.: Add for one month's more net traffic for the Manchester and Birmingham section of the line, only five months thereof being included in the Revenue Account, £1,000	543,929	4	4
Disposable Balance	£710,035	16	7
Receipts.	*£*	*s.*	*d.*
Balance of Capital Account	16,461	18	1
Balance of Stores Account	143,113	1	10
Balance of Outstanding Accounts	32,399	13	3
Balance in hand of bankers	518,060	3	5
	£710,034	16	7

The CHAIRMAN said: I have now to move the first resolution – that the Report now read, with the half-yearly statement of accounts appended thereto, be received, approved, and printed and circulated amongst the Proprietors in the usual way. Mr. LAWRENCE seconded the motion; which was carried unanimously.

The CHAIRMAN then moved the payment of a dividend of 5 per cent. on the stock of the late London and Birmingham and Grand Junction Companies, and 4 per cent. on the Manchester and Birmingham capital of £1,440,000.

Mr. LAWRENCE seconded the motion.

Mr. HOYES[7] asked if the dividend was free of Income-tax?

The CHAIRMAN replied, not on this occasion.

Mr. HOYES: Then the dividend is less than usual.

The CHAIRMAN said, that the Directors considered that to pay the Income-tax would make too large a deduction from the reserve fund. The hon. Proprietor should recollect that they had not uniformly paid it, only occasionally.

The resolution being carried, another was proposed for creating new stock to the amount of £4,687,500, to be raised in shares of £25 each, to be offered rateably to the Proprietors, in the proportion of one £25 share to every £100 share held in the Company. The resolution was carried unanimously; as was the following, directing the way the money should be paid, as detailed in the Report. In answer to questions, the CHAIRMAN said, they did not propose to take calls in advance, allowing interest, as they might be too much pressed with money. The new shares would partake rateably in any future creation. Two resolutions were then passed: the one appointing Abel Peyton[8] and Richard Earle,[9] Esqrs., to be Auditors, at a salary of £50 a-year each; and the other, appropriating 1,000 guineas each for a testimonial to Messrs. Stephenson and Locke.

Mr. CROSTHWAITE,[10] according to the provisions of the Act of Parliament they had to fix the remuneration to be given to the Directors; and he should propose that the same sum should be appropriated to them that they received before the amalgamation. It was with great pleasure that he congratulated them on that amalgamation having taken place, being one of those who had long since advocated such a measure as the means of putting an end to strife and jealousy. He should not, therefore, do his duty if he did not congratulate them on the completion of the amalgamation, as they would thereby get rid of the ill-feeling, which more or less was sure to exist while they were separate. He had always admitted the ability and energy with which they had worked while separate, which energy and ability he was sure would not be less now that they were united. They (the London and Birmingham) would now have the advantage of the talents of those who, on the Liverpool and Birmingham, had had more experience than they had, and who had always proved themselves good workmen. It was with great pleasure that he moved that the remuneration to the Directors should be the same as that previously paid to the Directors of the three Companies.

Captain WATTS,[11] having been connected with the Birmingham Company for fifteen years, had great pleasure in seconding the resolution. He was aware how well their affairs had been conducted, through good report and bad report, and he agreed with the Chairman, that great advantage would arise from their union. There was one point, however, on which he did not think their Company properly managed, and which had been mooted at the last meeting, that of allowing the Proprietors to pass along their own line to the meetings free. The gallant captain was proceeding at great length to show the supposed advantages of his proposition, when he was called to order. He accordingly gave notice of his intention to bring forward the question at a future meeting in a more regular form.

The resolution being carried,

The CHAIRMAN said: That it became the bounden duty of the Directors to acknowledge the obligations they were under to the Shareholders. At the same time he would assure them, that the salary was not so much an object to the Directors as the continuance of their approbation.

Mr. HOYES asked: Whether the Chairman could give the meeting any information as to the calls on the fifth and quarter shares?

The CHAIRMAN said: If he answered for the next twelve months it would be sufficient, as it would be almost impossible to pledge themselves further. There would be a call of £5 every three months on the quarter shares of the Grand Junction: and a call to the same amount on the London and Birmingham quarters in

July next year. It was not, at present, intended to make any call upon the fifth shares till the quarters were paid up.

In answer to a further question, the Chairman moved a resolution, that the paid-up capital on the £32 shares of the London and Birmingham Company be converted into stock. The resolution was carried unanimously, and thanks being voted to the Chairman, the meeting separated.

Notes

1 George Carr Glyn (1797–1873) joined his father's bank as a partner in 1819 and turned it into one of Britain's leading lenders to railways. He acted as treasurer for St. Katherine's Dock Company and the Globe Insurance Company and, in 1833, joined the board of the LBR. He remained chair when it became the LNWR in 1846 and held that position until 1852. He was Chairman of the Bankers' Clearing House and a Liberal MP from 1847 to 1868.

2 Richard Creed (1778–1867) was the original London secretary of the LBR from 1833 to 1838, then became Secretary and Treasurer of the entire company in 1838. When the LNWR formed in 1846, he shared secretarial duties with Henry Booth until he retired in 1848.

3 Charles Lawrence (1776–1853) was a wealthy Liverpool merchant with an interest in coffee and sugar plantations in Jamaica. He was Mayor of Liverpool in 1823–24 and the first chairman of the LMR when it opened in 1830. He became Glyn's deputy chairman at the newly-formed LNWR.

4 Robert Stephenson (1803–1859), son of the engineer George Stephenson, worked closely with the LBR throughout its early years. He entered politics in 1847, representing Whitby as a Conservative until his death.

5 Joseph Locke (1805–1860) trained under George Stephenson, with whom he worked on the LMR and Grand Junction railways. He represented Honiton as a Liberal MP from 1847 to 1860.

6 Henry Booth (1789–1869), a Liverpool corn factor, was a founding committee member of the LMR. He briefly served as secretary of the Grand Junction when it absorbed the LMR in 1845.

7 Alexander Hoyes was a Liverpool merchant and a frequent critic of British railways, particularly the Great Western's system of broad-gauge tracks.

8 Abel Peyton (1799–1887) was a Birmingham manufacturing chemist. Besides being auditor for the LNWR from 1846 to 1860, he was also a director of the Midland Railway from 1836 to 1857 and the Birmingham & Midland Bank.

9 Richard Earle (1796–1848) was a barrister and private secretary to the Earl of Derby; in 1839, he took over as manager of Derby's estates in Knowsley, Merseyside. He was a director of the North Union Railway from 1840 until his death.

10 John Crosthwaite, Liverpool merchant, was on the provisional committee of the Birmingham & Grand Junction Railway in 1845; also auditor of the Great Western, director of the Waterford & Dublin Railway, and provisional committee member for several Lancashire railways.

11 George Edward Watts, a retired naval captain who lived in Darlington in the 1840s, was a founding director of the Stockton & Hartlepool Railway. Besides airing his complaints at the LNWR meeting, Watts also pestered the North Midland, Midland Counties, Newcastle & Darlington Junction, and Great North of England Railways.

Editorial Headnote

Albert Life Assurance Company and Medical Invalid Life Assurance Society (1860)

The Medical, Invalid and General Life Assurance Society formed in 1841 on the novel plan of selling life insurance to "persons afflicted with particular maladies." A brainchild of the medical statistician Francis Neison (1815–1875) and the eminent surgeon Benjamin Phillips (1805–1861), it boasted support from William Farr (1807–1883), who made a name for himself at the Registrar General's Office as a pioneer in vital statistics and an advocate for extending the reach of life insurance. Phillips's brother Thomas, a mining magnate and barrister, joined its board in the 1850s and chaired the meeting announcing a merger with the Albert when poor health prevented Benjamin from attending.[1] The Albert Life Assurance Company started business in 1838 as the Freemasons and General but changed its name and expanded its clientele in 1849. In 1857, in the words of one contemporary, it "entered upon that wild career of amalgamation which ultimately destroyed it." It absorbed 21 companies over the next decade at a cost of £274,152, 28% of which went to the Medical Invalid, and it drained even more money by building a huge agency network. Although its payout must have seemed enticing to the Medical Invalid's investors, they were on the hook when the Albert failed in 1869. The Albert's shareholders, including those in its absorbed firms, were responsible for around £4 million in liabilities, including annuities, endowments, and substantial legal costs.[2]

Thomas Phillips's assurance that the Albert was "prudently managed and well conducted" would stand out as famous last words less than a decade later; its demise also cast doubt on his claim that mergers "had the effect of diminishing expenses." The one thing he did get right, at least from the Albert's perspective, was the positive impact of an insurance merger for multiplying policyholders. This was the case in India, especially after the Albert added to the Medical Invalid's extensive business there by purchasing the Family Endowment in 1861 and the Indian Laudable in 1865.[3] Phillips's speech was more noteworthy for what he left unsaid. His most important omission concerned India, where the Rebellion in 1857 had seriously damaged the Medical Invalid's finances and almost certainly left the company looking for purchase offers. The Albert merger came a few months after its Indian secretary, Patrick Tait, tried and failed (with the Family Endowment) to secure from the India Office £130,000 "paid on lives of persons actually assassinated . . . by the rebels in cold blood." To Tait's credit, he quickly turned things around in India after staying on as the Albert's "director of Indian business," and in fact, kept the company afloat for several years with an influx of profits from that quarter.[4] The Albert's failure contributed to two major changes in British life insurance. In India, it occasioned the rise of a Bombay-based office, the Oriental, with wealthy South Asian directors, which soon dominated the market there. In Britain, its collapse (along with that of the European) led to the passage of the Life Assurance Companies Act in 1870, which imposed uniquely rigorous reporting regulations on that sector.[5]

Notes

1 Medical Invalid prospectus (undated), prospectus collection, Institute of Actuaries, London; Cornelius Walford Papers, ME-METE (Chartered Insurance Institute, London, MS 9.92); Edward Walford, *The County Families of the United Kingdom* (London: Robert Hardwicke, 1869), 777; "Benjamin Phillips," *Lancet* 6 July 1861. On Farr and life insurance see John Eyler, *Victorian Social Medicine: The ideas and Methods of William Farr* (Baltimore: Johns Hopkins University Press, 1979), 84–90.

2 Cornelius Walford, *Insurance Cyclopaedia* (London: Layton, 1871–1880), 1: 46–48, 3: 159; Timothy Alborn, *Regulated Lives: Life Insurance and British Society, 1800–1914* (Toronto: University of Toronto Press, 2009), 60–63. Less than half of the Medical Invalid purchase money went to the shareholders; the rest enriched its secretary and an agent who arranged the deal: Philip Rawlings, "'A Sacred Trust for the Future': Regulating Insurance, 1800–1870," *Cambridge Law Journal* 77 (2018), 589.

3 Walford, *Insurance Cyclopaedia,* 1: 46–47.

4 *Post Magazine* 21 (1860), 76; *Post Magazine* 24 (1863), 25; P. M. Tait, *Anglo-Indian Vital Statistics* (London: East India Association, 1874), 21.

5 Alborn, *Regulated Lives*, 32, 64–69; Rawlings, "'A Sacred Trust,'" 587–599.

17

ALBERT LIFE ASSURANCE COMPANY AND MEDICAL INVALID LIFE ASSURANCE SOCIETY

Source: Albert Life Assurance Company and Medical Invalid Life Assurance Society (1860), *London Daily News*, 2 October 1860

ALBERT AND MEDICAL LIFE ASSURANCE COMPANY

Arrangements have been in progress for some time past for the purpose of uniting the businesses of the Albert Life Assurance and Guarantee Company and Medical Invalid and General Life Assurance Society. These arrangements having been completed, an extraordinary meeting of the proprietors of the Medical Company was recently held at the offices, No. 25, Pall-mall, when the recommendation of the directors to transfer the business to the Albert Company was unanimously adopted; there was a large attendance of shareholders, and the chair was occupied by Sir THOMAS PHILLIPS.[1]

Mr. SINGER,[2] the secretary, having read the advertisement and circular convening the meeting, correspondence, and resolutions of the two companies,

The CHAIRMAN said perhaps it might be considered necessary that he should briefly state the circumstances under which the meeting had been called; it was no light matter which had induced the directors to come to the resolutions which would be presently submitted for their consideration. The directors might be supposed to be attached to the institution, and to regard with some affection the objects for which it had been established, and the purposes which they believed upon the whole had been accomplished. The chairman then traced the rise and progress of the society down to the present period, and entered into minute details with regard to the results of its past management. The proposal made by the Albert Company was unsolicited, and of such a nature as to require respectful consideration at their hands, and was accordingly carefully considered. There were two questions which presented themselves to them: – 1. Was it desirable to amalgamate at all? and secondly, Were the terms offered advantageous to their share and policy-holders? As a general principle he believed amalgamations to be desirable, when fair and reasonable terms could be agreed upon. They had the effect of diminishing expenses, increasing the business, and reducing the necessity for competition; at all events the directors felt that the amalgamation now proposed was one which offered

DOI: 10.4324/9781003177715-20

considerable advantage to both the two important interests to be represented – the share and policyholders. He desired it to be clearly understood that the directors did not invite the offer. The directors had done nothing whatever to indicate any unfavourable impression of the position of the society, or anything that would in the least tend to depreciate the value of their property. Having regard to the diminished cost, to the increased business, to the elements that largely contribute to commercial prosperity, he believed that prudently managed, and well conducted, the Albert will by no means make a bad bargain. If the shareholders approved the terms offered, they would have the option of being paid off in cash, at the price agreed upon, or of taking that amount in Albert stock at par, upon which a dividend of 7 per cent. per annum has for some years past been paid. As regards the interest of the shareholders, the board soon came to the conclusion that it was for their interest to accept the terms proposed, and when he stated that the board held a very large proportion of the shares as their own, he thought their opinion was entitled to some weight. Then came the interest of the policy-holders, which involved two questions; first of all the probable profits, to be divided as bonuses among the participating policy-holders, which is one question – a question upon which they could only come to certain presumptive conclusions. Obviously if an amalgamated business be conducted with as much prudence, and with that reasonable amount of success which ought to attach to a considerably increased business, the profits ought to be commensurate with the altered state of things. Therefore, so far as regards the participating policy-holders, the probability is, that they will benefit not to a less but to a greater extent – that was the opinion the board had arrived at, after carefully considering the whole question, and consulting with Dr. Farr, whom he was glad to see present, and who had had a good deal of experience in vital statistics, and who, as they were aware, had presided over the department of Medical Statistics in their society. Then it became a question for them to consider whether the principles upon which the bonuses of the Albert were calculated were as much for the advantage of the policy-holders as the principle adopted by themselves, and they found that, substantially, there was more than their own for the participating policy-holders in the Albert; after deducting their share of the expenses, having regard to the proportion of business applicable to participating policies and to non-participating policies, it seemed to them that the policy-holders of the Medical would be in a more advantageous position than at present. Then came a question which was of considerable importance, and that was, the ultimate security of the policy-holders, comparing the probability of ultimate security in the one office and the other. Upon an examination of the list of shareholders in the Albert they found a proprietary which appeared to them to be of abundant responsibility; but they were not disposed to regard as perfect security the prospect simply of personal responsibility on the part of any men, however eminent or good may be their position, and they required from the Albert, on the part of their policy-holders, some clear tangible security beyond the probable security afforded by the personal condition of the proprietors; accordingly the Albert Company agreed that the whole of the accumulation in the life assurance fund of the Medical Company should be invested, for a period of ten years, as a further guarantee for the payment of the policies from time to time. Many of the proprietors present, who were well versed in life assurance operations, were aware of the numerous changes likely to take place within that period; beyond this, he thought the policy-holders would find it to their interest to accept from the Albert substituted policies in lieu of those they now hold; therefore, having regard to these circumstances, the meeting would see that there was ample protection and security for their policy-holders. The chairman then entered into a statement of the arrangement made with, and the duties in future of, the different officers of the society, and invited questions from the proprietors.

THOMAS COATES,[3] Esq., and other proprietors, being also policy-holders, then instituted stringent inquiries as to the present and future position of the policy-holders, all of which were satisfactorily answered.

The resolutions approving the amalgamation having been duly moved and seconded, were carried unanimously.

The second extraordinary meeting of proprietors was held at the office, 25, Pall-mall, on Friday, September 21st, and as on the former occasion there was a large attendance of proprietors.

Sir THOMAS PHILLIPS again occupied the chair. After the usual formalities had been gone through, the resolutions adopted at the former meeting for amalgamating the business of the two companies were confirmed.

The CHAIRMAN then stated that the directors felt it a duty devolving upon them to propose that the meeting should authorise them to expend no unreasonable amount of money in testifying their satisfaction and approval of the services of Mr. Singer, their secretary, who had been the servant of the society for nearly twenty years; it was always difficult to select one of many persons for a special compliment who in their several spheres might be equally deserving, but Mr. Singer had long been acting as the manager of the society, and had brought special qualities to their service, which he believed they as well as himself thoroughly appreciated; he had united to perfect integrity of character intelligence and undoubted zeal, and no one had been characterised by a greater desire to advance the interests of the society than their friend Mr. Singer. He moved "that the board of directors be authorised to expend 200 guineas in such manner as shall be most agreeable to the secretary," and then added, that the directors had not erred on the side of lavish expenditure. These things were not measured by the actual cost, but by the temper and spirit in which they were offered, and he believed the kindly spirit in which all would adopt the resolution would be of more value to Mr. Singer than the money value of the testimonial offered him.

Dr. Farr, Mr. Cantrell, and other proprietors having expressed their approval of the proposition of the chairman, and testified to Mr. Singer's merits, the resolution was carried by acclamation.

The CHAIRMAN then said there was another officer of the society deserving of a kindly expression of opinion, the solicitor, Mr. Sadler,[4] who had brought to the conduct of their business a constant and undeviating attention, which, in his position, is one of the most valuable of all qualities. He had always given personal attention to the business of the society; and had conducted it with considerable ability, deserving a cordial expression of the confidence and esteem of the proprietors. There were other gentlemen connected with the head office, medical officer, auditors, and others, but on the whole the board thought they should best discharge their duty, and that it would be most agreeable to them, not to extend any formal expression of their approval and thanks beyond the two officers named. The moderation with which these things are done constitute their great value, and he thought, on the whole, they would have done what was fitting and right on that occasion by assenting to the resolutions then submitted.

It was then moved, seconded, and resolved – "That, in the opinion of the shareholders, the directors should present Mr. Sadler, the solicitor of the company, with a substantial recognition of his valuable services."

Mr. Singer and Mr. Sadler having returned thanks at some length,

The CHAIRMAN then in highly complimentary terms referred to the valuable services of the directors of the Indian branch and their ndefatigable Secretary, Mr. Tait,[5] to whom they were much indebted, and to whom special allusion had been made at the last annual general meeting. The chairman then referred to the services of Mr. Cooper,[6] the accountant, and the staff of the society, gentlemen whose services are necessarily unobtrusively performed and for whose faithful services it was desirable to express their satisfaction.

A resolution embodying these sentiments was then put from the chair and carried unanimously.

On the motion of Mr. PIDGEON,[7] seconded by Mr. STREETER, a vote of thanks was passed to the chairman and board of directors for their past services, as well as the great care and attention bestowed in perfecting the present arrangement, which was gracefully and feelingly acknowledged by the chairman, amidst the strongest expression of satisfaction and hearty approval of the entire meeting, which then terminated.

Notes

1 Sir Thomas Phillips (1801–1867) was a trustee of the Medical Invalid from 1844 and a director as of 1859; after the Albert merger, he became a trustee of the new company.

2 Charles Douglas Singer had been the Medical Invalid's secretary and an "official associate" of the Institute of Actuaries since 1850; he stayed on as Secretary of the Albert Medical and Family Endowment in 1861.

3 Thomas Coates was a founding director of the Medical Invalid and a parliamentary agent who represented railway companies in India and Britain. He frequently appeared at Medical Invalid meetings to praise its performance.

4 R. R. Sadler, a solicitor specializing in property auctions, was a partner in the firm of Richardson, Smith and Sadler, which represented the Medical Invalid (as Richardson, Smith and Jones) from its founding in 1841. Smith died in 1849 and Charles Richardson retired in 1855, when Sadler formed a new partnership with Richardson's son Frank, which continued to represent the Medical Invalid until its dissolution. After the

Albert failed in 1869, Frank Richardson insisted that Sadler had not received £2000 (or any compensation) after the merger, as had been reported in 1860.

5 Patrick M. Tait joined the Medical Invalid as its Indian branch secretary in 1851, after previously working for the Scottish Union, East of Scotland, and National Mercantile insurance offices. He stayed on as the Albert's "Director of Indian Business" until its demise in 1869 and ended his insurance career as Managing Director of the Ocean Railway & General from 1872 to 1883. He published numerous articles on Indian insurance and vital statistics.

6 W. Stewart A. Cooper, accountant, also served as auditor of the Empire Life Assurance Company in the 1850s.

7 Possibly Jonathan Sills Pidgeon, a London stockbroker and director of the Star Life Assurance Society from 1859 to 1882.

Editorial Headnote

Alliance and Dublin Consumers' Gas Company (1866)

Private and public investment joined forces in early Victorian Britain to provide its rapidly growing cities with something approaching the requisite infrastructure for clean drinking water and gas for light, power, and heat. Such services blurred boundaries between taxpayers and consumers and challenged the notion that competition was always the most effective method of combining low prices with public safety. In the many cases where more than one company provided the same utility in the same city, they either created inefficiency, colluded to keep prices high, or both. Parliament attempted to rectify this for gas companies with the Gas Works Clauses Bill of 1847, which capped shareholders' dividends at 10 per cent to protect the pocketbooks of what it called "gas ratepayers." Local authorities, who themselves often ran factories that relied on the cheap provision of gas, frequently had the upper hand in these battles between city and company. By the end of the century, that dynamic often led to municipalization.[1]

Three gas companies formed in Dublin between 1823 and 1825: the locally owned Hibernian Gas Company and two London-based firms, including United General Gas. By that time, more than a dozen other British cities had erected gasworks, starting in 1812. United General bought a controlling stake in the Hibernian in 1826, and the other London firm failed in 1834. In 1836, the Alliance Gas Company reintroduced competition, but the price and quality of service continued to lag behind other British cities.[2] In 1844, Dubliners called for "a corporation gasworks" to improve matters. Although many supported municipalization, the city's elites settled on a new joint-stock company, which raised £150,000 to purchase the Alliance and improve its operations. In 1844, a prospectus of the Alliance and Dublin Consumers' Gas Company announced that "the consumers of gas in Dublin will be at once the buyers and sellers of the commodity."[3] Many of the most vocal of these consumers were the wealthy residents of Dublin's growing suburbs, who lobbied for better (and more expensive) gas lines to their streets and houses.[4] A new share issue in 1866 raised money to purchase the gasworks of the United General, which had recently lost its main source of revenue when the Dublin Corporation refused to renew its public lighting contract. At the same time, the Alliance and Dublin Consumers purchased the Commercial Gas Company, another local firm that Sir James Gray (1815–1875) had established in the 1840s to insure that "the artisan, after the labour of the day, could sit down to read by good light."[5]

Nearly all the directors who spoke at the reconstituted Alliance and Dublin Consumers' Gas Company's meeting were prominent Dubliners, and many sat on the boards of other Irish companies. Thomas Gresham (1787–1871) stayed on as Chairman of the Alliance and Dublin after the merger, overseeing a "complete monopoly" on the provision of gas to Dublin and its suburbs. Gresham had made a fortune building hotels and houses in the suburb of Kingstown; he converted the Gresham Hotel into a public company in 1835, pocketed £30,000, and retired. Besides helping to found (and later chair) the Alliance and Dublin after he retired, he sat on the boards of three other local firms, involved himself in numerous Dublin charities, and grew prize-winning potatoes and turnips on his suburban estate. Gray joined Gresham on the board after the merger; he had owned Dublin's main newspaper, the *Freeman's Journal*, since 1842; was a "leading spirit" of the Dublin Corporation and chaired its waterworks committee; sat on the boards of two local railways; and represented Kilkenny in Parliament. Directors who spoke at the meeting in 1866 included a Dublin alderman and three others who also served as directors or auditors of four different Irish railways, two Irish insurance offices, and an Irish bank.[6] With friends in so many high places, the company fended off calls to municipalize in 1872 and survived later attacks on its high prices and poor service in the 1880s. The firm persisted (under the name of Dublin Gas in later years) until 1987, when it handed over its assets to the state-run Bord Gáis Éireann.[7]

Notes

1 Martin Daunton, *State and Market in Victorian Britain: War, Welfare and Capitalism* (London: Boydell Press, 2008), 113–122.
2 Colum McCabe, "History of the Town Gas Industry in Ireland, 1823–1980," *Dublin Historical Record* 45 (1992), 33–35.
3 Charles J. O'Sullivan, *The Gasmakers: Historical Perspectives on the Irish Gas Industry* (Dublin: O'Brien Press, 1987), 37, 43.
4 Séamas Ó Maitiú, *Dublin's Suburban Towns 1834–1930* (Dublin: Four Courts Press, 2003), 103–104, 163–165.
5 O'Sullivan, *The Gasmakers*, 56–59; McCabe, "History of the Town Gas Industry," 35.
6 O'Sullivan, *The Gasmakers*, 59; *Wilson's Description of the New Royal Exchange* (London: Effingham Wilson, 1844), 71–72; George Walter Thornbury, *Old and New London* (London: Cassel, Petter, Galpin and Co., 1880), 1: 506; G. L. Barrow, "Justice for Thomas Mooney," *Dublin Historical Record* 24 (1970), 176; *The Joint Stock Companies' Directory for 1867* (London: Charles Barker and Sons, 1867), 1082, 1138, 1140, 1142, 1211, 1255; McCabe, "History of the Town Gas Industry," 67; *Proceedings of the Royal Dublin Society* 89 (1852): lxii, lv; *Freeman's Journal* 2 September 1870 and 10 April 1875.
7 O'Sullivan, *The Gasmakers*, 60–67; Gas (Amendment) Act, 1987, Irish Statute Book: www.irishstatutebook.ie/eli/1987/act/9/enacted/en/html.

18

ALLIANCE AND DUBLIN CONSUMERS' GAS COMPANY

Source: Alliance and Dublin Consumers' Gas Company (1866), *Freeman's Journal*, 2 October 1866

ALLIANCE AND DUBLIN CONSUMERS' GAS COMPANY

The first ordinary general meeting of the Alliance and Dublin Consumers' Gas Company, under the "Alliance and Dublin Gas Act, 1866,"[1] was held at one o'clock yesterday, at the company's offices, Grafton-street,

Mr. T. M. Gresham presided.

The Chairman said he presumed all the shareholders had already received the report and accounts for the past half year. They would, probably, therefore, take them as read (hear, hear).

The Secretary then read the advertisement calling the meeting, which was "to receive the directors' report and statement of accounts of the Alliance and Dublin Consumers' Gas Company, as incorporated under the 10th and 11th Victoria, chapter 42, for the half-year ending 30th June last; to sanction payment of dividend thereon to and amongst the shareholders of said company as so incorporated, and for the purpose of the acquisition of the works and other properties of the United General Gas Company, situate in the city of Dublin and counties of Dublin and Wicklow, according to the provisions of the Alliance and Dublin Gas Act, 1866; to authorise the creation by this company of further capital to the extent of, but not to exceed, 300,000*l*., as specified in the 27th section of said act of Parliament, and for that purpose from time to time to issue the requisite number of new ordinary shares of 10*l*. each in this company, and to take such other measures as shall be considered necessary in relation thereto; and for the election of directors of this company, in pursuance of the said Alliance and Dublin Gas Act, 1866, and to fix the periods at which the future half-yearly general meetings shall be held, and for the election of auditors, and to determine the remuneration of the directors, auditors, and secretary of said company."

The Chairman said the shareholders were all quite prepared for a great alteration in their company – an alteration which he thought would prove most conducive to their interests. Although they had taken possession of the works of the

DOI: 10.4324/9781003177715-21

other company, this was their own half-yearly meeting, and it was with its result they had to deal. In speaking of their own company, he wished to say that it had been and was a prosperous company (hear). Their works were in the best condition they could be, and their dividend was the same as last year. He hoped the new and large addition which they had taken into the concern since Saturday last would fulfil their expectations. He believed it would, and that – if not the next half year, at least the half year following – they would have a report satisfactory not only as regarded the carrying on of the operations, but also in reference to the pounds, shillings and pence, a matter important to them all. He believed that the result of the gas companies being amalgamated into the one great concern would make them realise an increased dividend, besides conferring substantial benefits upon the city (hear, hear). The first resolution he had to propose was – "That the seal of the company be affixed to the registry of shareholders, as enacted under the 10th and 11th Vic., cap. 42."

Passed unanimously.

The Chairman then proposed that the report and accounts for the past half year be received and adopted. Any question which shareholders desired to ask he would be happy to answer.

Alderman Moylan[2] seconded the resolution, which was passed unanimously.

The Chairman said the next resolution was, "That a dividend at the rate of 7s. per share, free of income tax, be now declared, and that pursuant to the powers of the Alliance and Dublin Gas Companys' Act, 1866, same be paid to and amongst the shareholders of that company, as incorporated under the 10th and 11th Vict., cap. 42, on and after Monday, the 22nd of October."

Mr. Reynolds[3] seconded the resolution, which was adopted.

The Chairman said he had now to propose what was perhaps the most important resolution. It was "That for the purposes of the acquisition of the works and other properties and effects of the United General Gas Company, situated in the county of the city of Dublin, and in the counties of Dublin and Wicklow, according to the provisions of the Alliance and Dublin Gas Act, 1866, this company shall create further capital to the extent of, but not to exceed, 300,000*l*., as provided in the 27th section of the said Act, and for that purpose from time to time to issue the requisite number of new ordinary shares of 10*l*. each in this company, and that the directors are hereby authorised to take all such measures as may be lawful and necessary in respect thereto, and for giving effect to this resolution and the objects embraced in it."

Mr. Molloy wished, before the resolution was passed, to say a few words, as a proprietor of the Commercial Gas Company. When they held their meeting to confirm the amalgamation, there was, he did not say a distinct pledge, but an implied understanding that the shareholders in the Commercial Gas Company would be put into the same position as if they had been original members of the Alliance Company. If that were carried out, they would for every 8*l*. they had paid up have received a 10*l*. Alliance share, with 8*l*. paid on it, and, besides, they would be considered to be entitled to any advantages that would arise from the distribution of the new shares. If they were partners in the company they were entitled, in his opinion, to all the benefits of that position. He would be glad to hear some explanation on that point.

Sir John Gray, M.P., said, as the duty had devolved upon him as a director of the Commercial Gas Company to make the statement to which Mr. Molloy referred, he had better state his views of the case, as he had stated them in the presence of Mr. Molloy at the Commercial Gas Company's meeting. He believed Mr. Molloy was confusing some figures. The statement made was that the proposition for the amalgamation of the companies would run thus – that the holder of five shares in the Commercial Company, with 1*l*. paid up, would be entitled to receive, on the passing of the act, or at such time as might be fixed by the clauses of the act, a scrip certificate of a 10*l*. share in the Alliance Company, with 5*l*. marked paid thereon. He spoke in the presence of some other members of the board, and they would remember that that statement was distinctly made on the part of the Commercial Gas Company. That statement was again and again repeated at several meetings and stated in the public papers during the discussion pending the passing of the bill, and the arrangement stood substantially in the bill at present. It made very little difference to the shareholder whether he received an 8*l*. certificate for 8*l*. paid or a 5*l*. certificate for 5*l*. paid, but, in point of fact, the undertaking of the Alliance Company and the arrangement and agreement made by the directors of the Commercial Company was, that for every five shares held, with 1*l*. paid up, the party would be entitled to one 10*l*. share, with 5*l*. marked paid thereon. There never was a deviation from that, and he was not aware that any statement was made with respect to the 8*l*., except, indeed, this – that, at the time he was speaking of, the Alliance share, with 8*l*. paid up, stood at a premium of from 2*l*. 10s. to 2*l*. 15s. The advantage to the Commercial Company in being amalgamated with the Alliance Company was extremely large. The shareholders in the Commercial Company felt then, and they felt now, that their property had been largely protected, and had received an increase in value which it otherwise would not possess by the amalgamation, and that it was now on a par in all matters with the Alliance Gas Company. They were joint proprietors with them in the whole amalgamated concern, and from January next their shares worth 5*l*. paid would bear the same ratio of dividend, pound for pound, as the old shares (hear, hear).

Mr. Molloy said he was perfectly satisfied that what Sir John Gray stated took place. But he thought that they were to be put into the position of original shareholders in the Alliance Company, and, if they were, they would be entitled to the benefit of the issue of new shares.

Sir John Gray said he should correct what was a misapprehension of Mr. Molloy on that point. It was impossible that new shareholders coming into the company could be placed in the position of old shareholders, the old shares being limited to a certain number. They came in as amalgamated, not as original, proprietors.

A Shareholder said that the resolution authorised the directors to take all the steps necessary for the raising of capital in order to effect a junction with the other company. In paragraph three of the report from the bottom it was stated that

15,000 of the new shares were to be allocated over 19,000 of the old shares that 2*l.* were paid on, and after that there was to be a further call of 2*l.* per share. The report also stated that the directors might exercise borrowing powers in the spring, and ask the sanction of the proprietors to issue bonds to meet the payment of the residue of the purchase money. If the people who advanced the money on the bonds paid the residue of the purchase money, he wished to know were there to be further calls to the proprietors who accepted the shares. The report stated that the company might issue bonds to meet the payment of the remainder.

Mr. Stevenson said that under the agreement with the Hibernian Company they were bound to issue a certain number of shares to them at par – 13,500, which would represent 135,000*l.* The remainder of the sum to be paid them would entirely depend upon the amount of the valuation to be arrived at by Mr. Hawkesley[4] and Mr. Barlow,[5] who were at present employed in Dublin making the valuation. The extreme value to be put upon the works was 270,000*l.*, and the minimum 240,000*l.* The board proposed to pay in shares 135,000*l.* to the Hibernian Company, to pay them 60,000*l.* in two calls, and the residue to be paid in spring, if it would be found from the then state of the money market advantageous to borrow. The matter was entirely for the proprietors, because the board could not issue bonds without calling a special meeting of the proprietors for that purpose. Although bonds might be issued in the spring, the payment of these bonds, when they became due, should either be provided for by a re-issue, or by calls on the proprietors.

Mr. Johnstone said that there were four descriptions of shares of the company – the first, their own eight pound shares; the second, the compensation to the Commercial Gas Company, 10*l.* shares, with 5*l.* paid up; the third, the new shares of 8*l.*, with 4*l.* paid up; and the fourth the 10*l.* shares, which were fully paid up. He wished to know how the dividends were to be distributed over them.

The Secretary (Mr. Stevenson)[6] said the distribution should be *pro rata*, and, with respect to the dividends, they would be equalised in proportion to the sum paid on each share – namely, 10*l.*, 8*l.*, 5*l.* and 4*l.*

Mr. Richard Martin,[7] High Sheriff of Dublin, said, owing to the alteration of the company, he believed it was necessary at this meeting to fix the renumeration to be given to the directors. He had, therefore, great pleasure in proposing the following resolution: – "That Joseph Boyce, James Brophy, David Drummond, Edward Fottrell, Thomas Michael Gresham, Edward Hudson Kinahan, Denis Moylan, Michael Bernard Mullens, William Reynolds, John Stokes, Sir John Gray, James Pim, and James Milo Burke shall continue to be the directors of this company, and that having referred to the great increase recently made to the duties and responsibilities of the effectual management of this company, the remuneration of each director shall be at the rate of 150*l.* a year, and that the future half yearly general meetings of this company shall be held on every 31st day of March and 30th day of September, unless when same may fall upon a Sunday, and then upon the preceding or following day, as the directors may determine.

Mr. J. B. Johnstone wished to know whether the act of Parliament stated that nine directors should continue in office.

Mr. Stevenson replied that the act of Parliament stated that the present board of directors should be re-elected at the first general meeting, but that after that they were to be reduced to nine by deaths or otherwise, and until they were reduced to eight no new director could be elected.

Mr. Johnstone – Are we limited to nine?

Mr. Stevenson – The act gives the number at 14, but nine is the minimum.

Mr. Johnstone – I beg, then, to move that the directors be named *scriatim*, and that they be voted for accordingly.

The Chairman – I am in the hands of the shareholders, and I stand in the position of a servant, to be dictated to by them; but I may observe that at a meeting of a railway company I once heard a motion made of the kind just now made, but it was overruled, and I may say negatived almost unanimously. It was a very unusual motion indeed. There are 13 directors, and if you wish I shall put their names singly before the meeting, because, of course, I am bound to do it (cries of no, no). He thought, however, that the feelings of those in the room were against such a course.

Mr. Thomas Clifford said he would second the resolution proposed by the High Sheriff.

The Chairman then asked the meeting to pass the resolution as it was read to them.

The resolution was unanimously adopted.

Sir John Gray moved the following resolution: –

> That, inasmuch as the duties and responsibilities of the secretary would be largely increased by the act of last session the salary of that officer be 1,000*l*. per annum.

He said that the salary of Mr. Stevenson at present was 800*l*. a year, and that that was paid to him when their rental was only 59,279*l*. Their rental for the future would be upwards of 149,000*l*. per annum, and although their business would thus be increased from 59,000*l*. to 149,000*l*. per annum, the only increase of salary which the directors proposed to give Mr. Stevenson was 200*l*. per annum as a recognition of the increased responsibilities which would devolve upon him and of the great services which he had already rendered to the company. He was sure that in a meeting of the Alliance Gas Company he need not speak of those services. They were there not only as directors and shareholders of the company, but as citizens, and as citizens they should acknowledge the services rendered to them by Mr. Stevenson in connection with the gas lighting of their city (hear, hear). When Mr. Stevenson took an active part in originating that company the citizens of Dublin were paying 10s. per 1,000 cubic feet of gas. As secretary and officer of this company, Mr. Stevenson was consulted by the directors and shareholders of the company, and the result was that the price of gas in Dublin became gradually reduced from 10s. per 1,000 feet to its present price of 4s. 6d. per 1,000 feet for 12 candle gas. Acting under the same able advice, the gas that would in future be supplied to them as citizens would be

16 candle gas, which would only cost the price now paid for 12 candle gas. He (Sir John Gray) made these observations as a citizen and not in his capacity as a director or shareholder in the company, and he believed they would all agree with him that they owed a great deal in pounds, shillings, and pence to Mr. Stevenson (hear, hear). It was principally to Mr. Stevenson they owed the position which they now held. It was he who first worked out the idea of amalgamating the companies, and they all knew how satisfactorily that idea was carried out (hear, hear). In the negociations which took place in Dublin and in London he (Sir John Gray) could bear his testimony to the value of the services rendered by Mr. Stevenson to the company, to the knowledge, ability and attention which he brought to bear on every part of the subject. It was proposed that the minimum price to be paid to the Hibernian Gas Company should be 260,000*l*. but after much careful manipulation, the minimum was brought down to 240,000*l*., the maximum to be 270,000*l*. In that transaction Mr. Stevenson had borne a great part and saved them a great deal. At this meeting the addition to the salary for their secretary might have been proposed by the directors without having previously intimated their intention in reference to it, but the directors thought it better to communicate their intention, which they did in the copy of their report sent to every shareholder of the company. The result was that he was in a position to say that they had received only one remonstrance, and that from a gentleman not living in this country but in Edinburgh, and who could not have been made aware of how much they owed to Mr. Stevenson. This gentleman was Mr. Herbert J. Hughes, who wrote to their chairman on the subject, and he (Sir John Gray) believed that Mr. Hughes would have been the first to come forward and support the resolution if he had known what they owed to Mr. Stevenson. He believed that, considering what Mr. Stevenson had done for the company and for the citizens of Dublin, they would unanimously adopt the resolution which he had the honour to propose to them (applause).

Mr. Molloy seconded the resolution. He said that the figures mentioned by Sir John Gray showed that their income had been now trebled, and consequently a considerable increase ought to be made to Mr. Stevenson's salary. He had great pleasure in seconding the resolution (hear, hear).

The Chairman said that he would have felt it his duty to bring the letter of the Scotch gentleman before the meeting, but that he knew that gentleman was not at all aware of the great and valuable exertions made by Mr. Stevenson in the interest of the company. There was in the room a gentleman to whom Mr. Stevenson had been previously opposed in the establishment of the Commercial Gas Company, and that gentleman told him (the chairman) that he believed if the whole concern were his own Mr. Stevenson could not have acted more thoroughly or more successfully in its interest. He could say that in his life he had never known a gentleman who had devoted his attention and ability to the duties of his position better than Mr. Stevenson did as secretary to that company. Indeed if the concern were his (the chairman's) no consideration would induce him to part with Mr. Stevenson. He would now put the resolution proposed by Sir John Gray and seconded by Mr. Molloy.

Mr. R. G. Collis[8] said he was sure that there was not a gentleman in the room who would not most willingly second that resolution, but he would take the liberty of asking the question whether the act of Parliament would allow of Mr. Stevenson being appointed as managing director of the company (hear, hear); if so he would propose that Mr. Stevenson be appointed its managing director (hear, hear, and applause). He thought that his proposition, if adopted, would be attended with advantage to the company.

Mr. Stevenson said he would take the liberty of answering the question so kindly put by Mr. Collis. He was extremely obliged to Sir John Gray for the manner in which he had proposed the resolution, and to Mr. Molloy who seconded it, and also to Mr. Collis, but he should say that the proposition just now made was untenable, because the act of Parliament provided that a certain number of directors should be elected; but it never contemplated such an appointment as that now proposed by Mr. Collis. He had to add that he was quite satisfied with the position which he now held, because there was nothing of the character of servitude attached to it, the directors having always treated him with the almost kindness and consideration (loud applause).

Sir John Gray said that it would be impossible under the act to adopt the proposition made by Mr. Collis.

Mr. Stevenson, in reply to a shareholder, said the act of Parliament provided that whatever additional capital was required should be called up at 2*l*. per share, with three months interval between each call.

The Shareholder wished to know, in the event of additional capital being raised, how it would be called up in the three different classes of shares.

Mr. Stevenson said the calls would be only on the shares of the United General Gas Company. Until all the capital required for that company was called there would be no call upon either the Alliance or Commercial Company's shares. The act of Parliament prescribed the liability. The Alliance shares, there being but 8*l*. paid on them, were liable to a call of 2*l*. more. The Commercial Company's shares having only paid 5*l*., were liable to be called up for 5*l*. more.

The Shareholder inquired whether the call would be in proportion to the different amounts of the shares.

Mr. Stevenson said that was a matter for the shareholders; the board could not give an answer. It would depend very much on the emergency that might arise.

Mr. D'Arcy said the secretary of the company had very properly been taken care of by the shareholders; he trusted that the other officers, whose duties were also increased, would have their salaries raised. He left the matter entirely for the board to deal with. He begged to move that John Hyland and Francis Askins, Esqrs., be elected auditors, and their salaries increased from 10*l*. to 15*l*. per annum.

Mr. Smith seconded the resolution, which was adopted.

Mr. John M'Namara Cantwell[9] said he had been entrusted with a resolution which he had great pleasure in moving. The principal business of the meeting had arisen out of an act passed last session. As their solicitor, having the carriage of that act, he was enabled to bear testimony to the truth and propriety of the resolution. The Messrs. Dorrington, of London, were their parliamentary agents, and as the chief member of that house, Mr. Challoner Smith took special charge of their bill. He was a gentleman of high station and great ability, and he was by far the largest proprietor in the Alliance Gas Company. The bill itself, regarded in a technical and professional point of view, was an extremely difficult bill in its constituent parts, and required the close attention of a man in London conversant with such matters. He (Mr. Cantwell), as solicitor to the company, felt bound to state that to Mr. Challoner Smith was due the greater part of the credit in connection with the preparation and conduct of the bill, and that to his care, skill, and zeal, they were mainly indebted for the successful carriage of the bill through all the parliamentary stages. Both as solicitor and shareholder of the company he, therefore, felt unmixed pleasure in moving –

> That the special thanks of this meeting are hereby given to Mr. Challoner Smith for his able, zealous, and effective services in promoting the act of Parliament obtained by this company in the last session of Parliament.

Sir John Gray claimed permission to second the resolution. He went over to London as the representative of the Commercial Gas Company, and it was in that capacity he first had the pleasure of meeting Mr. Challoner Smith. Nothing could exceed that gentleman's courtesy, fairness, and impartiality, while doing at the same time ample justice to the company he represented. When the agreement between the companies was completed he had many opportunities of witnessing the constant care and almost perpetual anxiety of Mr. Smith to have everything done for the advantage of the company with perfect fairness towards all parties (hear, hear).

Mr. Cantwell said he had omitted to mention that Mr. Smith was counsel, as he (Mr. Cantwell) was solicitor, to the original bill of the Alliance Company which had been so beneficially worked out for the last twenty years (hear, hear).

The Chairman said he was aware that Mr. Smith's services had been of the greatest advantage to the company, and he felt great pleasure in putting the resolution.

The resolution having been adopted,

Mr. Andrew Lee moved that the cordial thanks of the meeting and of the proprietors generally are due and hereby given to the board of directors for the attention they have bestowed on the affairs of the company, as manifested by the favourable accounts submitted to this meeting.

Dr. Brady[10] said he felt great pleasure in seconding the resolution. Passed unanimously.

On the motion of Mr. Fottrell the second chair was taken by Alderman Moylan, D.L.

Mr. Fottrell[11] then moved a cordial vote of thanks to Mr. Gresham for the manner in which he discharged his duties as chairman of the company.

The High Sheriff of Dublin seconded the motion, which was adopted unanimously, after which the proceedings terminated.

Notes

1 The Alliance and Dublin Gas Act, 1866 (29 & 30 Vict. C. 205) permitted the amalgamation of the Alliance and Dublin Consumers Gas Company with the Commercial Gas Company of Ireland, Ltd., and permitted the new company to acquire the gasworks of the United General Gas Company.

2 Denis Moylan (1802–1878), Dublin alderman, was "a merchant and man of more than average capacity in civic affairs," according to the *Freeman's Journal*.

3 William Reynolds was also a trustee and director of the Hibernian Joint-stock Bank.

4 Thomas Hawksley (1807–1893) was an English civil engineer who consulted gas and water projects throughout Great Britain, including a Dublin Corporation water scheme in 1861.

5 Thomas Greaves Barlow (1812–1872) was a consultant to the Oxford Gas Works and the editor of the *Journal of Gas Lighting*.

6 John Stevenson was Secretary of the Alliance and Dublin Consumers' Gas Company starting in 1847 and remained Secretary after the merger in 1866.

7 Richard Martin, High Sheriff of Dublin, also sat on the boards of the Dublin, Wicklow and Wexford Railway and the Patriotic Assurance Company of Ireland.

8 Robert G. Collis also sat on the boards of the Irish North Western Railway and the Cork & Bandon Railway.

9 John M'Namara Cantwell was a prominent Dublin solicitor who was active in the Home Rule Party during the 1870s.

10 Possibly Daniel Frederick Brady, MD, a Dublin magistrate.

11 Edward Fottrell (died 1898) served as a commissioner for the Dublin suburb of Rathmines for 25 years and also sat on the boards of the Hibernian Joint-stock Bank and the Dublin Exhibition Palace & Winter Garden Co.

Editorial Headnote

London & County Bank and London & Westminster Bank (1909)

The merger between the London & County Bank (LCB) and London & Westminster Bank (LWB) in 1909 capped a sustained period of concentration in British banking, dating back to the Barings crisis in 1890. Between 1890 and 1905, an average of ten banks annually joined forces, and 264 bank mergers transpired overall between 1870 and 1920. Most of this activity took place in the provinces, where Lloyds, Midlands, and Barclays absorbed smaller neighboring banks and staked a presence in London by buying private City firms. This merger movement paralleled and, in most cases, preceded similar movements in central Europe, Australia, and North America, while French and Scandinavian banks grew without engaging in much acquisition. Regardless of how it was accomplished, concentration generally improved stability and trust in financial institutions as well as expanding access to retail banking: the number of branches in England increased from 4570 in 1900 to 6573 in 1913.[1]

The merger of the LCB and LWB was exceptional in that both banks were roughly equal in size and stature, and both had head offices in London. Although the *Economist* noted at the time that this "produced a certain amount of headshaking" in the city, it made sense to its constituencies for several reasons. The banks shared common histories and cultures: they had formed within two years of each other, the LWB in 1834 and the LCB in 1836, as two of the first London joint-stock banks to appear after a new Bank of England Charter permitted this in 1833. Their boards featured a similar mix of merchant princes and influential MPs: in 1909, for instance, the politician George Goschen sat on the LCB's board, while his uncle, the merchant banker Henry Goschen, sat on the LWB's. The two banks also sported complementary branch networks, with the LWB focusing on the metropolis and its suburbs and the LCB, building on a string of amalgamations in the 1840s, attracting most of its deposits from the Home Counties.[2] As of 1909, the LCB paid substantially higher dividends than the LWB, with the result that it could afford to prop up the reserve of the new bank: at £4.25 million, compared to £3.5 million in paid-up shares, this was the largest in Britain.[3] Finally, the merger allowed both banks to catch up with their provincial rivals in the race to build nationwide branch networks. After combining forces, the new bank closely trailed Lloyds as the largest in Britain, and by 1914 – after opening 44 new branches and doubling its deposits from £70 million to £142 million – it stood with Lloyds and Midland among the largest three banks in Europe. By 1920, the so-called "Big Five" English banks – these three plus the National Provincial and Barclays – held 80% of deposits in England.[4]

Notes

1 Richard S. Grossman, *Unsettled Account: The Evolution of Banking in the Industrialized World since 1800* (Princeton: Princeton University Press, 2010), 111–127; P. L. Cottrell, "The Domestic Commercial Banks and the City of London, 1870–1939," in *Finance and Financiers in European History, 1880–1960*, ed. Youssef Cassis (Cambridge: Cambridge University Press, 1992), 47; Michael Collins and Mae Baker, *Commercial Banks and Industrial Finance In England and Wales, 1860–1913* (Oxford: Oxford University Press, 2003), 107–112.

2 T. E. Gregory, *The Westminster Bank through a Century* (London: Westminster Bank, 1936), 2: 2, 296; 1: 63–121, 322–330, 376–383.

3 "The Important London Amalgamation," *Bankers' Magazine* 88 (1909), 349.

4 Gregory, *Westminster Bank*, 2: 4, 306, 312, 316; Youssef Cassis, "Management and Strategy in the English Joint Stock Banks 1890–1914," *Business History* 27 (1985), 302; Cottrell, "Domestic Commercial Banks," 48.

19

LONDON & COUNTY BANK AND LONDON & WESTMINSTER BANK

Source: London & County Bank and London & Westminster Bank (1909), *Bankers', Insurance Managers', and Agents' Magazine* 88 (September 1909): 434–436 and 438–439.

LONDON AND COUNTY BANKING COMPANY, LIMITED

An extraordinary general meeting was held on August 6, at the Cannon Street Hotel, to consider the proposed amalgamation with the London and Westminster Bank.

Mr. J. Annan Bryce,[1] M.P., who presided, remarked that that occasion was one of the most eventful, if not the most eventful, in the history of the bank. The proposed union with the London and Westminster Bank had been described in the press as a marriage, and if he might be allowed to develop the metaphor, he would say that as the happiest marriages were those between persons of dissimilar characters, so the most fortunate auguries might be drawn from the results of a union between two institutions so different in their upbringing and conditions of activity. The London and County Bank had been from the first bred in the country and they derived the main part of their vigour from it, while their intended spouse was essentially town bred. The basis of the arrangement was the actual market price of the shares of the respective banks.

The London and Westminster shareholder was receiving no profit on the market price, and nothing whatever was being paid to him for goodwill. With regard to the London and County shareholders, he did not think they would suffer anything by the splitting of the shares; on the contrary, he believed that there would be a wider market for a share of the new and more manageable dimension of about £23 than for the, in these days, somewhat unwieldy bulk of £92, and consequently a relative enhancement of price. Under the rearrangement of capital the existing paid-up capital of the London and Westminster shareholders would be reduced from £2,800,000 to £1,500,000, and the difference would go to swell the existing reserves of the two banks, so that the total reserve of the joint concern would stand at £4,250,000, against a paid-up share capital of £3,500,000. The reserve would thus be far the largest possessed by any joint stock bank in this country. The name of the bank was to be changed to London County and Westminster Bank. The registered head office was to be the Westminster's head office in Lothbury.

DOI: 10.4324/9781003177715-22

The staffs of the two banks were to be amalgamated, and it was not intended that the interests or position of any member of either of them should be injuriously affected. The boards of the two banks were to be amalgamated, and one of the resolutions provided that their number should never be more than 27 nor less than 15. The number of 27 was made up of 12 directors from this bank and 15 from the Westminster.

Some shareholders might enquire, "Why do you ask us to sanction this amalgamation? Why not leave well alone?" The directors were, he hoped, not megalomaniacs, but sensible men, who knew that there was no point in bigness for its own sake. Therefore, when the proposal for amalgamation was mooted, they asked themselves precisely the same question; but after long and anxious deliberation they decided unanimously to recommend the shareholders to approve the conclusion at which they themselves had arrived that the amalgamation would be to their advantage. In these days of keen competition if one did not go forward one must go back. In the last ten years they had opened nearly 90 branches and added 38,000 to the number of their current accounts, but owing to the changed conditions of business the total balances had not advanced, while the expenses had increased, and they had only been able to maintain the rate of earnings by a greater economy in administration and by a more careful supervision of advances. A union with the Westminster Bank would, he believed, offer them an opportunity of increasing their earning power. They had a valuable connection, which the London and County Bank had lacked, in the City and in the Colonies, and the union of their forces and the enhanced prestige which would result would, the directors believed, enable them to utilise their means to greater advantage than either of them could do separately. It would no doubt be possible to effect economies in administration by the elimination of competition in the case of certain of their branches, but the effect of such changes must necessarily be gradual, and neither the local public nor the market need fear that there would be any diminution of facilities.

A discussion followed.

The chairman, in reply to Mr. Ord, said that it was quite true that the London and Westminster Bank had only earned 12 per cent., but their capital under the present arrangement would be reduced, and it would be perfectly possible to earn 20 per cent., and even more than 20 per cent., on the capital represented by the Westminster Bank's holding.

Mr. Alfred Faber[2] said he thought that 27 directors were far too many, and that £30,000 was an absurdly large sum to pay them in the way of remuneration. He also asked whether it was intended to appoint a chairman as well as a deputy-chairman.

The chairman stated that it was intended to reduce the number of directors as vacancies occurred to 20. He did not know of a single amalgamation which had taken place on equal terms where the directors had not been taken over bodily. He believed that it was the desire of the directors of the London and Westminster Bank that a chairman and deputy-chairman should be appointed, and that was certainly the desire of the majority of the members of the board of the London and County Bank. In reply to Mr. Walter Bowl,[3] he added that the amalgamation was not going to diminish the probability of paying a dividend of 20 per cent.

The solicitor having explained the provisions of the agreement,

The chairman proposed the various resolutions, which were seconded by Mr. Seymour Grenfell[4] and carried unanimously.

LONDON AND WESTMINSTER BANK, LIMITED

The half-yearly general meeting was held on July 21 at the head office, Lothbury. Mr. Arthur Hill,[5] who presided, observed that they had decided to act as trustees in public and private trusts, as well as custodian trustees. They had the power to do so, and as valuable customers had asked them to act in that capacity, the directors had felt that it would be to the advantage of the bank to do so, and they were now ready to accept the position. Their total figures showed an increase over those of the corresponding period of last year, and the number of current accounts had slightly increased, but they regretted that the profits had not been quite so good. The causes, however, were not far to seek. With such low rates of money the margin of profit was smaller, and seldom had rates been less remunerative than they were during the past six months. The Bank rate had averaged £2. 14s. 3d. per cent., against £3. 10s. 7d. per cent.; brokers' call money £1. 18s. 6d. per cent., against £2. 13s. 11d. per cent.; discounts, £1. 19s. 3d. per cent., against £2. 18s. per cent.; and Stock Exchange loans £2. 19s. 6d. per cent., against £3. 15s. per cent. These low rates necessarily reduced banking profits. With peace and cheap money they would in ordinary circumstances have had a considerable profit on their investments. He spoke for himself when he said that had we not had severe shocks to credit and a large creation of trustee securities, including the £4,000,000 Transvaal loan, guaranteed by the Imperial Government, the bank's Government and other securities would have shown a very handsome profit, instead of their having to keep £100,000 against depreciation of Government securities, and that would have more than compensated for the reduced profits on their money. Recently they had an opportunity of selling £500,000 of consols and £100,000 local loans, which they had replaced by other securities having a free market and yielding a better return. He was sure that every one must feel greatly indebted to Lord Rothschild,[6] who justly held the leading position in the financial world, for the action he had taken, supported by many others, to uphold the credit of the City – (hear, hear) – for there was nothing which required more delicate handling than credit and finance. He felt that every shareholder in banks, insurance offices, and, in fact, in every business depending on credit, must appreciate the action which had been taken with a view of restoring confidence and of avoiding the dislocation of business. In conclusion, he proposed the adoption of the report, in which a dividend was declared of 6 per cent. for the half-year. Mr. O. A. Benecke[7] seconded the motion, which was carried.

An extraordinary general meeting was held on August 6 at the head office, Lothbury, to consider a resolution for the amalgamation of the company with the London and County Banking Company.

Mr. Walter Leaf,[8] who presided, moved the resolution. They had, he said, met to consider a great amalgamation which the directors put before the shareholders as a step in the highest degree advantageous to the shareholders' interests. It was an amalgamation without precedent in the history of banking, and the new institution was one which – the Bank of England being, of course, *hors concours* – would, he ventured to say, stand second to no bank in the world. The reputation and magnitude of the London and County Bank were matters of world-wide notoriety. Fifteen years ago it stood second among the banks in the amount of its current and deposit balances, and the London and Westminster was third. Since then other banks had risen by successive amalgamations to the head of the list, and the London and Westminster Bank, although without any diminution of their business, had fallen to a lower place. The London and County was in about the same position. They both felt that nowadays mere size did act as an important element in bringing new openings for a bank's activity, and that prestige was one of the most valuable of a bank's assets. They had often been asked why they did not go to the country by amalgamating one of the first-class country banks. The reason was that their capital was too large. While in their last statement their paid-up capital represented 11 per cent of the liabilities, that of the London and County was under 5 per cent., and it certainly could not be said that the larger figure was necessary for the credit of their company, for the London and County Bank stood unquestionably in the very first rank. The effect of the company's disproportionately large capital was a lower rate of dividends, and that meant a smaller premium on their shares.

Explaining the advantages which the bank would derive from the amalgamation, he said that the shareholders of the London and Westminster Bank would get a capital value at least equal to that which they now possessed, established on a wider basis, better protected by reduced liability, and with a vastly increased reserve. Their undertaking would be open to an expansion of business in a direction from which they had been hitherto precluded. They would be in receipt of a dividend which, even if somewhat reduced in amount, would be far better secured from fluctuation. In addition, there were advantages which would be shared by both banks, and which had appealed to the board of the London and County Bank as sufficient to induce them to enter into the agreement. The shareholders of the latter company gained nothing from the shareholders of the London and Westminster Bank in the way of price, in reduction of liability, or in increase and steadiness of dividend.

The general consideration common to both banks which had made the combination a desirable one from both sides was the obvious advantage of increased resources with much greater elasticity in the employment of them. He was confident that the London market would have no reason to complain of any less readiness to meet its requirements. The board looked forward eventually to considerable economies in management.

Mr. O. A. Benecke seconded the resolution.

The solicitor having explained the terms of the agreement, a short discussion ensued.

The Chairman, in reply to questions, said that the reason for holding the meetings of the two banks at the same hour was to enable the two institutions to take the important step absolutely side by side. Whatever economies were effected in management would be carried out without discharging a single member of the staff. The combined board would number twenty-seven members, but as vacancies occurred probably several of them would not be filled.

The resolution was carried, there being only two dissentients.

Notes

1 John Annan Bryce (1843–1923) worked for the East Indian firm Wallace and Co. between 1875 and 1906 (first in South Asia and later in London), then, after retiring, represented Inverness in Parliament from 1906 to 1918.

2 Alfred Faber was a partner in Faber Brothers, insurance brokers, which became Willis Faber in 1893, and was a longtime Lloyd's underwriter.

3 Possibly Walter Bowl, a brewer based in Hook Norton, a village in Oxfordshire.

4 Charles Seymour Grenfell (1839–1924) was a longtime partner in Pascoe, Grenfell and Sons, prominent Swansea copper merchants and bankers. He joined the LCB board in 1881 and continued as a director after the merger until 1918. He also served as a director at Royal Exchange Assurance, Anglo-Italian Bank, London & Brazilian Bank, City & South London Railway, and National Mortgage & Agency Company of New Zealand. His father, Henry Riversdale Grenfell, was a Bank of England director.

5 Arthur Hill (born 1851) was a partner in Panmure Gordon, Hill and Co., with commercial ties to the United States, Europe, and Japan, then (from 1903) Speyer Brothers, an Anglo-German firm that specialized in issuing railway securities in the US and Mexico. He joined the LWB board in 1904.

6 Nathan Mayer Rothschild (1840–1915) was a London banker who took over his father's bank in 1879 and was a Liberal MP from 1865 until 1885, when he was raised to the Peerage and soon switched his loyalties to the Liberal Unionist party. In 1909, he took a leading role in opposing David Lloyd George's "People's Budget," leading to a veto in the House of Lords that delayed its passage by two years.

7 Otto August Benecke (1837–1922) inherited, in 1865 (with his brother and mother, who was the sociologist Max Weber's great-aunt), his father's Anglo-German chemical dying factory, Benecke and Souchay, selling his share in the partnership in 1893. He sat on the board of the LWB and its successor banks from 1875 to 1922, also serving as Director of London Assurance and as a Lloyd's underwriter.

8 Walter Leaf (1852–1927) gave up a classics fellowship at Cambridge to join his father's silk and ribbon business, overseeing its conversion to a limited liability company in 1888. He joined the LWB board in 1891 and became its deputy chair in 1909 after it merged with the LCB, then chair from 1918 to 1927. He published respected translations and criticism of Homer into the 1910s as well as an influential banking textbook in 1926.

Part 4

BUBBLES AND FAILURES

Editorial Headnote

United Chilian Mining Company; Chilian Mining Company (1826)

Latin American mining companies played a central role in the stock market bubble of 1825. More than 40 such firms were floated (and 29 formed) in 1825, with £24 million in nominal capital, of which shareholders parted with £3.5 million. Four of these focused at least partly on Chilé, which had been rich in silver in the previous century and would become the world's leading copper producer in the decades after 1825. Together with the Anglo-Chilean and Chilean & Peruvian companies, the United Chilian Mining Company (UCMC) and Chilian Mining Company (CMC) combined to issue nominal shares worth £4 million, of which £295,000 was paid up. All of them focused on Norte Chico, a mineral-rich and water-starved region north of Santiago that Chilé's new government had designated as a mining zone in 1810. Foreign investors succeeded there only if they hired local workers and adapted to traditional excavation methods. The favored approach of British capitalists in 1825 – to export British labor and machinery – led all four companies to go bankrupt by 1827.[1]

In May 1825, the UCMC's prospectus announced its aim to "work Mines in the rich provinces of *Coquimbo* . . . which are esteemed as rich as any in Chili or Peru"; for this purpose, it issued 10,000 shares worth £500,000.[2] Its main promoter was Herman Hendricks, an infamous character who moved to London in the early 1820s after working as a merchant in the West Indies. A stockbroker by trade, he arranged an ill-fated loan for the Colombian government in 1825 and, a year earlier, for the fictitious Central American state of Poyais. In 1826, he promoted the Thames and Lower Rhine Company, which the *Morning Examiner* described as "a scheme so nefarious, that even in a period when we have been saturated with every species of humbug and barefaced fraud, threw into shade all other proceedings of a similar nature." Coverage of the UCMC fiasco and another failed venture in Haiti was no less damning.[3]

In 1825, the CMC promised to apply "British capital, skill, and machinery" to mine "gold, silver, copper, lead, tin, and iron" in Chilé.[4] It was one of several mining ventures promoted by John Powles, who recruited Chilé's British plenipotentiary, Don Mariano De Degaña, to be its president. It had managed to raise only £75,000 of its proposed £1 million when the stock market crashed in December, and it limped along for another year before dissolving. Its chair, Charles Herring, whose banking partnership had also recently failed when Mexico and Colombia had defaulted on loans it had underwritten, called the meeting in November 1826 to end the company's misery.[5] In stark contrast to the UCMC meeting a few months earlier, however, both Powles and several shareholders were surprisingly upbeat at this assembly: they expressed faith in the value of the property and hoped a new company could be supported to resume mining operations there. Press coverage was also far more respectful than was the case with the UCMC: both Powles and Herring had friends in high places, as did the shareholders in attendance, including the eminent Huguenot broker James de Cazenove.[6] Although mining did ultimately pick up in Chilé, things went from bad to worse for the CMC's interests and personnel there. Of its three on-site commissioners, one killed himself in January 1827 on learning of the stock market crash and another drank himself to death in Santiago. The third, Charles Lambert (1793–1876), remained in Chilé until 1851 with much success, but not before involving his former company in extensive legal wrangles.[7]

Notes

1 John Mayo and Simon Collier, *Mining in Chile's Norte Chico: Journal of Charles Lambert, 1825–1830* (Boulder: Westview Press, 1998), 2–8, 12, 16–17; Claudio Velez, "Egaña, Lambert, and the Chilean Mining Associations of 1825," *Hispanic American Historical Review* 55 (1975), 637–645; Frank Griffith Dawson, *The First Latin American Debt Crisis: The City of London and the 1822–1825 Loan Bubble* (New Haven: Yale University Press, 1990), 102–107, 139–142.

2 Henry English, *A General Guide to the Companies formed for Working Foreign Mines* (London: Boosey and Sons, 1825), 64.

3 "Colombian Loan," *Morning Chronicle* 27 June 1823; "Poyais Loan," *Morning* Post 31 May 1825; *Times* 14 October 1826; Dawson, *First Latin American Debt Crisis*, 111–112, 130.

4 English, *General Guide*, 19.

5 John Woodland, *Money Pits: British Mining Companies in the Californian and Australian Gold Rushes of the 1850s* (London: Routledge, 2014), 19–20; Dawson, *First Latin American Debt Crisis*, 26–72, 87–90, 125–130.

6 David Kynaston, *Cazenove & Co.: A History* (London: B.T. Batsford, 1991), 11–12, 24.

7 Mayo and Collier, *Mining in Chile's Norte Chico*, 13, 19–20.

20

UNITED CHILIAN COMPANY; CHILIAN MINING COMPANY

Sources: United Chilian Company; Chilian Mining Company (1826), *London Times*, 18 April and 7 November 1826

London Times, 18 April 1826

UNITED CHILIAN COMPANY

Yesterday a meeting of the shareholders in the United Chilian Mining Company took place at the George and Vulture Tavern, Cornhill, for the purpose of receiving the deposits which had been paid upon the shares they held in the company.

At 12 o'clock, the hour appointed for taking the chair, all the shareholders were assembled, and perhaps the district of Duke's-place never poured out three or four dozen of meaner objects than were mixed up on the occasion with the noble persons whose names had been lent to give the Company a character.

At half past 12 o'clock some impatience was manifested, but Captain Curzon,[1] Lord Teynham's son, soon afterwards entered the room, and assured the shareholders that his father was detained by an unforeseen occurrence, but would be certainly at their command at two o'clock.

At half-past one o'clock his lordship[2] arrived, and immediately took the chair.

He addressed the gentlemen around him. He regretted that there had been no disposition manifested upon the part of any of the directors, with the exception of himself and his son, and Mr. Annichini,[3] to meet the proposal of the shareholders. He had merely to repeat that he and his son were ready to contribute their shares of the deficiency which had been complained of. The circumstance of the bankruptcy of Mr. Hendricks, the projector of the company, had, of course, interfered with the arrangements for paying off the deposits. Under all the circumstances, he thought it would be advisable to draw the money which was in the hands of the bankers, and distribute it amongst the shareholders as far as it would go. It was calculated that the amount in the hands of the bankers would pay 3l. 4s. per share. and afterwards an exertion might be made to induce all the directors to pay up the deficiencies, which amounted to 1l. 6s. per share, so that the shareholders might be at no greater loss than 10s. per share.

This statement excited considerable disapprobation.

DOI: 10.4324/9781003177715-24

A Shareholder declared, that he had expected from what occurred at the last meeting, that 4l. 10s. would be paid upon the shares this very day. He expected that the Directors would have assembled immediately after it was known that the shareholders were dissatisfied, for the purpose of making up the deficiency: but after all, the shareholders were as badly off as ever.

Lord TEYNHAM said the fact was, they formed no company at all. Mr. Hendricks was the proprietor of what was called the company, and had taken the whole responsibility upon himself, and he (Lord Teynham) and his son had signed the draughts for the 1,000l. of the money subscribed, merely for the purpose of dissolving it. He hoped the shareholders would take the 3l. 10s. per share; if not, they must adopt whatever course they thought most advisable.

Mr. ANNICHINI said, the shares ought to be paid off at par. He would do all he could to accomplish that object.

A Shareholder. – My Lord, I say I must have my property. If you *von't* pay me, I must go in my own *vay* to get it. It's a shame, my Lord – it's a shame.

Another Shareholder said, that the Directors might, if they pleased, look to Mr. Hendricks, but the shareholders must look to the Directors, and to them alone. It was understood that the money would be forthcoming this day, and now another postponement was aimed at. Was this worthy of a nobleman?

Lord TEYNHAM repeated, that he was willing to pay his proportion of the deficiency complained of; but he begged to know whether any one present thought him to be such an ass as to pay what ought to be contributed by nine directors. He knew nothing of the gentlemen in the direction, with the exception of his own son; and he had signed the draught while on a sick bed. God Almighty knew he derived no profit from the transaction; and God knew that he most earnestly wished he had never heard a word about the company. (A laugh.)

Several shareholders said, they expected to get the whole of their money back.

Lord TEYNHAM. – I shall do as I have stated. You would not be so unreasonable as to expect I should pay the whole deficiencies myself.

The Shareholders were almost unanimous in the opinion that his lordship ought to pay every farthing. They pulled out their shares, and said they were ready to receive their money. They came prepared, and they expected not to be any longer humbugged. One of them, however, observed, that his lordship would act a very foolish part in disposing of his property in such a manner to gentlemen, all of whom had embarked in the concern in the hope of a premium, and most of whom, he believed, had purchased the shares at a heavy discount.

Mr. ANNICHINI said, that Mr. Hendricks had stated as a reason for not coming to a settlement, that Lord Teynham and another director owed him between 400l. and 500l.

Lord TEYNHAM. – That belongs to another transaction. It has nothing to do with this; it refers to shares in another company.

A Shareholder. – My Lord, if I don't get the money for my shares what I paid, I'll bring an action against you, that I *vill*. Oh Lord! How can a Lord act in that 'ere *vay*.

Lord TEYNHAM, who sat with his hat off, close to the person who uttered this threat, and who sat with his hat on, respectfully assured him, that every thing should be done to get the whole of his money restored to him. In the mean time, his Lordship recommended that the Jew who had thus addressed him would be for the present satisfied with his share of the money which remained at the banker's.

"Ay," said the Shareholder, "I'll take *dat;* but if I don't get *de* rest I'll go into *de* court *wid* it."

Another Shareholder. – My Lord, here's a printer's bill of upwards of 50l.

Lord TEYNHAM. – Oh, I have nothing to do with that. God knows, I have enough to do with the shareholders.

A Jew Shareholder. – I hope, my Lord, you are not a director in any other mining company?

Lord TEYNHAM. – No, thank God. I never regretted any thing so much in my life as my connexion with city companies.

"Ay, ay," said one of the Shareholders, with a red face and dirty shirt, "you are a director for all that. Why, you belong to the Kentish Railway Company."

Lord TEYNHAM. – I am a Director, but it is an honorary one; I have no responsibility upon me.

The shareholder smiled familiarly at Lord Teynham, who said – "I have certainly acted most foolishly in giving my sanction to those things, but I have been punished for it. It has been a source of bitter regret. I have made every inquiry into the nature of the mining speculations since I have found myself in error, and I have ascertained, beyond a doubt, that mining in South America is all nonsense. I spoke with an intelligent Captain the other day upon the subject, and he assured me that in the new mining districts the roads were filled with broken carts, broken tools, and drunken Englishmen and Scotchmen." (Loud laughter.)

A Shareholder. – Well, my Lord, we'll thank you for the little that comes to us.

Lord TEYNHAM. – Now, gentlemen, there are 611*l*. wanting. That will be about 70l. a-piece amongst the directors. I am ready, and so is Captain Curzon, to pay a fair proportion.

A Shareholder. – Very well, my Lord, we'll take your share now, if you please.

Lord TEYNHAM. – Upon my word, you will not. You don't think that I'll pay without being indemnified.

"God bless you," said the shareholder, "you'll be quite clear. Come, you and the Captain here can give us your proportions, and that will be doing the thing decently."

Lord TEYNHAM would not consent, without being indemnified according to law.

A Shareholder then moved, that the sum of 3l. 4s. upon each share should be accepted by the shareholders in part payment of the deposit money.

This motion was agreed to unanimously.

It was also proposed, that on the 2d of June, the shareholders should again meet, for the purpose of receiving whatever might be collected from the directors.

This was also agreed to.

Some of the shareholders cried out, "I say, my Lord, my Lord, I wish we may get it." (Laughter, in which Lord Teynham joined.)

Here a gentleman who held shares called for a glass of brandy and water, and sat down next to Lord Teynham. "You had better, my Lord," said he, "send off to the bankers, for the little money there; we'll have it now, if you please."

"Ay, ay," said a Jew shareholder, "ve von't go vidout it. Go down, my Lord, to de bankers and get it."

Lord TEYNHAM then sent to the bankers, but word was brought back that the check must be countersigned by Mr. Hendrick.

The Shareholders, who were waiting with great impatience for the return of the messenger, were thunderstruck at this intelligence. They began to give all for lost.

A Solicitor, who attended upon the part of one of the directors, suggested the propriety of waiting until Mr. Hendrick's examination before the Commissioners of Bankrupts should take place, as it might come out before the Commissinners what had been done with the shares which had been purchas'd by the bankrupt by the desire of the directors.

Lord TEYNHAM said, there was no occasion for waiting, as the shares had been properly disposed of.

Lord TEYNHAM then said, he would himself go to the bankers. The shareholders cheered up at this intimation. His Lordship then left the room, accompanied by a shareholder on each side.

A Shareholder walked over to Captain Curzon, who was bareheaded, and said, "Well, Captain, any naval promotions this year?"

The Captain was astonished. He said he was not aware of any.

The Shareholder pulled his chair close to that of the Captain, and with his hat on, began to discuss the conditions of the naval power of France and of that of England. "The French," said he, "have 50 sail of the line ready to start, and if there is such a thing as a war, John Bull will have to look sharp."

The Captain observed, that there might be some difficulty in manning the French ships effectually.

His Lordship at this moment returned, and informed the meeting that all was right. There was a general cry of joy at this intelligence.

His Lordship then took the shares from the holders, who gave a receipt on the back of them, which is a complete bar to any future action for the recovery of the remainder of the deposits.

The first person who received a check from his Lordship, made but one spring towards the door, and he was out of sight in an instant.

The rest of the company were equally quick in their movements.

One of the shareholders, upon receiving his money, took his Lordship by the hand, "Well, my Lord," said he, "God bless you, I'll see you again on the 2d of June."

The business being concluded, Lord Teynham and his son retired. His Lordship having frequently during his exertions declared, that he had never derived any advantage from the Company, one of the Shareholders, upon leaving the room, said, "My skull and eyes! if I don't become a Director myself."

Between 1,000l. and 2,000l. was paid away in the room by his Lordship. He and his son, and Mr. Annichini, were the Directors upon whose responsibility the money was drawn.

London Times, 7 November 1826

CHILIAN MINING COMPANY

Yesterday a meeting of the shareholders in the above undertaking, was held, pursuant to advertisement, at the City of London Tavern, for the purpose of confirming a resolution passed at a meeting convened on the 16th of October, dissolving the company.

Mr. HERRING,[4] having taken the chair, read the minutes of the last meeting, which contained the resolution, stating, that in consequence of the proprietors not being willing to advance any more capital, the directors had recommended to the proprietors the necessity of dissolving the company forthwith:

The CHAIRMAN said it now only remained for the shareholders present to confirm the resolution, and he moved that this company be now dissolved, according to the provisions of the deed of settlement.

A Shareholder could not but regret that such a step as that of dissolving the company had been taken, the more so, as the mines they possessed in Chili were valuable. He was sorry that the altered state of the times had rendered it impossible to procure the necessary funds to carry on the concern with profit. He would be glad to know from the directors whether the mining operations could not be conducted with a limited capital?

The CHAIRMAN. – The directors had always entertained a most favourable opinion of the property in Chili; but the want of money compelled them to recommend the abandonment of the mines. Under all the circumstances, it was desirable that this company should be dissolved. If any gentlemen wished to establish a new company, they could do so with a limited capital.

Mr. POWLES[5] remarked, that many shareholders in the Chilian and Peruvian Mining Company, which had been dissolved a few days since, had likewise expressed such a wish. He was sure the mines would turn out profitable.

Mr. CAZENOVE[6] said he represented a great body of foreign shareholders, who were all sorry that the dissolution had been decided upon. He could guarantee that a large proportion of them would readily join in the formation of another company on a smaller scale.

The CHAIRMAN said, if another company was formed, it would commence with great advantages. Chili had been explored, and the best mines in the country had been obtained by the Chilian Mining Company. It had also obtained many privileges, which would revert to a new concern; among the most prominent of which was a considerable reduction in the duties by the Chilian Government. The directors would be very happy to meet, and join any body of shareholders, who were disposed to form another association. He then put the resolution for dissolving the company, which was carried, with only one dissentient voice.

A Shareholder (a foreigner), on the part of many shareholders abroad, expressed their thanks to the directors for their good management of the company's affairs. (Hear, hear.) He concluded by moving a vote of thanks to the directors. – Carried.

The CHAIRMAN, in returning thanks, said the directors throughout, only had the welfare of the proprietors at heart.

The Secretary observed, that should a smaller company be thought desirable by a body of the proprietors, the directors would be happy to receive communications on the subject.

Mr. POWLES remarked, that the proprietors in the old company would have the preference in a new company, should one be formed. – The meeting then separated.

Notes

1 Thomas Roper Curzon (1790–1833), captain in the Royal Navy (promoted from lieutenant in 1813), was the second son of Henry Francis Roper-Curzon.

2 Henry Francis Roper-Curzon (1768–1842) succeeded his cousin John in 1824 as the 14th Baron Teynham. See note to 3 (Welsh Iron and Coal).

3 Pompey Anichini, London-based East India broker, immigrated to London from Leghorn (Tuscany) and became a naturalized British subject in 1833.

4 Charles Herring was partner in a merchant bank with David Barclay and Christopher Richardson, all three of whom sat on the Chilean Mining Company's board.

5 John Diston Powles (1787–1867) was (in Benjamin Disraeli's words) "the creditor of every nation from California to China" in the 1820s. Born in Denmark, he entered business with his brothers in the early 1820s, and their firm partnered with Herring to broker a £2 million loan to Colombia in 1822. Into the 1830s, he promoted mining companies in Colombia, Mexico, Chile, and Brazil, typically purchasing a large proportion of shares and sitting on the company's board.

6 James de Cazenove (1744–1827), London merchant, stockbroker, and investment banker, immigrated from France and became a naturalized English subject in 1778. In the 1780s, he formed a partnership with his brother Charles and two fellow Huguenots, which (as he indicated at the meeting) supplied capital to British companies from "a great body of foreign shareholders." Although he died worth close to £48,000 in 1827, his firm went bankrupt four years after his death, suggesting that the 1825 crash may have weakened its finances.

Editorial Headnote

London, Chatham and Dover Railway (1866)

British railway construction in the 1860s primarily filled in gaps between the large trunk lines that had been built over the preceding three decades. Although these railways did attract some local investment, much of the capital they raised came from bonds issued by construction companies, which borrowed additional funds on their security. The business model of these "contractors' lines" was to flip them at a profit to trunk lines once they were complete.[1] The leader in this field was Sir Morton Peto, who leaned heavily on the discount house of Overend, Gurney to fund his projects. When that house failed in 1866, Peto declared bankruptcy, and the main railway he was working on at the time, the London, Chatham and Dover (LCDR), presented shareholders and bondholders alike with the prospect of expensive calls, delayed repayments, and proliferating litigation. When the dust settled, he owed £4 million on the nearly £6 million he had borrowed and spent, using the company's shares as collateral. *Punch* spoofed Peto and his gullible shareholders in a story about the fictitious company of London, Cheteam and Clover.[2]

The LCDR began life in 1853 as the East Kent Railway, changing its name when Peto appeared on the scene in 1859. The company formed with enthusiastic support from local Kent landlords, who had been miffed when the South Eastern Railway (SER) had failed to deliver on its promise of a branch line in 1847. Its original chair, Lord Harris, was a Kent fixture who had served as a colonial governor between 1845 and 1860, then joined the LCDR board when he returned to Britain in 1860. Other early directors who remained with the company after Peto arrived included retired army officers Sir John Maxwell Tylden and Lord Sondes ("the largest landowner between Rochester and Canterbury") and Faversham magistrate Charles Hilton. Under Peto's supervision, the company constructed expensive extensions of the line southeast to Dover and west to Victoria Station in London. This provided shorter travel times between London and Dover than the SER, which had been operating in a slipshod fashion since 1836. Besides running parallel lines for much of this journey, the two companies also plowed share capital into numerous and ultimately unremunerative rival branch lines.[3] To pay for these projects, Peto relied heavily on so-called Lloyd's bonds issued by finance companies, which charged 5–6% to raise money with minimal collateral; more than a quarter of the LCDR's outstanding debt in 1866 was in this form.[4]

When the LCDR held its biannual general meeting on 31 August 1866, six weeks into Peto's drawn-out bankruptcy declaration, the meeting adjourned from its usual location at the Westminster Hotel to the nearby St. James's Hall, with a capacity of 2000 people.[5] Angry debenture holders sat on either side of the company's shareholders, their perch in the galleys mirroring the LCDR's uncomfortable relationship between credit and share capital; they held a meeting on their own a month later at the London Tavern. Looming over the proceedings were the shadowy finance companies that had footed so many of Peto's costs. When the LCDR's directors raised £1.5 million in share capital to pay off these companies, holders of its £4.5 million in debenture stock protested, arguing that they should come first in the queue, and it took until 1870 for the competing claims to be sorted out in arbitration. Similar levels of chaos roiled the railway side of the fence. In 1868, when Parliament developed a plan for the LCDR, SER, and a third company to manage the London-Dover corridor jointly, LCDR shareholders jumped at the chance but the SER scuttled this plan. Instead, the LCDR continued to limp along, persisting in its inefficient competition with the SER. It took until 1923 for ordinary LCDR shareholders to earn a return on their investment.[6]

Notes

1 Timothy L. Alborn, *Conceiving Companies: Joint-Stock Politics in Victorian* England (London: Routledge, 1998), 203.

2 James Taylor, *Creating Capitalism: Joint-Stock Enterprise in British Politics and Culture 1800–1870* (London: Boydell Press, 2006), 183.

3 Philip S. Bagwell, "The Rivalry and Working Union of the South Eastern and London, Chatham & Dover Railways," *Transport History* 2 (1955), 66–68; Keith Lampard, "The Promotion and Performance of the London Chatham & Dover Railway," *Journal of Transport History* 3rd ser. 6 (1985), 51; Katherine Prior, "George Francis Robert Harris," *Oxford Dictionary of Biography Online*; "Deaths," *Gentleman's Magazine* n.s. 2 (1866), 533.

4 Harold Pollins, "Railway Contractors and the Finance of Railway Development in Britain – II," *Journal of Transport History* 3 (1957), 106–109.

5 "Sir S. Peto and the Representation of Bristol," *Saturday Review* 25 (1868), 380. On St. James's Hall, a concert hall that had been built in 1858, see Michael Forsyth, *Buildings for Music: The Architect, the Musician, and the Listener from the Seventeenth Century to the Present Day* (Cambridge, MA: MIT Press, 1985), 200–205.

6 Phillip Cottrell, *Investment Banking in England 1856–1881* (London: Routledge, 2012), 2: 427–429; Bagwell, "Rivalry and Working Union" 68–76; Lampard, "Promotion and Performance," 48.

21

LONDON, CHATHAM AND DOVER RAILWAY

Sources: London, Chatham and Dover Railway (1866), *London Times*, 14 August, 1 September, 29 September, and 28 November 1866

London Times 14 August 1866

The directors of the London, Chatham, and Dover Railway have issued a circular preparatory to the general meeting on the 31st inst., stating the position in which they stand, in consequence of the inability of the company to obtain new loans to replace the 400,000*l.* debentures which became due last month, or even to meet the half-year's interest payable on the whole of the company's debentures. A receiver has been appointed by the Court of Chancery, and an assignment has been made of the rolling stock, &c., to prevent its seizure and appropriation by any special creditors, but an effort to procure distinct Parliamentary powers to facilitate a readjustment in the interests of all concerned was unsuccessful, and cannot now be obtained till next year. Meanwhile an appeal is made to the forbearance not only of the debenture holders but of the claimants of the company, including about 700,000*l.* for land. United action is at the same time solicited from the shareholders, from whom the Board invite the fullest investigation.

London Times 1 September 1866

LONDON, CHATHAM, AND DOVER

The 27th half-yearly general meeting of this company was held yesterday. It assembled at the Westminster Palace Hotel, but at once adjourned *pro formâ* to the St. James's-hall, in order that a larger number of proprietors and debenture-holders might be enabled to take part in the proceedings. The body of the hall was about half filled with owners of stock, and the side galleries for about half their length were densely packed with holders of debentures. A few lady proprietors were also present. The chair was filled by Lord Sondes,[1] chairman of the company.

The seal of the company having been affixed to the register of shareholders,

The CHAIRMAN said he had to apologize to the proprietors for the report not having been sooner in their hands. That was owing to the illness of one of the accountant's staff, and to some other circumstances over which the Board had no control. The report showed an increase of receipts and also an increase in the working expenses. It

DOI: 10.4324/9781003177715-25

appeared that the number of passengers conveyed on the railway and its branches during the half-year ending June 30, 1866, was 4,901,444 – a fact which spoke strongly for the utility of their line. For himself and his brother directors he must express his regret at the unfortunate situation in which their railway was placed. Their difficulties had arisen chiefly from the fact of 400,000*l*. of debentures falling due when it was impossible in the state of the money-market to get them renewed. These and other responsibilities could not be met, and the directors had been obliged to request the indulgence of their creditors. Some of the creditors resorted to the Court of Chancery in order to have receivers appointed, and many actions had been commenced against the company. In consequence of these proceedings it was thought necessary by the Board that the rolling stock should be assigned, and held in trust for the company. No doubt it was within the knowledge of the proprietors that during the late Session of Parliament the Board applied for powers to enable the company to raise money to discharge claims which were pressing upon them. Their application received the approval of the Board of Trade, but the clauses which would have given it legal effect were objected to in the House of Lords, and owing to the late period of the Session it was found impossible to carry the matter out. They all regretted that the interest on the debentures had not been paid, and they felt still more on account of the inconvenience to which that non-payment had given rise. It was, however, satisfactory to know that the steps taken by the Board had prevented any interruption of the traffic, and that the interest on the debentures would ultimately be paid. The line was earning the interest of the current half-year. The Board were glad to find that the appointment of a committee of investigation was contemplated by the shareholders. The Board would welcome such committee and give it every assistance, and they would thankfully receive any suggestions from the committee for the improvement of the company's affairs. Every one must admit that the state of their affairs was unfortunate; but it was by no means irretrievable. Other companies had had to pass through the same or similar difficulties, and had got over them. The Board looked with much confidence to what would result from their metropolitan lines. After a careful consideration it was estimated that within seven years they would double their present traffic without any very considerable increase in their expenses, for it was to be remembered that the expense of a train was the same whether it was filled or only half filled. (Hear.) But what was absolutely necessary for the welfare of the company was provision for the payment of their debts. (Hear, hear.) He had to announce that by death the Board had lost two of their members – Sir J. Tylden[2] and Mr. C. J. Hilton;[3] and by retirement three – Sir C. Rich,[4] Sir C. Roney,[5] and Mr. G. F. Holroyd.[6] He begged to move that the report be adopted.

Lord HARRIS[7] seconded the motion.

A SHAREHOLDER remarked that many of the proprietors had not heard a sentence of the chairman's observations.

Sir J. CURTIS was not there to defend the directors; still less was he present to offer any ungenerous remarks on the course which the Board had pursued. He had not been in communication with a single individual on the subject of the meeting, If the directors had pursued bold schemes – and it must be admitted they had done so – they had not hid their candle under a bushel. It had been put on the housetops (a laugh), and if blame there was, other companies ought to take their share of it. The schemes of the London, Chatham, and Dover Company had met with great opposition from other companies; those schemes had been severely criticized; they had been subjected to rigid Parliamentary scrutiny, and yet they had been carried successfully through both Houses. Under these circumstances he hoped there would be no angry discussion at that meeting. (Laughter, and cries of "Time.")

Mr. SURGEY[8] observed that the order of proceeding which had been agreed upon ought to be carried out. ("No, no," and cries of "There has been no agreement.") An order of proceeding had been agreed upon by those gentlemen who thought that a committee ought to be appointed. ("No, no," and other interruptions.) He and those gentlemen came there to do their best for the company, and it was for the shareholders to say whether they would appoint them as a committee. In stock represented there and for which they held proxies they represented 4,300,000*l.* of capital, and he could assure the meeting that his and their wish was to benefit the debenture-holders as well the proprietors of stock. He had no wish to make any observations in disparagement of the Board, but he should feel it his duty to conclude his observations by moving, by way of amendment to the motion of the chairman, a resolution for the appointment of a committee of investigation. (Cheers.) As a matter of form, his resolution must be put by way of amendment. The amendment would be acceded to by the Board. Indeed, he might say that they themselves had requested the appointment of a committee. A committee was necessary for every one connected with the management – from the chairman to the boy who swept the offices. (Hear, hear.) The object of those who proposed it was to bring about public confidence in the company. Every one was aware that rumours most damaging to the welfare of the company were afloat, and they could not get rid of those rumours till they had an investigation by a committee. (Hear, hear.) It was his desire to make the company a prosperous one, and he had every confidence that they would arrive at that happy result. He was grieved that the debenture-holders should be in the position of not getting their money; and he thought that on the committee of inquiry two gentlemen, at least, should represent that class of creditors. (A cry from the debenture-holders, – "That is not enough.") They were rather sharp with him. He had said "two, at least;" but he would now observe that nearly every gentlemen whom he proposed to place on the committee represented the interests of a bondholder as well as of a shareholder. (Hear, hear.) He thought, however, that two at least ought to specially represent the bondholders. He was sure the directors would afford the committee every assistance; for he believed it was their desire that the committee should do all that was desirable. His own personal friends represented upwards of 2,000,000*l.* in the various securities of the company. He had been instrumental in getting them into what had proved to be a difficulty, and he felt bound to do all in his power to get them out of it. The gentlemen who had been active in promoting the arrangement for a committee had placed themselves in communication with Mr. R. Fletcher,[9] of Aberdeen, who, with other gentlemen, had been so successful in setting matters right in the case of the West Hartlepool Railway. The first cause of all the mischief was that the London, Chatham, and Dover Railway was a contractors' line. Indeed, all the cause of their difficulty was summed up in that statement. What had been the effect of the railway being a contractors' line? The contractors would have been glad to receive sovereigns from the directors; but as the directors could not give them coin they had to give them securities, and the contractors had to raise money on bonds and preference shares. When the contractors received 1,000,000*l*. of ordinary stock or of debentures, what did they do with it? Why, wanting money, they had to go to a broker and raise money on those securities. And did not that very much lessen the value of the securities and damage very considerably the credit of the company? (Hear, hear.) Afterwards, when the contractors had to offer the securities to the public, had they not to do so at prices which still further damaged the company? It was at once said, "Good gracious, here is the stock of the London, Chatham, and Dover offered at 80!" But the person who made that exclamation in a tone of blame as against the contractors took the stock at the reduced price, while another who blamed the company for not issuing it at a higher figure would not take it if it were so offered. (Hear, hear.) Then, when the stock would not be taken, "sales" had to be effected and prices declined still further. Unless these operations were carried on the works must be brought to a stand, and the line could not be opened at the promised time; while it must be admitted that as a consequence of such an arrangement the company and the contractors became most inconveniently one. (Hear, hear.) The contractors never had less in their possession than 1,000,000*l*. of stock, which they were always trying to get rid of, and the want of public confidence in the financial position of the company increased. When the credit of the company was gone it could no longer borrow money. Debentures having three years to run were issued. The custom was to renew debentures or borrow money upon them. They rarely or never represented money in any other way than by being renewed or taken up by others, or in having money borrowed on them. But persons refused to lend money in a time of financial difficulty such as that which we had been experiencing lately. The other day, during the worst period of that difficulty, a large amount of the debentures of the London, Chatham, and Dover Company fell due, and a heavy amount of interest was required to be paid. He expressed his opinion, in unison with that of other gentlemen, that it was the duty of the company to fulfil its obligations if possible, even at the cost of a future loss. He said he should not shrink from a prospective loss of 20,000*l*. or 30,000*l*. if the directors could raise money to meet their immediate liabilities; but so bad was the credit of the company, and such was the state of the money-market, that it was found impossible to do it. They had not at their back such a bank as that which Mr. Laurie,[10] the chairman of the Brighton line, described as having come to the aid of his company. [A Shareholder. – "Stick to the London, Chatham, and Dover."] It appeared to him that the company should act as a business firm would under similar circumstances – namely, go to their creditors and represent to them fairly the state of their affairs. He did not believe there were half-a-dozen present at that meeting who understood the position of the company;

but he thought he did understand it, and yet he did not look upon it in a desponding light. There was 1,000,000*l.* out in one way or another on land; but if the shareholders put him in possession of 50,000*l.* he would undertake to free them from all liability on account of that 1,000,000*l.* The land was worth much more than the amount for which it was security. With the 50,000*l.* he would redeem land which would sell for 70,000*l.*, and, having sold it for the latter amount, he would continue his operation of repayment and sale till the 1,000,000*l.* was discharged, and he should be very much surprised if at the end of six months he did not show a good balance after every debt had been wiped off the land. He based his opinion on the authority of statements made by Mr. Vigers,[11] their surveyor, who had sold some of their land at a profit of 20 per cent. Mr. Newman's[12] policy had been to get as much land in London as he could for the company. He believed it right to have borrowed money for that purpose; for in no case was the land likely to realize less than 20 per cent. profit. Again, judging from the results achieved by the Brighton Company, the London, Chatham, and Dover Company ought to take more on their 12 miles of Metropolitan Railway than on their line from London to Dover. [A Voice. – "When?"] Directly they had such mileage receipts as the Brighton Company had on their metropolitan lines. (A laugh.) Until their metropolitan system afforded the additional accommodation which the traffic required they could not expect such mileage receipts. Peace, honour, economy, and thorough good management were required by the company. (Hear, hear.) Why should they not make arrangements with other lines – with the Brighton, the South-Western,[13] and the South-Eastern lines? Why should there not be even amalgamation where it was feasible? (Hear, hear.) He did not see why two different trains should be run to Dover on two different lines when one would answer the purpose. In making these suggestions he wished it to be understood that, while he desired to serve the company, he was anxious that the public convenience should also be consulted to the fullest extent. He begged to move, –

1 "That a committee be nominated to investigate the company's accounts and affairs generally, and to report to an adjourned meeting to be held on the 15th of October next.

2 "That the following gentlemen be the committee, with power to add to their number, as well as to fill up vacancies, and to employ all the professional assistance which they may think necessary – viz., Samuel Hawksley Burbury,[14] 1, New-square, Lincoln's-inn; Thomas Alers Hankey,[15] London; William Hartridge,[16] 80, Old Broadstreet; Frederick Heritage,[17] 28, Nicholas-lane; William Edward Hilliard,[18] Cowley-house, near Uxbridge; Grosvenor Hodgkinson,[19] M.P., Winthorpe-hall, Newark; Augustus Thomas Hotham, 17, Calverley-park, Tunbridge Wells; Cornelius Surgey, 7, Finch-lane, London; and George Cavendish Taylor,[20] 42, Elvaston-place, South Kensington.

3 "That, considering the position into which the company has been brought under the past management, it is necessary that the Board of Direction be re-constituted.

4 "That a new Board of Directors be nominated at the adjourned meeting.
5 "That the present Directors be requested not to undertake any new works, or to resolve on any Parliamentary proceedings for next Session, without the sanction of the committee, and generally to confer with the committee on all questions of importance affecting the interests of the company."

Mr. H. De Grey Water,[21] in seconding the amendment, complained that the promises of the prospectus in regard to the mode of issuing certain stock had not been fulfilled.

Mr. Herapath[22] did not altogether concur with Mr. Surgey in the way in which he had brought forward his suggestion for the appointment of a committee. He respected that gentleman, but he did not think he ought to have come there with his committee cut and dry. ("Hear, hear," and "Oh, oh!") They had been paying interest on three times the amount of capital they ought to have paid on. He believed that all the losses incurred by blundering and mismanagement would be retrieved in time, owing to the extraordinary growth of the traffic; but it was his opinion that the present position of the company was entirely owing to the unparalleled, he might almost say the criminal, blunders committed in connexion with the issue of the capital. (Hear, hear.)

Mr. Rees,[23] who spoke amid constant interruptions, begged to remind the gentlemen by whom he was surrounded that they had gone into all the schemes of the company with positive enthusiasm. The directors had been blamed for not going forward with those schemes rapidly enough. He wondered Mr. Surgey did not blush when he told them he was so well acquainted with the company's affairs. He now came forward as the deliverer of the London, Chatham, and Dover Company; but if there was any one man to whom, more than another, these calamities were attributable, that man was Mr. Surgey. (Cries of "That's not the business," "Sit down," "Time," and counter-cries of "Hear, hear.")

A Shareholder. – We are not here to discuss Mr. Surgey's character.

Mr. V. Knight[24] suggested that the Chairman should call on Mr. Rees to sit down. They were there to consider the liabilities of the company.

A Shareholder would advise Mr. Rees not to sit down.

Mr. Rees would make such remarks as he thought fit, as long as he was in order. (Cries of "Sit down," "Go on;" amid which some half-dozen gentlemen in the body of the hall and in the gallery started to their feet.)

A Debenture-holder. – The honorable proprietor (Mr. Rees) ought not to go on when nobody wants to hear him. (Cheers and hisses.)

Mr. Rees intended to conclude with a resolution, but the meeting would first allow him to say a word in explanation. (Shouts of "No.") He moved a resolution to the effect that the meeting do adjourn till the 15th of October, in order to receive a further statement from the directors on that date containing more detailed particulars as to the liabilities of the company, and a specific plan of future action.

This resolution found no seconder.

Mr. KEMPE, a debenture-holder, rose to address the meeting, and his doing so gave rise to a very stormy scene. A number of the shareholders refused to hear him, on the ground that he had no right to speak: the debenture-holders cheered him and called upon him to proceed, and Mr. Kempe declared that he would be heard. Ultimately, on an appeal to the chair.

Lord HARRIS, the deputy-chairman of the company, said the legal adviser of the Board had advised the Board – and they were anxious to act on the advice – to hear any of the debenture-holders who might wish to speak, though, as a matter of legal right, they might not, perhaps, be entitled to address the meeting. (Cheers.)

Mr. KEMPE then called on the shareholders and the debenture-holders to work together. He complained that in the reports of railway directors there was always something kept back. In the report now before the meeting it was stated, "The accounts between the company and their contractors, Messrs. Peto, Betts, and Crampton, are under investigation, but will not be ready for the general meeting." He moved that the meeting be adjourned till those accounts had been taken.

Another debenture-holder expressed his full confidence in the proposed committee. Speaking for himself and his family, they were anxious to show forbearance; but the first thing which ought to be paid was the interest on debentures. (A laugh.)

Lord HARRIS said that with regard to the objection to their meeting being held before the accounts between their company and their contractors were made up, his answer was that under their Act they were obliged to hold their meeting about this time. He could assure the meeting that in consequence of the misfortunes which had occurred to them the directors had been living in a state of protracted agony. Their desire had been to meet the difficulty, and to pay the interest on the debentures. Up to the 30th of June they expected to be able to do so; but they then found that the only terms on which they could get money to pay that interest would be utterly ruinous to the company. They did not refuse to risk their private fortunes on the occasion, but they found that even such a step would be useless, and accordingly they thought it better to place the state of the case before the proprietors and the holders of debentures and ask their forbearance. (Hear, hear.) He had no doubt that if they could have procured from Parliament the financial powers which they applied for last Session they would have been able to settle their affairs, and that all parties would have been saved much trouble and expense. The directors felt their position very much, because they were sensible that it must shake public confidence in the Board. They were most willing that there should be a committee – an entirely independent committee – to investigate the entire case and report to the proprietors. He had nothing to say against any of the gentlemen proposed by Mr. Surgey. He trusted the committee would go fully into the company's affairs, and that it might be able to suggest some useful measures. He would observe that if a benefit had resulted to the country from the construction of the London, Chatham, and Dover line, he doubted very much whether that benefit would ever have been conferred had it not been for their contractors. A good deal had been said about mismanagement. He could not boast of much experience in matters of this sort, but he must express his conviction that every member of the Board had done what he honestly believed to be best for the interests of the concern. It seemed to be assumed that the present direction had come into the management of a flourishing concern and injured it by their proceedings. The real question was this – whether the construction of the Metropolitan Extension of the London, Chatham, and Dover line was a legitimate object? For two reasons he thought it was: – First, the scheme went through a most searching inquiry by two Parliamentary committees, who came to the conclusion that it was a legitimate one, and a scheme likely to be successful; secondly, it appeared from the receipts that the number carried over the extension was very large, and that the traffic was likely to increase very much. It was of importance that the line should have as many feeders as possible; so that looking to all the circumstances the undertaking appeared to him to be a very reasonable one. He could give an impartial opinion on the point, because when this metropolitan system was begun he was not a member of the Board, nor did he know anything about it. At the instance of his noble friend (Lord Sondes) he joined the Board, but he did so without any idea of speculation. The line ran through his own county, and he took an interest in it because it had long been an idea of his that the line from London to Dover should run in the old direction through Kent. He felt that he was more competent to look after the traffic of the line than after its finance. Having had no experience in the latter department, he, as well as other members of the Board, had been obliged to trust to those who had more knowledge of the subject. He had hoped until within the last few days that there was one humiliation which had been spared to the Board, for they had taken great pains to avoid it, but he was sorry to be obliged to inform the meeting that within the last four or five days the Board had been informed and had ascertained that there had been an over-issue of debentures to the amount of 128,000*l.* ("Oh, oh!") arising from the fact that the contractors had undertaken to redeem debentures on which money had been raised, but failed to do so. (Shouts of "Shame," and "Oh, oh!") He could assure the meeting that neither he nor any other member of the Board had been aware of it till within the last few days. (Renewed expressions of surprise and indignation.) The matter would be one of account as between the company and the contractors. These gentlemen stated that the money which ought to have been employed in the redemption of the outstanding debentures had been expended in meeting other obligations of the company, and the persons who held the over issues would have the money which they paid refunded to them as soon as possible. He would remind the meeting that the directors had had large dealings with the contractors, and, however the conduct of these gentlemen in reference to these debentures might be disapproved, it could not be denied that they had exerted themselves very strenuously in the interests of the company.

Another stormy scene followed on the statement of Lord Harris. Not less than 20 gentlemen were on their legs at the same moment, and from the debenture holders there was a unanimous and determined demand for further explanations.

Mr. BAXTER,[25] of the firm of Rose, Baxter, Norton, and Co., solicitors to the company, said that it was the custom of railway companies having debentures to issue to pledge those debentures when they wanted to raise money. When they issued their debentures to the public they took up the old ones which had been pledged. The directors of the London, Chatham, and Dover Company had acted in that way through their contractors, and as the debentures were issued to the public the contractors redeemed and withdrew those which were pledged; but in the case of some, on the city line alone, amounting to 128,000*l*., they had not followed that course. They got the money to take them up, but they said they were obliged to apply it to the payment of other demands against the company. ("Oh, oh!")

A SHAREHOLDER recommended the debenture holders to capitalize their interest for a year, and then take debentures at 5 per cent. per annum for ten years.

Mr. SCOTT, though a shareholder, had a larger interest as a debenture holder. He thought the present directors were not fit to manage the concern, and was glad that the Bank rate of 10 per cent. had pulled the company up. If it had not done so, they would have been ruined irretrievably in another year. He approved the appointment of a committee.

A SHAREHOLDER thought there ought to be some explanation of the retirement of Sir C. Roney and Mr. Holroyd.

A DEBENTURE HOLDER suggested that a committee consisting entirely of debenture holders should be appointed.

Lord HARRIS said the legal adviser was of opinion that it would not be competent to that meeting to appoint such a committee. The debenture holders themselves could do so subsequently, and he was sure the committee of shareholders would give them every assistance.

Mr. SURGEY said the committee of shareholders certainly would do so.

A DEBENTURE HOLDER begged to ask the directors pointedly and emphatically whether they could state positively and distinctly that there was no other over-issue of debentures except the 128,000*l*. on the city line. It was almost impossible to imagine that without the knowledge of the Board or their officers such an amount of debentures as 128,000*l*. could be issued on the city line in excess of the legally authorized amount, that being only 330,000*l*. Why, any charity-school boy of six months' standing, if he had a seat on the Board, ought to be able to detect an over-issue amounting to more than one-third of the entire amount which the Board were lawfully entitled to issue. It appeared to him that the effect of the operation was to make the contractors first mortgagees of the line.

The CHAIRMAN said the Board were perfectly satisfied that there was no further over-issue beyond that with which Lord Harris had acquainted the meeting.

Mr. BAXTER had investigated the matter, and its simple effect was that debentures to the amount 128,000*l*. lay in the hands of the parties to whom they had been pledged. There was no mortgage on the line. The holders of these 128,000*l*. worth of debentures would have the rights of other debenture holders. They were legal debenture holders. The disastrous consequence was that the 128,000*l*. worth which were last issued – that was the over issue – were illegal. The company were bound to pay back the money given for them, with all the interest; but the parties who possessed them did not possess the rights of debenture holders. (Cries of "Scandalous.")

A Debenture holder asked whether the directors were not personally liable to those persons to whom the illegal debentures had been sold.

Mr. Price said that Mr. Horace Lloyd, in replying to questions put to him by Lord Overstone,[26] as one of a Lords' committee, said there could be no doubt that in the case of an issue of debentures *ultra vires* the directors were personally liable. (Loud cheers and loud cries for Sir M. Peto.)

Sir M. Peto[27] said that when the city line was about to be made, debentures to the amount of 330,000*l*. were pledged for the purposes of the company, and at the request of the directors. For the money so raised his firm made themselves personally responsible by giving their promisory notes, in addition to the security of the debentures. When it appeared to the Board desirable to place the debentures permanently among the public that was done, and when the money was received for them the original debentures were redeemed to the amount of over 200,000*l*. But money to the amount of 128,000*l*. was received by his firm for debentures at the same time as engagements of the company, for which the firm also were liable, had come to maturity. This was in the period of the financial difficulty, and the company being unable to meet these engagements his firm was forced to apply the 128,000*l*. to that purpose, not being able to meet them by any other means. The proprietors would see from the large sum due by the company to the contractors at the time to which he referred that they were justified in believing they would be able to replace the money, the loan on the original debentures not coming to maturity for some time after. He admitted that the proceeding was an irregular one; but could assure the meeting that every shilling of the 128,000*l*. had been religiously applied to meeting obligations of the company. Not a shilling of indebtedness had resulted to the company from the irregular transaction; not a shilling's worth of damage had been done to the company; not a shilling of the money had gone into the pockets of his firm. The whole amount was applied for the purposes of the company. Debentures to the amount of the 128,000*l*. were now held for an original loan to the company, but, as that amount had been spent in discharging other obligations of the company, they were in no worse position for having to pay the money in the particular shape in which it was at present a charge. His firm regretted exceedingly the irregularity of the transaction, but the failure of the company to discharge enormous liabilities for which his firm were responsible placed them in a peculiar difficulty, and left them no other alternative but to collapse themselves and allow the company to collapse with them if they did not take the course of applying the 128,000*l*. to the discharge of the obligations which they had paid with it. He repeated that not a shilling of the money had been applied to their own purposes. (Hear, hear.) He felt it right to add that no director or officer of the company was cognizant of the transaction. If blame was to be incurred he was prepared to take it. (Cheers.) Certainly he should not allow it to fall on any honourable man who was not cognizant of the transaction. (Renewed cheers.)

A debenture-holder declared that he did not understand a word of the explanation of the hon. baronet, and he defied any one to do so.

In reply to a question from a debenture-holder,

Mr. BAXTER said that when he became engaged for the company, which was not very long ago, he was told there was no over issue. When the debentures were issued they were issued *en masse* in pledge for borrowed money. When money came in from the public for the debentures the contractors had funds given to them to cancel the old debentures, but to the amount of 128,000*l.* the old debentures were not cancelled.

There were loud calls for Mr. Baxter to name the person who had told him there was no over issue, and he replied that it was the general manager.

Mr. FORBES,[28] in obedience to loud demands from the debenture-holders, came forward and said he had made the statement to Mr. Baxter when that gentleman was beginning to investigate the affairs of the company. At that time he had no reason to believe there had been an over issue, and when the matter came to his knowledge subsequently he was perfectly astounded. He would observe, however, that the issue of debentures did not take place in his department, and he had nothing whatever to do with it.

Mr. W. E. Johnson,[29] secretary of the company, was then called on to explain. He said the contractors had acted for the company in the double capacity of financiers and contractors. ("Oh, oh!") An enormous amount of business had been transacted by them for the company. In issuing the debentures to which reference had been made the whole amount of the money had passed through their hands. As soon as the money came in from the public it was given to them to redeem the debentures on pledge. In the case of the 128,000*l.* it was directed to the general purposes of the company, instead of being directed to the special purpose of redeeming debentures to that amount. [A Voice. – "It was a fraud."] There was no knowledge of the application of the money in that way by any one on the part of the company. On the part of the directors, not one of them knew of the failure to redeem those debentures till within the last two or three days, and until the last 48 hours it appeared there was a probability of their being redeemed.

The amendment of Mr. Surgey was then carried amid much confusion, and the meeting hurriedly separated,

London Times, 29 September 1866

LONDON, CHATHAM, AND DOVER

A general meeting of the debenture holders of this company was held yesterday at the London Tavern to consider as to what steps should be taken for the protection of their interests; Mr. R. Hodgson[30] in the chair.

The CHAIRMAN, in opening the proceedings, said that the present meeting of debenture holders had been called in no hostile spirit to the company, or with any view to interfere with the province and duties of the committee of shareholders appointed at the company's meeting on the 31st ult. That committee owed its origin to a gentleman who took most active steps in obtaining proxies and otherwise from the shareholders to secure the nomination of such a committee, and those proxies would be available for any other purpose at the adjourned meeting in October. All then must have acquiesced even if the shareholders had consulted each one of the debenture holders in the advisability of the appointment of a committee of inquiry. Towards the end of the half-year the debenture holders found themselves in possession of the line. The shareholders had gone out of possession, and given up the management to them. The Legislature gave to those in possession the managing and working of a line. And when they took possession they found themselves without materials, without facts, without information. They were in great want of information and materials. Beyond the report they had nothing laid before them as to the state of the company's accounts, its traffic, its past transactions, its position, or its prospects. The committee appointed by the shareholders would, no doubt, enter into these matters on the shareholders' account, and in doing so would materially serve the bondholders by supplying information. He hoped that each debenture holder would be furnished with a copy of the report of the committee as soon as it was issued; and, if so, it would furnish each debenture holder with the figures and accounts of the past, and would give information which would enable him to form an opinion as to when he might be likely to be repaid his debenture and get his interest, or what alterations were to be made as regarded the line. Already a report had been circulated in the monetary world that a proposition would be made to the debenture holders to accept a 4*l*. per cent. debenture stock and 100*l*. ordinary stock of the company in lieu of the existing debenture debt. ("Oh!") It was this report, and other circumstances, which induced several large holders to meet together and call a general meeting for that day. With precedents before them as to the treatment debenture interests had met with by share interests, it was high time the holders averiging but 500*l*. holdings each should co-operate together and remain fast to their own interests. (Hear, hear.) The small nature of each debenture holding, the large nature of each share holding, the existence of a present organization among the present share capital, the entire absence of any similar system among the debenture holders showed the necessity for a close co-operation of the debenture holders. The shareholders of the company were the last persons who ought to call on debenture holders who had paid 20s. in the pound to abate 1s. of their just claims, for what had these shareholders done, and what had they got for their 12,500,000*l*. and 4,500,000*l*. borrowed on debentures? Why for this 17,000,000*l*. – a capital 4,000,000*l*. larger than that of the Great Northern, which had 437 miles miles open, and 4,000,000*l*. larger than the South-Western, which had its 529 miles – for this 17,000,000*l*. nominally raised the London, Chatham, and Dover Company had but 130 miles open to receive tolls from, and that, too, provided they first paid to the Victoria station 16,000*l*.; to the Crays line, 3,600*l*.; to the Sevenoaks line, 11,500*l*.; to the Sittingbourne and Sheerness, 7,000*l*. – in all 38,100*l*., or, at 20 years' purchase, 762,000*l*.; and to the lines they worked by statute, the excess over 50 per cent. – upon Metropolitans 26 per cent., City undertakings 8 per cent., of their gross takings; and to the lines they worked by agreement – Crystal Palace, 20 per cent.; Kent Coast, 36 per cent., which last year amounted to about 60,000*l.*, or equal together to a yearly rental of 98,100*l.* He referred then also to their former rivals, the South-Eastern, a company going through the same district. For their 15,767,739*l.* and the rents of the Greenwich and Reigate line, or 41,000*l.* a year, they had 291 miles open. Had the share capital been raised at 20s, in the pound, the 12,500,000*l.* would have given them as many miles and as good a system as those other lines; but they had barely received 12½ per cent. for their share capital. The general line was worked at 67·7 per cent., and Mr. Forbes and the directors told them no new company could get down its working expenses; while the South-Eastern and the South-Western were worked at 50, and the Great Northern and the Brighton at 52. The separate undertakings of the company showed still worse. On the Metropolitan, then, the working expenses were 76·1, while on the North London Railway, with nine miles of similar class, the expenses were but 51, and on the Underground Metropolitan but 39. It was owing to these results that the debenture interest was now. by the receiver, in possession of the line. They had removed the shareholders from the tolls, and practically had become "the shareholders." But they were "shareholders" without votes, without the power of being represented by proxies, without the power of a majority, with no collective existence. To remedy this – to give cohesion and combination among their debenture holders – he moved the following resolution: –

"That in order to protect the rights and interests of the debenture holders of the London, Chatham, and Dover Railway Company, a committee be formed consisting of Mr. Price, Mr. Peel, Mr. Harris, Mr. Broomhall, and Mr. R. Hodgson, with power to add to their numbers." (Hear.)

Mr. Wed seconded the proposition. He said that all the debenture holders had a power of action which they could exercise against the shareholders. It might be that many of the shareholders held some debenture stock, and then they would not agree with them. There must be a large number of shareholders who held debentures and who had also a debenture interest. It must be borne in mind that if they could not get the committee of debenture holders to act with them, they still maintained a power which the London, Chatham, and Dover Railway Company could not resist. He thought it would be better for them to get the debenture interest represented specially apart from any of the interests of the shareholders. He was not a debenture holder himself, but represented a large number of persons holding such stock. Their real position was, then, that they were the mortgagees of the whole undertaking and in possession of it. Their remedies were precisely the same as those of a person who had a piece of land mortgaged for a certain sum of money, the creditor of which failed to pay the money in arrear. They could not get their money, and he had little doubt but that the Court of Chancery would order the line to be sold. (Hear, hear.) The Vice-Chancellor appointed a receiver on the application of some of the shareholders of the company, and one individual debenture holder. He did not for one moment advocate the selling of the London, Chatham, and Dover Railway, but what he meant was that if they could not obtain their money themselves the Court of Chancery would sell the railway for a sufficient sum of money to pay the debenture holders, while the shareholders would have to find their money in the best manner they could.

A long discussion followed, in the course of which the resolution was adopted. The chairman moved the following resolution: – "That in order to put the present committee upon as efficient a footing as the shareholders' committee (who now had use of the company's funds and organization free of expense) and to enable the present committee to communicate their progress to the debenture holders, a subscription of 1s. per cent. be paid by each debenture holder to the account of the debenture holders' committee fund, London, Chatham, and Dover Railway Company, at Messrs. Deacon, Williams, and Labouchere,[31] bankers, Birchin-lane," which was carried unanimously.

London Times 28 November 1866

RAILWAY AND OTHER COMPANIES

London, Chatham, and Dover

A meeting of the common fund holders in this company was held yesterday at the London Tavern, for the purpose of considering the steps necessary to be taken to maintain their rights.

Mr. W. Hartridge, having been called to the chair, said that the meeting had been convened by himself and three other holders in the common fund of the undertaking. It had always been held that the common fund was a first charge upon the company after the payment of the working expenses. That had never been denied by persons in authority until very recently, when the common fund holders were assailed by certain debenture holders. In consequence of that he addressed the Board of Directors, inquiring whether it was their intention to take any steps in reference to the pending proceedings in the Court of Chancery; and in reply the Board stated that it was not necessary to take any steps in the matter. It was, therefore, thought by those who had convened the present meeting that the expense of conducting the proceedings should be borne by each holder according to the amount of stock held by him. He represented 20,000*l*. of the common fund stock, and those with whom he acted represented 115,000*l*. It was proposed that the committee to be appointed should take steps to place themselves in association with the directors in order that a general meeting should be held on the subject to ascertain what should be done. What they had in contemplation would involve a very heavy expense in Parliament and in the Court of Chancery to protect their property. They must endeavour to press upon the directors the necessity of maintaining all these sectional movements, and he contended that the persons at the head of those movements should take an active part in the reconstruction of the undertaking.

The present being a preliminary meeting for the objects he had named, he did not think that it would be advisable to enter generally upon the position of the London, Chatham, and Dover Company. Their sole object was to protect their position as shareholders in the "common fund" of the undertaking. He then moved that a committee of five common fund shareholders be appointed, with power to add to their number, for the purpose of maintaining the priorities of payment and other rights as specified by the London, Chatham, and Dover Railway (additional powers) Act, 1862, and to take such steps in Parliament, in the Court of Chancery, and elsewhere in relation thereto as they might deem necessary.

Mr. BURBURY, in seconding the motion, said that as a bill had been filed in the Court of Chancery against the Common Fund shareholders, it was felt incumbent upon them to take steps to protect their property.

The motion was unanimously adopted; and Mr. W. Hartridge, Mr. Burbury, Mr. W. Denison,[32] Q.C., Mr. Glover, and Mr. Tuke were appointed the committee, with power to add to their number.

A vote of thanks to the chairman concluded the proceedings.

Notes

1 George Milles (1794–1874), fourth Baron Sondes, was born George Watson and briefly served in the British Army, fighting at Waterloo in 1815. He succeeded to the peerage in 1836 and moved to East Kent, where he served in that district's yeomanry cavalry. Besides the LCDR, he held shares in the Faversham Public Rooms Company, which failed in 1871.

2 Sir John Maxwell Tylden (1787–1866) was an army officer who fought in North and South America, Madras, and Europe during the Napoleonic War and War of 1812. After retiring in 1825, he focused on local politics in Kent, serving as a JP and deputy lieutenant there.

3 Charles Jones Hilton (1810–1866) was a cement manufacturer in Faversham, East Kent, LCDR Director from 1853 until his death, and Chair of the Kent Coast Railway.

4 Sir Charles Henry John Rich (1812–1866) died in London in December 1866.

5 Sir Cusack Patrick Roney (1809–1868) was a civil servant turned railway secretary, first for the Cambridge & Lincoln in 1845 and later for the Grand Trunk Railway in Canada. He also sat on several railway boards and published *Rambles on Railways* shortly before his death.

6 George Frederick Holroyd (1823–1874) was educated at Cambridge and was the LCDR's first secretary through 1863. He later sat on its board and that of several other railway companies before becoming a barrister in 1873.

7 George Francis Robert Harris (1810–1872) became the third Baron Harris in 1845 then served as a colonial governor, first in Trinidad (1846–1854) and then Madras (1854–1859). Upon returning to England, he dabbled in politics but mainly remained at his family seat in Belmont, Kent.

8 Cornelius Surgey (1822–1915) was a stockbroker who specialized in raising money to purchase tea plantations in India. He was involved in a legal dispute in 1866 involving stock purchased in Overend, Gurney a day before it failed.

9 Robert Fletcher (1824–1883), Aberdeen chartered accountant, was auditor for five Scottish railways and Director of the West Hartlepool Railway, overseeing its absorption by the North Eastern Railway in 1865. He moved to London in 1867 to take charge of the LCDR reorganization, forming a partnership with Roderick Mackay.

10 Peter Northall Laurie (1809–1877) was a barrister and Chair of the Brighton and South Coast Railway (the "Brighton Company" he mentions in this speech), Deputy Chair of the Land Mortgage Bank of India, Governor of the Union Bank of London, and Director of five other south-coast railways.

11 Francis Vigers (1820–1895) was a London land agent and surveyor, in partnership with his brother Robert. Besides consulting on the LCDR's Metropolitan extension, he advised several dock companies and municipal public works.

12 George Gunnell Newman (1827–1885), one of the LCDR's solicitors, was part of the law firm Freshfields and Newman, which acted as parliamentary agents for several railways and also represented the Bank of England.

13 The London & South Western Railway originated as the London & Southampton in 1838, extending its services to Gosport and several London suburbs by 1860.

14 Samuel Hawksley Burbury (1831–1911) was a London barrister and mathematician.

15 Thomas Alers Hankey (1806–1872) was a partner in the private bank of Hankey and Co., which dated back to 1685 and was purchased by the Consolidated Bank of Manchester and London in 1865.

16 William Hartridge (1809–1885) was a London stockbroker.

17 Frederick Heritage was a London solicitor who also represented the Credit Foncier of England (one of the companies to which that the LCDR owed money).

18 William Edward Hilliard (1802–1871) was Director of the Equity and Law Life Assurance Society and the London Bridge Land Co. and joined the LCDR's board in 1867.

19 Grosvenor Hodgkinson (1818–1881) was a lawyer who, as a Liberal MP, represented Newark from 1859 to 1874.

20 George Cavendish Taylor (1827–1889) was also a director of the Hammersmith & City and East Gloucestershire Railways.

21 Henry De Grey Water (1807–1884) trained as a lawyer and owned a large estate in Shropshire.

22 Spencer Herapath (1822–1884) was a stockbroker who sat on the boards of several South American railways and was, up to 1865, Secretary for the Sheffield, Barnsley & Wakefield Railway. He was briefly involved with his father John's railway journal in the 1840s.

23 Rowland Rees (1840–1904) was a surveyor and engineer who consulted on several projects in Dover and spoke frequently at LCDR meetings. He emigrated to Adelaide in 1869, where he made his name as an architect and politician.

24 Valentine Knight (1792–1867) was a Surrey magistrate and landowner who frequently participated in railway shareholder meetings from the mid-1840s until his death.

25 Rose, Baxter, Norton and Co., besides being solicitors for the LCDR, represented the General Credit and Finance Co. and 12 other railways and had much experience arranging foreign bonds. Its partners included Philip Rose (1816–1883) and Dudley Baxter (1827–1875).

26 Horace Lloyd (1828–1874), a London barrister, appeared before a House of Lords committee in March 1866 and responded to questions from Lord Overstone (1796–1883) on behalf of the Chester United Gas Company to oppose a petition by the Flintshire Oil and Canal Company.

27 Samuel Morton Peto (1809–1889) trained as a public works contractor with his uncle, on whose death in 1830 he took over the business with his cousin. They filled numerous contracts for schools, churches, clubs, theatres, and docks before turning to railways in 1840, the same year they began work on rebuilding the Houses of Parliament. In 1846, he dissolved his partnership and devoted his full attention to railways; the fact that he no longer accepted government contracts allowed him to run for Parliament, and he successively represented Norwich, Finsbury, and Bristol as a Liberal between 1847 and 1868.

28 James Staats Forbes (1823–1904) was the LCDR General Manager from 1861 to 1873, then took over as chairman of the board from 1874 to 1899, when he became Manager of the Manchester and District line.

29 William Ezekiel Johnson was LCDR Secretary from 1863 to 1866, then left to be Secretary of the Kent Coast Railway in 1867.

30 Richard Hodgson (1804–1872) was a retired publisher, amateur astronomer, and self-appointed champion of LCDR debenture holders from 1866 until his death.

31 Deacon, Williams and Labouchere was a private London banking firm that lasted from 1771 until 1890, when it was purchased by the Manchester and Salford Bank.

32 Edmund Beckett Denison (1816–1905) was a lawyer and amateur horologist and astronomer; he was Queen's Council from 1854 through 1881 (he is listed on this committee as "Mr. E. B. Denison" in other publications, which list the other two members as John Glover and W. M. M. Tuke).

Editorial Headnote

City of Glasgow Bank (1878)

Founded in 1839, the City of Glasgow Bank (CGB) expanded quickly, with nearly 90 branches by the 1850s, and from early on, engaged in overseas investments to an extent that was rare among Scottish banks. Its exposure in the United States rendered it vulnerable in the financial crisis of 1857, when it briefly suspended business. Its extensive investment in New Zealand and Australian real estate resulted in major losses when the stock market again crashed in 1866. Finally, a flurry of unsuccessful American, Indian, and antipodal investments led to its downfall in 1878.[1] Like all joint-stock banks that formed before 1857, the CGB pledged unlimited shareholder liability to its depositors. Only a few such banks converted to limited liability after this became legal, and as of 1878, around 80% of English bank deposits and 64% of Scottish deposits continued to be backed by this protection. What was a protection for depositors, however, was occasionally a serious risk for shareholders.[2]

On 1 October 1878, the CGB closed its doors, and two days later, handed over its books to the accounting firm of Kerr, Anderson, Muir and Main; the fact that other Scottish banks agreed to accept its notes prevented a run on what remained of its assets. Four days before shareholders gathered at Glasgow City Hall on 22 October, the accountants reported an enormous gap between the bank's assets (£7.2 million) and liabilities (£12.4 million). On the same day, the bank's directors, manager (Robert Stronach), and secretary (Charles Leresche) were arrested for "culpable, reckless, and fraudulent trading and mismanagement"; Stronach and four directors would spend between eight and 18 months behind bars. Besides falsifying the bank's balance sheet, these men had also propped up the firm's share price by buying up stock, which increased the liability of its 1819 shareholders (holding an average of 4.7 shares each) from £519 to £613 per share. The first call on these shares, of £500 per share, bankrupted 599 investors, and after a final call of £2250 in April 1879, only 14% of its shareholders remained solvent.[3]

The shareholders who spoke at the meeting included a maltster, calico printer, property manager, corn factor, papermill owner, retired draper, ship broker, iron tube maker, bank manager, two coal masters, two gentlemen, two Presbyterian ministers, and four lawyers. This was close to a cross section: 30% of CGB shareholders in 1878 were gentlemen, manufacturers, or merchants and 40% were executors and trustees. Only 16% were women, compared to a national average of 30% among bank shareholders, and only 10% were professional men or clerks. This conformed to the bank's reputation as a high-risk, high-reward institution.[4] Speeches at the meeting ranged from businesslike to passionate, with all in favor of delivering swift justice against the guilty directors. That united front soon crumbled, as court-appointed liquidators faced off against trustees and other shareholders who tried to minimize their liabilities. More than 400 lawsuits took decades to wrap up. One such case concerned the Aberdeen manufacturer William Shirres, who had seconded a Glasgow preacher's motion to wind up the bank in 1878. In 1897, two years after he had died, his heirs were still in court, facing accusations that they had concealed assets from the company that had taken over the CGB's portfolio. Additional American lawsuits accompanied the liquidators' arduous efforts to recover the bank's far-flung assets.[5]

In the banking sector, the immediate consequence of the CGB failure was to ruin the Caledonian Bank, which owned four shares of CGB stock; the resulting wave of bankruptcies among its own investors produced a run on its deposits. Other banks' share prices fell in the wake of these two failures, especially in Scotland, but rebounded within a year. Although the failures did lead some English bankers to call for restricting interest rates on deposits, the only major legislative change was the introduction of compulsory internal bank audits. A wave of banks also switched to limited liability in the CGB's wake, although they reassured depositors by providing reserve liability – effectively capping shareholder responsibility at a fixed multiple.[6]

Notes

1 R. E. Tyson, "Scottish Investment in American Railways: The Case of the City of Glasgow Bank, 1856–1881," in *Studies in Scottish Business History*, ed. P. L. Payne (London: Frank Cass, 1967), 386–413; J. Forbes Munro, *Maritime Enterprise and Empire: Sir William Mackinnon and His Business Network, 1823–1893* (Woodbridge: Boydell Press, 2003), 253–277.

2 Graeme G. Acheson and John D. Turner, "The Death Blow to Unlimited Liability in Victorian Britain: The City of Glasgow Failure," *Explorations in Economic History* 45 (2008), 237.

3 Acheson and Turner, "Death Blow," 238–239; S. G. Checkland, *Scottish Banking: A History, 1695–1973* (Glasgow: Collins, 1975), 471; *Report of the Trial . . . against the Directors and the Manager of the City of Glasgow Bank* (Edinburgh: Edinburgh Publishing Co., 1879), 3.

4 Acheson and Turner, "Death Blow," 240–244.

5 Kenneth C. G. Reid, "Embalmed in Rettie: The City of Glasgow Bank and the Liability of Trustees," in *Judge and Jurist: Essays in Memory of Lord Rodger of Earlsferry*, ed. Andrew Burrow et al. (Oxford: Oxford University Press, 2013), 495–507; *Cases decided in the Court of Session, Court of Judiciary, and House of Lords* (Edinburgh: T. and T. Clark, 1897), 418–429; Saul Engelbourg, "John Stewart Kennedy and the City of Glasgow Bank," *Business and Economic History* 15 (1986): 69–82; Tyson, "Scottish Investment in American Railways," 406–411.

6 Checkland, *Scottish Banking*, 471–472; Acheson and Turner, "Death Blow," 247–252; Timothy L. Alborn, *Conceiving Companies: Joint-Stock Politics in Victorian England* (London: Routledge, 1998), 131–137; James Taylor, *Creating Capitalism: Joint-Stock Enterprise in British Politics and Culture, 1800–1870* (Woodbridge: Boydell Press, 2006), 221. For an overview and analysis of the aftermath of the CGB failure see Michael Collins, "The Banking Crisis of 1878," *Economic History Review* 42 (1989): 504–527.

22

CITY OF GLASGOW BANK

Source: City of Glasgow Bank, *Aberdeen Journal*, 23 October 1878

CITY OF GLASGOW BANK

Meeting of Shareholders

Appointment of Liquidators

An extraordinary general meeting of the City of Glasgow Banking Company was held in the Glasgow City Hall yesterday afternoon for the purpose of passing certain resolutions as to winding up the concern, and the appointment of liquidators. There was not a large attendance, only about three hundred persons being present, of whom half-a-dozen were ladies.

Among the gentlemen who took seats on the platform were Messrs Robert Young, G. W. Clark, John Blackley; A. B. M'Grigor, LL.D.; C. D. Donald, Wylie Guild, Rev. F. L. Robertson, Provost Christie (Stirling), James Muir, Naismith, &c.

Mr Robert Young[1] said – I have been requested before commencing the business to explain to you that, in the present circumstances of the directors of the bank, it is necessary that we should call attention at this meeting to section 11 of the articles of association and copartnery of the City of Glasgow Bank. This section provides that at all ordinary general meetings and special general meetings the chair shall be taken by the governor, or in his absence by the deputy-governor, or in the absence of both by the chairman of the ordinary directors, or in his absence by such other director then present as shall be elected by a majority of partners, by themselves or their proxies, in proportion to the number of shares held by them, respectively; or in case no director is present, then by such partner holding £100 shares of the capital stock; and the chair shall be taken by him before any other business is transacted. Now, I have great pleasure in moving "That Mr Robert Craig[2] of Craigcork, Newhattle Paperworks, by Dalkeith, be appointed to take the chair at this meeting."

On the motion of Mr Craig, Mr R. S. Aikman[3] was appointed as clerk to the meeting.

The Clerk having read the several notices,

DOI: 10.4324/9781003177715-26

The Chairman moved – "That the balance-sheet as at 1st October, 1878, and report relative thereto by Messrs Kerr, Anderson, Muir, & Main,[4] C.A., Glasgow, and Messrs M'Grigor, Donald, & Co.,[5] solicitors, Glasgow, dated 18th October, 1878, now laid on table, and of which printed copies have been circulated among the partners previous to this meeting, be held as read." It was, he said, beyond his power to give an account of their present position, but he hoped that the assets might turn out much better than was expected. (Applause.)

Mr Young, in seconding the motion, said – I suppose there is but one opinion in regard to this. You have all got a copy of it, and it would only add to our sadness to read it again. It is perhaps sufficient to refer to it in the short, succinct manner in which the chairman has done. It has been requested, however, that I should say a word or two in regard to it, and, first, as to the time for calling this meeting. Considerable complaints and doubt and uncertainty seem to exist in regard to the time taken up in calling this meeting. I believe the investigators have used every possible moment they had. You will remember that, by a certain section of the articles of association, section 46, it is provided that when the balance-sheets show that all the reserve and one-fourth of the capital of the company are lost, the directors shall call a special general meeting. These gentlemen, Dr M'Grigor and Mr Anderson, found, two or three days after beginning their investigation, that we certainly had lost more than one-fourth of the capital. Instantaneously they desired to call a meeting, and after consulting counsel they called it, giving the 14 days' previous notice required in these articles of association. I am sure that their task must have been a very onerous and a very difficult one, and it is one I believe they have discharged to the best of their ability, and for which, sad though the report is, we owe them our sincere thanks, That report it is useless for me to go over, or make sadder. It reveals that as far back as 1873 there commenced, unless it was commenced earlier, a system of fraud. (Hear, hear.) It was then certainly, and there is evidence in the hands of the Crown authorities and otherwise to show that, at all events, it culminated in 1873. In June, 1873, we find from this report that we were actually deceived to the extent of £973,000, and fictitious entries meant to deceive were actually inserted, and at that time a dividend of 10 per cent. was declared. Instantly thereupon we issued new stock, which was taken up by many shareholders. Since then, as the report says, this system has been regularly adhered to, the sum of £973,300 having been actually deducted from each of these accounts, so that up to this time that system seems to have been carried out. This report reveals further the systematic falsification of the amount of gold, and also an addition to our apparent assets by creating imaginary sums, and the practical result of this was that the shareholders were led to believe that the bank lent £1,126,764, and that they had in their hand securities absolutely more than was the fact by £976,000. Then there is the astounding fact brought out that the bad debts are estimated by the reporters to be £7,335,357, the debts of the principal debtors amounting in the aggregate to five millions and three-quarters, showing their estimated securities at a million and a half, so that there is actually shown at that time a deficit of four millions and a quarter, which in the balance-sheets has been carried forward as wholly good debts. This report reveals also an enormous amount of unwarranted and imprudent advances and purchases of properties in New Zealand, Australia, Rangoon, and India, and also railways in Canada and America. It reveals also that bad debts, known to be bad, had been rehabilitated and shown to us as good. Now, what has struck me in these different reports issued is that we seemed to have had a good business, and the report of the investigators, so far as the branches are concerned, seems to confirm that. I think it is hardly possible that any of the other Scotch banks have had such a lucrative class of business as we seemed to have possessed in these branches. The amounts of deposits are a handsome sum, and one which, under good management, might have produced a very large and profitable business for us. As recently as June, 1878, you know, we had a report which showed that £400,000 of ours was intact, and the directors then declared a dividend of 12 per cent.; and in face of this and in the short space of three months, we find that our capital is gone, and we are confronted with an apparent deficiency of £5,190,000. It is hardly possible to speak quietly with reference to such tremendous defalcations, that £5,200,000, we, the shareholders, are now called upon to make good. What the ultimate result may be I cannot tell. The deficiency is overwhelming, and the prospect appalling. The result of the liquidation will be to myself and to many – very many – of the shareholders ruin and misery; to all privation and suffering. Our money, perhaps our all, we must lose. But this is not the time, nor is this the place, to speak of the directors and officials, who are now criminally charged by the Crown authorities with fraud. But this, I think, we are at liberty to say, that our misfortunes have been greater than our faults. We have reposed our confidence in men who have proved unworthy of our confidence. We have believed in reports and balance-sheets which have turned out to be fictitious. We have lost much, but we have not lost all. We hope that, while losing our money, we have not yet lost our personal honour. We know we have the full sympathy of the public. We dare not ask to be relieved from any part of our debts. We must show that we are prepared to face our difficulties. (Applause.) We must have the most perfect honour, and a determination that we shall, if possible, pay everyone in full. (Applause.) I therefore now beg to second this motion. (Applause.)

Mr Alexander M'Cutcheon,[6] Newton-Stewart – Before this motion is put to the meeting I would wish to ask the reporters two or three questions. The first question is, whether they can tell us from an examination of the books and accounts of the bank any of the officials of the head office not at present included in any criminal charge. At present all responsible for or cognisant of (1) those enormous advances made at the head office, (2) the making up of the yearly statements, (3) the returns made to Government of gold in hand, and (4) whether the reporters had any special reason for limiting the scope of their investigations to the period since 1873. In my humble opinion enough has been shown, and there are ample materials at the office and in this report to raise the suspicion in the minds of the shareholders that the investigation must go further back than the year 1873, and that men who are not yet included in the criminal charge must be put in the dock as well as those who are now in the hands of the authorities. (Applause.) I humbly think, having studied this report with the utmost care, being a shareholder, unfortunately now ruined, and having been an agent of this bank for twenty-three years, and my all now gone, it is absolutely necessary, in the interests of public justice and morality, that a thorough, full, searching investigation of this bank's affairs should be made, and must go back, if necessary, even to the year 1857. Therefore I ask these questions with all respect – (applause) – 1. Whether, of any of the officials at the head-office that are not included in the criminal charge of the Government – if any are responsible for, or cognisant of (1) these enormous advances at the head-office; (2) as to the making up of the early returns or statements; (3) the returns made to the Government of gold on hand; and (4), whether the reporters had any special reason for limiting the scope of their inquiries to the period since 1873.

Dr M'Grigor – In answer to the first question, I may say that I think, in a matter affecting criminal liability, it would be most unbecoming in us to indicate suspicions. The time may come when the authorities may interrogate us and precognose us. We shall be ready then to give the very fullest information in our power – (hear, hear) – but it would be most unbecoming – and I think the gentleman who asked the question will on consideration see it to be unbecoming – for me, on a suspicion, to mention at a public meeting those who may be probably liable to a criminal prosecution. As regards the last question, whether we think that the transactions we have pointed out extend beyond the year 1873, there seems to be some misapprehension in the public mind. Our duty was simply to make a balance-sheet for 1878. Properly speaking, we had nothing to do, and certainly we had no time to do more than attend to the affairs of 1878. The reference to 1873 in the sheet occurs simply in this way. In making up our balance for 1878 we came upon a balance of £973,000 in the slump, which, in the inquiry as to what that sum represented, we traced back page after page of some three or four weekly-abstract ledgers of the bank till we came to June, 1873, and there we found an explanation. That is the reason we took 1873 as the date of the special charge in our report. We had no time, and it would involve an amount of time and an amount of labour thatis not easily expressed to those who are unacquainted with such matters to go into the position of the bank in any past year. That time, I have no doubt, will be given, and that labour will be given too. (Applause.) It will be given, no doubt, in liquidation, and I am much mistaken if it will not be given by the public authorities also. But you will see that the difficulty would increase with every year you went back. You have to apply to the assets and the liabilities and the debts in 1873, or 1872, or 1871 the same continuous wearying process we had to apply to the year 1873, and the difficulty would be increased proportionately.

The resolution was then put to the meeting and passed unanimously.

The Rev. F. L. Robertson[7] said – I certainly did not expect that I should have been called to the front and asked to move the first and most important resolution, but I have not shrunk, and shall not shrink either from this or any other duty which may be imposed upon me which can in the very smallest degree benefit the shareholders of this unfortunate bank. The motion I have to propose is one which, unfortunately, does not need a single word on my part to show the absolute necessity of putting it. It is to the effect "That it has been proved to the satisfaction of this meeting that the City of Glasgow Bank cannot, by reason of its liabilities, continue its business, and that it is advisable to wind up the same." There has been some talk of resuscitating the bank, but to attempt to resuscitate a bank which has not merely lost its capital, but has incurred liabilities beyond its capital, and beyond to the extent of five millions, is merely absurd. Well, now, we are met to-day under very adverse circumstances, called upon to face a crushing calamity, and it is for us in such a time of adversity to acquit ourselves like brave, courageous, and honourable men – (cheers) – so as to retain the confidence of our creditors, which they have been good enough to repose in us, and the respect of our fellow-countrymen. There is no good in sitting idly wringing our hands in despair. It is best boldly to look facts, ungainly and disastrous though they are, in the face, to grapple with them, and to determine what course in the circumstances it is best for the shareholders to follow. I shall not speak about the resolution. I have other and more important matters to speak of. With respect to the directors, I scarcely dare allow myself to speak, but I shall endeavour to restrain those feelings of indignation – just indignation – which stir in the hearts of every one of us, and speak calmly as a minister of religion ought to speak – (applause) – for those gentlemen have been faithless to the high office to which they were advanced. To the shareholders they have been disloyal to truth and to the first principles of morality. And, with respect to some of them at least, what deepens the discredit which attaches to their conduct is that they drove through the streets of the city arrayed in the garb of religiousness, and making long prayers when they were devouring the widow's portion, and erecting churches while wrecking homes. The day of reckoning has already dawned, and the majesty of the law is about to vindicate its claims. For my part, sir, I wish them no sorrow or heavier punishment than to be haunted night and day by the ghostly vision of the hundreds of happy lives they have wrecked and blighted, till all feeling of remorse lie kindled within their hearts, and they be driven to their Maker's presence to seek His forgiveness, and leave His presence determined to spend the utmost energies of their remaining years in some poor measure to undo the evil thereof. But with regard to the shareholders' duties and responsibilities – heavy duties and burdensome responsibilities to meet – our creditors here and in England have been good enough to repose trust in our honour. Let us show them that they have not misplaced their confidence. (Applause.) In a time of adversity it is for men to band together as brethren, and fight shoulder to shoulder. It is for every man to do his utmost in a crisis. For any shareholder to endeavour to elude or shrink from an endeavour, at any cost or sacrifice, to pay his just debts, and to meet the demands of his creditors, were simply to imitate the vicious example of our directors, which we are here to-day to reprobate and to condemn. It is a stern ordeal, but, passing through the ordeal, let us emerge from it with characters unstained and reputations unblemished. (Hear, hear, and applause.) The report is a sorrowful document, but it seems to me that there are not wanting here and there a few gleams of light. You will notice that the assets of the bank, though miscellaneous, are many of them of great value. Further, those of you who have carefully studied the report will also notice that there is a note appended, stating that the investigators have not credited the account with any of the dividends which may be drawn from the bankrupt assets. These dividends may be very large. I entertain a strong and sanguine expectation, not without very good grounds, that one estate alone – of one of our largest debtors – will yield a sum rather exceeding half-a-million, which will certainly improve our condition considerably. Though we were in ignorance of it before, we are possessed of an American railway in which those gentlemen or their predecessors in office were good enough to sink a million sterling, and they called that banking. There are policies to a large amount – £60,000. They are of value for that amount, and wicked men sometimes die – (laughter) – but I do not know whose lives are insured, but I will say that any man who deliberately obtains, by fair means or by false facilities, credits at a bank, to the ruin of the shareholders which he knows he cannot meet, he is most undoubtedly and unquestionably a wicked man. There are shares in a New Zealand Company, and I speak of this matter for this reason. These shares are of value if they are held. Everybody knows that if you force property into the market you sell it at a great sacrifice. If you force a million shares into the market you will not get a fair price if they are worth more. There is no use, as I said, wringing your hands in despair. Try and amend your fortunes if you can, and what I have to address to the shareholders and through the shareholders to the public, whose feelings of keen sympathy we have is: – To organise a company which shall be called "The City of Glasgow Bank Assets Company" with a capital of two millions, one million to consist of ordinary capital, and the other million to consist of debentures. Let that company purchase from these liquidators whatever assets they are prepared to throw into the market, and purchase these assets at their full market value, or rather above their full market value. Well, now, if this scheme were carried through, you would then be able to hand over to the liquidators the sum of two millions of money. And how would your account then stand? There are at the present moment available assets – bills current, money, and so forth – amounting to four and a-half millions. Well, now, if you would, by successfully floating this company, raise two millions, and if the shareholders would band together, and by a supreme effort in response even to a heavy call, raise £3,600,000, and add to that the sum that Messrs Smith, Fleming, & Co.'s[8] asset shows – viz., £600,000, and add to that again what I think the directors' assets will show – viz., £250,000, you would then have ten millions of money, and with that ten millions you would have to meet claims to the amount of £12,400,000. Then the liquidation will be brought into very moderate dimensions, indeed. The question is, Do you not think it is possible, nay certain, to float a scheme of this sort? The sympathy of the public is with you. Then the shareholders who are not ruined will come forward and share in it, because in itself it will be a good and profitable investment which would pay largely the shareholders. The trustees who are liable would come forward and take shares in it. The shareholders who held shares in the bank within the last year are interested, and would come forward and take shares in it; and if you get gentlemen, as I am sure you would, of high position and undoubted honour in the city of Glasgow to come forward as directors, and to act as trustees, I am perfectly certain that by the assistance of the shareholders in every country village and town, and with the sympathy which we have in England, you would within a month or two months float the whole capital, and be in a position to come forward and deal with the liquidators, and by so doing you would benefit all classes of the shareholders, the poorest and the richest, you would lessen the pressure of calls, and I feel assured that the scheme would meet with great success. I am perfectly aware that from my position as a minister of religion there are many who may be disposed to speak harshly of the position I have chosen to occupy. They may tell me I am mingling perhaps too much with secular affairs, but my reply is, that I do not care one rush for their opinion. (Applause.) My opinion is that well-doing is religiousness; and if our directors had taken to heart that opinion, and believed that religion consisted less in solemn phrases than it does in right doing and serving God in their day and generation, we would not to-day have been placed in the calamitous circumstances in which we stand. For my part, sir, I am not disheartened. I shall not abate one jot of courage. I have my brains to work with, and so long as the Almighty is good enough to prolong my days, and to continue to me health of body and soundness of mind, I shall work to the best of my capacity, and respond to every call made upon me, to the last I shall stand in the face of the world a solvent man. (Cheers.) If my services are of any value in promoting the scheme I shall, saving my sacred office, divest myself of every duty and trust, and devote my time and attention in pushing and forwarding the success of such a scheme, believing that in doing my humble little to lesson the appalling pressure of this calamity on many sore hearts I am serving my Maker and my Master as truly and well as when I am preaching the Truth. It will be a severe and stern ordeal through which we are called to pass, but in God's name and by God's blessing let us bravely and faithfully one to another struggle through it, and emerge with honour untouched and reputation unshaken. (Cheers.)

Mr Wm. Shirres,[9] manufacturer, Aberdeen, seconded the motion.

Mr Young said that if any persons in the area held proxies but were not entitled to vote, not being partners, he would be obliged if they would remove to the gallery, so as to prevent confusion.

A Gentleman in the gallery – Would you allow me to ask a question – Whether one who has a proxy for a shareholder to the extent of £300, and who is himself a shareholder to the extent of £100, is allowed to vote?

Mr Young – I am instructed to advise you that you would have a vote for the £300 proxy, but not for the £100 of your own.

The Gentleman in the gallery – Quite so. Then I may vote?

The motion was then put to the meeting and passed unanimously.

Treasurer John Wilson, Edinburgh, rose to move the next resolution. He said – It having become necessary that we should wind up the affairs of the City of

Glasgow Bank the question now arises – By what process shall we best gather the fragments of the wreck together, and best extricate ourselves from the fearful load of debt which the faithlessness of our so-called directors has laid upon us. The committee of shareholders, who have been to a certain extent taking charge of the initiation of to-day's proceedings, have carefully considered the various methods open for us to adopt under the Companies Act of 1862. That Act describes three modes of procedure. First of all, judicial liquidation. That means application to the Court of Session to appoint liquidators, and carry on the whole work under Court supervision. There is a second method, somewhat akin to that, but only under partial Court supervision, combined with a kind of voluntary liquidation, but after considering all the methods, the third method prescribed by the Act of 1862 has appeared to your committee the one which we ought to recommend to the shareholders to adopt, and that is voluntary liquidation. Mr Chairman, I believe, in England especially, there is some misunderstanding as to what voluntary liquidation means. It is there supposed to be a kind of quiet winding up about which the public are to know nothing; that it is a species of concealment of – haggling over the affair so as to make the bank's matters as little public as possible. Now that is a gross mistake. Voluntary liquidation has every species of publicity attached to it. It has the further advantage of being cheaper than the other two methods. It is also less trammelled by Court forms and legal forms. The liquidators have ample, full powers to do everything necessary for the best interests of the shareholders. So that, gentlemen, I think we are right to-day in recommending to you to adopt a voluntary liquidation in winding-up the affairs of this bank. A month ago I never dreamed of being here to-day to propose the winding-up of this institution. I can assure you that in Edinburgh and along the east coast this bank had always, up to a month ago, and, in fact, up to the day it closed its doors, done a first-rate business. Indeed, no other bank had more zealous or painstaking agents everywhere, or a more enthusiastic body of shareholders than the City of Glasgow Bank. So that everywhere, except in the bank parlour in Glasgow, this bank appeared to prosper. It was therefore with the utmost surprise that many of us in Edinburgh on Wednesday morning, on opening our newspapers learned, to our horror, that the bank had closed its doors. After the able speech delivered to you, I need not say any more than this, that I hope we will come out of this visitation with at least the honour of doing the utmost in our power to meet our debts manfully. I know that in doing that hundreds of our unfortunate shareholders must succumb. Many are now in the depths of bankruptcy, who a fortnight or three weeks ago were in affluence. But we will show to the world that although in difficulties, we are striving like honest business-men to do the best we can, I am therefore of opinion that we should now wind up the business by voluntary liquidation.

Mr Hugh Baird seconded the motion, which was agreed to.

Mr Wm. Thomson, Edinburgh, said he had to propose a resolution which necessarily followed upon that which the meeting had just adopted. The motion was: – "That the meeting proceed to appoint liquidators for the purpose of winding up the affairs and distributing the property of the company, and that each of them so appointed may act separately, and exercise every power which, by the Companies' Act of 1862, and Acts amending or extending the same, is conferred on liquidators, and that the remuneration to be paid to them, and each of them, as such liquidators, shall be left to be fixed by the following partners, who are hereby appointed a committee for the purpose, with full powers, namely: – Messrs John Wilson (treasurer), Edinburgh; J. H. Annandale, Lasswade; Robert Young, Glasgow; Archibald Russell, Glasgow; John Cunningham, Ardrossan; G. W. Clark, Glasgow; John Wilson, Glasgow." (Applause.) There was a difficulty connected with the amount of remuneration to be given to the liquidators. It should not be fixed before it was known what was the amount of the work to be done. Having confidence in their committee, they should leave the amount to be fixed by them.

Mr M'Cutcheon – Before this motion is put to the meeting, I beg to suggest that there should be an addition made to it to the effect that this meeting specially instruct these liquidators, in the exercise of their statutory powers, to direct their special attention to the state of the bank's books prior to the year 1877, and I have a special object in asking that that should be put as a rider to this motion, in order that these liquidators may bring to the front the men dealing in the bank's affairs before that time. Mr Young seems unnecessarily interfering with the Act. The simpler we can keep the resolution the better. The powers of the liquidators are enormous, and they may at once proceed without any pressure being put upon them, instantly to find out the culpability of parties, and whatever committee you appoint will take care not to give them rest either day or night. (Applause.) Mr M'Cutcheon urged that this rider should be put to the meeting.

Mr Young – I suppose it is far better to talk quite frankly in the matter. I have put it to Mr M'Gregor and Mr Naismith, and they tell me that such a thing is incompetent, and, being incompetent, we had better not put a vote on the matter to the meeting. Every shareholder will bring his influence to bear on the liquidators and also on the public prosecutor, and no liquidator will feel at rest himself unless he looks to the carrying out of the views my friend has indicated. (Applause.)

Mr J. Beckett, Glasgow, seconded the motion, which was then put to the meeting and declared carried unanimously.

Treasurer Wilson, Edinburgh, said he had been asked to nominate one of the liquidators, and he was sure they would all concur with him when he named Mr Anderson, accountant, Glasgow. That gentleman had had a fortnight's examination of the bank books, and he had shown great business ability, acuteness, and thorough work as an accountant, and fully capable of acting as one of their liquidators.

Councillor Downie, Glasgow, seconded the motion, which was likewise unanimously adopted.

Mr John Wilson, Glasgow, proposed another gentleman for this office. His name, he was sure, would recommend him to everyone present, as he stood at the top of his profession, and also carried immense influence in wide circles – Mr George Auldjo Jamieson,[10] of Edinburgh. (Applause.)

Mr G. W. Clark, Glasgow, seconded the motion.

The Chairman put the motion to the meeting, and afterwards declared it carried unanimously.

Mr Robert Young said – The committee you were kind enough to appoint sent a deputation to London, and, as a deputation, we had the full confidence of the committee. They were brought into contact with a large number of our creditors, representing about a million and a-half of money, or £1,600,000 of bills held by them in London, and when they asked what liquidators should be appointed, we condescended upon three names of gentlemen who we thought would receive support. Two of the gentlemen have been unanimously elected by you, and the third was a gentleman in whom we had equal confidence, but he has seen it his duty to decline to be put in nomination. Probably our London friends will not be pleased at this. I wish to explain that we were determined, if possible, to carry out the suggested arrangement, but were prevented doing so from the declinature of the gentlemen I have alluded to. Therefore, the fault is not ours, but that gentleman's. Then there have been applications made from London since we came home, by telegrams and letters, on behalf of no fewer than three other gentlemen, who have been recommended by sections of the London bondholders. So far as I can make out, I have reason to believe that they represent only very small holders, for by far the larger number of holders – representing probably 1¼ millions of money – could not have given us a warmer reception. They were perfectly satisfied after all the explanations were given to them that voluntary liquidation was a thing which they probably had not understood at first, but which in the end would be not only better for us, the shareholders, but certainly better for them also as creditors of the bank, securing a management at much less expense, and probably with more expedition, and certainly with a much better result in the end than under a judicial winding-up. Therefore, although some of these gentlemen, probably billbrokers, are dissatisfied, I think now, since the amount of deficiency is so overwhelming – at that time we thought it would be something like three millions, but now that it is over five, it seems to have startled them not a little, and probably has alarmed them somewhat, I hope there is no cause for alarm. Since we have not been able to carry this gentleman we had in view, we have carefully looked at other gentlemen, and have listened to the suggestions of gentlemen who ought to know, and there has been a unanimous feeling in favour of a gentlemen as a third liquidator – Mr John Cameron,[11] of the Clydesdale Bank of Glasgow. I have known Mr Cameron for between 22 and 23 years. I knew him when he was in the Western Bank,[12] and he was present during the whole of the liquidation of that bank, and was brought into contact with the four liquidators there, and had a very large amount of their confidence. I speak the unanimous sentiment of the shareholders when I say that a better liquidator – one with more sense – more clear-headed and firm – it would be impossible to have. He has the thorough confidence of our principal creditors, and I have pleasure in proposing that he should be associated with Mr Haldane in the painful work.

Mr Hugh Baird seconded, and the motion was unanimously adopted.

A gentleman in the gallery made some remarks which were inaudible at the platform, but no counter-motion was proposed.

The Chairman wished it to go forth to the public that they had had the confidence of the other banks throughout. They had that power over the shareholders as their creditors, but they had expressed their readiness to acquiesce in the appointment of any liquidators who might be selected, if they were merely acquainted with their names. It would, therefore, be furthering their own interests, as well as those of other banks, to appoint these gentlemen, who, he knew, were thoroughly trusted by the other banks. (Applause.)

Mr G. W. Clark proposed a cordial vote of thanks to Mr Robert Young, whom he was in a position to be able to praise highly. Indeed, thanks cannot at all pay anything like the gratitude which we owe Mr Young for the great services he has rendered to the shareholders. At a moment's notice, Mr Young has been called upon to do the work assigned. He has grudged no amount of time, or labour, or anxiety. I know that when he undertook to go to London as one of the committee he undertook a very arduous task; and, with the blandness of manner which you know characterises him, he succeeded very quickly in carrying with him all the gentlemen with whom he came in contact in London, as creditors, or owners of our bills. And therefore he has succeeded in bringing about the harmony we have here to-day, and, instead of being forced into a judicial liquidation, we have now adopted a voluntary liquidation, which will save our pockets, and the interests of all concerned. I therefore ask you to give Mr Young a vote of thanks for his services.

A Shareholder seconded Mr Clark's proposal, which was enthusiastically agreed to.

Mr Walter Paton, Glasgow, in proposing a vote of thanks to the chairman, remarked that he was in the unfortunate position of being the largest shareholder in the bank, and it said a great deal for him that he, being in such a painful position, should come through from the east coast and also attended other meetings. He had taken a great interest in the unfortunate business all through, and it was their duty to accord to him a hearty vote of thanks for the manner in which he had discharged his duties.

Mr Blackley,[13] in seconding, said – It is only those in a position similar to what I have been placed who can have the slightest idea of the comfort it has been to us to have Mr Craig associated with us. We have had every encouragement from him, and we have him very much to thank, along with Mr Young, for the cordiality and for the excellent arrangements that have been carried out, and have resulted in so harmonious a meeting.

The Chairman begged to thank the meeting most cordially for the honour they had done him.

Mr Robert Young also returned thanks for the appreciation of his services.

A Shareholder in the gallery said – I cannot, as no one in the body of the hall has said anything in condemnation of those directors, leave this meeting without joining most warmly in the eloquent expressions that have been put forth by Mr

Robertson and my excellent old friend Mr Robert Young. We have heard a great deal about vivisection lately. Was there ever such a cruel case of vivisection as that which has been perpetrated or performed by the directors of the City Bank. (Laughter.) It mattered not to them whether they performed their experiments on helpless childhood or helpless old age, provided they had a chance of securing their unhallowed gains. (Applause.) I believe that that board will be pointed to for many a long day as a lurid beacon to guard others from similar shipwrecks. What punishment they may get or deserve I know not – (a Voice – "The hangman") – but I just fear they will not get the punishment so beautifully described by Mr Robertson – the gnawing of their consciences – just simply because they have no conscience. (Laughter and applause.)

Mr Young – The Chairman has declared this meeting now finished, but an informal meeting will now be held, Mr Craig being still chairman.

Rev. Mr Mitchell, of Dunfermline – There is one motion which has not yet been put, and I, for one, should be very sorry that this meeting should separate without that motion being put and carried. There is a body of gentlemen to whom we are all deeply indebted – the joint-committee from the east and from the city of Glasgow, who have done so much at so great trouble and expense to mature the proceedings for the meeting, and I propose that a very cordial vote of thanks be given to the committee for the services they have rendered. (Applause.)

Mr Young said – There is no use in detaining you much longer; our object is now in regard to the committee. The committee which has acted has consisted of twenty gentlemen, ten of them being gentlemen from Glasgow and the West; eight were nominated in Edinburgh, including one from Dunfermline, one from Stirling, and the other two from Aberdeen. Mr Milne, of Aberdeen, has found it advisable to give in his declinature. He is a large shareholder, and it has excited him, as it has excited us all, and he has been unable to come here to-day. Mr Walker, his friend, has come along with Mr Shirress, and what we suggest would be is that the committee be reappointed in this way: – Appoint the following committee, of whom five shall form a quorum, to advise the liquidators in regard to any questions arising under the liquidation, with power to add to their number from the shareholders or the creditors, and to appoint a subcommittee: – Messrs Robert Craig of Craigesk, Dalkeith; Archibald F. Somerville, 11 Viewfield Terrace, Edinburgh; J. H. Annandale, Esk Tower, Lasswade; Treasurer John Wilson, 31 Drummond Place, Edinburgh; John Boyd, Edinburgh; William Thomson, Edinburgh and Leith; Provost Matheson, Dunfermline; Provost Christie, Stirling; George Walker, Aberdeen: – Shirres, Aberdeen; Hugh Baird, 134 St Vincent Street; G. W. Clarke, 29 Waterloo Street; James Becket, 16 St Vincent Place; John Wilson, 20 Buchan Street, Gorbals; John Cunningham, 127 St Vincent Street; Walter Paton, 73 Virginia Street; Archibald Russel, 68 Great Clyde Street; Rev. F. L. Robertson, 204 Bath Street; Robert Young, 107 Buchanan Street; and John Blackley, 88 Bath Street. In returning thanks for myself, and proposing this list, I think you should have included a vote of thanks to Mr Blackley; he is here, and without him I could not have got on. He has advised me and done everything we wanted.

Mr Blackley, in returning thanks, said that they had been as one voice at every meeting, and, so far as he was aware, they had one end in view, and they all united in carrying out the object they had in view.

The Chairman announced that the business was over, and the meeting thereupon broke up.

Notes

1 Robert Young was a Glasgow ship broker whose partnership dated to 1843.

2 Robert Craig (1807–1892) owned a paper mill in Newbattle, south of Edinburgh, which had been in his family since 1832 and closed in 1890. As of 1872, the mill employed 300 workers and produced 1700 tons of colored printed paper annually. His obituary referred to him as "the heaviest loser by the City of Glasgow Bank failure." He was a generous donor to his local Presbyterian parish.

3 Robert S. Aikman was a Glasgow legal secretary and later secretary to the City of Glasgow Bank Relief Fund.

4 William Anderson (1817–1889) started his career as an accountant in 1831, working for the Irvine Town Council, then, after moving to Glasgow, formed the partnership Kerr, Anderson and Co. with the father-son team of James and Henry Kerr in 1842; James Muir and John Thomas Main joined the partnership in 1874. The firm specialized in railway work, and Anderson was a founding member of the Glasgow Stock Exchange Association in 1844.

5 Alexander Bennett M'Grigor (1827–1891), "one of the best-known lawyers in the West of Scotland," earned his L. L. D. from the University of Glasgow and was a partner in M'Grigor, Douglas and Co., which his grandfather had founded in the late-eighteenth century. He acted as an agent in Glasgow for the Law Life Assurance Society and legal advisor for the City Union Railway.

6 Alexander M'Cutcheon was a lawyer who served, with A. Jamieson, as the City of Glasgow's branch manager in Newton-Stewart (near Dumfries). In that locality, he also served as justice of the peace, law agent, auditor of the sheriff's court, chief magistrate, school board member, sub-distributor of the stamp and tax office, Vice-Chairman of the local gas company, and agent for the Queen and North British & Mercantile insurance companies.

7 Frederick Lockhart Robertson (1827–1892) was the son of an Edinburgh doctor who was ordained in the Church of Scotland in 1851 and preached at Ayr, Bonhill (near Dumbarton), and Greenock until 1873, when he took over the impoverished St. Andrew's parish in Glasgow's East End. He used this position, which he held until his death, to promote education and housing reforms.

8 Smith, Fleming and Co. was a London firm trading with India, comprised of John Smith, John Fleming, Robert McIlwraith, and William Nicol. The firm owed the CGB close to £2 million when it failed.

9 William Shirres (1812–1895) was a "sagacious and successful draper" in Aberdeen, then, after retiring in the early 1870s, "employed his spare time in private accounting and ship management." His biographer reported that "he was a heavy sufferer through the City of Glasgow bank failure . . . but overcame this blow."

10 George Auldjo Jamieson (1828–1900) was a leading Scottish accountant. An Aberdeen native, he moved to Edinburgh in 1848, becoming partner in the firm of Lindsay, Jamieson and Haldane in 1858. He sat on the board of the Royal Bank of Scotland and the North British and Mercantile Insurance Company.

11 John Cameron was secretary of the Clydesdale Bank, which had formed in Glasgow in 1838.

12 The Western Bank of Scotland was founded in Glasgow in 1832 and suspended payment in 1857.

13 John Blackley was a factor (or property manager) on estates in Milton and Castlemilk in the north and south of Glasgow, respectively; he lived Springburn, bordering Milton.

Editorial Headnote

Great Britain Mutual Life Assurance Society (1881–82)

In October 1880, a Chancery judge approved two policyholders' lawsuits and ordered the Great Britain Mutual Life Assurance Society – which had formed in 1844 and sank into insolvency after purchasing the dregs of three failing companies – to be wound up.[1] Two weeks later, both the company's directors and a committee of policyholders appealed the ruling. Neither group denied that the company was insolvent; instead, they argued that the plaintiffs had invoked the wrong law. In 1870, Parliament had carved out an alternative to winding up insolvent life insurance companies, encouraging them, instead, to reduce their benefits and sell their business to another company if they could persuade a judge that this was viable. The directors and policyholders succeeded in convincing the Master of Rolls to wait for the results of policyholder meetings the following January, which would determine the will of the society's members.[2] Ahead of these meetings (one in Glasgow and one in London), the policyholder committee commissioned two actuaries and an accountant to provide an independent report on the company's finances. Although the company's directors disputed a few details, especially the valuation of its assets, they largely supported the policyholders' verdict, and almost two years later, the National of Ireland agreed to purchase the Great Britain's business, paying between 44% and 90% on claims depending on age and duration of policy.[3]

This result apparently marked a win for policyholders in a mutual insurance company (and the recently enacted legislation), even in the worst-case scenario of insolvency. The reality of policyholder input, in this instance, as well as the equitable division of remaining funds, was more complicated. Although the committee did represent five different British cities from the company's large national branch network, only a tiny fraction of the society's 10,000 members attended the meetings in Glasgow and London. Nearly a quarter of them lived in Germany, where the Great Britain Mutual had been doing business since the 1840s – and these people received no representation on the committee and only passing reference in any of the numerous public discussions of the company's fate. A second issue concerned younger and healthier members. Prior to the policyholder meeting, one naysayer warned that those "who are healthy enough to be reassured would rather take the surrender value" than agree to reduced benefits.[4] By the time the National of Ireland absorbed the Great Britain Mutual in December 1882, the latter company's premium income had declined to £21,039 from £61,108 three years earlier – suggesting that exactly this outcome had transpired.[5] In insurance terms, the Great Britain Mutual's reconstruction scheme was a classic case of moral hazard: from these thousands of policyholders' perspectives, a few pounds in lost premiums were nothing compared to the chance to switch to a well-established company that paid in full – and their decision to depart diminished the benefits that their older peers could claim by more than 25%.

Notes

1 "Law Reports," *Post Magazine* 41 (1880), 426. The three companies were the National Union (purchased in 1868), Imperial Guardian (1869) and Bristol and London Life (1875).
2 "Law Reports," 460. On the 1870 Act see Timothy Alborn, *Regulated Lives: Life Insurance and British Society, 1800–1914* (Toronto: University of Toronto Press, 2009), 63–74.
3 *Statements of Account and of Life Assurance and Annuity Business, and Abstracts of Actuarial Reports deposited with the Board of Trade under . . . the Life Assurance Companies Act, 1870* (London: Hansard, 1884), 204.
4 Law Reports," *Post Magazine* 43 (1882), 213; "Correspondence," *Post Magazine* 41 (1880), 476.
5 Editorial, *Post Magazine* 44 (1883), 377.

23

GREAT BRITAIN MUTUAL LIFE ASSURANCE SOCIETY

Sources: Great Britain Mutual Life Assurance Society (1881), *Post Magazine and Insurance Monitor*, 8 and 15 January 1881; 7 October 1882

Post Magazine and Insurance Monitor, 8 January 1881

GREAT BRITAIN MUTUAL LIFE

The following are circulars issued to the policyholders of the *Great Britain Mutual* Life Assurance Society. A meeting of those interested was held on Friday to consider the scheme of reconstruction, and we postpone our comments until we have had an opportunity of laying a report of that meeting before our readers: –

"101, Cheapside, London, E.C.,
"27th Nov., 1880.

"Sir, – The policy-holders will shortly receive the formal notice calling a meeting, and in the meantime the committee have thought it desirable to acquaint them with the facts that have rendered this step necessary.

"The policy-holders will probably have seen from the newspapers that two petitions had been presented to wind up the society. These petitions were heard before the Court last week, and a winding-up order was made, followed by the appointment of an Official Liquidator. The committee found that the directors were as much surprised as the members of the committee at the order having been made, and on Tuesday the committee instructed their solicitors to use every exertion to get the order set aside. Accordingly, on Wednesday, an application was made to the Court of Appeal, which the committee are glad to be able to report was favourably entertained by the Court, who unanimously discharged the winding-up order, and directed a stay of further proceedings until the policy-holders shall have had an opportunity of expressing their opinion as to the best course to be taken with the society.

"From the preliminary investigation which the committee have made, they feel that it will be inexpedient for the society to continue on its present basis; but at the same time they are convinced that nothing could be more disastrous in the interests of the policy-holders than a winding-up by the ordinary process of the Court, with an official liquidator. On this point the committee cannot do better than refer the policy-holders to the words of the Master of the Rolls and Lord Justices

DOI: 10.4324/9781003177715-27

Sir W. M. James[1] and Sir R. Lush[2] in giving judgment upon their application, an extract from which is annexed.

"The committee have accordingly directed their attention to devising some alternative to a winding-up, and they think that an endeavour should be made to take advantage of the provisions of sec. 22 of the Life Assurance Act of 1870, which provides that in lieu of a winding-up order, a general arrangement may be effected for a reduction of the policies. With this view, the committee have determined to institute a thorough investigation into the position of the society, by an independent actuary of the highest standing, and as soon as this investigation is completed (in regard to which every dispatch will be used), the committee will then be in a position to lay before the policy-holders a detailed scheme, and to make a further report to them as to the best course to be adopted in the common interest, either under the above Act or otherwise.

"The committee are of opinion that in the present condition of the society it would be difficult to commence any negotiations for the transfer of the society's business to another company; but when the policies have been reduced to the amount which the actual assets of the society properly warrant, the committee anticipate that arrangements can be made by which the business may be transferred on satisfactory terms, and all interests saved the disastrous consequences which a winding-up, pure and simple would entail.

"We are, Sir, your obedient servonts,

"W. Burrows (London), S. I. Da Costa (London), W. Blake Burke (Wolverhampton), R. Smith Casson (Birmingham), Jno. Elliott (Newcastle), A. Neilson (Glasgow), *Committee of Policyholders.*"[3]

"No. 101, Cheapside, London, E.C.,
"31st Dec., 1880.

"The committee of policy-holders are now able to present a further report in regard to the position of the society.

"As mentioned in their circular of the 27th November last, the Court of Appeal discharged the winding-up order which had been made and directed that a meeting of all the policy-holders should be called, in order that their views might be ascertained as to the course to be taken with reference to the society.

"The committee immediately put themselves in communication with the directors, and with Mr. A. H. Bailey[4] (the President of the Institute of Actuaries) and Mr. M. N. Adler[5] (the Actuary of the *Alliance* Assurance Company), and requested the latter gentlemen to advise in regard to the society's liabilities.

"Mr. Bailey and Mr. Adler subsequently informed the committee that it would be impossible to present an exact report of the society's position without making a detailed valuation of each policy, which would require at least three months, but that by a less extended investigation, founded upon the returns presented to the Board of Trade under the Life Assurance Companies' Acts, involving comparatively small expense and much less time, they would be able to inform the committee approximately as to the amount at which the liabilities would stand, if estimated with a view to the reduction of the policies under the Act of 1870, or a winding-up under the Act of 1872.[6]

"The committee decided that under all the circumstances it would be undesirable at the present moment to attempt to enter upon the detailed valuation, which would entail considerable expense, and could not be made available for any meeting at an early date.

"Provision having thus been made for ascertaining the amount of the society's liabilities, Mr. J. Young[7] (of the firm of Turquand, Young & Co.), who has had large and special experience in matters of this kind, was requested to report upon the assets of the society.

"With regard to the liabilities, the committee at the outset were informed by Mr. Bailey and Mr. Adler that the mode in which their valuation would be made differed so much from that hitherto adopted by Mr. Makeham,[8] the society's actuary (and by Mr. Woolhouse[9] in his report of Nov.), that the liabilities would inevitably be much greater than the amount at which they stood in the society's last valuation balance sheet (31st December, 1879).

"The valuations of Mr. Makeham and Mr. Woolhouse were based upon (amongst others) three data. 1st. The *Table of Mortality* used was that known as the "*Carlisle Table.*" 2nd. It was assumed that the society could obtain on an average 4½ *per cent. interest* on its funds; and, thirdly, the valuation was made by valuing the *gross premiums* with a deduction of about 10 per cent. for expenses and profits.

"On the other hand, Mr. Bailey and Mr. Adler have adopted: – 1st. The *Seventeen Offices Experience Table*;[10] 2nd. A rate of interest of 4 *per cent.*; and, 3rd, *A net (or "pure") premium*, valuation, *i.e.*, with a deduction of about 28 per cent. from the premiums for expenses and profits. The Life Assurance Companies Act of 1872 prescribes this method for valuing the policies of life assurance companies, and as this must be adopted if the society is wound up by the Court under that Act, it seems probable that the Court will require it to be applied in the alternative of a reduction under the Act of 1870. It appeared, therefore, to Mr. Bailey and Mr. Adler that they had no alternative but to make their valuation in accordance with the Act.

"Whilst the difference between the two methods is not great as regards the *table*, that arising from an assumption of 4 *per cent. interest* instead of 4½ per cent. is considerable, while the adoption of a *net premium* valuation is much more so.

"The committee are now informed by Mr. Bailey and Mr. Adler that they estimate the liabilities of the society to amount to about £340,000, and Mr. Young reports that assuming that to be the amount of the liabilities, and that the assets will be applied in meeting them *pari passu*, he estimates the value of the latter to be about £88,000.

"The difference between the amount of the liabilities and assets as thus shown, does not, however, necessarily mean, as it would in an ordinary trading business, that the society is insolvent to that extent and able to pay only about 5s. in the £, but is in part the result of the difference in the mode of valuation.

"As to the liabilities, the difference between the £340,000 and the £160,000 shown by the balance sheet of 1871, is accounted for in the main by the additional half per cent. interest, and the net premium valuation.

"As to the assets, the difference between the £160,235 shown by the balance sheet of 1879, and Mr. Young's estimate of £88,000 is chiefly accounted for as follows: –

(1) "In the item of "Mortgages on Property," Mr. Young excludes from the assets a sum of about £11,500, on the ground that under a winding-up or a reduction of policies the item would be so dealt with by the Court, although in the case of a solvent insurance company it might be treated as a good asset. A corresponding allowance has been made by the actuaries in their estimate of the liabilities.

(2) "In dealing with the items of loans upon policies, and the 21 per cent. abatement on certain premiums, Mr. Young has taken into account the fact that the assets of the society are insufficient to meet the liabilities, and estimating the amounts which will probably be received from the borrowers and the dividend which the assets will yield on the value of the policies, he arrives at a probable loss of £17,500.

(3) "From the item of £9,126 for "Outstanding Premiums," £7,000 has been written off, representing premiums on policies which have been allowed to lapse, but which were not previously written off, as the policy-holders had the right to revive their policies within twelve months free of fine, on producing satisfactory evidence of health.

(4) "various other sums, amounting in all to about £23,000 (including special foreign deposits to cover risks which are also deducted from the liabilities), should, in Mr. Young's opinion, be written off the assets as representing reductions in value. Part of this reduction is consequent on the insolvency of the company thus reducing the value of the assets and securities, which would otherwise have been considered good for the amount at which they stood in the society's books.

(5) "The actual cash payments out of the assets, since the beginning of the year, for claims, surrenders, and expenses (less receipts), is about £12,000.

"If, therefore, under a winding-up, or a reduction of policies, the liabilities must be treated as amounting in round figures to about £340,000, and the assets, as representing £88,000, it now becomes necessary to consider which is the better course – to wind up the society in the ordinary way, or to effect a reduction of the policies, – and it is upon these alternatives that an expression of the policy-holders' opinion is desired at the meeting which has been called for the 7th January next.

"To enable the policy-holders to form a judgment on the question, the committee append the following table, showing the reduced amount at which a policy for £100 would stand on the above basis, assuming the life at the time it was first

TABLE NO. 1—(REDUCED POLICY).

Age at date of Policy.	*Amount of premium.*			*Amount of reduced policy for £100 (on the assumption that the assets are ¼ of the liabilities) if the policy has been in force.*											
				7 years.			*10 years.*			*20 years.*			*30 years.*		
	£	s.	d.	£	s.	d.	£	s.	d.	£	s.	d.	£	s.	d.
20	1	18	10	99	19	10	95	3	0	77	13	0	61	9	0
30	2	8	4	96	5	0	89	13	0	69	14	0	53	13	0
40	3	5	0	92	2	0	84	12	0	62	14	0	47	17	0
50	4	14	10	88	9	0	80	4	0	58	1	0	43	11	0
60	7	9	0	86	3	0	76	13	0	53	19	0	–	–	–

TABLE NO. 2.—(DIVIDEND IN WINDING-UP)

Age at date of Policy.	*Amount of dividend to which a holder of a policy for £100 will (on the same assumption as in Table No. 1) be entitled on a winding-up, if his policy has been in force.*										
	7 years.			*10 years.*			*20 years.*			*30 years.*	
	£	s.	d.	£	s.	d.	£	s.	d.	£	s.	d.
20	1	4	0	1	16	0	4	6	0	7	14	0
30	1	16	0	2	14	0	6	6	0	10	11	0
40	2	15	0	4	1	0	8	16	0	13	12	0
50	3	18	0	5	13	0	11	8	0	16	7	0
60	5	5	0	7	8	0	13	16	0	–	–	–

insured was either 20, 30, 40, 50, or 60 years of age, and had been in force, 7, 10, 20, or 30 years, the same premium as heretofore still being paid.

"The amounts shown in the 3rd – 6th columns are made up of two sets of figures, the 1st depending upon the annual *premiums* payable in future under the policy; and the 2nd being the revisionary value of the *share in the assets* to which the policy-holder is entitled. The reduction is therefore, of course, less on the young lives than upon the old, the future premiums payable in the former case exceeding that in the latter, although the old lives receive a larger share of the assets than the young lives.

"To show the result to the policy-holders under a winding-up order the committee append a second table giving the amount to which the holder of a policy for £100 would be entitled in the event of a winding-up, without carrying into effect any reduction of the policies.

"It will be seen, therefore, that the result to a holder of a policy for £100, who was 40 years of age at the date of his policy, would be as follows: – If he is now 47 he would get a reduced policy for £92 2s. 0d., or on a winding-up £2 15s. in cash on the ultimate realization of the assets; or if he is now 50, 60, or 70 he would have a reduced policy for £84 12s., £62 14s., or £47 17s.; or in cash, £4 1s., £8 16s., or £13 12s. So far as the reduced amount of the policies is concerned, as shown in Table 1 (the net premiums only have been taken into account), the committee believe that in the working out of the society's business additional profits would be shown which would increase the amount of the policies. In regard to the share of the assets, however, the committee feel that, under a winding-up, Table 2 represents as sanguine a view as can fairly be taken, and that the assets are more likely in that case to realise less than more, irrespective of the heavy expenses which a winding-up by the court entails.

The committee are sure that the policy-holders will agree that it is most undesirable to wind-up in the ordinary way until every means have been exhausted for avoiding it. Whilst the committee do not overlook the fact that there are difficulties to be dealt with in carrying out the reduction, including legal questions as to the priority of various classes of claims, yet seeing the desire already shown by the court to assist the policy-holders in saving the society from being wrecked, the committee recommend to the policy-holders that they should assent to a reduction on the basis above shown, with the view of transferring the society's business to another company, the latter either undertaking the reduced liabilities or managing the business for a commission. Nothing can of course be done without the sanction of the court, which, before its sanction is given, will require to have before it a proper detailed valuation, such as that referred to at the commencement of this report. Assuming, however, that the policyholders generally agree to the reduction, the committee have strong hopes that it will not be found impossible to give effect to it, but unless a considerable majority of the policyholders do assent there will be no alternative but a winding up, with the disastrous result to each policyholder shown in the 2nd table.

"If you should be unable to attend the meeting a form of proxy is sent herewith which, as will be seen, leaves it open to a policyholder to express which of the alternatives he supports, and the committee earnestly beg that every policyholder will make a point either of attending the meeting or of previously returning this form to the committee duly signed. If, after all, it should be found impossible to effect a reduction, the committee will endeavour to arrange for the liquidation being conducted on a strictly economical basis; and in this view, and having regard to the remarks made by the Master of the Rolls (which the policyholders have already had before them), they would suggest to the court that it should not be left wholly in professional hands.

"W. Blake Burke, W. Burrows, R. Smith Casson,
S. I. Da Costa, John Elliott, J. Jelf, A. Neilson."
"London, 3rd Jan., 1881.

"The directors of this society have perused the circular of the 31st ulto. issued by the committee of policyholders, and they consider that an explanation of the circumstances in which the society is now placed is due from them, and that an expression of their opinion as to the course that should be adopted in the interests of the policyholders should be given.

"Shortly after the issue of the circular notice of the 2nd November last, stating the result of Mr. Woolhouse's valuation, a petition for winding up the society was filed by the representative of a deceased policyholder whose claim is disputed (on *bonâ-fide* grounds); and this was immediately followed by another petition and other proceedings on the part of holders of subsisting policies. A *prima facie* case was established *(ex parte)* against the society in consequence of the weakness of its financial position, as disclosed by the actuary's report which was read at the last annual general meeting. The directors thereupon, with the advice of their actuary, and the concurrence of Mr. Woolhouse, at once determined to propose to the members a reconstruction of the society upon the basis of a reduction in the sums assured.

"The directors, however, gave distinct instructions to the solicitors of the society, Messrs. Prideaux and Son,[11] to oppose the petitions, and they were greatly surprised to receive a notification from them at a special board (called at their request) only the day previous to the winding up order being made, that counsel had refused to carry them out, on the ground that in their opinion the present financial position of the society did not justify the opposition, and that the scheme of reconstruction suggested by the board ought to be considered in chambers.

"The directors desire it to be distinctly understood that they were in no way parties to the granting of the winding up order or the appointment of a provisional liquidator.

"The directors think there can be no difference of opinion that the determination come to by them, with reference to reconstruction, presented the only possible means of saving the funds from being gradually dissipated in meeting petitions for winding up the society.

"The principal difference between the valuation made by the society's actuary of the outstanding liabilities and that presented by the committee, arises from the large reserves which are made in the latter, both in the "loading" struck off in valuing the future premiums, and in the difference in the rate of interest assumed (viz., 4 per cent.), and that adopted by the actuary (4½ per cent.) and actually obtainable on the invested funds according to the society's past experience. The following statement, showing the result of the substitution (in the valuation of the society's actuary) of a reserve equal to that adopted in the valuation put forward by the committee, will put this matter clearly: –

Liability for sums assured under existing policies		£880,286 0 0
Value of corresponding future gross premiums	£806,631 0 0	
Less reserve as explained in committee's report	226,887 0 0	
		579,744 0 0
Net liability as above		£300,542 0 0
Net liability as in actuary's report		157,767 0 0
Difference		142,775 0 0

"This difference represents the excess of the above reserve of £226,887 over that shown by the society's actuary, viz., £84,112. It will be observed that the difference in the rate of interest is not taken into account in this statement.

"The directors do not dispute the propriety of the data adopted by Messrs. Bailey and Adler as the bases of a scheme of reconstruction; but they desire the members to bear in mind that the sources of profit, from the reserves above adverted to, will have the effect of making good, to a considerable extent, the reductions made in the nominal amounts of the policies.

"Mr. Young, in his valuation, has taken the assets of the society as on the 19th November, 1880 – the date of the winding up order; and he proceeds upon the assumption that the society may have to be wound up, and its assets realised at once. Hence the large portion of the property which is dependent upon the value of the several policies granted by the society in connection with such investments, has been greatly reduced in value.

"Upon the basis above explained, Mr. Young has made the deductions referred to in the committee's report, amounting to £71,000. Without expressing any opinion as to the necessity of so great a reduction, the directors think it important to remind the policyholders that the additional amount which will arise from this source (if an immediate realisation be avoided), will go to increase considerably the large reserves created by the severe method which it has been necessary to adopt in valuing the liabilities.

"With regard to the item of £23,000, referred to in Mr. Young's estimate, the directors think it well to explain that £7,000 represents the German and Italian securities, which are deposited with the Governments of those countries, and, although not realisable, are earning interest. The rest is mainly composed of agents' balances (received in 1880) – reductions in the values of house property and furniture, and in the amounts of half premiums on loan and cash balances.

"The directors have only further to urge upon the policyholders the great importance of their supporting the scheme of reconstruction by so large a majority as to render it certain of obtaining the sanction of the court.

"By order of the Board,
"A. W. DIXON, *Sec., pro tem.*"[12]

Post Magazine and Insurance Monitor, 15 January 1881

GREAT BRITAIN MUTUAL LIFE

The Scottish policyholders of the *Great Britain Mutual* Life Assurance Company held a crowded meeting in the Religious Institution Rooms[13] of Glasgow, on Monday, the 3rd inst. It was stated by Mr. J. M'Queen Barr,[14] Glasgow, that, in anticipation of the general meeting to be held in London on Friday, his firm had called them together. After some noisy demonstrations, Mr. M. C. Smart,[15] who appeared not as a policyholder, but as agent for the provisional liquidator, was permitted to take his place in the meeting. On the motion of Mr. PRITCHARD, the chair was taken by

Mr. BARR, who explained the present state of the company. Many of them were aware that the representatives of a policyholder who had been pressing the company for £5,000, which they refused to pay on the ground that when he insured he made false representations as to the state of his health, applied for the appointment of an official liquidator to wind up the concern. The company did not take any decided step in the defensive during the month at their disposal, and a provisional liquidator was nominated. One of the judges, in disposing of the petition, recommended that some arrangement should be made for reducing the amount of the contracts in order to save the expense of liquidation. With that expression of opinion he quite agreed, because the past history of liquidation showed it to have been simply ruinous in such cases. The policyholders, in the event of allowing the company to go into liquidation, would not receive 5s. in the £; indeed, he questioned if they would receive anything at all. What, as policyholders, they had to do was to devise the best means of saving themselves, and, in his opinion, that was to get the policies taken over at a re-valuation by some good, solvent office. To what was called the resuscitation of the present company he had the strongest objection, because they knew what the directors had done, and they could have no confidence in others in the same company. In answer to a question, the chairman said he understood a Scotch office had been approached on the subject of taking over the policies at a re-valuation, and had indicated that it would entertain the proposal.

Dr. NEILSON,[16] Glasgow, as a member of the committee which had proposed re-valuation, disclaimed any connection with the directors. The committee desired to avoid the expense of liquidation, and were taking steps for that purpose. On their instructions, two of the most eminent actuaries in the country had made an investigation into the affairs of the company, and, striking off from £60,000 to £70,000 of the assets, they left £88,000 applicable to the wants of the company. The value of a policy for £100 taken out at twenty years of age, and on which an annual premium of £1 18s. 10d. had been paid for several years, would, on a winding-up table, be £1 4s.; paid for ten years, £1 16s.; for twenty years, £4 6s.; and for thirty years, £7 14s. It was proposed to avoid the expense of liquidation, to put the policies in a saleable condition, and then to transfer them to some solvent company.

A POLICYHOLDER said the whole concern was what it had been said to be outside, "a big swindle;" while another expressed the belief that the management would turn out to be the most disgraceful thing of the present century.

Dr. NEILSON, in reply to questions put by policyholders, stated that the liabilities amounted to £350,000, and that the assets had been reduced from £160,000 to £88,000. Of that deduction, £11,500 had been on mortgages on property within the United Kingdom – (cries of shameful") – £17,000 odd upon personal loans, and so on. The sums invested in Government securities had been reduced by 23 per cent. It was explained, in answer to a question, that the premiums would in the meantime have to be paid to the provisional liquidator, or else the policies would lapse; but that in the event of liquidation being proceeded with the amounts would be returned in full.

Provost CUMMING,[17] Renfrew, remarked that they had heard enough to show them that they should avoid winding-up the company in a legal way. (Applause, and cries of "No.") It would be best, he thought, to reserve what remained of the money, and get some good Scotch office to accept the policies at a reduction. The insurance offices were, although not legally, morally in duty bound to assist them, as such a collapse weakened the credit of the whole of them.

Mr. J. CUMMING, Glasgow, said they should find out who were responsible for this calamity, and take steps against them.

Mr. PRITCHARD said they had not been told why or how the company came to grief. The funds of the society were to be applied for specific objects and not to be used in the purchase of Turkish bonds, on which £9,000 were lost, or to lend to another company £7,000 on personal security. The society had, continued Mr. Pritchard, in 1873 a surplus of over £20,000, in 1876 over £30,000, and in 1879 nearly £600. What had become of that reserve fund? What he wanted was a proper investigation of the management and the accounts. He moved – "That this meeting is of opinion that the present state of insolvency of the *Great Britain Mutual* Life Assurance Society, established in 1844, has been brought about by the mismanagement of the directors, and by the misapplication of the funds of the society; that a fit and proper person or persons be appointed on behalf of the policyholders alone, to inquire and report to them what has been the cause of such a calamity; and that until that report is put into their hands the policyholders decline to pledge themselves to any proposition that may be submitted to them by the directors of the society or otherwise."

The motion was seconded by Mr. CUMMING, and it was explained that it would keep the liquidation in abeyance.

Dr. NEILSON put it as an amendment that such a motion should not be received. It did not matter, he said, whether the funds had been misspent or not, as what they had to do was to preserve their property. This was seconded by Mr. WRIGHT, Glasgow, ex-agent of the company, whose appearance was the signal for a storm of disapprobation.

A POLICYHOLDER mentioned that three days before the concern went into liquidation the Glasgow manager, Mr. Cowan, told him that the concern was perfectly sound.

Dr. NEILSON withdrew his amendment, and substituted the following motion: – "That this meeting is of opinion that policyholders should at all hazards avoid liquidation, and adopt a system for the reduction of the value of the policies with the view of getting another company to take over the business.

On the conclusion of a good deal of talk, both motions were adopted. The meeting then separated, after a sitting of over two hours.

Meeting in London

A general meeting of the policyholders of the above company was held on Friday, the 7th inst., at the City Terminus Hotel, Cannon Street, E.C. There was a crowded attendance, and the proceedings lasted three hours.

Mr. PUNNETT (a director since the 22nd of June) presided, in the absence of the Earl of Kilmorey (the chairman of the society) on matters connected with his Irish estates. The report of the committee stated that they were informed by Mr. A. H. Bailey (president of the Institute of Actuaries), and Mr. M. N. Adler (actuary of the *Alliance* Assurance Company) that they estimated the liabilities of the society at about £340,000, and Mr. John Young (of the firm of Turquand, Youngs, and Co.), reported that, assuming that to be the amount of the liabilities, and that the assets would be applied in meeting them *pari passu,* he estimated the value of the latter at about £88,000. The difference between the amount of the liabilities and assets as thus shown was in part the result of the difference in the modes of valuation. As to the liabilities, the difference between the £340,000 and £160,000 shown by the balance-sheet of 1879 was accounted for in the main by the additional ½ per cent. interest and the net premium valuation. On the basis of the liabilities being £340,000 and the assets £88,000, the result to a holder of a policy for £100, who was 40 years of age at the date of his policy, would be as follows: – If he were now 47 he would get a reduced policy for £92 2s., or on a winding-up £2 15s. in cash on the ultimate realization of the assets; or if he were now 50, 60, or 70 he would have a reduced policy for £84 12s., £62 14s., or £47 17s., or in cash £4 1s., £8 16s., or £13 12s. The chairman said they must arrive at a definite decision upon some course. On the application of the committee, who were appointed through the action which the Board took directly the winding-up order was made, the Court discharged this order, but did not remove the gentleman who had been appointed provisional liquidator from being receiver, leaving this matter to stand over till the meeting had been held. No doubt, before the winding-up order was made, the directors had decided on a reconstruction of the society on the basis of a reduction of the policies. They did not dispute the propriety of the *data* adopted by Messrs. Bailey and Adler, nor did they wish to express any opinion on the necessity of so great a reduction as Mr. Young had made in the assets. During the past year, however, the assets which appeared in the balance-sheet of December, 1879, had been reduced, notwithstanding large reductions in expenses, &c., by excess of claims and outgoings over income to the extent of £12,000, and on the assumption that the society might have to be wound up and its assets realised at once Mr. Young had made deductions amounting to £71,000; but if the society continued, by itself or another society, several of the items dealt with by Mr. Young would be good assets. The committee showed what the result of liquidation would be.

Captain W. BLAKE BURKE, of the committee, after repudiating a statement that they were in harmony with the Board, moved a resolution to the effect that, in order to avoid a winding-up, the contracts of the society be so reduced as to enable the business either to be transferred to another company or continued under new management.

The motion having been seconded, a long and animated discussion ensued, in the course of which the feeling was generally expressed that anything would be preferable to liquidation. The past management of the society was severely criticized, and the necessity for a thorough investigation into its affairs was strenuously urged. The resolution was ultimately carried, and a committee of 12 was afterwards appointed to oppose any application for winding-up, to apply for an order reducing the society's contracts on such terms as they should think just, and requesting them to take all such steps as they might think desirable to obtain an investigation into the affairs of the society.

Post Magazine and Insurance Monitor, 7 October 1882

GREAT BRITAIN LIFE

The meeting of policyholders took place, as announced, on the 29th ult. at Cannon Street Hotel, and was largely attended. The Chairman was T. F. PUNNETT, Esq.,[18] a gentleman, it is only fair to state, who has undertaken the responsibility of a director since the company was in difficulties, and with the laudable desire to protect the interests of the members. It will be seen that considerable soreness exists in reference to the older management, and, if we are not mistaken, preference would have been given to a simple transfer of the business. Our report is taken from the *Citizen* newspaper. Full particulars of the arrangement were given in our issue of May 13th last.

The CHAIRMAN entered at some length into the history of the society during the past few months. The first resolution passed at the last meeting, he said, affirmed the desirability of avoiding the winding-up of the society, while the policyholders expressed the hope that the society might be reconstructed, or the business transferred. The affairs of the society were laid before Vice-Chancellor Hall,[19] and Mr. John Young, accountant, prepared a scheme for the reduction of policies in accordance with a resolution passed. Policyholders attended the court and approved of the scheme of re-construction, and the directors were prepared to-day with a definite proposal. They had two courses – they might either carry on their own business, or associate themselves with another society and work it united with another, and guaranteed by another society. This second company would work the society's business, and pay its claims out of the funds, but in case of these being insufficient then the company would step in and meet the claim. They had found a company willing to undertake this in the *National* Assurance Company of Ireland, who would give the necessary guarantees. Particulars were given in an abstract of the agreement; and on the transaction being concluded, the *Great Britain* Mutual Life Assurance Society would cease to grant policies. One-fifth of the profits would belong to the company, and four-fifths to their own society. But in the first year the company would take only one-tenth. The company had guaranteed the whole of the liabilities of the *Great Britain* Assurance Society. There would be three trustees, one of whom would be appointed by their society. He then proposed that the agreement between the *Great Britain* Assurance Society on the one part, and the *National* Assurance Company of Ireland on the other, be confirmed, and be declared binding on the society. At this stage of the proceedings there was some little excitement, which lasted for several minutes. Several policy-holders detailed their connection with the society, and each declared that his was a hard case. One affirmed that his policy was not worth five shillings, notwithstanding that he was expected to continue his payments from year to year. Another wished to know how it came to pass that £6,000 had been spent in reconstructing the society. The Chairman explained that, in regard to the value of policies, the *National* Assurance Company of Ireland had guaranteed to meet all liabilities, whilst Messrs, Bailey and Adler had reported that the funds of the society itself were sufficient to meet every liability. With respect to the expenditure of £6,000, he pointed out that every item had been passed by the Court. The motion was then carried, with but three dissentients. The Chairman next proposed that Mr. John Young, of the firm of Turquand, Young, and Co., Coleman Street, be appointed to act as trustee on the part of the society. This was seconded and carried unanimously. A series of resolutions respecting the duties of the trustee and his salary – which was fixed at 100 guineas per annum – &c., were subsequently agreed to. Afterwards Dr. Bentham read the report of a committee appointed at the last meeting, and who had made inquiries as to where the society's funds had gone, and the proceedings terminated.

Notes

1 Sir William Milbourne James (1807–1881) was a Welsh-born judge who was called to the bar in 1831 and was appointed Vice-Chancellor of the Court of Chancery in 1869, where he left his mark in decisions concerning company and bankruptcy law.

2 Sir Robert Lush (1807–1881) was called to the bar in 1840, specialized in commercial law, and was a judge on Queen's Bench between 1865 and 1880. He was appointed to the Court of Appeals shortly before his death.

3 William Burrows was one of the parties who sued to delay the GBM's winding-up order in 1880. S. I. Da Costa was a shipping agent and a leading member of Lloyd's of London. Capt. Walter Blake Burke and Richard Smith Cason were on the committee of management of the GBM's Midland (Birmingham) branch. John Elliott was a Newcastle iron manufacturer.

4 Arthur Hutcheson Bailey (1823–1912) was actuary of the London Assurance Company from 1861 to 1895 and a leading member of the Institute of Actuaries.

5 Marcus Nathan Adler (1837–1911) was a German-born actuary who worked at the Alliance Assurance Company from 1857 until his death.

6 The Life Assurance Companies Act, 1870 (33 and 34 Vict. ch. 61), and the Act to Amend the Life Assurance Companies Acts, 1870 and 1871 (43 and 36 Vict. ch. 41), passed amidst the failures of the Albert and European insurance companies. Sections 4–7 of the latter act included new provisions for winding up companies, which the policyholder committee was seeking to use.

7 John Young (1826–1888) was a partner in the accounting firm of Turquand, Young, and Co.

8 William Matthew Makeham (1826–1891) acted as actuary and Secretary for the Great Britain Mutual between 1873 and 1880. His main claim to fame was "Makeham's Law" (1867), an algebraic formula used in smoothing raw mortality data. He was a longtime consulting actuary for the Church of England Life Assurance Company.

9 Wesley Stoker Barker Woolhouse (1809–1893) was an eminent mathematician who gained a reputation for consulting numerous life insurance companies that subsequently failed.

10 The Seventeen Offices table, completed in Britain in 1842, was the first mortality table that aggregated records from more than a single insurance company and formed an industry standard into the 1870s.

11 Walter Prideaux (1806–1889) was a London solicitor who practiced with his two sons, Walter Sherburne Prideaux (1846–1928) and Arthur Robert Prideaux (1857–1932).

12 Arthur W. Dixon was the GBM's accountant until 1880, when he replaced Makeham as its secretary.

13 The Religious Institution Rooms in St. George's Place, Glasgow, hosted numerous voluntary society meetings since the early 1860s.

14 John M'Queen Barr was a Greenock accountant.

15 Michael Cray Smart (1813–1901) was a Tewksbury alderman.

16 Archibald Neilson (1825–1918) was a Glasgow physician who was also active in local politics.

17 Daniel Cumming was a wool merchant and Provost of Renfrew from at least 1874 through 1880.

18 Possibly Thomas F. Punnett, a London merchant.

19 Sir Charles Hall (1814–1883) was called to the bar in 1838 and was a dominant figure in chancery litigation through 1873, when he joined William James as vice-chancellor in Chancery Court.

BIBLIOGRAPHY

This list includes all secondary sources except for reference works (e.g., biographical dictionaries), and no primary sources.

Acheson, Graeme G., Gareth Campbell, John D. Turner, and Nadia Venteeva. "Corporate Ownership and Control in Victorian Britain." *Economic History Review* 68 (2015): 911–936.

———, Gareth Campbell, and John D. Turner. "Active Controllers or Wealthy Rentiers? Large Shareholders in Victorian Public Companies." *Business History Review* 89 (2015): 661–691.

———, Gareth Campbell, and John D. Turner. "Who Financed the Expansion of the Equity Market? Shareholder Clienteles in Victorian Britain." *Business History* 59 (2017): 607–637.

——— and John D. Turner. "The Death Blow to Unlimited Liability in Victorian Britain: The City of Glasgow Failure." *Explorations in Economic History* 45 (2008): 235–253.

Alborn, Timothy. "The Moral of the Failed Bank: Professional Plots in the Victorian Money Market." *Victorian Studies* 38 (1995): 199–225.

———. *Conceiving Companies: Joint-Stock Politics in Victorian England.* London: Routledge, 1998.

———. "Persuading by the Numbers: The Balance Sheet in Late-Victorian Financial Journalism." In *New Economics and its Writing*, ed. John Davis (Durham: Duke University Press, 1998), 212–230/

———. *Regulated Lives: Life Insurance and British Society, 1800–1914.* Toronto: University of Toronto Press, 2009/

———. *All That Glittered: Britain's Most Precious Metal from Adam Smith to the Gold Rush.* New York: Oxford University Press, 2019.

Alderman, Geoffrey. "The Railway Companies and the Growth of Trade Unionism in the Late Nineteenth and Early Twentieth Centuries." *Historical Journal* 14 (1971): 129–152.

Amini, Shima and Steven Toms. "Accessing Capital Markets: Aristocrats and New Share Issues in the British Bicycle Boom of the 1890s." *Business History* 60 (2018): 231–256.

Armstrong, John. "The Rise and Fall of the Company Promoter and the Financing of British Industry." In *Capitalism in a Mature Economy Financial Institutions, Capital Exports and British Industry, 1870–1939*, ed. J. J. Van Helten and Y. Cassis (Aldershot: Edward Elgar, 1990), 115–138.

Bagwell, Philip. "The Rivalry and Working Union of the South Eastern and London, Chatham & Dover Railways." *Transport History* 2 (1955): 65–79.

———. *The Railway Clearing House in the British Economy 1842–1922*. London: Allen and Unwin, 1968.

Barnes, E. G. *The Rise of the Midland Railway 1844–1874*. London: Allen and Unwin, 1966.

Barns, Margarita. *The Indian Press: A History of the Growth of Public Opinion in India*. London: G. Allen and Unwin, 1940.

Barrow, G. L. "Justice for Thomas Mooney." *Dublin Historical Record* 24 (1970): 173–188.

Beaumont, Robert. *The Railway King: A Biography of George Hudson*. London: Headline Publishing Group, 2002.

Belich, James. *The New Zealand Wars and the Victorian Interpretation of Racial Conflict*. Auckland: University of Auckland Press, 2015.

Bielenberg, Andy. "The Irish Brewing Industry and the Rise of Guinness, 1790–1914." In *The Dynamics of the Modern Brewing Industry*, ed. T. Gourvish and R. G. Wilson (London: Routledge, 1998), 90–106.

Bignold, Robert. *Five Generations of the Bignold Family*. London: B.T. Batsford, 1948.

Black, Iain S. "Money, Information and Space: Banking in Early-nineteenth-century England and Wales." *Journal of Historical Geography* 21 (1995): 398–412.

Blake, Robert. *Esto Perpetua: The Norwich Union Life Assurance Society*. Norwich: privately published, 1958.

Bordo, Michael J. and Eugene N. White. "A Tale of Two Currencies: British and French Finance During the Napoleonic Wars." *Journal of Economic History* 51 (1991): 303–316.

Bowen, H. V. *The Business of Empire: The East India Company and Imperial Britain, 1756–1833*. Cambridge: Cambridge University Press, 2006.

Bowley, Tim. *Activist Shareholders in Corporate Governance: The Australian Experience and its Comparative Implications*. Oxford: Hart, 2023.

Braggion, Fabio and Lyndon Moore. "The Economic Benefits of Political Connections in Late Victorian Britain." *Journal of Economic History* 73 (2013): 142–176.

Burkert, Mattie. *Speculative Enterprise: Public Theaters and Financial Markets in London, 1688–1763*. Charlottesville: University of Virginia Press, 2021.

Burns, Patricia. *Fatal Success: A History of the New Zealand Company*. Auckland: Heinemann Reed, 1989.

Burton, Anthony. *Joseph Locke: Civil Engineer and Railway Builder, 1805–1860*. Barnsley: Pen & Sword Transport, 2017.

Butler, L. J. *Copper Empire: Mining and the Colonial State in Northern Rhodesia, c. 1930–64*. Houndmills: Palgrave Macmillan, 2007.

Callow, Edward. *Old London Taverns: Historical, Descriptive and Reminiscent*. New York: Brentano's, 1901.

Campbell, Gareth and John D. Turner. "Substitutes for Legal Protection: Corporate Governance and Dividends in Victorian Britain." *Economic History Review* 64 (2011): 571–597.

——— and John D. Turner. "Dispelling the Myth of the Naïve Investor during the Railway Mania, 1845–1846." *Business History Review* 86 (2012): 3–41.

Carter, Rand. "The Drury Lane Theatres of Henry Holland and Benjamin Dean Wyatt." *Journal of the Society of Architectural Historians* 26 (1967): 200–216.

Cassis, Youssef. "Management and Strategy in the English Joint Stock Banks 1890–1914." *Business History* 27 (1985): 301–315.

———. *City Bankers, 1890–1914*. Cambridge: Cambridge University Press, 1994.

Checkland, S. G. *Scottish Banking: A History, 1695–1973*. Glasgow: Collins, 1975.

Christopher, John. *London's Historic Railway Stations Through Time*. Stroud: Amberley Publishing, 2015.

Clapham, John. *The Bank of England: A History*. Cambridge: Cambridge University Press, 1966.

Cockerell H. A. L. and Edwin Green. *The British Insurance Business: A Guide to its History and Records*. Sheffield: Sheffield Academic Press, 1994.

Collins, Michael. "The Banking Crisis of 1878." *Economic History Review* 42 (1989): 504–527.

——— and Mae Baker, *Commercial Banks and Industrial Finance In England and Wales, 1860–1913*. Oxford: Oxford University Press, 2003.

Cottrell, P. L. "The Domestic Commercial Banks and the City of London, 1870–1939." In *Finance and Financiers in European History, 1880–1960*, ed. Youssef Cassis (Cambridge: Cambridge University Press, 1992), 39–62.

———. *Investment Banking in England 1856–1881*. London: Routledge, 2012.

Cowgill, Rachel. "'Wise Men from the East': Mozart's Operas and their Advocates in Early Nineteenth-Century London." In *Music and British Culture 1785–1914*, ed. Christina Bashford and Leanne Langley (Oxford: Oxford University Press, 2000), 39–64.

Darley, Gillian. *John Soane: An Accidental Romantic*. New Haven: Yale University Press, 1999.

Daunton, Martin J. "Inter-Union Relations on the Waterfront: Cardiff, 1888–1910." *International Review of Social History* 22 (1977): 350–378.

———. *State and Market in Victorian Britain: War, Welfare and Capitalism*. London: Boydell Press, 2008.

Dawson, Frank Griffith. *The First Latin American Debt Crisis: The City of London and the 1822–1825 Loan Bubble*. New Haven: Yale University Press, 1990.

Dennison, S. R. and Oliver MacDonagh. *Guinness 1886–1939: From Incorporation to the Second World War*. Cork: Cork University Press, 1998.

Dillon, Malcolm. *The History and Development of Banking in Ireland from the Earliest Times to the Present Day*. London: Effingham Wilson, 1889.

Dunlavy, Colleen. "Corporate Governance in Late 19th-Century Europe and the US: The Case of Shareholder Voting Rights." In *Comparative Corporate Governance: The State of the Art and Emerging Research*, ed. K. J. Hopt et al. (Oxford: Clarendon Press, 1998), 5–40.

Edwards, John Richard. *A History of Corporate Financial Reporting in Britain*. London: Routledge, 2019.

Engelbourg, Saul. "John Stewart Kennedy and the City of Glasgow Bank." *Business and Economic History* 15 (1986): 69–82.

Erikson, Emily. *Between Monopoly and Free Trade: The English East India Company, 1600–1757*. Princeton: Princeton University Press, 2014

Eyler, John. *Victorian Social Medicine: The ideas and Methods of William Farr*. Baltimore: Johns Hopkins University Press, 1979.

Foreman-Peck, James and Robert Millward. *Public and Private Ownership of British Industry, 1820*–1990. Oxford: Clarendon Press, 1994.

Forsyth, Michael. *Buildings for Music: The Architect, the Musician, and the Listener from the Seventeenth Century to the Present Day*. Cambridge, MA: MIT Press, 1985.

Frankel, Oz. *States of Inquiry: Social Investigations and Print Culture in Nineteenth-Century Britain and the United States*. Baltimore: Johns Hopkins University Press, 2006.

Freeman, Mark, Robin Pearson and James Taylor. *Shareholder Democracies?: Corporate Governance in Britain and Ireland before 1850*. Chicago: University of Chicago Press, 2012.

Freeman, Michael J. *Railways and the Victorian Imagination*. New Haven: Yale University Press, 1999.

Froide, Amy. *Silent Partners: Women as Public Investors during Britain's Financial Revolution, 1690–1750*. Oxford: Oxford University Press, 2017.

Frykenberg, Robert Eric. "Modern Education in South India, 1784–1854: Its Roots and Its Role as a Vehicle of Integration under Company Raj." *American Historical Review* 91 (1986): 37–65.

Fulford, Roger. *Samuel Whitbread 1764–1815: A Study in Opposition*. London: Macmillan, 1967.

Galbraith, John S. *Crown and Charter: The Early Years of the British South Africa Company*. Berkeley: University of California Press, 1974.

Gopal, Priyamvada. *Insurgent Empire: Anticolonial Resistance and British Dissent*. London: Verso, 2019.

Gourvish, Terence R. "A British Business Elite: The Chief Executive Managers of the Railway Industry, 1850–1922." *Business History Review* 47 (1973): 289–316.

Gramm, Jeff. *Dear Chairman: Boardroom Battles and the Rise of Shareholder Activism*. New York: Harper Business, 2016.

Gregory, T. E. *The Westminster Bank through a Century*. London: Westminster Bank, 1936.

Grossman, Richard S. *Unsettled Account: The Evolution of Banking in the Industrialized World since 1800*. Princeton: Princeton University Press, 2010.

——— and Masami Imai. "Taking the Lord's Name in Vain: The Impact of Connected Directors on 19th Century British Banks." *Explorations in Economic History* 59 (2016): 75–93.

Harris, Ron., *Industrializing English Law*: *Entrepreneurship and Business Organization, 1720–1844*. Cambridge: Cambridge University Press, 2000.

———. "The Private Origins of the Private Company: Britain 1862–1907." *Oxford Journal of Legal Studies* 33 (2013): 339–378.

Harrison, A. E. "The Competitiveness of the British Cycle Industry, 1890–1914." *Economic History Review* 22 (1969), 287–303.

———. "Joint-Stock Company Flotation in the Cycle, Motor-Vehicle and Related Industries, 1882–1914." *Business History* 23 (1981): 165–190.

Hawke, G. R. and M. C. Reed. "Railway Capital in the United Kingdom in the Nineteenth Century." *Economic History Review* 22 (1969): 269–286.

Hawkins, K. H. and C. L. Pass. *The Brewing Industry: A Study in Industrial Organization and Public Policy* (London: Heinemann, 1974.

Henry, Nancy. *Women, Literature and Finance in Victorian Britain: Cultures of Investment*. Cham: Palgrave Macmillan, 2018.

Hodges, Clive. *Cobbold and Kin: Life Stories from an East Anglian Family*. London: Boydell and Brewer, 2014.

John, A. H. *A Liverpool Merchant House: Being the History of Alfred Booth and Company 1863–1958*. London: Routledge, 1959.

Johnson, Paul. *Making the Market: Victorian Origins of Corporate Capitalism*. Cambridge: Cambridge University Press, 2010.

Jones, Geoffrey. "The Growth and Performance of British Multinational Firms before 1939: The Case of Dunlop." *Economic History Review* 37 (1984): 35–53.

Judge, David. *Representation: Theory and Practice in Britain*. London: Routledge, 1999.

Kelly, Joseph. "The Problem of Anti-Slavery in the Age of Capital: Britain and Transatlantic Slavery, c. 1833–1888." University of Liverpool Ph.D. dissertation, 2018.

Kindleberger, Charles P. *Economic Response: Comparative Studies in Trade, Finance, and Growth*. Cambridge, MA: Harvard University Press, 1978.

King, Frank H. H. and Sara Joynes. *Survey Our Empire! Robert Montgomery Martin . . . A Bio-Bibliography*. Hong Kong: Centre of Asian Studies, 1979.

Kynaston, David. *Cazenove & Co.: A History*. London: B. T. Batsford, 1991.

———. *Till Time's Last Stand: A History of the Bank of England 1694–2013*. London: Bloomsbury, 2017.

Laidlaw, Zoe. "'Justice to India – Prosperity to England – Freedom to the Slave! Humanitarian and Moral Reform Campaigns on India, Aborigines and American Slavery." *Journal of the Royal Asiatic* Society 22 (2012): 299–321.

Lampard, Keith. "The Promotion and Performance of the London Chatham & Dover Railway." *Journal of Transport History* 3rd ser. 6 (1985): 48–63.

Laurence, Anne, Josephine Maltby, and Janette Rutterford, eds., *Women and their Money, 1700–1950: Essays on Women and Finance*. London: Routledge, 2009.

Loftus, Donna. "Capital and Community: Limited Liability and Attempts to Democratize the Market in Mid-Nineteenth Century England." *Victorian Studies* 45 (2002): 93–120.

Mackintosh, Iain. "The Rise and Fall of the Georgian Playhouse 1714–1830 – A Cautionary Tale." *AA Files* 4 (1983): 16–28.

Makepeace, Margaret. *The East India Company's London Workers: Management of the Warehouse Labourers, 1800–1858*. Woodbridge: Boydell Press, 2010.

Maltby, Josephine. "Hadfields Ltd: Its Annual General Meetings 1903–1939 and their Relevance for Contemporary Corporate Social Reporting." *British Accounting Review* 36 (2004): 415–439.

———, Janette Rutterford, David R. Green, Steven Ainscough, and Carien van Mourik. "The Evidence for 'Democratization' of Share Ownership in Great Britain in the Early Twentieth Century." In *Men, Women, and Money: Perspectives on Gender, Wealth and Investment, 1850–1930*, ed. David R. Green et al. (Oxford: Oxford University Press, 2011), 185–206.

Matthews, Derek, Malcolm Anderson, and John Richard Edwards. *The Priesthood of Industry: The Rise of the Professional Accountant in British Management*. Oxford: Oxford University Press, 1998.

Mayo, John and Simon Collier. *Mining in Chile's Norte Chico: Journal of Charles Lambert, 1825–1830*. Boulder: Westview Press, 1998.

McCabe, Colum. "History of the Town Gas Industry in Ireland, 1823–1980." *Dublin Historical Record* 45 (1992): 28–40.

McCartney, Sean and A. J. Arnold. "George Hudson's Financial Reporting Practices: Putting the Eastern Counties Railway in Context." *Accounting, Business and Financial History* 10 (2000): 293–316.

McGowen, Randall. "Managing the Gallows: The Bank of England and the Death Penalty, 1797–1821." *Law and History Review* 25 (2007): 241–282.

McQueen, Rob. *A Social History of Company Law: Great Britain and the Australian Colonies 1854–1920*. Farnham: Ashgate, 2009.

Michie, R. C. "Options, Concessions, Syndicates, and the Provision of Venture Capital, 1880–1913." *Business History* 23 (1981): 147–164.

Morecraft, Nigel Edward. *The Origins of Asset Management from 1700 to 1960*. Cham: Palgrave Macmillan, 2017.

Munro, J. Forbes. *Maritime Enterprise and Empire: Sir William Mackinnon and His Business Network, 1823–1893*. Woodbridge: Boydell Press, 2003.

Nevill, Ralph. *London Clubs: Their History and Treasures*. London: Lancour Press, 2008.

Newman, E. K. "The Origin and Development of Company Meeting Reports." *Journal of Advertising History*, 6 (1983): 6–14.

Newman, Ian. *The Romantic Tavern: Literature and Conviviality in the Age of Revolution*. Cambridge: Cambridge University Press, 2019.

Newton, Lucy. "The Birth of Joint-Stock Banking: England and New England Compared." *Business History* Review 84 (2010): 27–52.

——— and P. L. Cottrell. "Joint-Stock Banking in the English Provinces 1826–1857: To Branch or Not to Branch?" *Business and Economic History* 27 (1998): 115–128.

Nicholls, Peter. "Labour, Management, and Control: The Early Railway Industry in Britain." In *A Business and Labour History of Great Britain*, ed. Michael Richardson and Peter Nicholls (Houndmills: Palgrave Macmillan, 2011), 9–31.

Ollerenshaw, Philip. *Banking in Nineteenth-Century Ireland: The Belfast Banks, 1825-1914*. Manchester: Manchester University Press, 1987.

Ó Maitiú, Séamas. *Dublin's Suburban Towns 1834–1930*. Dublin: Four Courts Press, 2003.

O'Sullivan, Charles J. *The Gasmakers: Historical Perspectives on the Irish Gas Industry*. Dublin: O'Brien Press, 1987.

Palmer, John E. C. and Harold W. Paar. "Transport." In *Victorian Periodicals and Victorian Society*, ed. J. Don Vahn and Rosemary T. VanArsdel (Toronto: University of Toronto Press, 1994), 179–198.

Payne, P. L. "The Emergence of the Large-Scale Company in Great Britain, 1870–1914." *Economic History Review* 20 (1967): 519–542.

Pearson, Robin. "Shareholder Democracies? English Stock Companies and the Politics of Corporate Governance during the Industrial Revolution." *English Historical Review* 117 (2002): 840–866.

Phillips, Andrew and J. C. Sharman, *Outsourcing Empire: How Company-States Made the Modern World*. Princeton: Princeton University Press, 2020.

Phillips, Maberly. *A History of Banks, Bankers, & Banking in Northumberland, Durham, and North Yorkshire*. London: Effingham Wilson, 1894.

Phoofolo, Pule. "Epidemics and Revolutions: The Rinderpest Epidemic in Late-Nineteenth Century Southern Africa." *Past & Present* 138 (1993): 112–143.

Pollins, Harold. "Railway Contractors and the Finance of Railway Development in Britain – II." *Journal of Transport History* 3 (1957): 103–110.

Powell, Jim. *Losing the Thread: Cotton, Liverpool and the American Civil War*. Liverpool: Liverpool University Press, 2021.

Preda, Alex. "The Rise of the Popular Investor: Financial Knowledge and Investing in England and France, 1840–1880." *Sociological Quarterly* 42 (2001): 205–232.

Rapp, Dean. *Samuel Whitbread (1764–1815): A Social and Political Study*. New York: Garland, 1987.

Rawlings, Philip. "'A Sacred Trust for the Future': Regulating Insurance, 1800–1870." *Cambridge Law Journal* 77 (2018): 570–599.

Raynes, Harold E. *A History of British Insurance*. London: Sir Isaac Pitman & Sons, 1948.

Reid, Kenneth C. G. "Embalmed in Rettie: The City of Glasgow Bank and the Liability of Trustees." In *Judge and Jurist: Essays in Memory of Lord Rodger of* Earlsferry, ed. Andrew Burrow et al. (Oxford: Oxford University Press, 2013), 489–508.

Ridgway, Robert H. *Summarized Data of Gold Production*. Washington: US Government Printing Office, 1930.

Ritchie, Leslie. *David Garrick and the Mediation of Celebrity*. Cambridge: Cambridge University Press, 2019.

Robbins, Michael. *George and Robert Stephenson*. Oxford: Oxford University Press, 1965.

Roden, Andrew. *Great Western Railway: A History*. London: Aurum Press, 2010.

Ross, David. *George and Robert Stephenson: A Passion for Success*. Stroud: The History Press, 2010.

Rungta, Radhe Shyam. *The Rise of Business Corporations in India, 1851–1900*. Cambridge: Cambridge University Press, 1970.

Rutterford, Janette. "'Propositions Put Forward by Quite Honest Men': Company Prospectuses and their Contents, 1856 to 1940." *Business History* 53 (2011): 866–890.

———. "The Shareholder Voice: British and American Accents, 1890–1965." *Enterprise and Society* 13 (2012): 120–153.

——— and Leslie Hannah. "The Unsung Activists: UK Shareholder Investigation Committees, 1888–1940." *Business History Review* 96 (2022): 741–775.

Ryan, R. J. "A History of the Norwich Union Fire and Life Insurance Societies from 1797 to 1914." Ph.D. dissertation, University of East Anglia, 1983.

Shannon, H. A. "The First Five Thousand Limited Companies and Their Duration." *Economic History* 2 (1932): 396–424.

Supple, Barry. *The Royal Exchange Assurance: A History of British Insurance 1720–1970*. Cambridge: Cambridge University Press, 1970.

Televantos, Andreas. *Capitalism Before Corporations: The Morality of Business Associations and the Roots of Commercial Equity and Law*. Oxford: Oxford University Press, 2020.

Taylor, James, *Creating Capitalism: Joint-Stock Enterprise in British Politics and Culture, 1800–1870*. Woodbridge: Boydell, 2006.

———. *Boardroom Scandal: The Criminalization of Company Fraud in Nineteenth-Century Britain*. Oxford: Oxford University Press, 2013.

———. "Privacy, Publicity, and Reputation: How the Press Regulated the Market in Nineteenth Century England." *Business History Review* 87 (2013): 679–701.

Thomas, W. A. *The Provincial Stock Exchanges*. London: Frank Cass, 1973.

Thornbury, George Walter. *Old and New* London. London: Cassel, Petter, Galpin and Co., 1880.

Trebilcock, Clive. *Phoenix Assurance and the Development of British Insurance*. Cambridge: Cambridge University Press, 1985 and 1999.

Trussler, Simon. *The Cambridge Illustrated History of British Theatre*. Cambridge: Cambridge University Press, 1994.

Tyson, R. E. "Scottish Investment in American Railways: The Case of the City of Glasgow Bank, 1856–1881." In *Studies in Scottish Business History*, ed. P. L. Payne (London: Frank Cass, 1967), 387–416.

Vallance, Aylmer. *Very Private Enterprise: An Anatomy of Fraud and High Finance*. London: Thames and Hudson, 1955.

Velez, Claudio. "Egaña, Lambert, and the Chilean Mining Associations of 1825." *Hispanic American Historical Review* 55 (1975): 637–663.

Wahl, Cheryl. "The Business of Settlement: Land Companies and Colonization in the British Empire, ca 1800–1850." Ph.D. dissertation, City University of New York, 2010.

Wahrman, Dror. "Virtual Representation: Parliamentary Reporting and Languages of Class in the 1790s." *Past and Present* 136 (1992): 83–113.

Walford, Cornelius. *Insurance Cyclopaedia*. London: Layton, 1871–1880.

Watson, Katherine. "The New Issue Market as a Source of Finance for the U.K. Brewing and Iron and Steel Industries, 1870–1913." In *The Evolution of Financial Institutions and Markets in Twentieth-Century Europe*, ed. Y. Cassis, G. Feldman, and U. Olsson (Aldershot: Scolar Press, 1995), 209–248.

———. "Banks and Industrial Finance: The Experience of Brewers, 1880–1913." *Economic History Review* 49 (1996): 58–81.

Watson, Susan. *The Making of the Modern Company*. Oxford: Hart Publishing, 2022.

Westall, Oliver M. "Entrepreneurship and Product Innovation in British General Insurance, 1840–1914," in *Entrepreneurship, Networks and Modern Business*, ed. J. Brown and M. B. Rose (Manchester: Manchester University Press, 1993), 191–210.

Withers, Hartley. *National Provincial Bank: 1833 to 1933*. London: National Provincial Bank, 1933.

"Winchester House in Old Broad Street." londonpicturearchive.org.uk

Woodland, John. *Money Pits: British Mining Companies in the Californian and Australian Gold Rushes of the 1850s*. London: Routledge, 2014.

Worth, Katherine. *Sheridan and Goldsmith*. London: Macmillan, 1992.

Yenne, Bill. *Guinness: The 250-Year Quest for the Perfect Pint*. Hoboken: John Wiley and Sons, 2007.